TEACHING INTRODUCTION TO THEATRICAL DESIGN

Teaching Introduction to Theatrical De___ ___ a week-by-week guide that helps instructors who are ne___ ___ teaching design, teaching outside of their fields of expertis ___ ___ looking for better ways to integrate and encourage non-de___ ___rs in the design cla___ ___ This book provides a syllabus ___ ___ foundational theatr ___ ___illustrating process ___ ___ application of the princi___ ___ ___tumes, sce___ ___ ___ights, and sound.

This b___

- Lessons, activitie___ ___at develop the knowledge and skills ___ ___ the stage.
- A companion website w___ ___ion videos and downloadable versions of instr___ ___ents.

- Examples of short plays to teach theatrical design more effectively.

Eric Appleton is an Associate Professor of Theatre and Dance at the University of Wisconsin–Whitewater. He has been a freelance lighting and set designer since 1994.

Tracey Lyons is currently a Lecturer at the University of Wisconsin–Whitewater. She has previously been on the faculty of the University of North Dakota and Del Mar College.

TEACHING INTRODUCTION TO THEATRICAL DESIGN

A PROCESS-BASED SYLLABUS IN COSTUMES, SCENERY, AND LIGHTING

Eric Appleton and Tracey Lyons

Routledge
Taylor & Francis Group
NEW YORK AND LONDON

First published 2017
by Routledge
711 Third Avenue, New York, NY 10017

and by Routledge
2 Park Square, Milton Park, Abingdon, Oxon OX14 4RN

Routledge is an imprint of the Taylor & Francis Group, an informa business

Library of Congress Cataloging in Publication Data
Names: Appleton, Eric, author. | Lyons, Tracey, author.
Title: Teaching introduction to theatrical design : a process based syllabus in costumes, scenery, and lighting / Eric Appleton and Tracey Lyons.
Description: New York : Routledge, 2017. | Includes bibliographical references and index.
Identifiers: LCCN 2016016947| ISBN 9781138193253 (pbk : alk. paper) | ISBN 9781315639499 (ebk : alk. paper)
Subjects: LCSH: Theaters—Stage-setting and scenery—Handbooks, manuals, etc.
Classification: LCC PN2091.S8 A685 2017 | DDC 792.02/5—dc23
LC record available at https://lccn.loc.gov/2016016947

ISBN: 978-1-138-19325-3 (pbk)
ISBN: 978-1-315-63949-9 (ebk)

Typeset in Univers
by Keystroke, Neville Lodge, Tettenhall, Wolverhampton

Visit the companion website: www.routledge.com/cw/appleton

Printed and bound in India by Replika Press Pvt. Ltd.

Contents

Figures

Preface

This book grew from conversations with peers and colleagues. These conversations revealed a distinct set of common issues many of us face when designing introductory design courses, especially in smaller departments or for designers new to teaching and teachers new to design.

First, a frequent theme was the tendency of instructors to cut and paste course materials from a broad range of texts rather than selecting and sticking with a single book. There are plenty of good design textbooks available, but beyond a handful of exercises at the end of chapters, there is little guidance in *how* to use content as progressive and meaningful hands-on components of an introductory class. This book seeks to resolve this issue, not by replacing comprehensive design texts in the classroom, but by proposing pedagogical strategies through which an instructor can organize classroom interaction with whatever texts are favored.

Another issue that arose in those conversations was what constitutes introductory level content. The course that we teach at the University of Wisconsin–Whitewater introduces scenery, costume, and lighting design in the space of a single semester. That's roughly five weeks apiece for each field. Many current textbooks feature material that can span several semesters' worth of classes in each design field. There's not usually any clear indication where the introductory material ends and intermediate or advanced work begins. Even though an instructor might not feel obligated to get through an entire book in a single course it's hard to figure out where to stop. For an introductory course the instructor must determine how deeply, in the time allotted, he or she can delve into the various design fields as well as strike a balance between concepts, communication, planning, and technical know-how.

The content of this book is based on classroom experimentation. In our seven years of developing and revising this course we have wrestled with the question of what we can realistically expect our students to achieve in ten one-and-a-half-hour sessions per design field, especially since it's the only formal design course currently listed in our curriculum. The students of our Fall 2015 session contributed images of their projects to demonstrate the variety of skill levels and the range of achievement we have come to expect from year to year.

A third concern was the ratio of design to non-design students in the average introductory course. In order to keep classes populated at adequate enrollment levels, design courses are often requirements for non-design students. However, the introductory design class that is foundational for a program's handful of design students can become a slog for the majority of non-design students, especially for those with limited drawing skills. The challenge is to introduce necessary fundamental skills for the design students while ensuring that the non-design students remain interested and engaged. Our solution has been to focus on the process of design, integrating only what technical skills are required to complete the projects at hand in the time we have. While the conceptual part of art and design is not always a linear activity, theatre production is. Structuring the class to parallel the step-by-step forward movement of the typical production process not only provides design students with real-world foundational steps, but allows non-design students to better understand how all the parts of production develop in tandem.

Finally, the nature of theatre production means that designers don't usually get to work with other designers in their respective fields, unless it's as an assistant. The same is often true in academic theatre programs: a department at a smaller school may have only two instructors — one whose duties are directing and teaching history, the other overseeing all the technical aspects. Indeed, someone trained as a director or historian may also be assigned to teach a design course. There is seldom opportunity to observe an experienced instructor teaching in one's own field of expertise. While sharing syllabi occurs (and is fostered by such bodies as the Education Commission of the United States Institute for Theatre Technology), syllabi are usually limited to announcing goals and broad topics; they don't help the instructor figure out how to achieve those goals or teach those topics – nor are they meant to. We have chosen to structure this book in a syllabus format and then fill in the gaps to serve as an example not only of what we teach, but how, and why we do it in a particular order. Each chapter covers two class sessions (again, at about an hour and a half duration per session), presenting concepts and exercises in the order we approach them. Since we've been developing this course over several years, we've accumulated a catalog of digressions and extra exercises from which to choose depending on how the class goes on a given day. We've included as many as possible. It would be impossible to include them all in a normal class session, but we hope they will spark variants useful to the reader's individual situation.

You are the person best positioned to understand the aims, needs, and resources of your institution and department. You are the person best situated to understand the needs and goals of your students. As part of an ongoing teacher-to-teacher conversation, use this book to design the class that brings your strengths forward, confronts and overcomes weaknesses, and assists you to stretch and explore as a teacher while offering a fulfilling experience for your students.

If you are new to the design classroom; if you are being asked to teach a design craft outside of your field; if your design class comprises mainly young actors, directors, and stage managers; if you've inherited a course structure that tries to fit the only discussion of lighting, scenery, and costumes your students will get into a single semester – please, read on. We have a lot to talk about.

Acknowledgments

This book is the result of years of teaching. We'd like to acknowledge that our students are the reason this book came to be, and have helped form the content as we revised our course semester by semester. We'd like to thank the students of Fall 2015 who were willing to share their projects with an audience beyond the safety of the classroom: Annie Kailhofer, Rick Grischow, Molly O'Hearn, Madeline Mehnert, Kelsey Smyth, Mason Ronan, Bridget Kelly, Nick Grischow, Eric Guenthner, Lilliana Gonzalez, Peyton Reigstad, Stephanie Graf, Stephanie Ruch, Abigail King, Allison Lozar, Casey Bunbury, Erin Quist, Bergen Hansen, and Amanda Kramer. We've also asked for and included some images and items from friends, collaborators, and colleagues, and would to thank Rachelle Miller, Don Smith, Keith Pitts, Brandon Kirkham, Brandy Kline, Thomas C. Umfrid, Aaron Bridgeman, Matt Hamel, anc Olivia Leigh. We appreciate our colleagues in the Theatre/Dance Department at the University of Wisconsin–Whitewater in their recognition and accommodation of this writing effort in the midst of a full academic year of teaching and production. Rick and Spencer, thanks for support on our home fronts. Finally, we'd also like to thank Meredith and Stacey at Routledge for shepherding us though this whole process.

Introduction

In developing any course, there is much planning and preparation that happens before the class meets for the first time. Before we get to the course content as laid out in each chapter, we'd like to discuss the rationale behind some of our teaching choices so that as you encounter each step in our process you have a better sense of how our course, and teaching, have evolved over the years.

As is the case in many theatre departments, we inherited this class and a syllabus for this class. Previous instructors had developed approaches that worked for them and for the period in which they taught. However, times change, approaches to theatre change, and for better or for worse students now come into the classroom with different expectations and work ethics than in previous decades. Teaching approaches themselves change, and as an instructor learns more about the craft of teaching, she or he will want to try new things to better facilitate student engagement. We changed things bit by bit, year by year. Even though we individually revised the content of our respective sections, this book truly had its origins as the two of us started sticking around to observe each other's sessions. The course became a true teaching collaboration rather than three stand-alone sections linked by a common meeting time.

Furthermore, design classes do not exist in a vacuum, but have relationships with other courses in the curriculum. Changing the content and approach in one course can strengthen or loosen ties with other courses, and the instructor seeking to revise a class can benefit greatly by considering the larger curricular picture. We chose to look for places where the Introduction to Design course could be more overtly connected to student experience in other classes, the departmental productions, and outside activities like KCACTF.

What follows will discuss the organization of this book, assessment of student creative work, how and why we select plays for use in the class, how student portfolio development can be fostered through the various projects, and finally, some books that we've found useful.

The Organization of This Book

Teaching itself is a learning experience. Those versed in current assessment jargon use the term 'closing the loop' to discuss those actions identified and taken to improve teaching. In a nutshell, that means identifying specific things the instructor wants the students to master but for some reason they are not quite doing so. The mechanics of the class must be investigated, specifically examining and evaluating those activities believed to lead students toward demonstration of that mastery. The instructor will be able to find places where more time should be spent on a topic, where more effective exercises might help students absorb the concepts; they may even re-examine the ultimate goals of the class itself. There are compromises to be made, as often having both breadth *and* depth may not be easily managed in the space of a single semester.

If you've glanced through the table of contents, you'll have noticed that we placed costume design first. When we inherited our class, scenic design was approached first, then costumes, then lighting. It was an order of approach we had experienced before and appeared to be standard in an all-in-one class. This can be rationalized from a historically hierarchical standpoint – scenery is first because it comprises the largest and most apparent physical feature of the performance space. Costumes come next because with scenery, costumes both create and inhabit the physical space of the stage. Light is treated last because both in history and the production process it's a relative latecomer, tying together the other design compo-nents. The assumption is that scenery and costumes need to do their work before lighting can really start making decisions.

After a couple of years of teaching the course in the more standard order, Tracey suggested we experiment with making costume design the first field introduced to the students. It has remained first ever since. Pedagogically, we feel that scenic design is less divisible than costumes (or even lighting). In set design, a student is asked to create a whole world on a stage, from scratch, in four weeks, with no prior experience in doing so, *and* this happens while in a feedback cycle with perhaps unfamiliar graphic skills like drawing, drafting, and model build-ing. Moving costume design into the first slot means that students now develop a project that is perceived by them as less formidable; a handful of costumes as opposed to a com-plete set. Topics like design elements, the use of metaphor, and basic research can be introduced, practiced, and applied more effectively on a project of less daunting size.

In class, we have found it effective to weave exercises and instructor presentation together, doing our best to avoid long periods of lecture. We'll use that approach throughout this book. Presenting the bones of the topic and then moving right into an exercise means that students immediately use what they have just learned and are more likely to retain it. Each chapter will be arranged to present material as we do in a given session.

Throughout this book we have scattered boxes with teaching tips and quotes where their content is relevant to the day's activities. Illustrations will accompany many projects, including samples of actual student work. We do use the work of professional designers to exemplify particular points in class, but for an instructor attempting to gauge what comprises solid introductory work and what does not, these images are of less value and will therefore be kept to a minimum in this book. Images of Broadway-level designs can be inspirational, but we don't want students feeling that after one semester they should be turning out work of that caliber. We find it useful to keep the work generated by students through the years in the classroom, using a range of student achievement both as teaching aids and as concrete examples of the type of work we expect of the students.

Our Formula

Combining both the framing topics and the structural order we've adopted for the class, we have a formula which applies to both the macro- and micro-level projects. We'll discuss each of these topics in more depth as they arise in each chapter.

1. Analysis
2. Design Metaphor
3. Design Elements
4. Research
5. Render (Design Mechanics)

This list reflects both the order in which these topics are intro-duced to the class, and the order in which we ask students to work through their projects. For example, for the 'drink-can label' exercise in Chapter 1 (see Figures 1.23 through 1.26) stu-dents analyze the text (in that case, soda), distill their reaction into descriptive terms that suggest particular design elements (line, texture, etc.), consider the context and meaning of their choices, and draw a ogo that expresses their sensation of the soda through the intentional use of design elements. For later, larger projects, places for improvement will be identified and students will be asked to revise and resubmit their work.

We are upfront with the students about this formula, and hope that as the semester moves along these steps become second nature. Structured practice early means that risks can be taken later with more confidence, with an understanding of *why* those risks should be taken. To paraphrase Martha Graham from the 1957 documentary *A Dancer's World*: discipline in learning your craft now permits freedom of expression later.[1]

Creativity and Evaluation

Grading art and design projects can be a tricky proposition. There are few absolutely right or absolutely wrong answers. Rather, there are approaches that work and those that work even better. Of course, the question then becomes what exactly is meant by something *working*? You might find yourself facing students who protest that you are stifling their creative impulses, that your teaching method is unfairly my-way-or-the-highway, or that you simply don't understand their out-of-the-box thinking. Critiquing and grading projects can end up seeming rather subjective to both the student and the instructor.

Design is about problem solving. Granted, in the theatre we want to solve problems in creative ways, but 'creativity' is such a slippery concept so tied to personal worth and self-esteem that framing discussion of a project by commenting on how 'creative' it is usually ends up being counterproductive, not just for the individual student but for the climate of the class in general. A focus on the steps of the process and the progress that engagement with the steps engenders is, we feel, the more constructive path.

Our class has, at its foundation, the development and application of critical thinking skills, not self-expression or the explosion of innate, raw talent. Some of that may come into play, but expression without critical self-awareness quickly leads to self-indulgence. It's our belief that anyone can learn to do things like historical research or close readings of a text. If a student chooses to costume *Antigone* in 1860s American Old West style it's not the creativity of the choice that gets evaluated; what matters is how the student follows through with research and applies that research to the needs of the text. The student must be able to adequately explain how and why the text of *Antigone* allows the choice of 1860s American Old West as a format that clarifies and explicates the action of the play. Maybe they will convince you. Maybe they won't. They still have to try. Even if you don't agree with their decision, letting them push through to the end so that the flaws (or successes) become manifest can be an excellent learning experience. A project that reaches a conceptually creaky final resting state can still receive an 'A' if the process steps are clearly engaged, and the student supports choices with research and textual evidence.

Our current homework and project guidelines will be included at the point they are assigned. Methods of instructor critique and grading can be found where assignments are turned in and discussed.

Selecting Plays for Use in Class

When we inherited the class, students were allowed to make their own choice as to which single play they would work on throughout the scenic, costume, and lighting sections. This meant that if the class had twelve students, we as instructors had to know all the twelve plays. While it was hoped that all the students would read all the plays being used, that was seldom the case. Having meaningful classroom discussions about projects as they developed was limited, since students were unfamiliar with the texts the others were using. We decided to limit the numbers of plays used in any given semester to three, with the requirement that all students were to read them. Only after discussion of all three texts would they choose which one to work on.

Exploration within parameters is an important teaching concept in our class. Students should have a certain degree of freedom to ensure ownership in their work, but too many choices can mean loss of focus, or focus on something other than the desired lesson objectives. By limiting the number of plays used, the students have time to read them all. They are discussed in class, and as the projects progress not only are students able to ask each other about choices made, but they also get to see the various directions possible even though they're all working on the exact same play. The problems we are trying to solve often have multiple, quite workable solutions and seeing this in action helps prevent students from locking in on a single, immutable 'right' answer for a play.

There are several criteria we use when choosing plays each year. We look at texts the students read in other parts of the department's curriculum, such as script analysis or theatre history courses. Taking a play familiar from an acting or English class perspective and looking at it from a design standpoint can be an eye-opening experience for students.

We also see what our region of the Kennedy Center American College Theatre Festival has put forward for that year's unrealized design projects. We have found KCACTF to be an excellent resource, and use their design presentation guidelines to structure project presentations. Sometimes a student's class work can translate into a presentation at the regional KCACTF festival, giving them a chance to present their work to a fresh set of viewers. By participating in the festival they also have the opportunity to observe how their peers at other institutions approach the same material. Even if your institution does not participate in KCACTF's conference or response activities, we encourage familiarity with their website and the practices the organization espouses.

We try to select plays for pedagogical practicality rather than for literary content or historical merit. Whether or not it also appears on a reading list for a theatre history course, we might use *A Raisin in the Sun* less because it's an Important American Play than because there's grounding in a very specific time and place: a cramped apartment on the South Side of Chicago in the late 1950s. Students can research that and readily link that research to the needs of the world of the play. An instructor can call out a student on a piece of clothing that a character in that play cannot wear because it's from the 1970s rather than the 1950s. If too many windows appear on the set it means that the student hasn't read the play carefully enough. On the other hand, there *are* non-realistic visual places you can take that play – for instance, exploring the ramifications of showing the city around the apartment. The bonus of a play like *A Raisin in the Sun* is that you also get specific social undercurrents that feed directly and urgently into design choices because they drive the play's plot.

Intro to Design can also introduce contemporary scripts, or plays that students should know but are unlikely to be mounted by your department. If your students aren't generally exposed to plays by a diverse range of minority voices, this course is a good place to get a few on the reading list. New and unfamiliar voices often require young designers to explore beyond their comfort range.

Each year, we try to select one play that tends toward naturalistic solutions, one that could tend toward more abstract or presentational solutions, and one that is fun and unexpected. If one play asks for a lot of lighting looks, one should have only a handful. If one play features fairly familiar contemporary costume, another should go deeper into period and style. Students can then choose the play that most appeals to them from whichever design field interests them most and presents those challenges they feel most comfortable tackling first. When taken together, the three plays offer the students variety and achievability.

Currently, we use full-length plays for the final projects, though the use of one-acts and ten-minute plays has been discussed. If we had more time, or could focus on a single field, shorter plays would be an excellent way to incorporate focused projects on particular design elements.

Play trios from past years of our course include:

- *Pseudolus* (Plautus), *The Royal Hunt of the Sun* (Peter Shaffer), *Leading Ladies* (Ken Ludwig)
- *Angels in America Part One: Millennium Approaches* (Tony Kushner), *A Raisin in the Sun* (Lorraine Hansberry), *The Three Sisters* (Anton Chekhov)
- *The Piano Lesson* (August Wilson), *The House of Blue Leaves* (John Guare), *The Hairy Ape* (Eugene O'Neill)
- *Boeing Boeing* (Marc Camoletti), *On the Verge* (Eric Overmeyer), *She Stoops to Conquer* (Oliver Goldsmith)
- *Getting Married* (George Bernard Shaw), *Jeffrey* (Paul Rudnick), *Rashomon* (Fay Kanin and Michael Kanin)

Changing the plays from year to year has a number of benefits. The class remains fresh for the instructor while maintaining constancy in the syllabus, broadens the reading of the department as a whole, and prevents students from passing down project components from year to year. Plus, if you are able to display student work in your building's public areas, variety provides interest, and potential students can see the breadth of the department's curricular investigations.

After making their choice of play, our students use that play for their costume and scenery projects. At the beginning of the lighting section, they are then assigned one of the other students' play choices for their lighting project. For example, student X designs costumes and scenery for *Pseudolus*, but then must design lighting for student Y's scenic and costume design of *The Royal Hunt of the Sun*. Students get to work on plays they did not choose or possibly do not even like, which models professional life. Not only will they have to pose questions about their classmates' work, but they will have to face those very same issues with their own work as they field questions from their own lighting designers. It becomes not just an exercise in design, but also in collaboration.

The Classroom

We are fortunate in our classroom space; before we joined our department, earlier faculty members assembled a room that well supports the department's design and technology teaching efforts. Our classroom contains drawing tables, blackboards, bulletin boards, projection equipment, a small light lab, and a small computer lab. On the other hand, in the past both of us have taught courses in a variety of less than optimal spaces.

As we have written this book, we have done our best to keep in mind that not every department or institution has the same classroom resources available that we do. If you have no projection equipment, you may find yourself making a lot of color photocopies. If no costume shop is accessible, it will be necessary to visit your local fabric and crafts stores. If you have no light tables, tracing paper will do.

Most of the exercises and activities in the costume and scenic sections of this book will work well as long as the students have space to draw and draft, whether on a drawing table, or a table with a portable drafting board. However, for the lighting section to be most effective some sort of light lab needs to be assembled. We work with dolls as models in the light lab, which means that the size of the lab need not be huge; hardware store clip-lights clamped to a light wooden frame sitting atop a table can work quite well.

A chapter on sound can be found at the end of the book. We do not teach a section on sound in our single semester design course, but find that our pedagogical approach to costume, scenery, and lighting can also aid those students interested in sound design. To work with sound in the classroom, a playback system is necessary. While a tablet or phone may not offer the highest quality of sound, the dramaturgical aspects of sound design can still be explored with those devices.

Portfolio Development

For a designer, the portfolio is an important communication tool when seeking employment. It contains samples of the designer's work, showing completed projects and materials that contribute to an understanding of the designer's process. By reviewing the portfolio, a potential colleague or client can get a sense of whether the designer is stylistically the right person for the job as well as a sense of his or her collaborative qualities.

Building a portfolio, particularly at the undergraduate level, is an activity that can easily fall through the cracks. As students reach the end of their senior year, they begin to realize that portfolios are part of the upcoming job interview process and discover that they haven't saved anything from their production work to put into it. Getting design/tech students to think about building their portfolio should happen as early as possible. Students should get into the habit of updating their portfolios after every production they are involved with, replacing older placeholder or classroom work with their most recent achievements.

A student portfolio serves many uses:

- Tracks the learning process
- Informs students of their improvement through the semester
- Models the collection of work kept by professional designers
- Creates a ritual for the presentation of work in the future
- Gives students a platform by which to introduce themselves to employers even before graduation.

We ask students to save everything produced from this class regardless of how they feel about it. This collection, from note cards to swatched renderings to storyboards, represents the journey of the student designer.

Your own portfolio can serve as a valuable example to the class. Walk your students through it as you would when presenting yourself to an artistic director or other potential client. Explain which show is about to be rotated out and why. If you're in the process of adding a recent show, bring in all the parts and pieces you've collected and lay out the page as a demonstration.

If you're new to design in general and do not have a portfolio of your own, there are organizations whose websites, commissions, and bulletin boards can direct you to images their members have posted to share, or put you in contact with designers willing to share portfolio items with your class. Three to start with are:

- The Kennedy Center American College Theatre Festival (KCACTF) (www.kcactf.org)
- United States Institute for Theatre Technology (USITT) (www.usitt.org)
- United Scenic Artists Local USA 829 (www.usa829.org)

If you are able to bring in guest designers, whether for production work or a short classroom visit, be sure to ask them to bring along their portfolios.

Building a good portfolio, like anything else, requires practice and experimentation. Above all, the student needs items to put in the portfolio. At the end of each chapter, we will offer suggestions and exercises on how that week's projects and exercises can be used to guide students through the process of building a portfolio.

Book Recommendation

Show Case, by Rafael Jaen (published by Focal Press), is a handy reference tool, full of do's and don'ts not just on portfolios but on resumes, vitae, business cards, and the general presentation of work to clients across the entertainment industry.

Books We Want to Share With You

At the college level, many of us are designers who moved sideways into education. We've trained extensively in one field and are now being asked to teach other design fields, to be a technical director, or even start directing.

As we backfill our education, the two of us constantly discover books and texts and films that people in other fields know to be essential building blocks but for some reason or another were never mentioned in our own, now distant, educational experiences. Throughout this book we periodically recommend texts that we hope are useful for someone catching up in a particular field. Some of these texts are still in print; others may be moldering in a forgotten corner of your institution's library. Whether you press them, complete, into the hands of your students or introduce excerpts for use alongside classroom exercises is up to you – but we find these texts to be useful ladder rungs laid by those who have gone before us.

Here are three books to start with that we feel address foundational issues in teaching theatrical design:

The Dramatic Imagination, by Robert Edmond Jones

Jones is still the mystic high priest of American stage design. In this book of breathless inspiration, he ties it all together – acting, design, direction, history – and urges the reader to seek *theatricality* in the theatre. For many students, the idea that theatre is born from the marriage of the dirt of Craft with the clean burning flame of Art is a revelation. "Does this mean we are to carry images of poetry and vision and high passion in our minds while we are shouting out orders to electricians on ladders in light-rehearsals? Yes. This is what it means."[2] Let his book inspire you in low moments.

Art and Fear: Observations on the Perils (and Rewards) of Artmaking, by David Bayles and Ted Orland

This book is a reminder that making things is hard and fraught with peril, but remains an eminently worthwhile pursuit. It explores the ramifications of putting yourself and your art out into the world, addressing issues of craft, inspiration, competition, habits, failures, acceptance, and approval and why anyone should do art in the face of seemingly insurmountable odds. "Q: *Will anyone ever match the genius of Mozart?* A: *No.* Thank you – now can we get on with our work?"[3]

A Practical Handbook for the Actor, by Bruder, Cohn, Olnek, Pollack, Previto, and Zigler

This is a solid, practical guide to the nuts and bolts of acting in language anyone can understand. Since designers design environments to be inhabited by actors, it's good to have some essentials at one's fingertips, especially since design classes in many smaller programs will have a high proportion of acting students.

A final note: We do not believe in 'weeder' courses. Our class must serve *all* the students of our department. Therefore, it's important to us that every student, through discipline and hard work, can be successful in developing their first designs. Their designs will not all be polished, detailed, or risk-taking. We do our best to measure success by examining students' engagement with the *process* of design, acknowledging that every student starts the course at various levels in different skills. By the end of the semester they will not be accomplished designers, but they will be better *at* design.

Notes

1. *A Dancer's World*. Dir. Peter Glushanok. WQED, 1957. Film.
2. Robert Edmond Jones, *The Dramatic Imagination* (New York: Theatre Art Books, 1941, 21st printing 1994), p. 128.
3. David Bayles and Ted Orland, *Art and Fear: Observations on the Perils (and Rewards) of Artmaking* (Santa Cruz, CA & Eugene, OR: The Image Continuum, 2014), p. 114.

Section I

Costume Design

Chapter 1

Organizing Principles of the Class and Week 1

Session by Session Framework

As we examined the course, we realized that our exercises and discussions fell under one of five basic topics. We use these five topics to frame classroom activities.

- Design Elements: The building blocks of visual expression: Line, Shape, Form, Space, Color, and Texture
- Design Metaphor: Our primary tool to distill the script so that design becomes a poetic parallel of the play
- Script Analysis: Creating a vast and deep understanding of the script
- Research: Developing the design through the collection, comparison, comprehension, and utilization of all things relevant to the design
- Design Mechanics: The broad swath of communication and graphic methods used to express a design, such as drawing, painting, drafting, and model building.

Section by Section Framework

In tandem with determining the five framing topics of the course, we sought a chronological ordering to the conceptual work and accompanying projects that could be applied to all three sections (costume, scenery, and lighting) of the class.

The through-line from section to section begins with the assigning of three full-length plays. Email script details to students prior to the start of the course. They may need the extra time to obtain the materials and to read them at a leisurely pace.

Because of our rural location and a desire to relate the classroom to the world beyond, a project that researches professional designers is integrated into each section. Ideally, each student would research a costume designer, a set designer, *and* a lighting designer, giving a presentation on each at the end of the corresponding section. If your classroom time, like ours, doesn't have room for every student to present in each of the three sections, assign one presentation to each student. We split the class into thirds and have each take a costume, lighting, or scenic designer's name from a hat.

We knew we wanted to retain a final project of reasonable scale as the capstone of each section. This project had to be large enough to be an achievement, yet small enough that all the students, with diligent work, would be able to complete it (more guidelines in later chapters) in the five weeks allotted. Once we determined what we wanted students to achieve in each final project, we worked backwards through the weeks to determine what building blocks had to be placed in what order.

In our class, the costume, scenery, and lighting sections have these commonalities:

- Fundamental concepts, and the structure of learning them specific to each category of design
- Low-stakes exercises
- A mid-level project
- Student research projects that discuss a Broadway- or regional-level designer's work
- A guest artist from the professional field recently discussed
- The presentation of a final project with components often completed throughout the section.

Each class period starts with the broad picture of design and applies the lessons through group discussions and hands-on projects. Often these projects are in the form of low-stakes exercises.

Projects that require more instruction, are multi-step, or take several class periods are placed mid-way through the content of each five-week section. These mid-level projects create confidence through the complex application of newly developed skills.

Having a systematic process means that risky exploration takes place within an increasingly familiar process-structure. For us, developing a coherent, repeatable structure was an important step in fostering student success.

Supplies Needed

Instructor supplies:

- Classroom collage material: images cut from magazines. Avoid images with text or human faces.

Student supplies:

- 3" x 5" unlined notecards
- Scissors
- Tape or glue stick
- Drawing utensil (this is a personal preference; ink pens or pencils will suffice)

For the first few weeks, we will often supply smaller items ourselves until the students have had a chance to get to local office and art supply stores. A list of required materials and tools is distributed with the syllabus on the first day of class and can be found in Appendix B.

The framing topics of this week are:

- Design Elements

  - Introduction of Design Elements
  - Expanding Students' Design Vocabulary
  - Connecting Design Elements and Vocabulary through Exercises

- Design Metaphor

  - Introduction of Design Metaphor
  - Exploring the Literal and Poetic Meaning of Metaphors through Exercises
  - Applying Design Metaphor to a Dramatic Text

TEACHING TIP

Lecture, Demonstration, or Discussion?

The model of lecturer/note-taker has been the backbone of academy learning for centuries, but doesn't fit well into the hands-on learning environment we try to foster in our design classroom. We strive to engage students in discussion by asking for feedback, encouraging interruption, and testing by doing. If an answer can be given in multiple ways, we may preface discussion by saying, "I'm going to go around the room and everyone is likely to have a unique answer." When writing on the board, we may start a sentence and not finish it. Students will know to shout out the answers. We respond with "yes, ok, you have a piece of it," or "dig deeper" rather than providing the missing piece ourselves. Note taking is important, but we don't view it as an excuse to avoid participation in the discussion. In-class projects verify that the student has absorbed and can demonstrate information from the presentation, rather than create a set of notes to be filed away or reviewed in the future.

Discussion: Introducing Design Elements

On Day 1, we explore a handful of specific design elements that will serve the students as the framework for all future observation, discussion, and creation of visual material. In class, while we isolate the elements and sometimes intentionally omit one in an effort to provide more focus, the others remain present by inference.

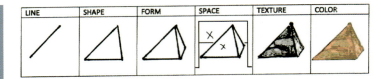

Figure 1.1 Progressive Treatment of Design Elements

"But a line, shape, texture, or color is a concrete actuality. These elements are more real than the objects they represent. Their effect does not depend upon an appeal to our intellect but to our primary instincts, which are deeper, more fundamental. They make a direct visual impact; they evoke an immediate, vigorous response. The elements and principles of design that govern their relationship are, therefore, real and powerful forces. If we would control and direct these forces, we must understand the elements and principles of design."[1]

Maitland Graves, *The Art of Color and Design*

TEACHING TIP

The similar sounding but differently defined phrase *principles of design* is often discussed in other books. The *principles of design* refer to the compositional use of the design elements – where things are placed and their relationships to each other. At our introductory level, we want our students to achieve a conscious understanding of the tools to make design (design elements) but absorb the use of those tools (principles of design) at a more visceral level. Principles such as symmetry and balance are introduced and named as opportunity arises, but limited class time generally does not allow a deeper or more formal discussion of composition.

Various texts, media, and artists define their lists of design elements differently, though there tends to be a handful of core terms common to all. Our short set of elements (listed below) serves our teaching and the students' learning very well, as it is inclusive without redundancy.

Figure 1.1 illustrates a progressive approach to the design elements. We introduce them by drawing this progression on the board to demonstrate how each successive element connects to the previous ones, and so builds complexity.

- Line: How to get from one point to another; an edge
- Shape: The 2D area defined by a line or the intersection of lines
- Form: The 3D area defined by a line or the intersection of lines
- Space: The volume of the form or the volume not within the form (negative space)
- Texture: The qualities/finish of a surface
- Color: Any variation of the visible light spectrum, inclusive of white and black.

The images in Figures 1.2 through 1.7 are relatively quick and basic treatments of each element, using computer programs such as Paint and SketchUp as well as personal photographs. Hand-drawn images, items culled from the internet, and actual objects can all be used to demonstrate each element. A bent coat hanger, for instance, can illustrate line (in both 2D and 3D permutations), shape, and form. A pipe cleaner adds texture to line. Fabric samples allow students a more tactile encounter with textures.

TEACHING TIP

Tracey once took a tap dancing class where the teacher used the last five minutes of each class period to demonstrate a new tap move. At first, it seemed infuriating to present something and give no time to practice. The teacher's methodology was to introduce the step, let it stay with a person, and revisit the item when the idea of the dance move was no longer new, even if the specifics were unknown. It worked. Because of the effectiveness of this style, Tracey puts a great deal of emphasis on early and thin introductions, feeling that the details of a concept are often best when added to a familiar foundation of vocabulary.

Book Recommendations

In-depth analysis of design elements common to theatrical usage can be found in any number of textbooks, such as Kaoime E. Malloy's *The Art of Theatrical Design* (published by Focal Press), or *The Magic Garment: Principles of Costume Design*, by Rebecca Cunningham.

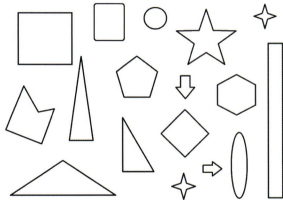

Figure 1.3 Shape

Figure 1.2 Line

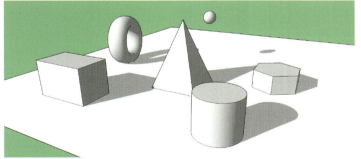

Figure 1.4 Form

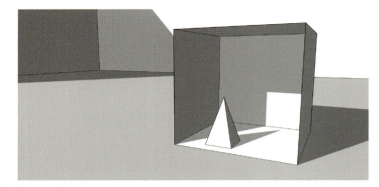

Figure 1.5 Space

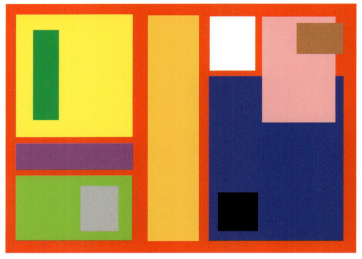

Figure 1.7 Color

Figure 1.6 Texture

Discussion: Exploring Design Elements

Within each of these six design elements comes a host of variation and associations. As we introduce them, a brief definition is accompanied by blackboard or slide image exploration of that element. Students are asked to describe the qualities of a straight line, a wavy line, a jagged line before straying into the application of emotional inferences: for example, what are the physical attributes of a line with regular points as opposed to one with irregular points? This is the first occasion students observe something and are asked to describe what they actually see before jumping to association and connotation. Only after the physical attributes of the element are exhausted do we move on to what that diagram or image suggests. There is a *difference* between the object itself and the associations it carries. We tell students that if you know that a particular type of line carries a particular connotation and why, it can then be *intentionally* applied in the creation of a garment's or environment's specific qualities.

If time allows, follow up the introduction of each design element with pieces of art or graphic designs that speak to that element. For example, the drawings and etchings of Albrecht Durer, Rembrandt, and Andy Warhol present a sense of line's expressive potential.

Work with your students to build up their descriptive vocabularies. For example: "The lead character is in a pink dress with soft lines and a full skirt." This statement notes the color, line, and space of the garment and hints at the texture. It is a more effective description than: "She wears a pretty dress that flatters her figure." Model the vocabulary that best suits you and your students' needs.

From now on, whenever an image is discussed, use the design elements to initiate description of the content. This begins a semester-long conversation that allows students to practice translating images into words, and words back into images. Almost every session from this one forward will review the design elements in some brief manner.

Figure 1.8
Color is a Sledgehammer. Which of These Girls is Passionate? Which One is Melancholy? Which One is Sad?

Hands-on Projects with Design Elements

To fit all of the exercises from each chapter of this book into one semester would require skill and endurance exceeding our own. Each chapter will present an exhaustive number of activities, many of which explore the same parameters but in slightly different ways. Choose from them. This is your course; use those things that will work best for you and your students in the time you have together.

The following exercises are small-scale, low-stakes explorations of each element. Their goals are to:

- Help students become more comfortable with drawing
- Begin expressing textual qualities through graphic means
- Reinforce design vocabulary.

Exercise: Developing Students' Vocabulary

Prepare projectable images, each of which prominently features one of the six design elements.

- Ask the students to call out the dominant design element.

  - If there is a difference of opinion, ask the students to support their decision with evidence from the image.

- Ask for adjectives that describe the action or inaction of the main elements.
- Exhaust their vocabulary on that element before moving to the next one.

Focus on what is actually in the image, rather than how the students *feel* about the image, or what cultural connotations they might discern.

Exercise: Building Presentation Skills for Designers

Put students in pairs. Assign a collection of related images to each pair (see Figures 1.9 through 1.14 for examples).

- Ask them to isolate a dominant design element from each collection of images and make a list of words that describe how the design element is used.
- Each pair, with equal contributions from both students, presents their image collection to the class and explains what element they addressed and how it is revealed throughout the collection of images.

Since communication is an essential part of designing for the theatre, this will be only the first among many presentations to the class.

Exercise: Take Nothing for Granted

Ask students to look around the room.

- Find a particular design element and describe it.
- Consider how it contributes to the overall mechanics and atmosphere of the space.

Figure 1.9 Line

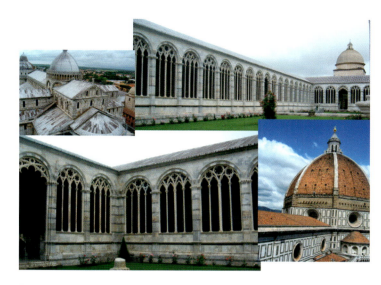

Figure 1.11 Form

Figure 1.10 Shape

Figure 1.12 Space

We are surrounded by colors and textures we take for granted – even institutional cinderblock has qualities to be explored and exploited – and being aware of the details around you means that you can use them later. We are surrounded by research materials every moment of the day.

Figure 1.13 Texture

TEACHING TIP

Drawing and painting are often daunting to beginners, especially to the non-design students in class. As scholars ourselves, we're interested in the idea of low-stakes practice. That is to say, many of the exercises we employ have little effect on the student's final grade and the mere finishing of these tasks keeps the student on track for learning. If a student is unskilled at color mixing, there is still great opportunity of success and no harm (no depletion of the overall grade) for trying. It's necessary to ensure that projects are achievable within the range of abilities of the class, but also that the projects stretch abilities without convincing the student that painting and drawing skills are only natural born talents. There have been plenty of student meltdowns, or apologies for something considered inadequate. We ask them if they've ever done the task at hand before. Usually they say no. Then we tell them to adjust their expectations and dig back in. Instilling confidence is sometimes more important than accomplishment.

Figure 1.14 Color

Exercise: Evoking Emotional Response through Design Elements

This exercise involves the interpretation of subjective terms and how the various design elements can be used to evoke them. It can help break some of the preconceptions students have about certain compositional elements by getting them to use those elements counter to how they might be used to experiencing them. It also helps introduce the idea that there are often many different routes to the same destination. There are any number of variations to this exercise, and it can be a good quick design element refresher. The use of 3 x 5 notecards is preferred.

Some examples:

- Using only straight, vertical lines, on three separate cards evoke a sense of: 1) isolation, 2) happiness, and 3) anger.
- Using only circles, on three separate cards evoke a sense of: 1) anger, 2) euphoria, and 3) melancholy.
- Using only squiggly lines, on three separate cards evoke a sense of: 1) boredom, 2) joy, and 3) fear.

Figure 1.17   Straight Lines/Isolation (Annie Kailhofer)

Figure 1.15   Circle/Anger (Annie Kailhofer)

Figure 1.18   Straight Lines/Isolation (Molly O'Hearn)

Figure 1.16   Circle/Anger (Rick Grischow)

Figure 1.19   Squiggly Lines/ Sadness (Madeline Mehnert)

Figure 1.20   Squiggly Lines/Sadness (Rick Grischow)

After the students complete three or four, collect them all but keep them anonymous.

- Ask the students to gather around, and randomly select a few to discuss. Don't announce the emotion that was the subject of the card, but let the class determine the artist's intention.
- Be sure they use design element language to explain their conclusions. What words describe the observed line, shape, form, space, color, and texture?
- Note similarities and differences between the cards. Part of the fun of this exercise is to see how students succeed with very different techniques.

The notecard exercises are equally about individual work and audience perception, so be sure to follow up the drawing with observation and discussion. This critical reflection and forum of public discussion shares the students' discoveries and develops new ideas. Dexterity with the use of design elements and the associated vocabulary contribute toward building better design skills.

TEACHING TIP

For many in-class exercises, we employ very short time limits. This not only helps the session roll forward at a steady pace, but prevents students from getting hung up on seeking the 'correct' answer or becoming paralyzed in over-thinking a response. Quick responses often bring forward gut-reactions, and one of the purposes of this class is to examine gut-reactions and understand why they contain the content they do.

Exercise: Less Control, More Designing

On a piece of paper, ask students to write down the name of a geometric shape.

- Have them fold the paper over to hide the name of the shape.
- Pass the paper to another student, who writes down an emotional state, then passes it to a third student.
- The third student uses a blank note card and attempts to evoke the emotional state using only the named geometric shape.

Limit time to prevent over-thinking. Collect all the cards.

- Ask the class to gather around; select a few cards for discussion.
- Ask the students what emotional state they thought was being evoked and why.
- How did the arrangement of shapes contribute to expressing the state?

When the discussion has gone as far as it can:

- Ask the student who drew it what emotional state was given.
- Were they surprised at the other students' conclusions? Why or why not?

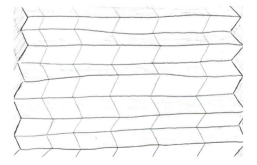

Figure 1.21 Parallelogram/Despair (Madeline Mehnert)

Figure 1.22 Triangles/Euphoria (Molly O'Hearn)

Book Recommendation

For further exploration of design principles (as opposed to design elements) we recommend *Visual Grammar,* by Christian Leborg. This highly diagrammatic book is sure to suggest a wide range of exercises and in-class projects.

Exercise: Design a Drink Logo

This is a low-stakes drawing exercise, and since it focuses on descriptive terms and connecting them with basic design elements, it's not about drawing ability but instead about becoming familiar with the tools just discussed. We use this exercise to close the class session in which design elements were introduced.

Bring in a soft drink or other beverage (poured into a non-labeled container) and opaque plastic cups. Be sure to ask about allergies, sugar, and caffeine sensitivities. Supply colored pencils or markers for the application of color.

Pour individual small samples and have the students taste the drink.

- Using the elements of design, instruct them to write down terms that describe their taste experience. They should not attempt to figure out what brand of beverage they just tasted; the focus should be on what they experienced directly.
- For example:

  - **Line** – smooth, wavy, or sharp
  - **Shape** – round, circles, melted, liquid
  - **Form** – bubbles
  - **Space** – overwhelming, dwarfing
  - **Texture** – reflective, slippery, sticky
  - **Color** – brown, caramel, black

On a notecard, and with a brief time limit, have the students create a logo for the soda by expressing their list of adjectives as design elements.

- Ask them to try to evoke the sensation of tasting the drink in their logo.
- Do not allow them to use any word other than 'drink' (and perhaps not even that) in their logo.

The card can be taped into a cylinder for presentation.

When everyone is done, have the students present their logos to the rest of the class. Ask the class to identify evident design elements, how each are used, and how they work together to create an overall effect.

Figure 1.23   Descriptive Words: Fruity, Vacation, Refreshing, Smooth, Tangy, Thin, Soft, Roundness (Kelsey Smyth)

Figure 1.24   Descriptive Words: Circular, Curvy, Citrus, Bright (Mason Ronan)

Figure 1.25   Descriptive Words: Smooth, Relaxed, Playful (Bridget Kelly)

Figure 1.26   Descriptive Words: Smooth, Easy, Thin, Cool, Watery, Bubbly (Eric Guenthner)

This is an early project, and some students will struggle with translating adjectives into design element building blocks. If pictorial images appear on the logo it may be less a response to the dynamic qualities of the flavor than an automatic pictorial association. This is okay, though, as these automatic images can spark further investigation. What is it about the lines, textures, and shape of the palm tree that connect it to the flavor of the drink? Is a drawing of an orange the only or best way to express a citrus flavor? What are the physical attributes of an actual orange?

The soda can exercise is the final effort of our first day of class.

Discussion: Concept and Design Metaphor

We use the idea of *design metaphor* as a through-line for thinking about a play. Design metaphor differs significantly from the more traditional idea of design concept, and we feel it provides a more narrowly defined, more helpful text-based foundation for beginning designers.

Metaphor is the implied relation of two different things, transferring meaning from one to the other without explicit connective words such as 'like'; for example, "All the world's a stage." Metaphor is a poetic parallel to an object or event, and design is a visually poetic parallel of the script. We define a design metaphor as *a brief, expressive, poetic parallel relating a script's dramatic arc to an active external visual image.*

'Concept' is a term applied to the overall stylistic approach of a production, and represents an effort to coordinate both the visual and performance components into an integrated whole. At first, this may sound similar to the idea of a 'poetic parallel.' Concept, though, tends to be something applied *to* a production and serves the explication of themes or audience expectation.

The problem with concept is that we, as educators, often ask students to consider the destination before examining the journey. The destination transmutes into themes and meanings and overshadows all subsequent work on the text, distilling the experience of theatre into a meaning delivery system where the first moment foreshadows the inevitable end and undercuts the suspense that creates interest. For example, a set design for *The Crucible* that displays obvious gallows imagery from the beginning is, yes, using a symbol derived from the text, but is applying that concluding image to the journey of the play. By considering theme and meaning (and the symbols that stand in for them) right off the bat, we risk losing sight of plot and character and start bending things to accommodate the destination rather than the journey. A designer may end up with visuals that are blunt and superficial rather than woven into the fabric of the play itself.

In the Mordecai Gorelik quote above, nowhere does he mention the *meaning* of the scene. Instead, he discusses *action* – what is going on in the scene. No matter how much historical verisimilitude is to be found in the scenery, the room doesn't become a living theatrical environment until it's connected with the life of the moment through the actors. Something is going on that puts the Sisters in a state of feverish excitement. How does their room speak to this moment? It's a scene of *raging fever.*

> "It is the *dramatic metaphor,* probably, which sums up, for each setting, all the thoughts which the designer may have. This metaphor is a piece of dramatic compression. Thus, the attic bedroom of the *Three Sisters* is not only an attic, not only a bedroom, not only a European room, not only a room of the period of 1901, not only a room belonging to the gentlefolk whom Chekhov wrote about. On top of all that, it may be, for the designer, the scene of *raging fever.* There is a fire going on outside. The whole house is restless, tossing about in this fire-atmosphere, unable to sleep . . . . Rightly done, the setting has an electric effect on the audience."[2]
>
> Mordecai Gorelik, "Designing the Play," from *Producing the Play*

The consideration of a script as a whole is an enormous undertaking, and development of a useful metaphor that speaks to the entirety of the text takes time. Often only after the first reading can a designer overlook the thrill of the story and read for larger scale. A metaphor suggested in the first reading might later slip away in favor of something that speaks to another, even more exciting aspect of the text. Some metaphors offer better visual components. Some metaphors are dated and not part of the students' common cultural literacy.

Eventually, we ask our students to distill the text into a single metaphor that speaks to the whole arc of the play; the journey rather than the destination. This condensed, visually rich statement then becomes a powerful tool that can be used to explicate and unify character and environment in service to the plot.

Table 1.1 presents a side by side comparison of Concept vs. Design Metaphor:

Table 1.1

Title of Play	Brief Plot Summary	Possible Concept, and Rationale	Possible Design Metaphor
Sweeney Todd, The Demon Barber of Fleet Street	A barber returns to London to reclaim his former life and take revenge upon those who wrong him.	Steampunk, to highlight industrial qualities of London at the time and present the play in a way contemporary audiences can identify with.	All the characters are trapped in a wasteland, starving for things that they have been denied.
She Stoops To Conquer	A wealthy young woman poses as a servant to get to know her shy suitor, leading to a variety of romantic misunderstandings.	Circus elements, to emphasize the three-layer plot and constant larger-than-life, frenetic activity.	Blinded by expectations, the characters only begin to see the value of each other when they must actually seek in darkness for each other.
Radium Girls	Young factory workers are poisoned by radioactive paint and must face down a major corporation in their quest for justice.	Clocks and Time, since the young women were poisoned painting watch-faces and are in a race against time.	Grace and the other radium girls are butterflies who learn that the ripples they cause can eventually become hurricanes.
The Tender Land	On the eve of her high school graduation, and prompted by a brief fling with a traveling farmhand, Laurie leaves home to truly begin her life.	Adapt the work of artists like Grant Wood and Thomas Hart Benton to illustrate the world of simple, hardworking Midwestern farmers.	The farm is a prison for Laurie's spirit, and she yearns to escape into the world she can see beyond its bars.

Hands-on Projects with Metaphor

The goals of the following exercises include:

- Becoming more aware of how we already use poetic language (metaphor) in everyday life
- To consciously make use of metaphor
- Connection and application of design elements to a given metaphor

"The greatest thing by far is to have command of metaphor."[3]
Aristotle, *The Poetics*

TEACHING TIP

Start a class session with a brief review of the previous session's major points followed by a quick run-down of specific goals for the day. This not only gives the students an expectation of the impending discussion and activities, but helps keep you on track as well.

Exercise: The Literal and Poetic Parts of Metaphor

Write a metaphorical statement, such as "The apple doesn't fall far from the tree," on the board.

- Engage the students in the literal meaning. Walk through the words. What is an apple? Where is it at the beginning of the action? When the apple lands, why "isn't it far from the tree?"
- Discuss the poetic meaning. What does the apple represent in the poetic meaning? What does the apple's fall symbolize? What, in the metaphor, is the relationship between the apple and the tree? What is the meaning of the short distance between the two?

Exercise: From the Poetic Back to the Literal

A web search will lead you to a number of language sites that discuss metaphor and provide many examples.

Prepare a worksheet listing a selection of statements containing metaphors with multiple choices as to that metaphor's meaning. For example:

We all would have had a second helping if George hadn't been such a hog.

George was compared to a hog because:

a) He looked like a farm animal
b) He lived on a farm, where people eat heartily
c) He ate gluttonously
d) His personal cleanliness was atrocious

After students make their choices, discuss the literal and poetic meaning of each metaphor.

Exercise: Independent Analysis of Metaphor

Distribute a list of common metaphorical sayings. Again, web searches will help you compile it. Some examples:

- He had ants in his pants
- She was the rotten apple in the barrel
- He was armed to the teeth
- It was her Achilles' heel
- That's easier than shooting fish in a barrel
- It was more fun than a barrel full of monkeys

Ask students to explain the meaning of each and its common usage. (There are always a few sayings that baffle students because they have fallen out of use amongst members of their generation or geographic region.)

Exercise: Linking Design Elements to Metaphor

The student designers now combine their new skills in the application of descriptive language. Offer a metaphorical statement to the class. For example:

Sweeney Todd's desire for revenge leads him down a dark tunnel of inhumanity.

Ask the students to offer descriptive terms that provide further visual flavor to "a dark tunnel of inhumanity." Some possible responses:

- **Line** – heavy, thick, straight, twisted
- **Shape** – circular, repeating, linear
- **Form** – tunnel, tube, straight
- **Space** – claustrophobic, imposing, endless, cylindrical, cavernous
- **Texture** – slippery, slimy, rough, gritty, sticky
- **Color** – muted, plain, dark, black, red, crimson, grey

None of these terms is more correct than any other, and if a student offers an unexpected descriptive term, be sure to dig a bit and get her or him to explain the full context of the choice.

TEACHING TIP

Collage is a powerful visual tool that circumvents students' fears of inadequate drawing skills. Designers can use collage at any number of points in the design process, from jumpstarting stalled thinking, to exploring the relationships of disparate visual elements, to communicating character and environmental details to other members of the production team. We find it useful to have a box in the design classroom cabinet filled with newspaper and magazine clippings that can be brought out at a moment's notice for both planned and impromptu exercises. As you fill your box, avoid images with text or people as students will often gravitate toward those as shortcuts to audience comprehension – *telling* the viewer what the collage is attempting to evoke rather than actually *evoking* the sensation.

Exercise: Deriving Design Elements from Metaphor to Support Visual Choices

The list of terms generated in the previous exercises can inform a student's choices in the formation of a collage.

If you have a box of classroom collage material, distribute handfuls of pictures to each student. Only the images at hand can be used. We want the student to *evoke* the sensation of the metaphor.

- Present a metaphor (you can use the one used in the previous exercise)
- Have the students make a short list of design element terms drawn from the metaphor
- Direct the students to use the limited number of available images to *evoke* the sensation of the metaphor.

  - Assign a time limit of about five minutes.
  - They may rip or cut images.
  - They may alter the texture of the images by crunching or wrinkling.

Collect the collages and present them, one at a time, to the class.

- Ask the class to determine which design elements are most prominent.
- Ask which descriptive terms from the list are most evident.
- Discuss how the collage visually evokes the metaphor's poetic meaning.

Exercise: Metaphor Journals

As students go about their day, they should listen for the metaphors sprinkled into everyday conversation. If someone uses a metaphor, the student should remember the statement, note the context, and write it down. At the opening of subsequent class sessions, we will ask if anyone heard any good metaphors in the time since we last met, and then discuss that metaphor's literal and poetic meanings.

This project can evolve into the review and application of design elements. For example, a student presents a metaphor from their journal: "That project was a grand slam."

- Dissect the literal meaning and the poetic parallel.
- List each of the design elements and explore creative words that apply to the concepts, in light of the metaphor. "What kind of LINE would describe a grand slam?"

We have found that the creation of a physical journal helps students keep this project in mind. Two pieces of paper, folded over and stapled down the fold, becomes an instant journal they can put in their packs, carry throughout the week, and make frequent entries in.

TEACHING TIP

The ability to talk about design comes with practice. Allow students to present their work and ideas without any penalty. Bring students to the front of the room often for small and specific presentations. For example: the students have been working on costume renderings for half an hour. Ask each student to show their work to the class, say what they were doing (focusing on a term or topic) and then allow them to sit back down. If the student's presentation misleads or wrongly presents ideas, try to make your comments sound like a reiteration for clarification. To make serious comments about sub-par in-class work, we turn to private feedback.

Exercise: Application of Metaphor to Text

Distribute a piece of flash fiction, one-minute play, monologue, or poem.

Ask the students to use a metaphorical statement to describe the arc of action or atmosphere of the piece. This can be a quick class opener throughout the semester to review the use of metaphor.

- "It feels as if the character is shouting at the audience from the bottom of a well."
- "She's trapped on a roller coaster and can't get off."
- "He's just waiting for the other shoe to drop."

This exercise can be expanded upon by adding a notecard component that focuses on expressing individual design elements or evoking qualities through collage.

Homework: Read the Plays

Since the students will select one of the three assigned plays for their costume design final project and will need to be able to discuss each other's work, we end the week by reminding the students to read all three plays. They should be ready to take a brief quiz during the next session to see how well they've read the plays. They should also bring their copies of all three plays to the next few class sessions to aid in-class exploration of the scripts.

Building a Student Portfolio

The following items, generated by the exercises in this chapter, can be used to begin building student portfolios. We ask students to save everything produced from this class regardless of complexity. The portfolio, from notecards to swatched renderings to storyboards, represents the journey of the student designer.

The portfolio is an ongoing project, and should be revisited a few times a year to add new projects and remove older ones. At the beginning, students will have mostly classroom work to put in their portfolios. As classroom projects become larger and more complex, those latest projects will replace the early efforts. When the work is part of a realized production, those pieces will, in turn, be prominently featured.

Decide whether you wish students to build paper or electronic versions, depending on how much time and energy you expect them to invest. If your department advocates a specific platform or format, or includes a portfolio review as part of the curriculum, have the students work within those parameters.

If you want students to assemble paper portfolios, two alternatives can be offered:

- If the student is pursuing design as a career, an actual portfolio case can be purchased. 22" x 17" is a good size (it should fit under a bus or airplane seat). Be sure it has removable, plastic-sheathed pages. As projects are added, affix them to separate sheets that can be slipped into the sheathed pages. This way projects can be added, removed, or moved around without having to buy new pages.
- A three-ring binder with a healthy supply of plastic sheet protectors is useful for students who wish to begin assembling portfolio materials without the cost of a larger artist's portfolio case. The drawback is that everything must be reduced to 8½" x 11" or smaller.

Figure 1.28   Sample Larger Format Portfolio Case

Figure 1.29   Sample Portfolio Pages in a Three-Ring Binder

Figure 1.27   Sample Portfolio Pages in a 22" x 17" Portfolio Case

In this digital age, electronic portfolios are popular and widespread for a number of reasons, not least of which is convenience. Occasionally students are able to build a website through which portfolio items can be viewed. We don't require *or* discourage students from building an electronic portfolio, but

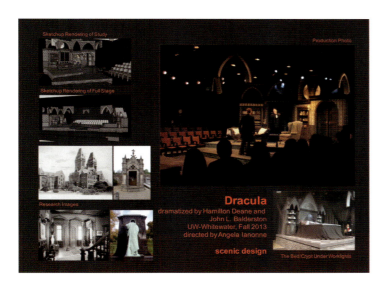

Figure 1.30 Sample PowerPoint Portfolio Slide

Figure 1.31 Sample Layout of a Soda Can Project Portfolio Page

note that effective layout techniques remain pertinent regardless of format.

Portfolio Exercise: Laying Out the Drink Project

This is another opportunity to slip in the use of compositional principles. Have the student arrange the items on a 8½″ x 11″ piece of paper before moving onto electronic formats.

If you wish your students to build a practice portfolio as part of the course, for this week's exercise:

- Scan or photograph the drink exercise; crop as needed.
- Write a brief caption, including the descriptive words that generated the design.

- Create a title block for the project that includes name of student and date of completion.
- Format a page or slide with the image, caption, and title.
- Discuss background colors and fonts that augment the content without distracting from it.

Notes

1. Maitland Graves, *The Art of Color and Design* (New York: McGraw Hill Book Company, Inc., 1951), pp. 3–4.
2. Mordecai Gorelik, "Designing the Play," in *Producing the Play*, ed. John Gassner (New York: The Dryden Press, 1941), p. 314.
3. Aristotle, *The Poetics*, tr. S.H. Butcher (New York: Hill and Wang, 1961), p. 104.

Chapter 2

Week 2

"A playwright is a craftsperson, and a play may be said to be designed and built, unit by unit, action by action, word by word. Each play has a finite number of units, even when the multiplicity and complexity of the units seem to be infinite and defy analysis.

Because plays are constructed from units you can examine, they are open to analysis. You may search for the nature and structure of the play by correctly identifying the parts and by perceiving the patterns in which the playwright has arranged the parts."[1]
Rosemary Ingham and Liz Covey, *The Costume Designer's Handbook*

- Pencils for drawing
- Poster board
- Ruler/straight edge
- Ultrafine-tipped black markers
- Light box, window, computer screen (any of these, in order to see through one sheet of paper and onto another; used to transfer images)

Supplies Needed

Instructor supplies:

- Croquis (human figure outlines, defined in this chapter)
- Handouts of fashion components (Figures 2.9 through 2.12)

Student supplies:

- Graph paper (useful for costume plot and costume chart but not required)
- Unlined paper
- Tracing paper (useful for drawing on top of other layers, but often not required)

The framing topics for this week are:

- Assigning the Costume Design Final Project
- Script Analysis

  - Discussion of Script Analysis
  - Using Script Analysis to Further Develop Design Metaphor

    - Unpacking Design Elements from the Design Metaphor

  - Creating the Costume Plot

- Metaphor

  - Continued Discussion of the Metaphor Journal Assignment

- Design Mechanics

  - Applying Script Analysis Tools to Delineate Individual Characters
  - Drawing Clothing on the Human Body

- Research

  - Using Research Images to Draw Clothing on the Human Body
  - Assigning the Presentation of a Professional Designer

In Chapter 1, the focus was on some of the foundational tools needed to understand and create design. This chapter continues to build upon design elements and metaphor, and includes exercises that are less theoretical and more directly applicable to the specifics of the costume design project assigned to the students. As noted earlier, this book targets teaching three design fields in just one semester, and for each field of study a design is substantially completed and presented. To connect the theoretical and the practical, we introduce the costume design final project at the beginning of Week 2.

Introduction of the Costume Design Final Project

Although early in the costume design process, it is necessary to define the costume section's final project (due in Week 5). Introducing the project in the first weeks means that students become familiar with the names of its components prior to knowing how to accomplish each task; still, this will help them connect day-to-day classroom activities to the requirements of this comprehensive piece of work. The next four weeks are designed so that the students progressively generate all the items necessary for the display of their project.

The components of the costume design final project are mounted to poster board or sheets of foamcore, and consist of the following:

- A title block

  - Name and author of script
  - Student's name and their title (in this case: Costume Designer)

- Metaphor statement
- 50 research images
- Research image used as a color palette
- Costume plot (optional)
- Script analysis by character (optional)

- Five costume renderings

  - Painted
  - Computer-aided titling

    - Name of script
    - Name of character (may include act/scene information)

- Fabric swatches

The five costume renderings can be either for five different characters, or may include multiple costumes for a single character as determined by the Costume Plot. The formatting of the presentation boards follows KCACTF Region III's current guidelines for conference presentations.

In Chapter 5, there are more details about the oral presentation of these projects, images of completed projects, and a rubric for evaluation.

The Kennedy Center American College Theatre Festival (KCACTF) holds eight regional conferences (and one national conference) each year. A component of the conference is the presentation of Regional Design Projects. Although the format is loosely defined by KCACTF, the designs at the festival have been our inspiration for the format of visual and oral presentations required in our classroom. For more information about other aspects of KCACTF or Regional Design Projects, consult their website (www.kcactf.org), and your region's website.

Script Analysis

The start of the costume design final project, as with any theatrical design, is script analysis.

In Week 1, we approach design metaphor before script analysis because we feel the first reading of a script is to gain the "flash."[2] That term is credited to seminal lighting designer Jean Rosenthal (considered by many to have originated the role of the American lighting designer), who urges us to read the whole play quickly, in one sitting, without care of details or worrying about technical demands. Even if the play is familiar, she says one should attempt reading it as though for the first time. By first having students become familiar with metaphor and understanding how design is a poetic parallel to the script they now are better situated to recognize a 'flash' of their own. Rosenthal also notes that the "flash" is an if-and-when proposition. If it comes, it's a guidepost for the rest of the process. If it doesn't, more work is certainly required. Make sure that students understand first impressions are subject to change through later discoveries.

Book Recommendation

First-hand conversations with important designers about their work and process can often be difficult to track down. Babak Ebrahimian's *Sculpting Space in the Theatre: Conversations with the Top Set, Light and Costume Designers* offers a series of interviews that discuss the approaches and work practices of a variety of designers. Backing up classroom activities with voices from outside the classroom is a good way to show skeptical students the larger context of your pedagogy.

Within the idea of metaphor and design concept, there is wide variation in how designers work with the script after their initial encounter with it. The following are ideas expressed by some major designers or design teachers. Each demonstrates their unique approach, all of which keep the script at the center of the process.

- Rebecca Cunningham, costume designer, feels that the second reading should focus on the language and imagery of the play.[3]
- Darwin Reid Payne, scenic designer, notes that visual images are formed during and after the reading of the play (he doesn't specify first, second, third, or multiple readings), with the next step being an attempt to set these images on paper as rough diagrams to explore plans of movement.[4]
- Howard Bay, scenic designer, begins labor on his second reading by taking notes and making diagrams – in rough scale – to "anchor large rhythms of the drama and forestall the chaos of total immersion in the details."[5]
- John Conklin, scenic designer, suggests a close reading, looking for "clusters of metaphors, recurring imagery, and key words."[6]
- Susan Hilferty, costume designer, looks for rhythm and timing to help establish the "essential nature of the world."[7]
- Michelle DiBucci, sound designer, says that she reads the play several times, focusing on story and characters the first time through. After that, she begins to take notes as thoughts pop into her head. "I have found that if it is undecided what 'sound world' the play will have, then the answer is often in the play itself."[8]
- Beverly Emmons, lighting designer, echoes Rosenthal: "I read the play; even if it's familiar, I'll read it again. I take care not to have opinions. Then I go to the first meeting with the director. Usually, at that point, the universe of the play has been developed in conversation with the director and scenic designer."[9]
- Phil Lee, sound designer, marks up the script with possible places for sound to occur. In his first meetings with the director, he says that his first priority is to LISTEN (his emphasis) and then revisit the script with the results of those meetings in mind.[10]
- The fifth edition of Parker, Smith, and Wolf's popular textbook *Scene Design and Stage Lighting* informs the reader that "it is impossible to set down universal rules for developing a design idea: there are as many methods as designers."[11]

Throughout a lifetime of designing and teaching, these and other masters of design must be encountered and read. While each one offers a variation on the steps of overall design process, they all *have* a process. Students should understand that even for the masters of their crafts, the final design does not spring fully formed from their heads after their first encounter with the script. There is long and deep engagement with the play that starts with reading it for the first time, then steadily grows more complex depending on design field, personal experience, and the needs of the production. In this book (as in our class) we try to reference the breadth of script analysis approaches while keeping the parameters within the reach of one semester (15 weeks).

TEACHING TIP

What becomes clear from the examination of professional designers' processes is that as one becomes more experienced and skilled, process steps merge. Working methods naturally shift and adapt toward those that give the best results in the shortest amount of time. Not until a designer dismantles the process in an attempt to lead a student through it do they realize just how much has become second nature. What has become intuitive for an experienced teacher and designer may appear illogical and mysterious to a novice. Don't assume any part of your own process is obvious.

Quiz: Reading Comprehension

At the start of the second or third session, before any discussion of the texts, we administer a reading comprehension quiz on all three plays. This ensures that students have read the plays and the class can indeed move toward the costume, set,

and lighting final projects that involve the plays. This is the only quiz given during the semester, and the only purely quantitative grade the students receive. The percentage that this quiz contributes to the final grade is low (five percent) which means that failing this quiz does not prevent a student from earning an 'A' through diligent work on subsequent assignments. Our experience has shown that many students automatically tend to assume quizzes and tests factor heavily toward the final grade regardless of their weight as noted in the syllabus. This quiz therefore becomes a low-stakes assignment that nevertheless serves as a wake-up call.

Devise ten or so questions per play, keeping the focus on plot points and structure. Try to include a certain level of detail that will point out the flaws of reading an internet summary or published notes condensation as well as suggesting the sorts of things that designers might start looking for in a text. Below are some sample questions.

Sample Quiz Questions

- (*Jeffrey*) Jeffrey meets Steve for the first time at the gym. Where does he run into him the second time?
- (*Leading Ladies*) Who owns the house in which most of the action takes place?
- (*Leading Ladies*) When Jack and Leo begin their scam, what do they intend to gain because of their fraud?
- (*She Stoops to Conquer*) When Marlow and Hastings arrived, they didn't think they were at the Hardcastles' house, they thought they were at _____.
- (*On the Verge*) How many male actors are required to cast this play?
- (*On the Verge*) At the beginning of Act Two, the explorers happen upon "fallout from the future." What shape does this fallout take?
- (*She Stoops to Conquer*) Who created the hairstyle worn by Mrs. Hardcastle?
- (*Boeing Boeing*) Over how many days does the action of the play take place?

- (*Boeing Boeing*) Bernard's plan to remain engaged to all three women relies totally upon the airlines they work for adhering to something. What is it?

After the quiz is collected, we review the questions in class and launch into a discussion of the texts. The following exercises assist in starting that conversation.

Hands-on Projects with Script Analysis

Exercise: Lasting First Impressions

Using their memories of the script, ask the students to make two lists:

- Remembered images, phrases, and situations
- Other descriptive terms that repeated or seemed otherwise prominent

Set a short time limit (four to five minutes) for this exercise. When the time limit elapses, have the students compare and contrast their findings with the rest of class. Note what features are remembered by most, and what that prominence may or may not mean for further exploration.

Exercise: Reactions into Metaphor

Referencing the lists from the 'Lasting First Impressions' exercise, students now experiment with creating a preliminary metaphor.

- Using gut-reactions and remembered images, develop a metaphor statement.
- Share and discuss these metaphors with the class.

The more successful metaphors transform those remembered fragments into something a bit more cohesive and global.

Look for action and movement rather than a static, symbolic image. Work at turning static images into a statement that applies to the arc of the play. For example, if a student offers "the sun" as a major recurring image from the play, ask what the sun does, and if the application of this image remains constant throughout the play. The sun rises, the sun sets, the sun can be obscured by clouds, the sun can blind someone who looks directly at it; what sun-related action can be used to best describe the journey of the play?

TEACHING TIP

For many students metaphor is still unfamiliar territory. This exercise should focus on developing metaphor muscles rather than on 'correct' or 'incorrect' metaphors. Very few students will arrive at a polished metaphor by the end of the session. Conclude the session by reviewing the connections between metaphor, script, and design.

Discussion: Unpacking the Play

Draw students into a conversation that starts from 'the flash' and moves into the specifics of the script. Ask the students to address basic script analysis questions:

- How does the action in the play begin (the inciting incident)?
- What *happens* in the play?
- What are the major plot points?
- What decisions are made by particular characters at these major plot points?

- What about the world changes at these major plot point moments?
- How does the play end?
- Who is the main character (protagonist)?
- Is that character the same one who keeps the action rolling (catalyst)?
- Who or what is the villain or obstacle (antagonist) and how does it/he/she engage the protagonist?
- How do the characters change in the course of the play? Who were they at the beginning and how are they different at the end?
- Was the protagonist a willing participant in the learning process?
- Did the world around the protagonist bring about their change or did they bring change to the world? Or both?

This conversation segues into the issue of the stakes of the play. If Scrooge does *not* become a better man by the end of his ghostly visitations, what happens to him? What happens to *the world*? Try to get the students to articulate clearly what they perceive to be the overall ramifications of the play.

Continue the discussion by moving away from plot and into style and language.

- Were there any writing idiosyncrasies?
- What does the style of the writing say about the dramatist's intention?
- If heightened language is an important stylistic element of the play, *why* did the playwright use it that way?
- How does that specific language serve the storytelling? How does heightened or idiosyncratic language affect designing the play?

"The first step in playscript analysis is to move from an understanding of the play in terms of what appeared to be happening in the early readings to a rigorous examination of the facts that are contained in the play, facts that are there to tell you precisely what is happening. In your search for script facts, collect only what is there."[12]
Rosemary Ingham and Liz Covey, *The Costume Designer's Handbook*

Book Recommendation

Backwards and Forwards: A Technical Manual for Reading Plays, by Alan Ball, is a fine and fast read when looking for a starting point with script analysis. However, do not underestimate the importance of exposure to many, many scripts as a lesson about understanding theatre. By reading a lot of plays the student (and designer, and teacher) builds their own body of first-hand knowledge, generating their own questions and seeking their own answers. This permits a more informed and critical interaction with opinions deemed to be authoritative. Often one has to know something prior to learning what others think.

Discussion and Homework: Combining Metaphor and Design Elements to Create a Metaphor Statement

The assignment, due next class session:

- Write a design metaphor statement suggested by one of the three full-length plays. This will be used in developing the costume design final project.

We find the success rate of first metaphors – ones that address the arc of the play as well as contain a potent visual image – to be around 20 percent of those presented. This may sound grim, but it *is* a starting point, and with specific and frequent feedback, success grows. A certain degree of statement evolution is expected as the costume project moves forward.

TEACHING TIP

For many students, discussing their work in an open forum is intimidating and frightening, especially if they feel they are being judged. There is a difference between judging work and evaluating work, and the teacher needs to be sure that public response to work, especially fragile early work, remains constructive. In the first weeks of class, as the students are getting to know you and each other, show by example that the room is a safe place to express *informed* opinion, that risks can be taken, and that it is the work being evaluated – not the student's worth being judged.

- Ask students to volunteer their work. There will usually be at least one brave student willing to go first.
- Use the first volunteer to demonstrate your standard critique process; try to be consistent from student to student so they know what's coming when it's their turn. After the first few volunteers, it will be easier to call students by name and have them step forward.
- Use a series of questions to get the student to explain their choices, such as: "I'm curious about that – tell me why you made that choice." If some aspect of the work is problematic, the line of questioning should make it apparent without the instructor having to state that something is good or bad.
- When opening responses to the rest of the class, ask them to respond to specific points about the work at hand. General responses can quickly get too personal.

Below are two frequent metaphor pitfalls, followed by suggestions to aid improvement:

- **The partial sentence metaphor**: "He was shooting fish in a barrel."

  - Who is the subject of this metaphor? Who is the 'he' in the sentence?
  - What action in the script parallels the act of shooting or shooting fish?
  - What is the quality of action that shooting fish in a barrel expresses?

  Try to lead the students (be sure to open this to the whole class, not only the student who brought in the partial metaphor) to a more developed statement, such as: "In Jane Austen's *Pride and Prejudice*, Charles Bingley's wealth made finding a wife as easy as shooting fish in a barrel." Even though this may not provide the most useful imagery through which to view *Pride and Prejudice*, it still connects a metaphor with a more active story arc.

- **The mixed metaphor**: "The folk tale, *Jack and the Beanstalk*, is a cat and mouse game with the thrills of a roller coaster."

  - Two metaphors usually muddy a design, rather than bring clarity. Lead the student out of the mixture with questions such as:

    - Is there anything in the text's mechanics or visuals that seem to favor one metaphor over the other?

  - Explore differences and similarities.

    - What is the nature of the thrills of a cat and mouse game? (*hiding, seeking, cruelty. . .*)
    - What is the nature of the thrills found on a roller coaster? (*speed, climbing and dropping. . .*)

  - Is there another metaphor that could work better than the two already chosen? Willingness to abandon an okay idea for a better idea is a good lesson to learn.

- By focusing on a character's journey rather than a descriptive plot blurb, a more informative, global metaphor could develop: "Jack learns that magic is a double-edged sword of wealth and responsibility."

After discussing the metaphor itself, link design elements to the design metaphor. This will underscore the need to have a strong visual quality to the metaphor. Present a metaphor to the class and ask them for descriptive words that connect to the visuals suggested by the metaphor. As suggestions are made, place them under the design element they are most related to, as in the example below:

Design Metaphor: "Nora's shackles of responsibility are unlocked when faced with the choice of blackmail or truth."

Design Elements inspired by the metaphor:

- **Line:** thick, hard, strong, binding
- **Shape:** square, small
- **Form:** boxed, tight, limiting
- **Space:** small, outgrown, crowded
- **Texture:** rough, uncomfortable, itchy
- **Color:** unhealthy, blaring, blinding, orange, dark orange, yellow-green

We prefer students to write their statements in paragraph format, rather than turning in bullet-point lists. This is to practice both overall writing skills and how to present their thoughts as a cohesive whole. Have them create a metaphor statement by weaving the metaphor and design elements into a narration similar to the following example:

- In Henrik Ibsen's *A Doll's House*, Nora's shackles of responsibility are unlocked when faced with the choice of blackmail or truth. To depict this in my designs, the lines will be thick, hard, and strong, with shapes and forms that box and oppress the characters. Nora's relationship with Torvald has been outgrown. She feels uncomfortable and itches for something to change. Colors depicted will be unhealthy, blaring, blinding, orange, dark orange, yellow-green. The design echoes the constraints put upon Nora by herself and by others.

TEACHING TIP
Two Cautionary Situations

First, when writing a metaphor statement, students may fall into the old habits of plot summary, thematic responses, or personal critique (I hated this play, I loved this play. . .). We mark up this first attempt without penalty and tell them to revise and resubmit. Taking the time to do a task well can be more valuable than receiving a passing grade on a weak argument.

Second, at this point don't let students jump prematurely to descriptions of how they intend to use the design elements on specific costume components: "Jack's costume will have long, sharp, pointed sleeves with jagged piping and shiny, metallic shoes." This means they've made their mind up about certain things before they've done any research or detailed character analysis. Things may yet change.

This metaphor statement will be the litmus test for the evaluation of student success. If a student declares that the lines of the design should be straight, sharp, parallel, and balanced, expect their finished renderings to contain the use of that design element as described. If the student defines the use of line as thick, heavy, weighted, and dominant but a design using chiffon fabric and soft, scalloped edges is drawn, the work is unsuccessful.

The edited version of the metaphor statement is a component of the costume design final project.

Homework: Using French Scenes to Dig Deeper into Detail

A French Scene breaks down a script by noting when any character exits or enters the stage.

Using French Scenes is a way to divide the script into small portions that make it easier to identify plot logistics. Entrances and exits often denote a change in character objectives or the completion of an objective, as well as delineating some stage mechanics such as the need for doors or isolated playing areas.

The goals of this assignment are:

- To engage in and strengthen the skills required for a 'close reading' of the play
- To organize and clarify thoughts about the play
- To increase familiarity with the intricacies of the plot
- To better understand the characters' relationships to each other
- To identify elements noted, described, and inferred by the script that might be useful to designers
- To create lists that will serve as references for further design mechanic activities.

Some students have been introduced to the concept of French Scenes in previous courses, but some review may be necessary to create confidence in using them as a tool for theatrical design. Begin the homework project in class. Working through the first page or two of one of the scripts will model the thinking needed to extract the information necessary to complete the work. Indeed, some of the subsequent costume exercises and assignments will not be possible unless the student finishes working through their breakdown.

We expect this assignment to be turned in at the start of the next session. Before collecting this assignment, be sure that students have retained a copy for themselves. The French Scene breakdown will assist in the creation of the costume plot. Figure 2.1 is a handout specific for a French scene breakdown used in scenery and lighting design. It is valuable to show how the different designers adjust this tool to their specific needs. Figure 2.2 is a French scene breakdown used as a first step for costume designers to create a costume plot.

A French Scene analysis is necessary to complete the process of costume design. To that end, it could be required as a component of the final costume design project.

Script Analysis Homework: French Scene Breakdown Guidelines

1) Break the script into French scenes. A French Scene is a unit of the script delineated by an entrance or an exit – whenever the number of people on stage changes. Some French scenes will be long, some may be very short; in some a lot may happen, in some very little may happen. If there is a quick series of entrance and exits (as in a farce), it may be necessary to group them together. Be sure to note page numbers.

2) Create a chart outlining:

   a) the character(s)' goal(s) (if the play has a large cast, focus on the main characters)
   b) the obstacle to achieving that goal
   c) what that character(s) does to overcome the obstacle
   d) whether there is success in obtaining that goal
   e) the result of that success or failure (what happens next because of it)

3) For each French scene, list everything that describes the characters and the environment. Is there mention of weather? A character's age? The color of someone's clothing? The food that is being eaten? Scents? Sounds?

Sample chart:

The Beauty Queen of Leenane, by Martin McDonagh
Scene One, French Scene 1, pages 3–11

Character	Goal	Obstacle	Action	Results
Mag	To make Maureen do everything for her (control);	Maureen	Nag, Wheedle, Complain; Guilt-trip	Maureen storms out; seemingly backfires
Maureen	Escape	Duty as a daughter (guilt?)	Finally gives Mag piece of her mind	Storms out; is this as far as she's willing to be pushed?

Things Noted that Describe the Environment:

- *rural cottage, west of Ireland*
- *long black range, box of turf, rocking chair*
- *door to hallway*
- *sink, cupboards*
- *dinner table, two chairs*
- *small TV, electric kettle, radio*
- *crucifix, framed picture of John and Robert Kennedy*
- *heavy black poker, touristy tea towel with inscription*
- *raining heavily*
- *porridge and tea – warm brown sludge*
- *Mag, stout, early seventies, tight perm, grey hair, shriveled red left hand*
- *Maureen is Mag's daughter, wearing coat, was shopping*
- *Pg. 7 – Maureen notes the smell of the sink*

Figure 2.1 French Scene/Script Analysis Homework Guidelines Needed for the Scenery and Lighting Sections

Discussion: The Costume Plot

A costume plot is a chart that transitions script analysis into design mechanics. Costume plots aid in the costume design process by allowing the costume designer, at a glance, to determine the number of costumes needed, when quick changes occur, and which characters will appear on stage together at any given moment.

The following figures (2.2 and 2.3) show the difference between a French Scene breakdown and a costume plot.

In the French Scene breakdown for *Yankee Tavern* (Figure 2.2), Adam and Janet start the show (French Scene 1). A few pages later Ray joins them (French Scene 2). When Ray later exits, it creates French Scene 3.

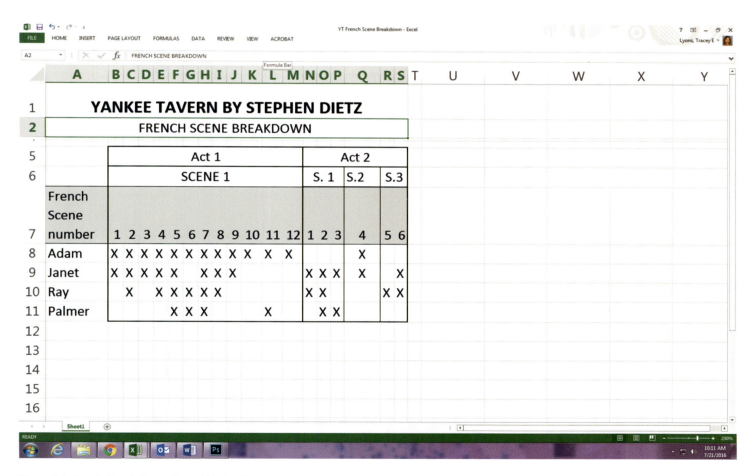

Figure 2.2 Sample French Scene Chart of *Yankee Tavern*

A costume plot substitutes the indication of a character's appearance with a number that references the costume. Be sure to number costumes sequentially as they appear, but always retain their number if the character wears the exact same costume in another scene. In the example costume plot, note that the 'X' indicating the appearance of a character has been replaced by their costume number. In Act 2, French Scene 1, Janet is in a new costume, indicated by a number different than that of her first appearance.

Homework: The Costume Plot

Assign the creation of a costume plot. Number costumes sequentially by their appearance. The costume number will

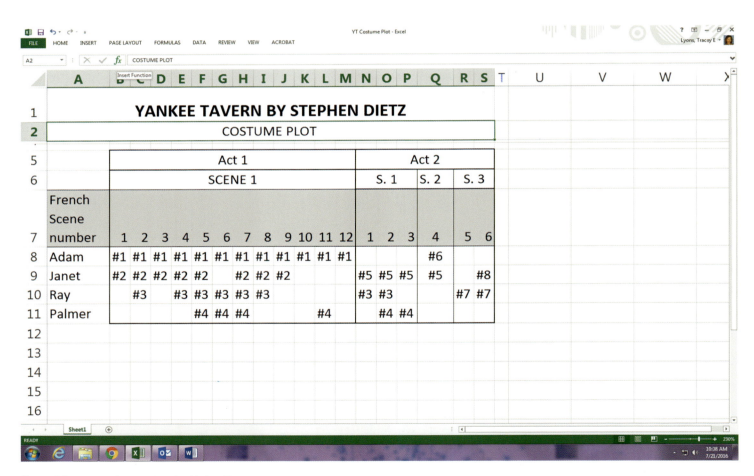

YANKEE TAVERN BY STEPHEN DIETZ

COSTUME PLOT

French Scene number	1	2	3	4	5	6	7	8	9	10	11	12	1	2	3	4	5	6
	Act 1 SCENE 1												Act 2 S. 1			S. 2	S. 3	
Adam	#1	#1	#1	#1	#1	#1	#1	#1	#1	#1	#1	#1				#6		
Janet	#2	#2	#2	#2	#2		#2	#2	#2				#5	#5	#5	#5		#8
Ray		#3			#3	#3	#3	#3	#3				#3	#3			#7	#7
Palmer					#4	#4	#4			#4				#4	#4			

Figure 2.3 Example Costume Plot for *Yankee Tavern*

serve as a placeholder in the chart, indicating that the character is on stage in that scene.

This exercise:

- Yields a useful worksheet in organizing the play (particularly for costume designers)
- Yields an estimation of the number of costumes required for a play
- Will help students determine which five characters/ costumes they wish to use for the final project
- May be displayed on the costume design final project.

This project can be completed using computer programs such as Excel or Word. If students do not have access to these programs, have them use graph paper.

Since this a distillation of the information discovered in the French Scene analysis homework, it can usually be done in tandem with that assignment and due the same session.

Discussion: Script Analysis by Character

Designers need to comb through a script in search of all possible information offered about every single character. There is more to understand about a character beyond apparent aspects such as era, class, and location (more about these research topics later). Every word about a character, said by them or said about them by another, contributes toward answering the question: who is this person? Since one of the primary functions of costume design is the condensed expression of character, this question is of vital importance to the designer.

A script analysis by character will be assigned as homework. Use a short play excerpt to demonstrate the extraction of character information. For example, in the following exchange from Henrik Ibsen's *Hedda Gabler*, there are clues to concrete physical appearances as well as inferences that can lead to a better understanding of a character's personality traits. The costume designer needs to find them all.

Tesman: Yes, aren't they, uh? But Auntie, take a good look at Hedda before you leave. See how charming *she* is!

Miss Tesman: But George dear, there's nothing new in that. Hedda's been lovely all her life.

Tesman: But have you noticed how plump and buxom she's grown? How much she's filled out on the trip?

Hedda: Oh, do be quiet!

Miss Tesman: Filled out?

Tesman: Of course, you can't see it so well when she has that dressing gown on. But I, who have the opportunity to – [13]

From this dialogue, we learn that Hedda is wearing a dressing gown at that point in the play (and it's important to note that it's from dialogue rather than stage directions). Both Tesman and Miss Tesman agree that Hedda is 'lovely' and 'charming' and that she has been this way her whole life. But we also learn that Tesman believes Hedda has 'filled out' while Miss Tesman sees no change. While the costume designer may not make a decision at this moment, the question has been raised as to whether the designer wants the audience to agree with either Tesman or Miss Tesman regarding whether – and to what extent – Hedda is indeed buxom and filled-out. How buxom is she, compared to Miss Tesman? How buxom is she that a gown could conceal it? We also learn that Tesman is apparently quite willing and able to discuss, with his aunt, a woman's figure in front of that woman; what kind of man does that make him?

This step is a fact-finding mission, accumulating evidence that will guide later research efforts.

Homework: Script Analysis by Character

- Using one sheet of paper per character, place the name of the character at the top.
- Reread the script, stopping to note on the corresponding sheet of paper anything within dialogue, or a functional stage direction, that describes a character (avoid cast list character descriptions and focus on evidence in the text itself).

Mary
- Motherly
- Leader
- Lots of skirts
- Heftier
- Lavender
- Pg. 84 whips off skirt

Alex
- Unique
- Free spirit
- Pants!
- Sassy
- Kodak
- Blue
- Pg. 77 pedal pushers + surfboard +cooler + basket+ egg beater
- Pg. 81 motorcycle leathers

Fanny
- Tiara and blonde wig
- Child like
- Umbrella
- Hand-tinted picture postcards
- Prisoner in a kaleidoscope
- Pink
- Loves cool-whip
- Pg. 71 50s cocktail dress and blonde wig + egg beater
- Pg. 77 50s sun dress and egg beater ----- white boots
- Pg. 81 dressed for bowling

ALL 3
- Machetes
- Umbrellas
- Egg beaters
- Belts
- Beaded handbags
- Feathers of some kind

Grover
- Fanny's husband
- Midwest
- Broker
- Large black oval carved African mask

- "Suit"
- Silly
- Alcoholic-Recovering
- New shoes

Alphonse
- Cannibal
- Uniform
- German pilot
- Jungle
- Heavy accent
- From Alsace-Lorraine

Gorge Troll
- Alex <3
- Young man
- Leather jacket
- Jeans
- T-shirt
- Sideburns
- Greased back hair
- Riddles
- Blue

Yeti
- Cold
- Only yells

Gus
- Fresh faced
- American
- Boy
- Baseball cap
- Gum
- Boundless energy
- Works at a gas station
- Dirty
- 50s

Madame Nhu
- Psychic
- Long finger nails
- Beautiful/slightly ferocious half mask
- Mask- "Asian eyes, high cheek bones"
- Black hair
- Feminine

Figure 2.4 Example of a Script Analysis by Character, Page 1 (Lilliana Gonzalez)

- Frightening
- Low voice
- French and Asian accent
- Mysterious
- Cross dressing?

Mr. Coffee
- White suit
- Elegant
- Gentleman
- Smoke
- With silver case
- Mysterious
- Angel?

Nicky Paradise
- Fanny <3
- Neon signs
- Palm trees and streamers
- Gaudy
- Flirtatious
- Plays piano
- Pg. 82 bowling outfit

Figure 2.5 Example of a Script Analysis by Character, Page 2 (Lilliana Gonzalez)

- If desired, this information can be reformatted into a table or chart for ease of reference. The example in Figures 2.4 and 2.5 present a student's character breakdown formatted as columns of bullet points.
- At the next class session, share notes and discuss discoveries with the rest of the class.

This homework is, once again, a low percentage of the total grade. The instructor's evaluation considers whether the student analyzed each character and how complete (compared to your own reading of the text) each list appears. This, also, is an assignment that can be completed in tandem with the French Scene breakdown and costume plot, or, depending on the abilities of the class and the time available, assigned with a separate deadline.

The script analysis by character assignment is an optional item to display on the costume design final presentation because while necessary to do, it's not often one of the design tools shared in a production meeting. However, remember that you are creating a class that best suits the needs of your specific situation.

Session Break: End of Week 2, Day 1.

Homework and Review: Metaphor Journal Follow Up

The following can be a quick review option at the start of a session.

- At the start of class, have students pair up and share metaphors from their metaphor journals.
- One student asks these questions of their partner:

  - What was the context of the metaphor's use?
  - What is the literal meaning of the phrase?

  - What is the meaning in its poetic parallel?
  - What kind of imagery does your metaphor evoke?

If desired, increase metaphor journal content by assigning one or two metaphor entries per day.

Homework Follow-Up: Costume Plot and Script Analysis by Character

After generating the costume plot and individual script analysis by character sheets, the students should be in a good position to decide which characters they would like to use for the final costume project. In our course, students pick five costumes. Designing lead characters is encouraged. If a lead character has a metamorphosis, the resulting sequence of costumes can be a very fruitful design exercise.

Ask students which characters appeal most to them as subjects for their final project. Discuss character groupings such as family members, friends, master and servant, and employer and employee. These relationships offer opportunities to explore how costume can both link characters as well as delineate difference.

Design Mechanics: Drawing Clothing on the Human Body

In a course like this you will be rushing your students through an incredibly condensed crash-course in graphic expression. Knowing that your students will range from the laissez-faire to perfectionist, aim for the center. The given amount of time will always be inadequate. We've created projects with variety to keep both the speedy interested and the slower from despair. We find that these exercises help build the student's skills and confidence without turning into an avalanche for either instructor or class.

TEACHING TIP

Anxiety is the perception of great danger and fearing the inability to cope. A portion of teaching drawing is mitigating anxiety. People say "I don't know how to draw" as frequently as they declare "I don't know how to do advanced math." We believe neither to be a gift bestowed at birth; rather, that drawing skills are steadily improved through practice. While it's unlikely any of us will become the next Michelangelo, it doesn't mean that we should live without trying.

When teaching drawing, be encouraging to a fault, thus removing the danger. Knowing that anxiety may be a big barrier for your students, withhold individually directed tips; even the most benign criticisms can extinguish a student's confidence at this stage. In the first days of design mechanics, we give drawing tips to the whole group by drawing on the board or overhead projector. Tracey notes that looking back on her education, watching a teacher draw was very rare. Now a teacher herself, she strives to make each step of her process transparent.

Drawing the human body is an essential tool for the costume designer, but can also be the designer's (and instructor's) Achilles' heel. Learning to draw the human figure well can take extended periods of practice and study; the instructor's challenge is to get students drawing reasonably proportioned human figures in a very short amount of time, especially when many of the students have minimal sketching experience. In order to use class time for exploring costume design rather than developing advanced drawing skills, we employ low-stakes activities, drawing short-cuts, short-term goals, and loads of positive reinforcement to help students become proficient enough to render their designs.

We teach costume rendering using **croquis**. A croqui is an outline drawn from a human form. Be careful of where your croquis originate. Images of humans published in fashion magazines or fashion drawings are often highly manipulated and of no use to the costume designer. While drawing costumes on very narrow and leggy croquis may make beautiful, elegant images, the costume constructed from them for a real body will, unfortunately, look significantly different from the rendering.

TEACHING TIP

Sample croquis are provided in this book (see Figures 2.6 through 2.8) but creating a collection of your own is easily done. Pay a student for an hour of their time. Provide a unitard or t-shirt and shorts for this photo shoot. Use a high contrast background (e.g., black unitard with white sheet as a background). Have the model move around slowly while you snap dozens of digital photos. Sort the photos and delete anything that won't work as a pose for costume design work. Tape a piece of lightweight paper over the printed picture and begin drawing.

A costume designer should build an image library by adding new models as time and funding permits. A variety of physical types will allow a greater range to introductory work, as students will not have to figure out how to turn a young, slender figure into a heavy-set elderly person.

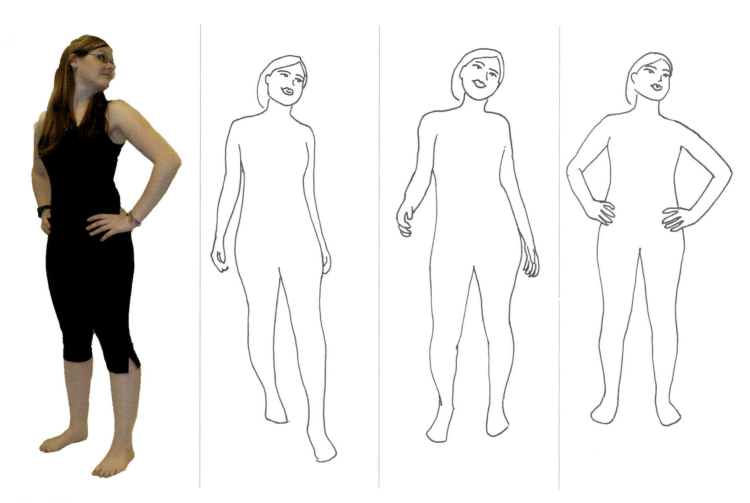

Figure 2.6 Sample Female Croqui

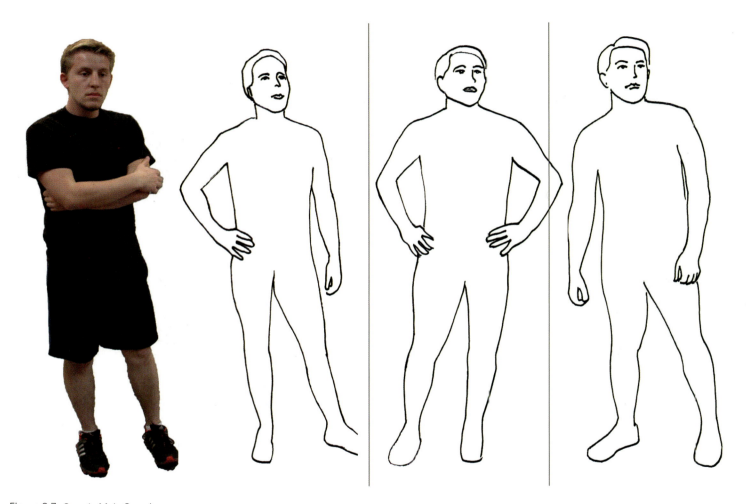

Figure 2.7 Sample Male Croqui

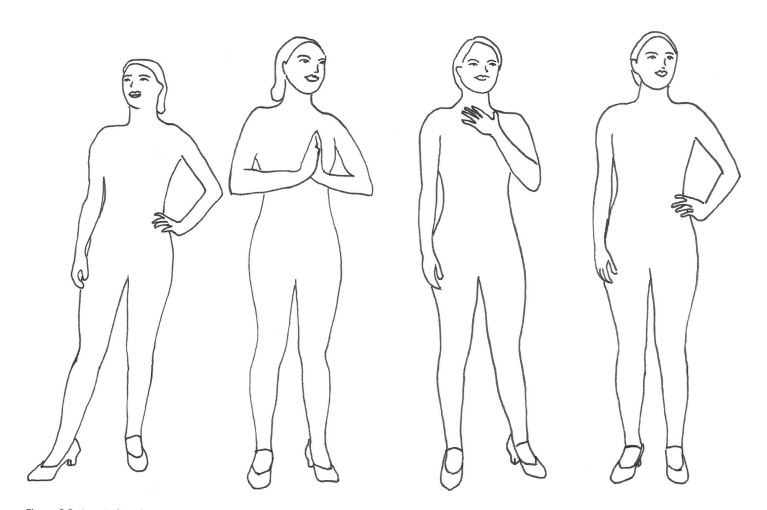

Figure 2.8 Sample Croqui

Book Recommendation

Students who intend to pursue costume design as a career should be directed toward life drawing courses. For an in-depth exploration of figure drawing as applied to theatrical design, *Drawing and Rendering for the Theatre*, by Clare P. Rowe (published by Focal Press) offers useful tips and exercises.

Launch right into working with the croquis and drawing fashion components. If you don't allow the students time to fret or feel inadequate – at this point, they're essentially tracing things – they're more likely to plunge right in and discover that they're drawing despite thinking they can't.

Demonstrate by first transferring the croqui onto a piece of tracing paper, and with a page of fashion components handy (see Figures 2.9 through 2.12), add items like collars or sleeves. Be sure that you have copies of images and examples of items you wish the students to draw; even though they are surrounded by sleeves in real-life, interpreting that reality onto a 2D surface adds yet another layer of complexity. Students may also be unaware of the variety of sleeve options available, and no one in the room may be wearing the puffy sleeve they would like to draw.

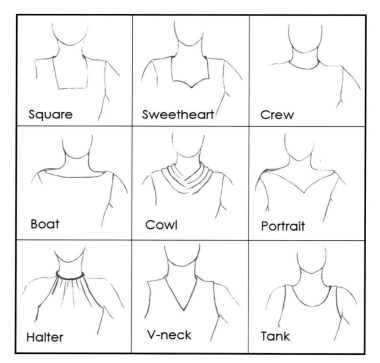

Figure 2.9 Sample Necklines

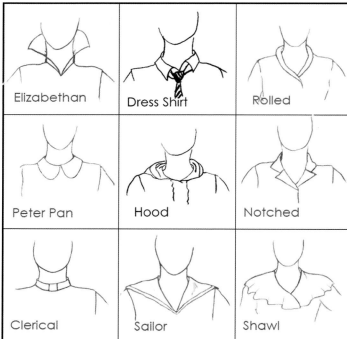

Figure 2.10 Sample Collars

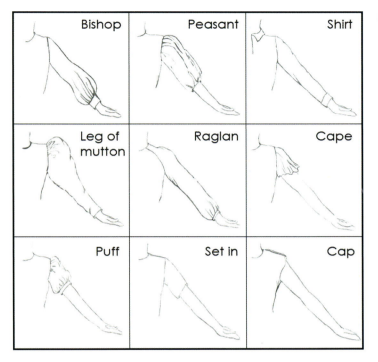

Figure 2.11 Sample Sleeves

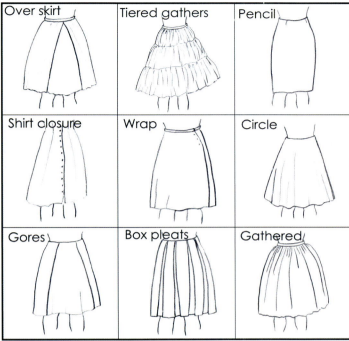

Figure 2.12 Sample Skirts

FIRST TIME COSTUME DESIGNER DRAWING TIPS

- In clothing construction, the difference in a person's body measurement and the measured garment is called 'ease.'
- Avoid making the costumes appear too snug on the body. Fabric frequently hangs away from the body at hemlines.
- Depict the ease of the garment by having sleeves hang off the wrists, pants glide over the legs, and shirts blouse at the waist. Drawing garments without ease can give them an undesired unitard look.

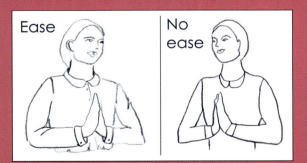

Figure 2.13 Unitard versus Garment with Ease

- Create the illusion of three dimensions by starting collars and cuffs with the hint of the garment coming from the back of the body.

Some students will begin their drawings by tracing the full croquis onto their lightweight paper and then add clothing pieces; others will jump into drawing the clothing pieces, assembling the garment on the tracing paper with the croqui beneath. Whichever works best for that student is fine.

Unless the garment is sheer, the body should not be visible under the clothing. Students can keep the body outline for the drawing process but should erase those guidelines upon completion of the garment.

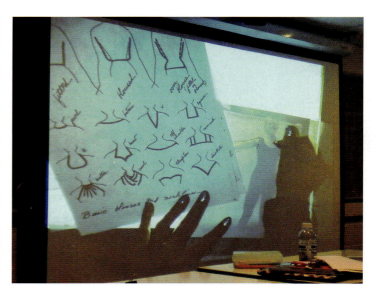

Figure 2.15 Tracey Demonstrates Transferring Fashion Components to a Croqui

Figure 2.14 How to Add Ease to a Drawn Sleeve

Exercise: Overcoming the Blank Page

For this exercise provide:

- Printed croquis
- Fashion components handouts (Figures 2.9–2.12)

Figure 2.16 Lilliana Adds a Puffy Sleeve to Her Croqui

Ask students to combine various sleeves, skirts, necklines, and collars, using the examples from Figures 2.9 through 2.12. Get them drawing. As you walk around the classroom, if a student has trouble interpreting an item, pause the class and demonstrate on the board or projector.

Exercise: Overcoming the Blank Page, Variation #1

- Give students three descriptive words that describe qualities of line.
- Have students create designs that use line in the manner described, using fashion components from the handout as a foundation.
- Share and discuss results with the class.

Figure 2.17   Some of the Images Distributed as Part of Variation #2

Exercise: Overcoming the Blank Page, Variation #2

- Provide pictures of furniture, sculpture, jewelry, or other 3D objects (see Figure 2.17).
- Have the students draw costumes that share characteristics of line, shape, form, and space with the object (again, use the fashion components handout as foundation for choices).
- Share and discuss results with the class.

Figure 2.18   Casey Uses an Art Nouveau Object to Inform Her Costume Choices

Figure 2.19   Casey Shares Her Art Nouveau Derived Rendering with the Class

Homework: 'Twenty-One Black Dresses'

Using the skills introduced in the preceding exercises, we move on to the first mid-level project of the semester, 'Twenty-One Black Dresses.'

The impressive results from this project:

- Bolster confidence through practice and evident accomplishment
- Employ and refine skills at incorporating research into content
- Generate conversation about design
- Create a beautiful piece of art.

This exercise also introduces the concept of using a research image to inform a design. We don't formally introduce research at this point, preferring to first let students experience how it can directly inform their work. Later, when we discuss research as used by designers, it will be a less abstract concept since they have already had some practice.

Students are allowed one week to complete this assignment. Each student works on the project individually. A demonstration is done in class by the instructor.

- On poster board, draw lines that divide the paper into twenty-one portrait boxes; set aside.
- Use a croqui that fits into a single box (if the box measures 7" x 3", use a croqui that is 6.25" x 2"). See Figure 2.20.
- On unlined paper or tracing paper, using pencil, create an interesting outfit (there aren't many parameters for these outfits; students may draw from the handout of fashion components or other sources). See Figure 2.21.
- Transfer the drawing onto the poster board. This can be done by lightly shading the back of the page with a pencil, positioning the croqui in the appropriate box, and then firmly tracing the drawing so that a graphite outline is left on the poster board. Or, if available, a light table can be used as shown in Figure 2.22.

Figure 2.20 Laying Out Boxes on Poster Board

Figure 2.21 Creating a Drawing on Tracing Paper

Figure 2.22 Transferring a Drawing Using a Light Table

- Strongly encourage students to work each outfit separately, as opposed to putting twenty-one sleeves down, then drawing twenty-one different necklines, etc. The composition of each outfit should be developed as a whole.
- Reiterate that the content of each dress does *not* have to emerge fully formed from the imagination. If a student wants to draw an element but is not sure how to go about it, stress research (look at pictures that inform). Having the research image right there on the drawing table as you work is very valuable.

Book Recommendation

For the best of books on drawing clothing on the human form we recommend *Dynamic Wrinkles and Drapery: Solutions for Drawing the Clothed Figure* by Burne Hogarth. His work is beautiful to look at, and easy to digest. This text and drawings were a cornerstone of Tracey's education on drawing.

- On the poster board, use a fine-tipped marker to blacken in the outfit. Depict highlights with unblackened areas. Larger markers, although faster, lose definition and description. Tracey supplies each student with a starter marker.
- Include faces, hands, hair, and shoes (hats are nice too) with each creation. Demonstrate drawing the minimum facial features desired, as this can be very intimidating for students.

Figure 2.23 Examples of Minimal Facial Features

Assigning Professional Designer Presentations

Our rural location means limited access to guest designers and few close opportunities for students to see professional non-academic work. To help bridge the gap between academics and the profession of design, we have created the Professional Designer Presentation project.

The main portion of the presentation should be images of the professional designer's work (renderings and/or photographs of the actors in costume) and presentation of what is observed by first describing the items using design element vocabulary. This can lead to comparing and contrasting the designs for a range of characters within a single production, and how the design elements unify or distinguish individuals and groups. Costumes from at least two different shows should be presented. Even if a show is unfamiliar (and nothing should stop a student from reading the plot or at least consulting a summary or synopsis), the student should be able to analyze what is observed in the costume and connect the findings to an expression of character. In addition, the student will briefly discuss the designer's philosophy, process, and any mention of insight into theatre as a whole.

We provide the students with a handout to guide the focus of the presentation:

- Presentation length is limited to 15 minutes.
- Neatness counts; know your material.
- Quotes from and interviews with the designer are the best source of direct information and are encouraged to be included as part of the presentation.
- Show and discuss no fewer than two but no more than four examples (an example is the whole of a single work, not a single photo of a single costume) of their production work. Be able to address the following:

  - What characterizes their work?
  - Discuss their use of line, shape, form, space, texture, and color.

  - Do they rely more heavily on some design elements than others?
  - Does the designer talk about how they use design elements?

The presentation should address the following concerns:

- What does your designer feel is the role of design in a production?
- Do they have a design philosophy, and what is it?
- What do they hope to add to a production through their design?
- Give examples of their use of design metaphor and research.

Early in the semester, we match students with a designer in a specific field. Since designers don't often create a wealth of easily accessed content, we do some searching on our own to make sure enough information can be found to support a presentation. For this same reason, we coach the students to begin accumulating information early. This can allow for the shipping time on articles or inter-library loans. We also encourage students who struggle in the face of scant information to seek help from the instructor; we might have a book or article to lend.

Some students fixate on bibliographic information such as lists of awards, early life history, and academic credentials. While personal history may be of passing interest, guide students to focus on analyzing the designer's body of work.

Since this is a research project, we do have a bibliography requirement and the grade is released only after a hardcopy bibliography is received. At present, we require no fewer than five sources, properly cited in MLA format.

Thoughts on the evaluation of the Professional Designer Presentations can be found in Chapter 5.

Portfolio Development Projects

Portfolio Project: Costume Plot

The portfolio-quality costume plot includes the name of the show, costume designer, theatre, and date on the chart. All items are clearly visible and legible. If the plot was created as a table with software, it can be directly imported into a graphics program like PowerPoint for electronic portfolio formats. If paper is preferred, copying and resizing may be necessary to fit it onto a portfolio page.

The instructor may choose to include the student's costume plot in the poster presentation of the costume design final project.

Portfolio Project: Designer's Metaphor Statement

In the portfolio, a statement helps the viewer better understand the designer's goals and choices, particularly if the designer does not present the material in person. Use a larger (12–14 pt) font to print out the one-page document. At the top of the document is the title of show and name of designer.

This document will be included in the final costume project.

Portfolio Project: Drawings Influenced by Art and/or 3D Objects

Display one of the costume line drawings from one of the 'Overcoming the Blank Page' exercises next to the image or prop that influenced the design. Students may photograph, scan and print, or photocopy the supplied image for incorporation into their portfolio. Include a titled caption that briefly explains the exercise.

Overcoming The Blank Page

This costume design exercise was inspired by tulips.

Artist's Name
Date

Figure 2.24 Sample 'Overcoming the Blank Page' Portfolio Page Layout

Notes

1. Rosemary Ingham and Liz Covey, *The Costume Designer's Handbook* (Portsmouth: Heinemann Educational Books, Inc., 1992), pp. 5–6.
2. Jean Rosenthal and Lael Wertenbaker, *The Magic of Light* (Boston: Little, Brown, and Company, 1972), p. 60.
3. Rebecca Cunningham, *The Magic Garment* (Prospect Heights: Waveland Press, 1989), pp. 37–38.
4. Darwin Reid Payne, *Scenographic Imagination* (Carbondale: Southern Illinois University Press, 1993), p. c31.
5. Howard Bay, *Stage Design* (New York: Drama Book Specialists, 1974), p. 92.
6. Babak Ebrahimian, *Sculpting Space in the Theatre: Conversations with the Top Set, Light and Costume Designers* (Burlington: Focal Press, 2006), p. 32.
7. Ebrahimian, p. 56.
8. Deena Kaye and James Lebrecht, *Sound and Music for the Theatre: The Art and Technique of Design* (Burlington: Focal Press, 2009), p. 233.
9. Ebrahimian, p. 42.
10. Kaye and Lebrecht. p. 231.
11. W. Oren Parker, Harvey K. Smith, and R. Craig Wolf, *Scene Design and Stage Lighting* (New York: Holt, Rinehart, and Winston, 5th edition, 1985), p. 74.
12. Ingham and Covey. p. 11.
13. Henrik Ibsen, *Hedda Gabler,* tr. Rolf Fjelde, *Ibsen: Four Major* Plays (New York: New American Library), p. 230.

Chapter 3

Week 3

As theatre practitioners we know that juggling thoughts and actions is all part of the design process. Teaching the gestalt and synthesis of design is equally hard as doing it yourself. This chapter sets the teaching of design elements, metaphor, and script analysis on the back burner, although they continue to inform the work. Part of the philosophy of the course outlined in this book is creating tangible evidence of understanding the material by applying the newly acquired skill set to realized work. This chapter begins to bring seemingly divergent topics back to the script through design mechanics and research.

The framing topics for this week are:

- Design Mechanics

  - Introduction to Costume Rendering Format
  - Experimentation with Color and Color Media
  - Discussion of 'Twenty-One Black Dresses' Project
  - Combining the Pieces to Draw a Design

- Research

  - Discussion of Research Approaches

Supplies Needed

Instructor supplies:

- Color copies of a standard color wheel (see Figure 3.10)
- Prepared blank croquis
- Fashion components (see Figures 2.9 through 2.12)

Student supplies:

- Access to a computer with Microsoft Word or Photoshop software
- Cardstock or Bristol board
- Tracing paper
- Watercolor paints
- Brushes
- Cups for water
- Paper towels
- Pencils for drawing

Costume Drawing Definitions

Rendering any drawing or painting that is intended to depict a costume

Line Drawing an unpainted sketch or nearly finalized drawing that depicts the costume

Swatch small pieces of fabric, usually 2" x 2", usually attached to a rendering, depicting the fabric and trim choices for that costume

Croquis the photos of human beings used as templates for the renderings. Using fashion sketches will create renderings with inaccurate proportions

Exercise: Overcoming the Blank Page, Variation

We begin this week with some drawing review.

Be sure students have their handouts of fashion components. This exercise asks students to:

- Use a physical object as a research image
- Extract design element information from the object
- Translate that information into features that inform clothing choices.

The prop storage room is down the hall from our classroom, which makes this variation logistically easy. A box of small, random objects works equally well.

- Venture into the prop room where students pick an object that they feel has some sort of connection – psychologically or physically – to the play they have chosen for their costume design final project.
- Students create several different drawings of costumes inspired by the prop, using different design elements found on the items as new starting points for each drawing. This is *not* the same as drawing a costume *for* a character in the play.
- Explaining their choices and implementation, students present their drawings to the class.

Figure 3.1   Example of Costume Developed from 3D Object (Bridget Kelly)

Discussion: Costume Renderings

Costume renderings are the main communication tool the designer uses to present the totality of a character's appearance to the director and members of the design team, as well as to express intentions to the costume shop. Finished costume renderings for a realized departmental production are shown as an example in Figure 3.2. Since trial and error is an important component of student development, we have found it useful to show students how to import drawings into a software program and create rendering templates. While every rendering must be attended to as a unique piece, we present some tips and shortcuts that allow for easier layout and duplicating of the line drawing. If students are painting their rendering on a copy of the line drawing, the fear of catastrophic mistake is lessened since it is easy to re-print another line drawing for a second or third attempt.

While costume renderings are as individual as the designer and the character being developed, there are commonalities to formatting. Be sure to have examples of finished renderings to share with the students. Present a range of professional renderings as well as those generated by previous (and current) students. As noted in the introduction of this book, consult the websites and bulletin boards of organizations such as USITT and USA Local 829 for examples; even if work has not been publicly shared, you can contact designers who might be willing to allow the use of their work in the classroom.

Book Recommendations

Some useful books about costume designers that feature renderings include:

- *The Performing Set: The Broadway Designs of William and Jean Eckart*, by Andrew B. Harris
- *The Stage is All the World: The Theatrical Designs of Tanya Moiseiwitsch*, organized by T. J. Edelstein
- *The Designs of Willa Kim*, by Bobbi Owen

Figure 3.2   Student Costume Rendering from the UW–Whitewater Production of *Three Excellent Cows* (Stephanie Ruch)

If you wish to incorporate computer-based technology in student work, be sure to go through the following steps with the class before sending them to their computers.

Hands-on Exercises with Costume Renderings and Computer Software

A Polished Product in Microsoft Word

As well as the image of the character, a finished costume rendering contains the title of the play and the name of the character. The following exercises demonstrate two techniques that accomplish this effect. Some students may already know or develop variations in using the software; since technology varies and individuals embrace it at different levels, achieving the result is more important than memorizing the prescribed process. If possible, work the demonstration in class and move to having students title a rendering immediately.

Begin by scanning (preferred) or photographing the drawing. Use one of the drawings created in the previous exercises. (As you insert the image, keep in mind that the drawing is placed so that the title, character, and fabric swatches can also be accommodated.)

Continuing in Microsoft Word, the steps are as follows (numbers noted correspond to the screen shots):

- Open a new document. Open Program; Blank Document (#1); Create (#2).
- From the tabs at top, click INSERT (#3). Click PICTURE (#4).
- Search (#5), select (#6), and INSERT (#7) the image of your drawing.
- You may need to hit ENTER (the button on your keyboard) to deactivate the drawing in Word (#8).

Once the drawing is placed satisfactorily, add text, as diagrammed in Figure 3.4:

- From the tabs at top, click INSERT (#9). Click TEXT BOX (#10). Experiment and play with different TEXT BOX styles (#11).
- Once inserted, move the text box to the desired area; it's best if the four-way arrow (#12) appears to help shift all of the points of the text box.
- Click on the written directions to highlight the words (#13). Click DELETE (from your keyboard buttons) and type the name of the show.
- Highlight the text within the textbox to affect changes (#14). Adjust the font (#15) and point size (#16) to fit the style of your show.
- Repeat the INSERT/TEXT BOX steps to add the name of the character (#17).
- Often it is necessary to add Act/Scene notation with a character's name, as this informs the viewer of the appearance of the costume in the order of the play.
- Create continuity by choosing the same font for both show title and character's name. By making the show title larger, it emphasizes the importance of the title over the character. Unify a group of renderings by placing the title of the show and each character's name in the same location on each rendering.
- Use white space on a rendering for the placement of example fabrics (swatches) (#18).

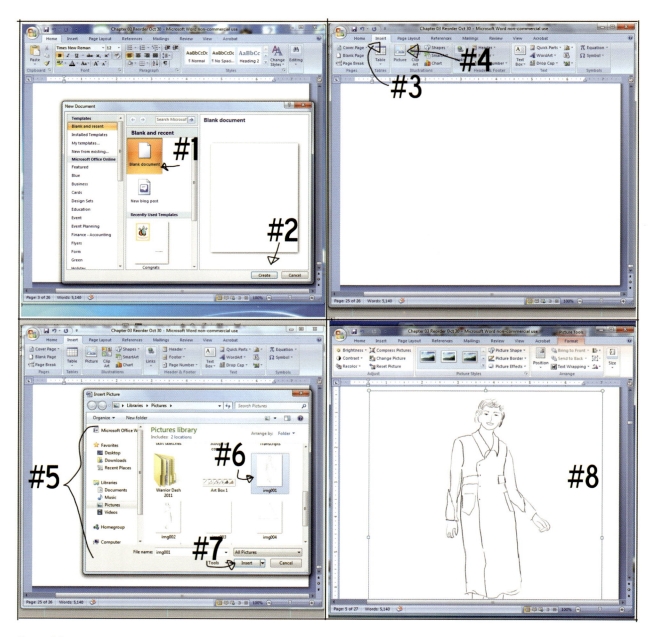

Figure 3.3 Grid of Screen Shots Showing Drawing Insertion

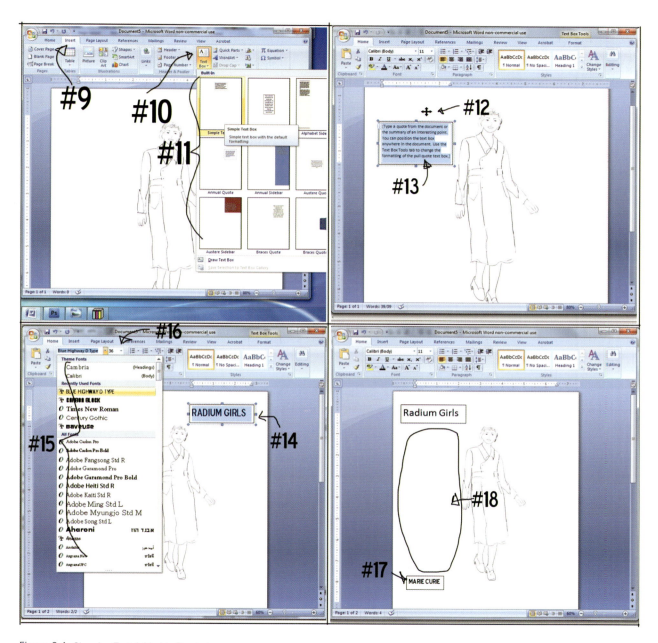

Figure 3.4 Showing Text Added to Renderings

TEACHING TIP

It is a struggle to add value and learning during an in-class work day. Knowing the wide range of learning styles in a classroom can feel like a no-win situation, and Tracey offers the following suggestions to prevent a workday from becoming scattered and unfocused.

First, diminish chatter that deviates from the subject matter. Helping a fellow student is great; recounting Friday night, not acceptable. Second, circulate. This can be difficult when someone's body language may lead you to think that they don't value your attention or that they fear your criticism. Lastly, try to spend at least two minutes with each student. To the extroverts, answer their questions and listen while they talk through difficulties. To the quiet students, ask open-ended questions such as: "What do you want to accomplish with your work-time today? How has this process been going for you? What new things are you learning?" When finished talking with each student, start from the beginning and visit each one again.

By spending a few minutes with each student, you give them in-depth, hands-on, one-on-one teaching time. In addition, the students not in discussion with you enjoy bigger segments of uninterrupted time in which to work quietly.

A Polished Product in Photoshop

Adobe Photoshop is a Pandora's Box of possibilities and approaches. The following titling and labeling demonstration is just one of the many means to this end.

First, create a template for the title and character names. Second, insert the drawing. Of course, the process can also be achieved by labeling the drawing, as explained in the Word document version, but the Photoshop template can save time, especially on a show with a large number of renderings.

The following are the steps for creating a title block template (see Figures 3.5 and 3.6):

- Open Photoshop. Click FILE (#1); from the pull-down menu click NEW.
- A pop-up window will appear. Make adjustments that will reflect the incoming image.

  - Adjust units of measurement (inches) to match the item scanned (#2).
  - Next, indicate the size of your drawing's paper (#3). If you drew on art paper, adjust to 9. If you use printer paper, adjust your image size to 8.5.
  - Adjust height to reflect the paper size of the drawing too.
  - Adjust the resolution (#4). My items scan in at 300 pixels/inch.
  - Once finished with the changes to the popup menu, click OK (#5).

- A blank document will appear. Add the play's title by grabbing the TEXT BOX tool (#6).
- Click onto the document at the desired placement of the first letter of the play's name.
- Type in the show title. While text is highlighted (#7), adjust font style (#8) and point size (#9).
- To deactivate the TEXT BOX, grab the MOVE TOOL from the menu (#10).
- Create a NEW LAYER for the TEXT BOX that will contain the character's name, by clicking the LAYER (#11) tab from the top. Select NEW (#12) from the pull-down menu. Click on LAYER (#13) from the second-tier pull-down menu.
- You may be given a prompt to name each layer. (Tracey never bothers with this and just lets the default name remain.) Click OK.

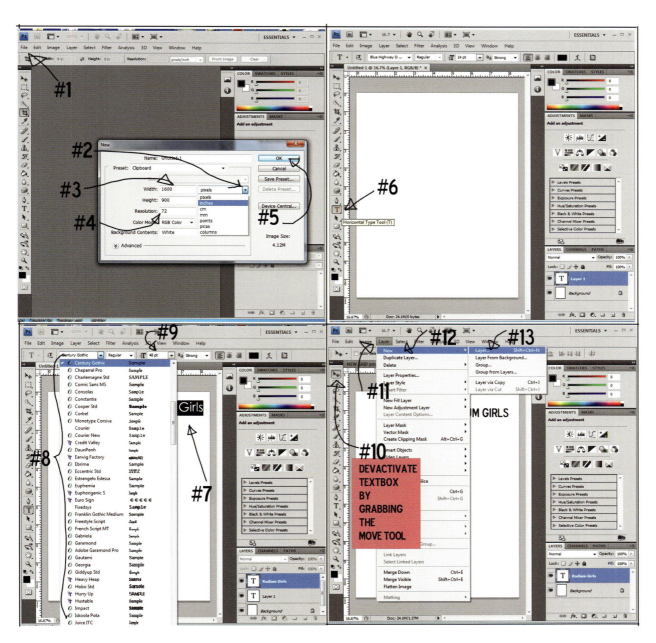

Figure 3.5 Building a Text Template, Part 1

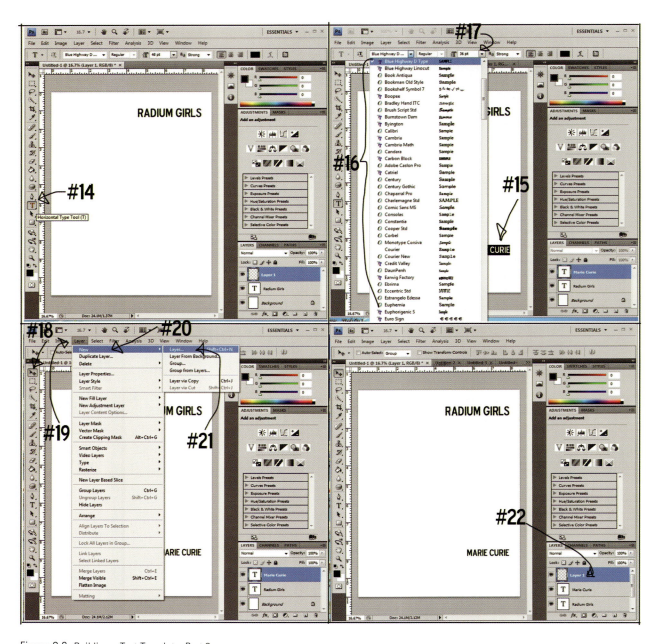

Figure 3.6 Building a Text Template, Part 2

- On this second layer, create a TEXT BOX for the character's name by first grabbing the TEXT BOX tool from the icons at the left (#14). Then, click onto the document at the desired placement of the first letter of the character's name.
- Type in the character's name. While text is highlighted (#15), adjust font style (#16) and point size (#17).
- To deactivate the TEXT BOX, grab the MOVE TOOL from the menu (#18).
- Create a NEW LAYER for the incoming drawing, by clicking the LAYER (#19) tab from the top. Select NEW (#20) from the pull-down menu. Click on LAYER (#21) from the second-tier pull-down menu.
- The new layer is highlighted (#22).

Save this file as a template. A set of steps will be included for quickly adjusting the template to reflect the names of other characters.

Now that the template is completed, an image can be prepared (see Figure 3.7):

- Begin by opening the drawing in Photoshop. Click FILE (#1). On the pull-down menu select OPEN AS SMART OBJECT. Search (#2), select (#3), and OPEN (#4) the image.
- Isolate the drawing from the background. Grab the QUICK SELECTION tool from the icons at the left (#5). Verify that the '+' symbol is selected from the menu above (#6).
- Start inside of the drawing, selecting many segments with your mouse. (With a left side click, press, and hold down the mouse for about an inch. Release and repeat to grab many different segments comprising the whole of the drawing.) Come near to but not crossing out of the drawing, until you have grabbed all of the drawing. When finished, a line that looks dotted and jumping surrounds the drawing.

- Tips:
  - To undo the last selection, click EDIT from the tabs, and click on UNDO.
  - To undo an area or selection further back in the process, switch to the (-) icon at the top row. Until deactivated, the areas cleared while programmed with (-) will be taken away from the active image. Return to the (+) icon to resume selecting the image.

- With the image surrounded by the dotted and jumping line, right click on the image. Scroll to LAYER VIA COPY (#7). This ensures that none of the background will travel with the image to the text template.
- Grab the MOVE TOOL (#8) from the tool box at the left. Select the image.

The next steps combine the prepared image with text template (see Figure 3.8):

- With MOVE TOOL selected (#1), grab image. Keep the left side of the mouse clicked and drag the drawing out of the current file (through the top) (#2).
- Keep dragging the image out of this file and into the text template. Hover the mouse on the title of the opened text template file (#3).
- The text template will appear.
- Release the image (releasing the button on the mouse) and it will appear in the text template (#4).
- The move tool (or any other maneuver) can only be accomplished within the highlighted LAYER. Highlight any layer that needs to be adjusted (#5).
- Prior to presentation, include a horizon line for the character (#6). This can be done by hand after the drawing is printed/painted.

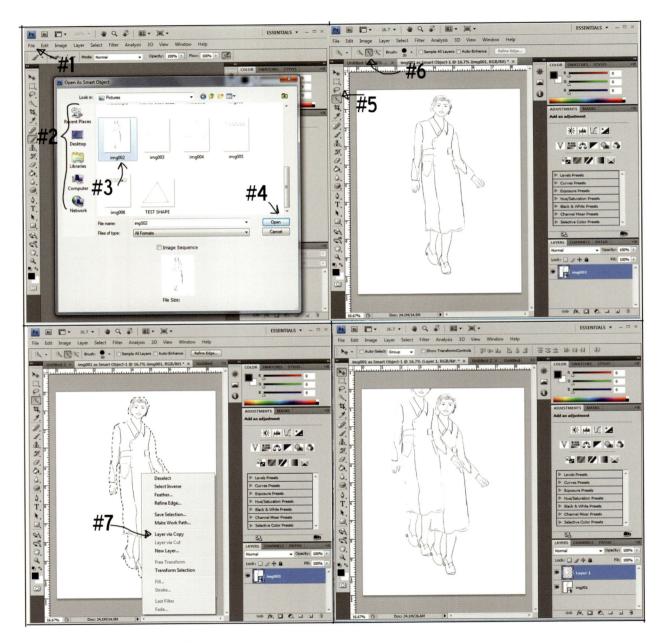

Figure 3.7 Adding a Drawing to the Text Template

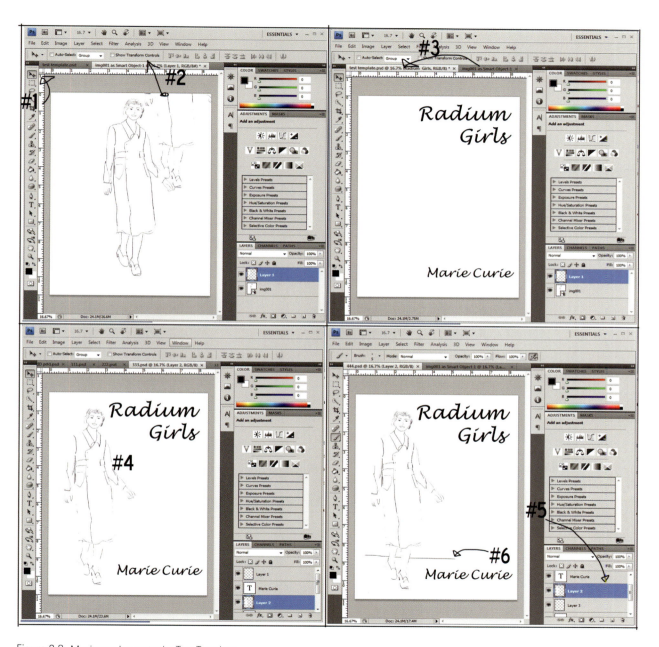

Figure 3.8 Moving an Image to the Text Template

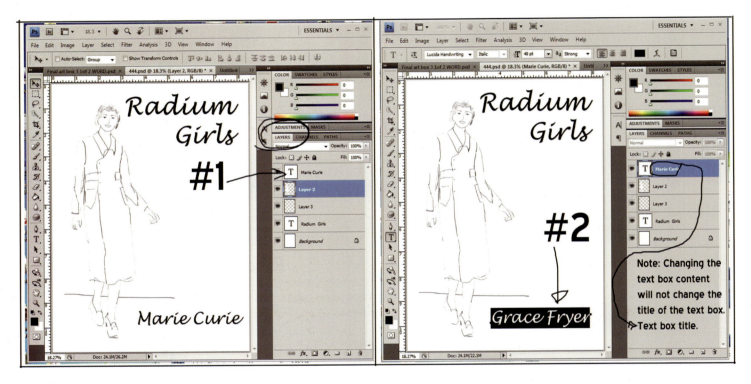

Figure 3.9 Changing the Name of a Character

The next steps change the character's name on the text template (see Figure 3.9):

- In Layers, double click on the [T], located next to the name of the character's name (#1) that you wish to replace.
- This will highlight the current character's name (#2) and allow you to type in the new character.

Exercise: Using Software to Create Rendering Templates

Be sure that each student has a scanned copy of a rendering. If it was not possible to scan drawings generated in class, bring a sample line drawing. If students do not know how to use the scanning equipment available, be sure to demonstrate. Provide a list of computer labs on campus that have the programs, scanners, and other equipment needed.

If you have classroom computer access:

- Ask each student to add a show title and character's name to a scanned line drawing using either Word or Photoshop approaches.
- Circulate among the students as they work.
- Discuss obstacles.
- Review, asking each student to make suggestions for success to the group.

Presenting unpainted drawings can denote flexibility in the yet to be formalized designs. Adding show and character names gives in-progress ideas a more professional appearance.

Homework: Completed Rendering Template

Assign one complete unpainted rendering template. It should include a line drawing, title, and character. This should be due the next class session.

This is primarily a check-in assignment, ensuring that students understand the layout process and can move on to laying

out all the renderings for their final project. Be sure to ask students to share their work with the class, as well as discuss problems they ran into and solutions they can offer their classmates.

Session Break: End of Week 3, Day 1.

Discussion: Introduction to Color Media

Color is, of course, an extremely powerful design element, which is one of the reasons we focus on monochromatic line, shape, and form in the first major project. By reinforcing the sense that other design elements can go far in expressing emotive qualities, students are a little less likely to go straight to bold color to get their point across.

Since most of our students have not had any formal training on color theory, we combine an introduction to the color wheel with learning to manipulate one of our favored media, watercolor. Although a little difficult to master, the medium is readily available, inexpensive, and cleans up easily. With practice, watercolors represent the qualities of fabric beautifully and make for lovely costume renderings.

Begin with a quick overview of the standard subtractive color wheel. We draw one on the board and ask the students to name what colors go where.

- Primary, Secondary, Tertiary Colors for Paint

  - Primary: Red, Blue, Yellow
  - Secondary: Violet, Green, Orange
  - Tertiary: such as, Blue-Green, Red-Violet, Yellow-Orange

- Complementary Colors (placed opposite to each other on the wheel)

  - Such as: Red/Green, Blue/Orange, Yellow/Violet

- Combination of Complementary Colors

  - What is meant by this? Mixing the colors?

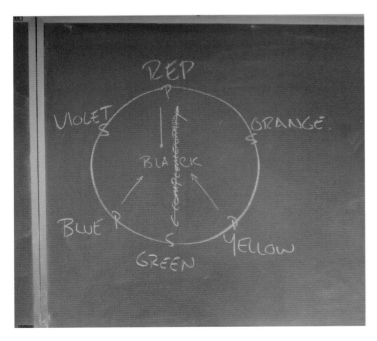

Figure 3.10 Color Wheel Diagrammed on the Blackboard

Book Recommendations

For an exploration of the color wheel from a teacher's perspective, Chapters 5 and 6 of Betty Edwards' *Color: A Course in Mastering the Art of Mixing Colors*, can be quite useful. While she uses oil paints instead of watercolors, the sample principles apply. *The Watercolor Book: Materials and Techniques for Today's Artist*, by David Dewey, has a good section on the color wheel that directly addresses the use of watercolor.

We don't do a lot of demonstration before the following watercolor exercise, preferring to foster first-hand student discovery.

Exercise: Painting a Color Wheel

- Distribute color copies of the color wheel image (Figure 3.11).
- Prepare each student for painting.

  - Cover the desks with protective paper if necessary.
  - Each student should have paper (cardstock or Bristol board is preferred)
  - Although students are asked to purchase sets of watercolor paints, we have some available in the classroom.

    - Depending on the quality of watercolor set purchased, students will notice that they do not have exact matches of many of the colors required for this exercise. This will both prompt experimentation in mixing, as well as demonstrate the limitations (or the opportunities) of the equipment at hand.

  - Cups of water
  - Paint brushes

- Direct the students to paint a color wheel for themselves, based upon the one they have been given. Ask them to try to match the colors as closely as their set of paints allows.
- Have them discuss their struggles, both as the exercise progresses and at the end.
- Ask the students to give technique advice to the rest of the class based on their experience:

  - How did you succeed in creating the correct hue?
  - How were you able to prevent one color from running into the next color?
  - How is saturated color created?
  - How is a pale color or shade created?

Scenic Design Vocabulary

Hue The name of the particular (pure) color

Chromaticity The intensity of the color

Value How light or dark is the color (compared to a greyscale that goes from pure white to pure black)

Tone Color plus grey

Tint/pastel Color plus white

Shade Color plus black

"Mixing color is great fun, from the subtle tones of a string quartet to a full orchestra playing a twenty-four-color Beethoven symphony."[1]
Marian Appelloff, *Everything You Ever Wanted to Know About Watercolor*

Figure 3.11 Color Wheel Handout

Exercise: Color Representation

This exercise continues to ask students to interpret the color they observe using the tools available.

Project an image with a limited color palette or distribute individual color copies of the image (in plastic page protectors). Provide a line drawing on cardstock that includes most of the major lines of the image. See Figures 3.12 and 3.13 for examples. The students should have to fill in a few blanks.

- Ask the students to do their best to duplicate the colors within the image.
- When complete, lead a discussion about the best practices discovered by the students.

Figure 3.12 Sample Image and Drawing for Color Representation Exercise

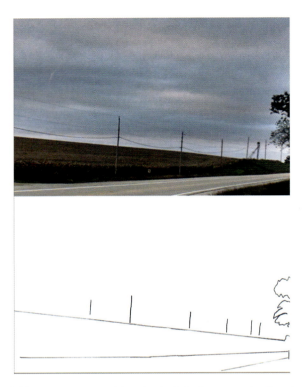

Figure 3.13 Sample Image and Drawing for Color Representation Exercise

Figure 3.14 Sample of Student Watercolor Work (Abigail King)

Figure 3.15 Sample of Student Watercolor Work (Bridget Kelly)

Figures 3.14 and 3.15 show completed exercises by students.

Homework Follow-up: 'Twenty-One Black Dresses' (the mid-level assignment for the costume design section)

When the students hand in the assignment, hang the posters around the room. We use bulletin boards in the hallway. Let them see their huge accomplishment. We use the following questions to open discussion:

- What was your favorite part of the project?
- What would you do differently next time?
- What advice would you give to students who do this project next year?

To generate a discussion about the drawings:

- Write the following descriptors on the board, and then hand out slices of sticky notes for the students to copy the terms onto:

  - Villain
  - Princess
  - Rock Star
  - Puritanical
  - Business woman
  - Mother
  - Sister A
  - Sister B
  - Sexy

- Direct the students to attach flags to other students' boards near the outfit that best matches the description. Students might flag some drawings with same, similar, or opposing words. All choices create opportunity for discussion.

TEACHING TIP

We find that everyone takes a step forward on this project, and often *within* the project as the final sketches are usually more assured than the early ones. Remind students not to compare the quality of their sketching to that of their fellow students; if comparisons must be made, stress that they should only compare their present work to their own work of a week ago. When publicly discussing the work, be sure that it's the dress being discussed and not line control or wobbly proportion (unless that seems to be part of the dress itself).

Figure 3.16   Students Attach Label Flags to the 'Twenty-One Black Dresses' Boards

Figure 3.17 Discussing the Label Flag Placement

After the labels have been placed, ask general questions, such as:

- Why did you think that outfit was sexy?
- What about this dress is business-like?

As the class warms up, ask more specific questions (related to design elements) to direct the discussion:

- What about the line in this drawing made you think that it matched this Sister A with that Sister B?
- What in the shape of this outfit says Puritanical?
- You have labeled this one Villain and this one Rock Star. What design elements support your decisions?
- What is it about the form in this outfit that describes a Princess?

Grading and evaluation of the 'Black Dress' project is done as per the rubric pictured in Figure 3.21. As a milestone project, the percentage of the costume section grade is accordingly greater.

TEACHING TIP

Big assignments can generate big feelings. If not diffused, they can influence the rest of the class period. Tracey notes that in some classes she will arrive early to chat with students who want to discuss the project. In other circumstances, going around the room and having each student note something that they learned and something that they wish they had done differently can focus their work back to learning. In most cases, students just want a moment to be heard.

TEACHING TIP

'Twenty-One Black Dresses' is usually the first assignment which at least one student does not complete. We stress to the students that there is much to discuss even in partially completed work, and that if nothing is presented, nothing can be discussed. Will the project receive an 'A'? No, but feedback and a 'C' is better than no feedback and an 'F.'

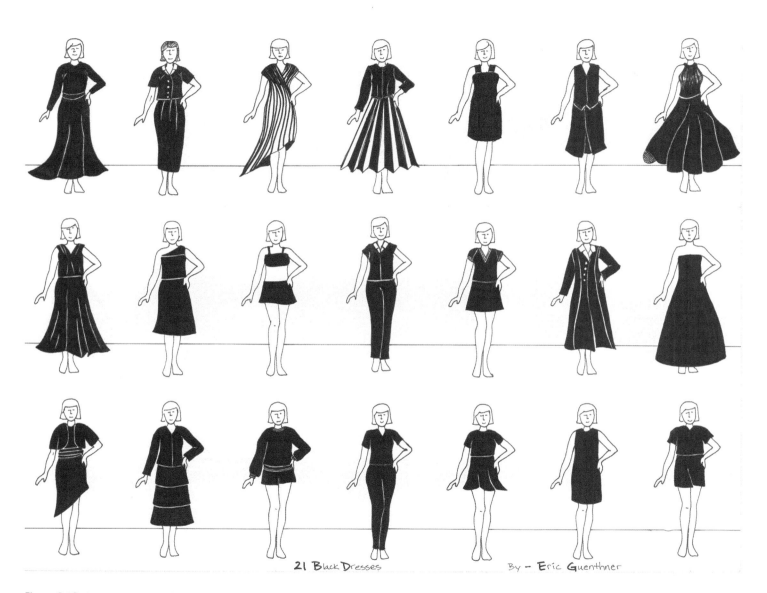

Figure 3.18 Completed 'Twenty-One Black Dresses' Project (Eric Guenthner)

Figure 3.19 Sample from Completed 'Twenty-One Black Dresses' Project (Kelsey Smyth)

Figure 3.20 Sample from Completed 'Twenty-One Black Dresses' Project (Casey Bunbury)

Student: _____

Followed the directions – 21 black rendering on one sheet

MINIMUM EFFORT	SOME EFFORT	AVERAGE	GOOD	EXCELLENT
1 – 4	5-8	9-12	13-16	17-20

Variety of looks on each rendering

MINIMUM EFFORT	SOME EFFORT	AVERAGE	GOOD	EXCELLENT
1-7	8-13	14-18	19-24	25-30

Attention to detail – finished quality

MINIMUM EFFORT	SOME EFFORT	AVERAGE	GOOD	EXCELLENT
1-7	8-13	14-18	19-24	25-30

Figure 3.21 'Twenty-One Black Dresses' Rubric

'Twenty-One Black Dresses,' Exercise Variations

The following exercises are all variations that combine 'Twenty-One Black Dresses' with color experimentation, providing practice that will contribute toward choices on the final project. Depending on the time available, use one or two as in-class exercises or assigned as homework.

Exercise: 'Twenty-One Black Dresses,' Variation #1

This exercise can be a first step in using color to achieve a particular goal, and by limiting the palette students are not paralyzed by choice. This is also an incremental movement toward full-fledged costume rendering.

Transfer the outline of one of the twenty-one outfits onto Bristol board or cardstock.

- Using three colors, without mixing or tinting, paint the outfit.
- Discuss the results with the class:

    - Why did you choose that palette for that dress? How do those colors heighten (or otherwise change) the effect of the dress?

Exercise: 'Twenty-One Black Dresses,' Variation #2

Transfer the outline of one of the twenty-one outfits onto Bristol board or cardstock.

- Using any/all colors paint the outfit.
- Discuss the results with the class:

    - Why did you choose that palette for that dress? How do those colors heighten (or otherwise change) the effect of the dress?

Exercise: 'Twenty-One Black Dresses,' Variation #3

Transfer the outline of one of the twenty-one outfits onto Bristol board or cardstock.

- Select a piece of artwork that utilizes a limited color palette.
- Using only colors that reflect those used in the artwork, paint the outfit.
- Discuss the results with the class:

    - Why/how did you decide to use which part of the color palette on which part of the outfit? What was your intended result? How do those colors heighten (or otherwise change) the effect of the dress?

Exercise: 'Twenty-One Black Dresses,' Variation #4

Pick one of the twenty-one outfits and transfer it twenty-one times to a new sheet of poster board.

- Using three colors, without mixing or tinting, paint each outfit differently.
- Discuss the results with the class:

    - How do you create variety with a limited palette? How do you create unity with a limited palette? Are there outfits that fare better or worse from the limited palette?

Exercise: 'Twenty-One Black Dresses,' Variation #5

Pick one of the twenty-one outfits and transfer it twenty-one times to a new poster board.

- Using any/all colors paint each outfit.
- Discuss the results with the class:

    - Why did you select those colors for a particular outfit? Are there outfits that ended up with similar palettes? Why?

Discussion: Further Research for Designers

> "The first phase of costume research begins as soon as you have read the script — and sometimes even during the first reading — as you start to imagine the characters in action and to dress them in historical garments pulled from your own memory . . . In the second phase you set out systematically to discover new facts to add to those you already possess."[2]
>
> Rosemary Ingham and Liz Covey, *The Costume Designer's Handbook*

Research is chocolate for the brain. To research is to travel the globe or to jump to a different time. One of the joys of being a designer is the constant seeking of new and interesting things that may inform a design in progress. What is not used is often kept anyway, as it might be of use someday. If you don't know something, how do you know whether or not you can use it?

Filtered through research, ideas can become truly interesting and unique, and are no longer instinctive responses constrained by the boundaries of personal experience and memory. With further research beyond the text of the play, all the information acquired about a subject is synthesized, distilled through metaphor, and employed to tell the story of the script.

In an academic setting, students are faced with a variety of research practices, depending on subject, department, and even instructor. Theatrical research tends to be eclectic in reach and range, actively seeking the happy accident or a surprise while browsing. Research might involve looking up historical photos, but it might also involve creating a collection of your own photographs that resonate with a script. Reading about the period, author, or history of the script's past productions is a great foundation. Gather whatever visual material seems even remotely pertinent. Encourage students to look past the first couple of pages of web search images. As the students collect material, have them sort the research images into groups such as:

- Those that apply directly to the script
- Those that resonate with but are not specifically connected to the script
- General useful historical context
- Abstract items that speak to character psychology.

The research cycle might begin afresh as information needs to be gathered not just about the script, but also about each specific character, and each costume. The students have already compiled lists of character attributes and physical details about character gleaned from the text; research, both textual and visual, can now be applied. In Chapter 2, the dialogue excerpt from *Hedda Gabler* noted that Hedda wore a dressing gown. The task now at hand is to consider how the costume designer finds the information that will lead to not only a period-appropriate garment, but the garment that Hedda, in this production, *should be wearing at that moment*. The design metaphor and the design elements suggested by the design metaphor help winnow the research items to those that best fit the desired parameters.

Discussion: Where Do Designers Go to Do Research?

Go through the following points one by one and see what responses the class can come up with before offering a suggestion or direction. Use one of the plays assigned in class as an example.

If *A Raisin in the Sun* is assigned, what are the best places to find information on living conditions for African-Americans on the South Side of Chicago in the 1950s?

- What type of information should be acquired?
- What exactly do you need to know about the subject?
- Who are the experts in this area?
- Is there a person or group you can contact?
- Is there a museum or historical society that can be consulted?
- How is online research different from traditional library research?
- How do you know a source is reputable?
- What can a library offer that the internet cannot, and vice versa?
- What should you avoid when looking for information?
- What is primary research and what is secondary research?
- Is it first-hand evidence, or someone *else* looking at the first-hand evidence?
- Which might be better under what circumstances?
- Think abstractly. What information might not seem overly applicable but interesting?
- List the pros and cons of getting lost in your research.

    - New authors, artists, painters may be uncovered.
    - Experts from that era or recent discoveries about a historical time may be found.
    - The deviation from your topic may only yield results that don't apply to your subject.

- The scope of research should be from large to small. It may be too early to focus on trim or lace until you know the silhouette.
- How could a design metaphor affect this process?

"In the play *She Stoops to Conquer* the characters swing gently from one decadence to another." Possible artists of decadence:

- Jean-Honoré Fragonard
- Francois Boucher
- Marguerite Gérard

TEACHING TIP

For discussion purposes, Eric likes to break research into two broad categories: 'physical' and 'psychological.' Physical research includes anything that informs the reality of the play, such as geographical location, period silhouette, styles of door trim, and photos of weather conditions (what, where, and when). Psychological research includes all those items that speak to mood, atmosphere, and the inner workings of characters, such as a piece of abstract art that connects to the metaphor statement and can then be used to inform color palette or textures. Psychological research is usually applied to physical research to connect it more meaningfully to the play's heightened stage environment.

Exercise: Library Fundamentals

TEACHING TIP: PARTNERING WITH LIBRARIANS

At our school, the librarians are very willing to pair with classes. It's worth a call to see if a partnership can be developed at your institution. Some of our most ambitious library partners have built online portals for the class, which include hints and tips on conducting research. Some libraries offer in-class mini-seminars on library resources.

In order to demystify the library, we use the following exercise to inform the students about various rich pockets of information, and to have a little fun too.

Before the class meets, select a variety of materials from every major section of your library. For example, find a book in the oversized section that features a painter or photographer of importance, a costume history book, an old bound copy of an obscure magazine, and the biography of a playwright. Place a sign-in sheet in each book/magazine.

- Distribute the names of the publications and the author/authors.
- Students look up the location of the book within the library.
- Students find the books on the shelves and sign the slip of paper.
- Discuss the process with the class:

  - What new things did they discover in the library?
  - Were they in a rush to find the item, or did a leisurely pace allow for any new discoveries?
  - Are there tips or tricks in finding materials that can be shared with the class?

Figure 3.22 Tracey Indicates a Visual Research Element to be Used in a Drawing

Discussion: Combining the Pieces to Build a Design

The culmination of this whole process is the combination of design elements, design metaphor, script analysis, and research to create a drawing that reflects the chain of discovery. In explaining this design mechanic synthesis to the students, Tracey draws while she talks.

Equipped with croquis and tracing paper, a few pieces of visual research, a metaphor, and the listed use of the design elements, review the character's description with the class. Keeping the research in sight, ask what kind of hair has the line, shape, form, space, color, and texture that speaks to the description of the character. Draw it. What kind of neckline underscores the meaning of the metaphor as defined by the elements of design, and informs the traits of this character? Draw. Create sleeves, hems, and other shapes that form the garment, using the research, applying all previously developed skills as the garment takes shape.

Figure 3.23 Adding the Visual Research Element to the Croqui Tracing

This is the moment when all of the plates are spinning at once. Designing in this process never allows for the omission of script, metaphor, design elements, research, or even design mechanics.

Homework: Visual Research that Informs the Script

Students now have a familiarity with some basic research techniques. Ask them to do research in support of their costume design final project.

- Students must gather at least ten images per costume rendering to be referenced for the costume design final project (five designs = fifty images total). Extra images are allowed and revising and changing the images prior to the costume design final presentation is encouraged.
- Strong research comes from a big variety of sources and covers a wide range of applicable topics.

Portfolio Development Projects

This chapter generated a lot of work (although we recognize that attempting all of the exercises is very unlikely). Choose one or more of the projects and have the students display the work as a portfolio page. A more substantial piece such as 'Twenty-One Black Dresses' might be an item that remains in the student's portfolio for quite some time; the color wheel is more of a placeholder, providing practice in layout and labeling.

Portfolio Project #1: 'Twenty-One Dresses' Project and Variations

- Photograph or otherwise digitize the poster board of 'Twenty-One Black Dresses.'
- Label and include a short description with title of the project.

Portfolio Project #2: Color Wheel

- Digitize or print the painted color wheel.
- Label and include a short description with title of the project.
- Label each of the colors.

Portfolio Project #3: Painting for Color Matching in an Image

- Digitize or print the painted images.
- Label and include a short description with title of the project..

In-class exercise
Matching colors to
a painting.

Medium:
Watercolor
on cardstock

Time Limit:
15 minutes

Figure 3.24   Example of Portfolio Project Layout (Portfolio Example References the Work of Bridget Kelly)

Portfolio Project #4: Pieces of the Final Project

This is preparatory work that will aid the presentation of the final costume project, both in-class, and as a major portfolio piece.

Organize the paperwork generated in the early stages of the final design project.

- Feature the design metaphor paragraph, including the use of the design elements
- Display the costume plot and individual character analyses (optional)
- Organize the research images
- Make notations where needed and label all of the pieces

Card Stacking

In advertising, making a long list in support of an item is 'card stacking.' Creating symmetry in your portfolio entries creates a tidy appearance and serves to card stack your qualifications. These projects, presented professionally, are the long list of skills that support a student's claim to be a theatrical designer.

Notes

1. Marian Appelloff, *Everything You Ever Wanted to Know About Watercolor* (New York: Watson-Guptill Publications, 1992), p. 28.
2. Rosemary Ingham and Liz Covey, *The Costume Designer's Handbook* (Portsmouth: Heinemann Educational Books, Inc., 1992), p. 49.

Chapter 4

Week 4

"Of all the skills required of a costume designer, the ability to draw figures and illustrate garments meaningfully is one of the most essential. The designer must be able to work out ideas and convey to the director, the actors, and the costumer the real proportion, emotional content, and construction detail necessary for each to understand the aspects of the costume that most affect them."[1]

Rebecca Cunningham, *The Magic Garment*

Supplies Needed

Instructor supplies:

- Three different pieces of fabric measuring roughly one square yard each
- Images to use for swatching project (Figures 4.4 through 4.7)
- Scrap bins of fabric

Student supplies:

- Unlined notecards
- Watercolor paint (brushes, water, cups)
- Scissors
- In-progress designs for in-class work session

In the previous weeks, the students have engaged with design information in a variety of formats, building up a picture of the design process dot by dot. By now, the dots should be so close together that there is little struggle to connect metaphor, design elements, script analysis, and research. The information from the script, distilled through the process outlined in this book, will begin to manifest itself through the choices made by the student. A student with this solid foundation will logically begin to design.

The framing topics for this week are:

- Design Mechanics

    - Choosing Fabrics (Swatching)
    - Analyzing a Painting For a Color Palette
    - Painting Fabrics
    - Painting Renderings
    - Applying All Classroom Work on Costume Design Final Project

This week, we focus on the student's technical abilities to express their ideas as costume renderings. While there are a number of structured exercises offered this week, time is carved out, especially in the second session, for in-class work on the final costume project.

Costume Shop Vocabulary

Selvage the manufacturer's tightly woven edge of fabric that prevents it from unraveling

Grain all threads parallel to the selvage

Cross Grain threads perpendicular to the grain

Discussion: Swatching

A costume designer begins to define the fabric through the drawing. The drapes, folds, edges, textures, and colors depicted in the rendering suggest qualities of the fabric. However, the rendering is in a tiny scale and therefore cannot completely tell the whole truth. A bold pattern may maintain its qualities at a great distance from audience members; at the same distance subtle patterns may merge and blend into a sense of texture without particular definition.

TEACHING TIP

For the scope of this class, gloss over the specifics of draping, weave, and fiber content. We do not find that time allows more than a glancing nod to the names and qualities of the myriad fabrics available. In reality, fabric choices for produced scripts require the consideration of dozens of variables. For this introductory course, the range of acceptable fabrics is very broad.

Exercise: Depicting Fabric with Paint

The following exercises help students understand what happens to fabric patterns when seen at a distance as well as begin to understand how to choose patterns that best suit what they have drawn.

Choose a few different pieces of fabric that have rather small prints: stripes, patterns, or plaids. Allow a minimum of one yard of fabric per each example (keep the fabric from year to year to expedite your preparations).

- Hang each fabric fifteen feet away from the students (use a hallway if needed).
- Ask the students to describe the fabric.

  - What colors do they see? Are there any designs on the fabric? How does the light hit the fabric? Are folds sharp and stiff or soft and flowing?

- Using a notecard (this adds the challenge of scale) and watercolors, have the students paint their perception of each piece of fabric.

Figure 4.1 Photograph of Three Different Fabrics (Each with Inset Detail Image) Taken at 15' Away

- Discuss the exercise.

  - Did you attempt to depict pinstripes or plaids in scale?

- Bring the fabric closer to the students in increments of five feet.

  - What changes about the perception of the fabric as it gets closer?
  - What are some of the challenges costume designers face because of the changes in the appearance of fabric as the viewer moves closer or further away?

Figure 4.2 Example of Student's Painting Depicting the Fabrics of Figure 4.1 (Abigail King)

Book Recommendation

If you are teaching this section and have a minimal knowledge of fabric basics, Chapter 7 of Rebecca Cunningham's *The Magic Garment* serves as a good introduction. You'll find information on the source, characteristics, and typical usage of common fabrics, as well as tips on how to incorporate fabric textures into renderings.

Exercise: Swatching a Painting

Begin with a review of some of the lessons learned from depicting fabric with paint.

- The details on fabric fade with distance and reduced scale.
- Patterns, even if undetectable from a distance, make fabric more dynamic.
- Colors mix, blend, or disappear when viewed from a distance.

The following exercise introduces the skill of choosing fabric for a costume. On a finished costume design rendering, a swatch or small sample of fabric is placed next to the drawing of the character. The intention is to clarify the fabric selected and aid in the depiction of the costume design.

Figure 4.3 Close-Up of Fabric Swatches Secured to a Rendering

Provide students with paintings that depict several types of fabrics. We use images like the examples provided in Figures 4.4 through 4.7 for this swatching project. We have the luxury of many scrap bins of fabric in our costume shop, but a single box loaded with fabric samples will also work for this exercise.

Each student:

- Identifies the various fabrics evident in the painting
- Selects the closest possible fabric match for each layer of cloth depicted in the painting.
- Cuts each swatch to a 2″ x 2″ square. Swatches should not have any selvage.
- Presents choices to the class.

  - How did their knowledge of loss of detail, and scale contribute to their fabric choices?

Figure 4.5 *Mrs. Hugh Hammersley*, by John Singer Sargent (The Metropolitan Museum of Art, Gift of Mr. and Mrs. Douglass Campbell, in memory of Mrs. Richard E. Danielson, 1998)

Figure 4.4 *Lady Guildford*, Copy after Hans Holbein the Younger (The Metropolitan Museum of Art, Bequest of William K. Vanderbilt, 1920)

Figure 4.6 *The Old Musician*, by Edouard Manet (Image courtesy of the National Gallery of Art, Washington)

Figure 4.7 *Antoine-Laurent Lavoisier and His Wife,* by Jacques-Louis David (The Metropolitan Museum of Art, Purchase, Mr. and Mrs. Charles Wrightsman Gift, in honor of Everett Fahy, 1977)

Some students may rush to color match without consideration of texture. As they pull fabric samples, circulate and ask what specific qualities led them to make their selections. By learning what makes fabric interesting now, they can make better choices for their costume design final project.

Two variations of this exercise ask students to choose fabric:

1. for shoes, hats, wallpaper, carpet, cushions as seen in the painting
2. to represent non-fabric items, such as tables, lamps, or wooden surfaces.

TEACHING TIP

There is a right way and a wrong way to cut a swatch from a larger piece of fabric. The correct way maintains the maximum amount of usable fabric for future projects. Cutting a swatch incorrectly can render a long piece of fabric useless. Conserve fabric by cutting on the furthest edge, rather than from the center, and near other cut-up edges rather than from a squared-off corner. The 2" x 2" square should not include the selvage. Cut the fabric on the grain and cross grain unless there is a specific reason to adjust the direction of the weave.

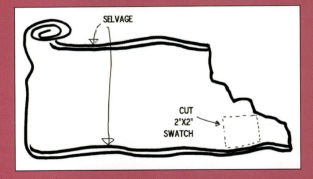

Figure 4.8 Diagram of Proper Swatching Cut

Figure 4.9 Abigail Swatches Her Renderings

- Using the fabric swatches, paint the line drawing. Attempt to depict the color and texture of each fabric.
- Students present results to the class
- Discuss the effects of the color, texture, and pattern of each of the fabrics, and why the student chose each fabric's placement and proportional use on the rendering.

For a variation, have students swap swatch sets and have them paint another set of line drawings.

Exercise: Colors in Harmony on a Rendering

This exercise reverses the process of picking fabric from an existing painting. Instead of pulling information from an image, students are asked to use a pre-existing color and texture palette to create a rendering. Provide line drawings or croquis on cardstock paper for ease of use with watercolors. Figure 4.10 depicts some examples of costume line drawings.

TEACHING TIP

The exercise 'Colors in Harmony on a Rendering' can start with the group of swatches gathered from 'Swatching a Painting.' Since our long class sessions allow for extended projects, the logic of each exercise is a little clearer when they are connected.

Figure 4.10 Sample Line Drawings for Use in Colors in Harmony on a Rendering

Figure 4.11   Results of Painting Line Drawings Using Swatches (Stephanie Graf)

Figure 4.12   Results of Painting Line Drawings Using Swatches (Peyton Reigstad)

Book Recommendation

For an excellent exploration of creating color harmony in painted work, as well as suggestions for advanced color exercises, see Chapters 8 and 9 of Betty Edwards' *Color: A Course in Mastering the Art of Mixing Colors*.

"The strange thing about color harmony is that, whether one is trained or untrained in color, we are aware that some color combinations please us greatly, even though we may not know why they please us or how to produce such combinations."[3]
Betty Edwards, *Color: A Course in Mastering the Art of Mixing Colors*

Discussion: The Color Palettes of Master Painters

Picture the classical kidney-bean-shaped wooden board held by oil painters. On that board are all the blobs of color intended for use on the current project. Painters seldom start with equal parts of all three primary colors (red, blue, yellow) and attempt to mix all their desired hues from them; instead, they select a range of more specific colors that will provide the desired degree of harmony.

In many great works of art, a limited color palette provides the maximum dramatic effect.

Consider the painting shown in Figure 4.13, Raphael's *The Alba Madonna*. The number of base hues is fairly limited. The range of shades, tints, and tones of each of these colors is also limited. For example, the blue of the sky is related to the blue of the Madonna's outer garment. The skin of the figures has a pinkish tone that relates it to the pink (which is a tint of red) of the Madonna's undergarment. The greens of the distant hills have a bluish cast that relates them to the sky, while the ground color appears to be a mixture of brown and green, which relates it to the background landscape as well as the fur worn by the child on the left, the Madonna's hair, and the tree stump she leans against. The eye is drawn to the center of the painting by the Madonna's pink garment, which is unlike anything else in the painting. By controlling the number of colors, their intensities, and their proportion in the whole of the painting, artists guide the viewer's eye through the work, indicating where to look first and which items within the painting should be seen as being connected.

Using the proportions of a limited color palette already worked out and mapped in a great painting can help the designer arrange and balance color, since the painter has already demonstrated the effectiveness of that set of color choices.

Exercise: Extracting Color Palettes from Paintings

This first exercise focuses on identifying and discussing the range of color used in painting. Assemble a selection of images from artists like Raphael, Titian, Jan Van Eyck, Hans Holbein the Younger, Fra Angelico, Cosimo Tura, Verrocchio, and Sandro Botticelli (see Figures 4.13 through 4.16 for examples). Use these images to lead a discussion on the use of a color palette:

- What colors are used?
- Is there a wide range of colors?
- Within a single color, is there a wide range of saturation?
- Are the whites really white? Are the blacks really black?
- What is the degree of contrast among the colors?
- Which color is used most?
- Which color is used least?
- Which colors are found next to each other?
- How are individual colors distributed around the painting?
- How does that distribution impact the viewer's focus?

Figure 4.13 *The Alba Madonna* by Raphael (Image courtesy of the National Gallery of Art, Washington D.C.)

Figure 4.15 *Edward VI, V/hen Duke of Cornwall* by the Workshop of Hans Holbein the Younger (Image courtesy of the National Gallery of Art, Washington D.C.)

Figure 4.14 *The Annunciation* by Jan Van Eyck (Image courtesy of the National Gallery of Art, Washington D.C.)

Figure 4.16 *The Adoraticn of the Magi* by Fra Angelico and Fra Filippo Lippi (Image courtesy of the National Gallery of Art, Washington D.C.)

Exercise: Connecting Color Palette to Design Metaphor

This exercise will create one of the components of the costume design final project and influence the painting of the final project's costume renderings. This can be a homework assignment, due at the next class session, or a short in-class research exercise, where students are given access to art books and online sources and asked to find an image within a given time limit.

- Select a painting that satisfies the following qualifications:

  - Contains a color palette that supports the choices delineated in the metaphor statement
  - Has meaningful content, such as coming from the same era, style, or other historical/dramaturgical connection

- Present the artwork to the class, explaining how the image fulfills the two criteria above.

  Test the color choices found in the image against the paragraph written by the student that describes their design metaphor and how they plan to use the design elements. For example, if the statement describes color as being bright, light, airy, and natural, but the student presents Hans Holbein the Younger's painting of Hermann von Wedigh III (Figure 4.17), the choice is unsupported. If the student feels strongly that the painting does exhibit relevant connections to the text, encourage the student to dig deeper. Is there a specific portion or detail of the painting that is felt to work? Would the student be better served by finding a work that expands upon that detail? If the student finds the image overwhelmingly compelling, is it time to go back and re-examine and revise the metaphor statement?

Figure 4.17 *Hermann von Wedigh III*, by Hans Holbein the Younger (Image courtesy of the Metropolitan Museum of Art, New York, bequest of Edward S. Harkness)

Exercise: Analyzing the Amounts of Colors Used in a Limited Palette

The preceding exercises gave clarification to color selection. Now we more specifically explore the proportion of each color to the overall costume design.

Using the painting from the exercise, 'Referencing a Limited Color Palette':

- Have each student list all of the colors depicted in the selected painting.
- Have each student assign a percentile coverage amount to each color in the painting.

- For example: Jean-Honoré Fragonard's *A Young Girl Reading*:

  - Green/brown = 25%
  - White with p nk highlights = 20%
  - Orange/yellow with red highlight = 15%
  - Yellow with grey shadows = 11%
  - Brown/brunette = 8%
  - Caucasian flesh tone = 6% (Flesh could arguably be omitted as your actors will provide their own skin.)
  - Mauve = 5%
  - White with highlights and shadows = 5%
  - Wood brown = 2%
  - Red = 2%
  - Extra light pir k = 1%
  - Dark yellow = 1%

- Discuss each student's results:

  - Which color draws the eye most?
  - Which colors are accents?
  - Is the color with the largest area the most important color?
  - How can the student use these proportions for each costume?
  - How can the student use these proportions for the entirety of the design?

Session Break: End of Week 4, Day 1.

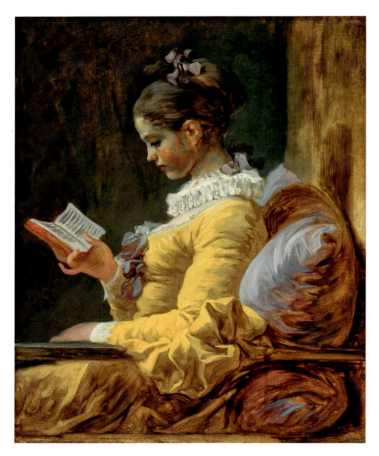

Figure 4.18 *A Young Girl Reading* by Jean-Honoré Fragonard (Image courtesy of the National Gallery of Art, Washington D.C.)

TEACHING TIP

Ongoing homework assignments like the costume design final project need frequent goal posts. By having students regularly bring their progress to class, you can prevent problems before they become a crisis. Our design class is not meant to weed out students, but to expose all students in the program to design in general and theatrical design specifically; therefore, we don't want anyone to stray too far. By checking in regularly, we can actively and intentionally encourage the students and support their growth.

In-Class Work Session: Costume Design Final Project

For each design section, we like to include a certain amount of in-class work time for the final project. Clearly state what you expect students to bring to the work session. For the costume final project work session, these are some of the tasks we expect to occur:

- Swatching
- Final layout of rendering templates
- Applying color and texture to renderings.

Be sure to circulate. Ask specific questions that clarify intentions. Offer judicious technical advice. If things are going well, watch, be present, be available.

By the end of the work session, you should have a good sense of how far along each student is on the final project.

If you prefer a more structured work session, the following exercises require students to arrive with a certain amount of finished work in hand.

Exercise: Painting the Renderings for the Costume Design Final

With their set (we require five) of line drawings finished, direct students to paint the renderings. Be sure they bring multiple copies of each line drawing to accommodate trial and error.

- Students should mirror the color palette of the chosen piece of art in their renderings.
- Students are encouraged to re-print and re-paint drawings as needed. They should feel free to experiment and make mistakes on their way to presenting their best effort.
- Remember that each rendering includes the show's title, the name of the character, act/scene notations if needed, a horizon line, and space for the fabric swatches.
- As students complete renderings, discuss the work with the class and invite the students to share their newly discovered best practices.

Figure 4.19 Lilliana Works from Her Research Images

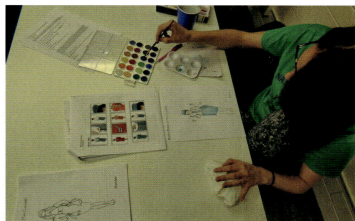

Figure 4.20 Kelsey Paints Her Renderings

Exercise: Swatching the Renderings for the Costume Design Final

Some professional designers choose their fabrics prior to painting; some paint first and shop for fabrics second. Since either way is acceptable, allow your students to find comfort in creating their own path.

- With painted or unpainted renderings in hand, the students pick fabrics for their designs.
- Swatches are cut into 2″ x 2″ squares and attached to the renderings.

Figure 4.21 Two Different Student Renderings with Swatches (Hastings from *She Stoops to Conquer*, by Abigai King, and Gabriella from *Boeing Boeing*, by Kelsey Smyth)

Figure 4.22 Example of Tape Holding Swatches that Flip Up

- Fabrics are displayed with the fabric lowest on the body lowest on the stack of fabrics.
- The fabric swatches are usually staggered to show a little of each fabric.
- Tape holds fabric to the rendering. A best practice allows the fabrics to flip up to expose lower layers. Both a 'hinge' created with clear tape placed on the bottom side of the fabric and a small loop of tape at the top of the underside of the swatch allow for easy access of each swatch.

Portfolio Development Projects

This chapter was a direct progression of exercises, both stand-alone and as part of the development of the final costume design project. Any of these can serve as portfolio projects. Smaller projects can share a single larger portfolio page with a collective title for the work.

Portfolio Items from In-Class Work

Painting Fabric from a Distance

- Display the notecard painted to depict the fabric at 15' away.
- Provide photographs of the fabric both from a distance and from close up.
- Include a short description, with title, of the project.

Swatching a Painting

- Photograph or otherwise reproduce the inspirational artwork.
- Photograph the well-cut and displayed swatches.
- Identify which swatch applies to which part of the artwork.
- Include a short description, with title, of the project.

Colors in Harmony on a Rendering

- Display the renderings painted using the palette generated from the fabric swatches.
- Include the swatches or a photograph of the swatches.
- If the student didn't generate the line drawings, they may wish to credit the other artist.
- Include a short description, with title, of the project.

Portfolio Items from Costume Design Final Project

The Color Palettes of Master Painters

- Alongside the color palette inspirational artwork, display the list of colors and their percentage of use.
- Include a short description of the project.

Painted Renderings for the Costume Design Final

- Scan or photograph each rendering, with the swatches included.
- Include a short description, with title, of the project.

Depicting Process

The polished final product of student work will speak well of the design skills; however, the hook for many that land a design job is the depiction of their *process*. As students assemble their portfolios be sure to encourage the inclusion of items like analysis statements, research, and layers of steps on the display page. Because good process can be applied regardless of the individualized nature of each project, the portfolio will be able to speak of the presenter not just as a technician, but as a collaborative person with whom others will be eager to work.

Notes

1. Rebecca Cunningham, *The Magic Garment: Principles of Costume Design* (Prospect Heights: Waveland Press, 1989), p. 147.
2. Lynn Pecktal, *Costume Design: Techniques of Modern Masters* (New York: Back Stage, 1999), p. 177.
3. Betty Edwards, *Color: A Course in Mastering the Art of Mixing Colors* (New York: Jeremy P. Tarcher/Penguin, 2004), pp. 85–86.

Chapter 5

Week 5

> "You learn it from a book to a certain extent –
> you know how to read a script from a book –
> but if you don't do it, you'll never learn it."[1]
> Theoni V. Aldredge, quoted in Lynn Pecktal's *Costume Design:*
> *Techniques of Modern Masters*

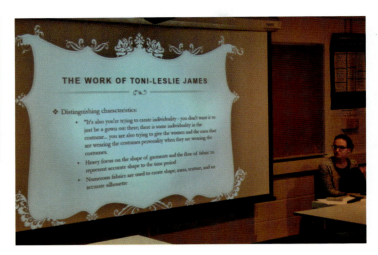

Figure 5.1   Kelsey Presents Costume Designer Toni-Leslie James to the Class

Within the two projects of this week, we will address all of the framing topics:

- Formal Presentation of a Professional Costume Designer

  - Metaphor
  - Design Principles
  - Script Analysis
  - Research
  - Design Mechanics

- Formal Presentation of Student's Final Costume Design Project

  - Metaphor
  - Design Principles
  - Script Analysis
  - Research
  - Design Mechanics

Costume Designer Presentations

Throughout the previous four weeks a classroom environment has evolved. Students have discovered and become skilled in speaking about scripts, design elements, metaphor, research, and design mechanics. These skills now serve them in a project that brings the pieces together in a presentation. As assigned in the earlier chapters, students present their research on and discuss the work of a professional designer.

TEACHING TIP

Modeling desired behavior is an underlying theme of all teaching. To that end, Tracey will periodically do mini-presentations of designers from the past (we ask the students to present on contemporary designers). It can be a great five-minute interlude between projects or the start or conclusion to a class. By discussing what she sees and how the designer used the design elements, students gain a great deal of information. They gain a snapshot of information about a historically relevant designer. Students observe a designer speaking about design and the instructor is modeling the type of information intended to be included in the student's presentation.

Evaluating the Students' Presentations on Professional Designers

The Rubric

Take each component of the assignment, create a value proportionate to the whole, and develop a scale indicating success. Students will know exactly where their work shone and where they need to improve. Alone, however, a rubric can lack detailed feedback as to what might account for the deduction from a perfect score so be sure to include, in writing, your fuller response. We have also used the rubric as a handout to the presenter. This information, given to a student a few class periods prior to the presentation, can help them do some self-evaluation.

Using a Rubric for the Evaluation of the Costume Designer Presentations

During the student's presentation, make relevant notes in each section. Quote the student's presentation. Use this information later for a reminder as to the specifics of the material. Evaluate later. This way, 'average' is determined at the conclusion of the day after all the students have presented. This also gives the instructor an opportunity for reflection before assigning a point value.

Theatre Arts 242 T – TH 9:00–10:45 / COURSE TITLE: Introduction to Design   Student: _____

Explanation of: "What does your designer feel is the role of design in production?"

No Information	Below standard	Average	Good	Excellent
0	1–3	4–6	7–9	10

Notes:

Explanation of: "What does this designer hope to add to a production through their design?"

No Information	Below standard	Average	Good	Excellent
0	1–3	4–6	7–9	10

Notes:

Was the designer's philosophy stated and explained?

No Information	Below standard	Average	Good	Excellent
0	1–3	4–6	7–9	10

Notes:

Display examples of this designer's work.

No Information	Below standard	Average	Good	Excellent
0	1–3	4–6	7–9	10

Notes:

continued

Using the visuals, analyze the characteristics of these designs.

No Information	Below standard	Average	Good	Excellent
0	1–3	4–6	7–9	10

Notes:

Analysis of the design principles:

No Information	Below standard	Average	Good	Excellent
0	1–3	4–6	7–9	10

Notes:

What did the designer say about design elements?

No Information	Below standard	Average	Good	Excellent
0	1–3	4–6	7–9	10

Notes:

Statement or comments concluding the presentation.

No Information	Below standard	Average	Good	Excellent
0	1–3	4–6	7–9	10

Notes:

Overall Presentation. Organization. Quality.

No Information	Below standard	Average	Good	Excellent
0	1–3	4–6	7–9	10

Notes:

Bibliography

No Information	Below standard	Average	Good	Excellent
0	1–3	4–6	7–9	10

Notes:

Total Grade:

Presentation by a Guest Artist

> "Bringing in guest lecturers with a variety of backgrounds, personalities, and success stories was identified as a good way to get students motivated and informed. The students generally believed that introducing undergraduates to guest lecturers can also help them build connections. Students with specific interests such as design, stage management, and touring said they had received 'trade secrets' and interview techniques from lecturers in their chosen fields."[2]
>
> Ashley Harman, "Student Perspectives on Theatre Technology and Design Education," published in *Inspired Teaching, Essays on Theatre Design and Technology Education*

If it is possible and if time allows, this class session is an excellent time to bring in a guest designer. Connecting students with an outside professional designer reinforces your material and creates an excellent capstone event for the section. Some professionals may have many ideas or topics from which they will wish to speak, others may be less structured. Be prepared with open-ended questions that could guide your guest. Here are some suggestions:

- How did you get your first professional design job?
- Where do you start your script analysis process?
- Do you have any tips or best practices for research?
- Do you develop a metaphor to guide your design choices?

- What advice do you wish you had been given when you were in your first design course?
- Allow for students to ask questions too.

Remember to treat your guest as a VIP. Perhaps they would like a tour of the facilities or a cup of coffee. There might be value in having this guest speak at other classes throughout the day. A thank you note goes a long way.

With a third of the students presenting, and a thirty- to forty-minute presentation from a guest designer, this concludes the first half of Week 5.

The Costume Design Final Project

TEACHING TIP

This is the final day of costume design course work, and the presentation of the capstone project within this subject matter should be a celebration. Even at various levels of success, every student learned about design, and specifically costume design. There should be a big emphasis on the journey, the process, the personal growth, and the vast amount of work required and completed. Have the students look at their accomplishments and at the achievements made by their peers.

The Kennedy Center American College Theatre Festival (KCACTF) has been a big influence on our teaching and this course. This regional conference gave us the basis of thought for developing a curriculum that incorporated unrealized designs.

For our final projects, we duplicate the visual and verbal formatting of our region's annual conference. Just like the conference format, our students give a three- to five-minute presentation that walks the viewer through the metaphor, use of design elements, application of research, and results shown in the final renderings. Even though we have seen many of these pieces in progress, we may ask leading questions such as, "What led to the use of metallic colored fabric?" or "Why have you moved away from your initial ideas?" Critiques are delivered in writing on the rubric. Distribute your time evenly to each of the students. A rush to the finish is never fair or desirable.

Rubric for the Costume Design Final Project

Theatre Arts 242 T – TH 9:00–10:45 / COURSE TITLE: Introduction to Design   Student: _____

Poster

Title of show, author, designer

Minimum Effort	Some Effort	Average	Good	Excellent
1–4	5–8	9–12	13–16	17–20

Notes:

Does the metaphor show through the use of design principles in the renderings?

Minimum Effort	Some Effort	Average	Good	Excellent
1–7	8–13	14–18	19–24	25–30

Notes:

Clarity of content: color palette painting, research near renderings, metaphor paragraph labeled

Minimum Effort	Some Effort	Average	Good	Excellent
1–7	8–13	14–18	19–24	25–30

Notes:

Five Renderings

Well drawn, with detail, hair, hats, shoes

Minimum Effort	Some Effort	Average	Good	Excellent
1–7	8–13	14–18	19–24	25–30

Notes:

Painted

Minimum Effort	Some Effort	Average	Good	Excellent
1–4	5–8	9–12	13–16	17–20

Notes:

Swatched: almost every layer indicated with fabric. Fabric that supports design principles

Minimum Effort	Some Effort	Average	Good	Excellent
1–4	5–8	9–12	13–16	17–20

Notes:

Title blocked with show, character name, size of figure dominates that page

Minimum Effort	Some Effort	Average	Good	Excellent
1–4	5–8	9–12	13–16	17–20

Notes:

Oral Presentation

Introduction of self and project AND conclusion at the end of the presentation

Minimum Effort	Some Effort	Average	Good	Excellent
1–4	5–8	9–12	13–16	17–20

Notes:

Summary of metaphor

Minimum Effort	Some Effort	Average	Good	Excellent
1–4	5–8	9–12	13–16	17–20

Notes:

Presentation of how metaphor is indicated in design principles in the renderings and choices made by designer

Minimum Effort	Some Effort	Average	Good	Excellent
1–4	5–8	9–12	13–16	17–20

Notes:

Final Grade:

Notes:

The Costume Design Final Project's Continuation

We offer every student, but do not require them to take, an opportunity to continue, outside of class, further development of their designs. Fully completed un-actualized designs are allowed to compete at our region's KCACTF. The timing works in our favor as we teach this course in the Fall semester with the KCACTF conference falling three weeks after the conclusion of the semester.

Guidelines for the Continuation of a Project for Competition at KCACTF

"Regional Design Projects are intended to serve Region III student designers with the opportunity to showcase their work for non-realized design projects, and to receive response to their work that will help them improve their design skills and grow as designers."[3]
KCACTF Region III website

Students will now work outside of the class in a one-on-one mentor relationship with the instructor, toward the goal of achieving a completed design of high quality for competition at the KCACTF regional festival. If you are a mentor, make clear the responsibility lies with the student and that the opportunity to attend KCACTF is the reward.

- Using a calendar, have students divide the remaining work into segments and assign due dates.
- Schedule weekly or bi-weekly meetings to address success and deficiencies.
- Pad in some time for corrections and improvements.
- Plan a session where other faculty members will give informal feedback to the student in a 'mock' presentation.

Funding KCACTF

The price to attend the conference is reasonable but hardly free. Travel, hotel, and meals are a serious consideration too. At this time, we are able to draw funding from our university's Undergraduate Research (UR) Fund. The UR program is a model that best fits the hard sciences but generously supports our creative work when it is framed as research. There are a few added steps to secure the funding, such as a written abstract and an afternoon of presentations on campus. All are a good mix of liberal arts training in higher education with the added benefit of raising the profile of theatre within our campus. Challenge yourself to find funding for the KCACTF conference within your university.

With KCACTF the only constant from year to year and region to region is change. The nature of a rotating, volunteer-led group drawn from a variety of institutions means that things remain in motion. Professional and academic theatre changes too, so guiding students with the full knowledge that they must remain open to new approaches, ideas, and guidelines is good training. There is a culture of competition at KCACTF, not unlike our experiences in professional settings. It can be an excellent wake-up call for students to see what they will face after graduation.

Figure 5.2   Bridget Kelly Presents Her Costume Design Final Project

Figure 5.3 Eric Guenthner Presents His Costume Design Final Project

Figure 5.4 Kelsey Smyth Presents Her Costume Design Final Project

Portfolio Development

This is the pinnacle of the costume design work and the final project should be prominently displayed in the portfolio. An opportunity to present other information, previously excluded, can add support to the design. As always, the intent of the design should be clear and the application of that intent into the design will be the litmus test by which success is gauged.

Depending on the preferred format, the student will find it necessary to convert the project materials either into a size dictated by the paper portfolio, or digitize elements for electronic presentation.

Encourage students to condense the material to be displayed on either two facing paper portfolio pages (22" x 17" is a good size) or two sequential PowerPoint (or equivalent) pages.

Here are some considerations when creating portfolio pages that represent your costume design final project:

- Background surfaces and textures should enhance, rather than distract from, the content.
- White space is important; don't crowd or overlap content unless there is a compelling reason to do so, such as the visual connection of research images to a particular final rendering.
- On renderings, if the boundary between background and image is unclear, consider using borders or changing the background.
- Prioritize and be consistent with image size to avoid visual confusion; if something is important, it should be easy to find.
- Include labels (unless, like the renderings, the labels are part of the image).
- A good rule of thumb is to begin with an image of the finished product, and then organize subsequent material to show how it was achieved. For costume portfolios, consider including the one or two most interesting or essential full-sized renderings with fabric swatches, and high-quality reduced-size scans or color photocopies of the remainder to

illustrate character relationships and groupings (the breadth of the whole show).

Regardless of delivery system, the portfolio pages should include:

- A Title Block

  - Name and Author of play
  - Name of Designer
  - Date of Design
  - Name of Director (if extant)
  - Name of Venue (if extant)

- Design Statement (condensed to a single paragraph)
- Renderings
- Research Images, clearly related to the appropriate renderings

- If a costume had a particularly interesting development process that illuminates the designer's approach, a short sequence of drafts and sketches can be included, with brief explanations of the steps.

Notes

1. Lynn Pecktal, *Costume Design: Techniques of Modern Masters* (New York: Back Stage, 1999), p. 19.
2. Erik Viker, *Inspired Teaching: Essays on Theatre Design and Technology Education* (Syracuse, NY: United States Institute for Theatre Technology, 2013).
3. KCACTF Region III, Design, Technology and Management (http://www.kcactf3.org/projects_info.htm, n.d. Web. 28 Mar. 2016).

Section II

Scenic Design

Chapter 6

Week 6

"For the present, however, the scene-designer
remains what he has always been: one member
of a group of interpreters. As such he must,
usually in four weeks' time, construct a home
or a palace . . . transport any corner of the five
continents or any number of Arcadias to the
theatre, provide any object that the actors must
touch or handle, whether a throne or a kitchen
chair, a dead sea-gull or the Sphinx, and out of
paint, glue, canvas, gauze, wood, and papier
mâché create a world real enough to house the
conflicts of human beings."[1]
Lee Simonson, *The Stage is Set*

During the past few weeks, focus has been upon the character
and the world that character inhabits as reflected by the choices
made by the costume designer. We now turn our attention
directly to that world inhabited by the characters, and how, step
by step, the scenic designer begins assembling a meaningful
environment.

The structure of this section repeats that of the costume
portion:

- Fundamental concepts
- Low-stakes exercises
- A mid-level project
- Student research projects that discuss a Broadway- or
regional-level designer's work
- A guest artist from the professional field recently discussed
- The presentation of a final project with components completed throughout the section.

Unless a student feels strongly otherwise (or a design
metaphor has proven totally ineffective), the design metaphors
developed for the final costume design project are retained for
the scenic design final project. Except for review and minor
revision, we do not revisit design metaphor in any extensive
manner as it is a tool that should already be in constant use.
Rendering (design mechanics) is limited to graphic tasks that fit
within the time available and best address scenery as a three-
dimensional element, allowing students to produce their final
project in five weeks.

For this first week of scenic design, the framing topics
are:

- Script analysis
  - Examining the qualities of various environments and
  analyzing them via design elements
  - Examining examples of scenic design and analyzing
  them via design elements
  - Discussion of what makes an effective, meaningful storytelling environment
  - Revisiting script analysis, this time with an eye toward
  scenic clues

- Research
  - Discussion of what physical elements are essential to
  telling a story
  - Determining the sizes of real objects

- Design Mechanics
  - Using a scale rule to measure and lay out items
  - Building the three-dimensional stage house for the mid-
  sized design project

Supplies Needed

Instructor supplies:

- Projectable images for discussion (see Figures 6.1 through 6.4)
- 3 x 5 notecards
- Line Measuring handout (see Figure 6.16)
- Groundplan reduced to 8½" x 11" paper
- Handout with Small Stagehouse directions (see Figures 6.22 and 6.23)
- Hair spray or workable fixative (to fix charcoal drawings)
- Projectable images of Scenic Designs
- A short play (a ten-minute play works well; see Appendix C for ones we use in class)
- Handout for 'Sizes of Real Things' homework

Student supplies:

- Architectural scale rule
- Drawing charcoal
- Drawing pencil
- 24" T-square
- Two sheets of 20" x 30" black foamcore
- X-Acto knife
- Steel straightedge (used with X-Acto to cut foamcore)
- Tacky glue

This list comprises materials for both the instructor and students. Our classroom cabinet contains a number of emergency tools, such as T-squares and drafting triangles. We stress to the students that sharing equipment makes everyone who is doing the sharing work more slowly, and that there is no guarantee that the forgotten tool will happen to be in the cabinet when needed.

Scenic Design Vocabulary

Background The region in a composition containing items that appear to be behind other items or appear furthest from the viewer

Foreground The region in a composition containing items that appear to be in front of other items or appear nearest to the viewer

Symmetry When a composition of items on one side of an axis is mirrored on the other side of the axis

Balance An equilibrium and stability achieved by arranging objects with different sizes so that an equal 'weight' is perceived on either size of an axis

Value The lightness or darkness of a color, especially when compared to the graduated steps moving from white through grey to black

Sittable Used to denote anything on a stage which can be sat upon before a specific furniture type has been determined

Dramaturgy (also, dramaturgical) According to director John Caird: "the craft of analyzing the structure of dramatic texts and the theatrical style in which they are performed . . . may be used more loosely to describe the dramatic structure of a play or the theoretical basis of a production"[2]

Discussion:
The Purpose of Scenery

The scenic designer physically organizes the performance space to create an environment in which the story can most effectively be performed. The designer must make sure that the world created on the stage underscores, supports, and otherwise engages the choices with which characters are faced, as the rationale of an actor's choice is linked to the environment in which the character is shown to exist. If the apartment in *A Raisin in the Sun* is large and spacious, for example, the play's motivation is undermined. Shape and space become essential tools for building this world; the tighter, the more cramped the apartment, the more of a pressure cooker it can become. The audience understands exactly why the Younger family wishes to escape it. Even an empty stage is a choice and can underscore vulnerability, isolation, and exposure, or be a stylistic choice to strip things down to a barebones focus on language, relationships, and the performer's body.

Everything on the stage must have a purpose, whether contributing toward psychology and atmosphere (e.g., set dressing) or providing physical barriers and entrances (e.g., walls and doors). A knickknack placed on an occasional table must reflect the history of the room; the owner of the room placed it there for a reason. The audience's expectations of what can occur in a room dotted with ceramic statuettes of frolicking shepherdesses may be very different from one decorated with taxidermied squirrels. Similarly, a couch placed dead center of the stage facing the audience creates very different possibilities for blocking (and therefore the expression of relationships) than a couch at an angle off to the side, or two separate chairs placed side by side. The placement and style of furniture reflects not only economic and social status, but determines how easy it is for characters to be intimate with one another – or, conversely, how easily they may escape one another.

The exercises and discussions to follow are designed to get students thinking about the details of an environment, and how those details coalesce to create meaning in a space.

Discussion: Describing Environment

It's important to broaden students' sense of what scenery can be, as well as to get them looking at scenery with a more critical

Book Recommendation

Philosophically, our approach to teaching scenic design is in line with that of the New Stagecraft practitioners and how their ideas have percolated down through American set design aesthetics.

The New Stagecraft is a name applied to the stage design movement that came to prominence in America during the 1920s and 1930s. It was a reaction against the then-current ultra-realism as well as an embrace of more abstract European scenery. It also drew inspiration from the advent of electrical stage lighting, and the revelatory ways of using it suggested in the writings of designers Adolphe Appia and Edward Gordon Craig.

The New Stagecraft looked beyond the basic physical requirements of a play and sought to express the play's deeper psychological workings through the environment as experienced by both the characters and the audience. In many cases, this meant stripping away anything that could be considered excess, making sure that everything on stage had a distinct purpose in being there. In other cases, it meant looking to symbols or abstraction – indeed, creating a visually poetic parallel to the action of the play. Robert Edmond Jones' scenic design for *The Man Who Married a Dumb Wife* is considered a seminal New Stagecraft design, as he abandoned realism in favor of a fanciful storybook look to the scenery and costumes that exemplified the *spirit* of the story.

For an opinionated history of scenic design culminating in the ideas of the New Stagecraft written by one of the major scenic designers of the first half of the twentieth century, we suggest *The Stage is Set*, by Lee Simonson.

eye. Before looking at the artificial contrivances that are theatrical environments, we examine real places and spaces through the lens of the design elements.

The following exercises serve a number of purposes:

- To sharpen observation skills
- To expand vocabulary for color and composition
- To understand that we make cultural assumptions about viewed objects based on personal experience
- To learn to use those cultural assumptions as intentional tools for design.

The first scenic design session begins with a review of the design elements by looking at a series of images. See Figures 6.1 through 6.4 for examples. Compositional terms such as background, foreground, symmetry, and balance are employed, as well as color terms like value and palette. Once a term is introduced, try to include it in the discussion of each image thereafter. The following steps provide structure for these explorations:

- *Observe.* Say nothing; just look. Search for detail. Explore all corners of the image.
- *Describe.* Stick with what is actually there. Use design elements and compositional terms to guide description. Don't jump to emotional or culturally-based responses.
- *Analyze.* Discuss how the image is arranged and how the elements work together to create an effect on the viewer, whether intended or not.
- *Interpret.* Discuss what kind of activities or events might take place in this environment, and how the design elements noted contribute to the mood and atmosphere of the environment, enabling the events to have a specific quality. Determine what elements are essential to the creation of the atmosphere. If students have cultural or personal associations that color their experience of the locale, discuss what might enhance or diminish the experience of the locale for those viewers who do not share that cultural or personal experience.

Discussion: Composition Influences Perception

A relatively simple abstract image works well as a starting point. We use a bold, high-contrast Mark Rothko painting. The students are asked to identify what they see as the most dominant design element, and it's not always the same for every student. Have the students support their choice by describing, with as much detail as possible, that applicable portion of the image.

When the conversation reaches a state of rest, the next slide presents the same painting, but turned on its side. Axes of symmetry change, balance shifts, even color relationships can change. Students may have to be led through the obvious – such as previously horizontal lines becoming vertical – and it's interesting to watch as assumptions about the sameness of the images (you 'just' turned it on its side) evolve into more complex considerations.

The next few images viewed have been chosen with a dominant design element, such as line or color, in mind (Figures 6.1 through 6.4).

Figure 6.1 Discussion Image #1

Figure 6.2 Discussion Image #2

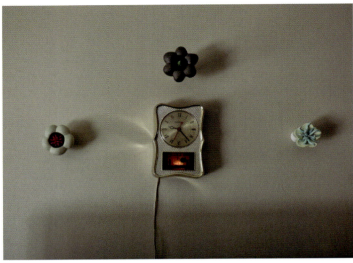

Figure 6.4 Discussion Image #4 (Artwork by Rachelle Miller, Included by Permission)

Distribute charcoal and blank 3 x 5 cards to the students. Charcoal works better than pencil for this exercise because it's much easier to draw a wide range of line weights, as well as create various textures and grayscale values.

- Show the class a photograph with a strong, dominant design element (a forest with large, vertical tree trunks works well for the first image, such as Figure 6.1).
- Ask the class to identify the most dominant design element (line) and how it works in the image (thick, bold, dark, vertical, placed in the foreground).
- Each student then distills the image down to *only* that single design element and draws a simplification of the image on their card.
- Share and discuss.
- Repeat with other images as time allows.

This short exercise is useful for short start-of-class review purposes, and can be repeated throughout the scenic design section. We also use a variant in the lighting design section.

Figure 6.3 Discussion Image #3

Exercise: Essential Gesture Drawing

This short drawing exercise helps students observe images more closely and interpolate design elements and composition from research into their own work.

Figure 6.5 Sample Charcoal Gesture Sketch Based upon Figure 6.1

Figure 6.6 Who Lives in This House? Why?

Discussion: Detail Contributes Meaning

The next series of photos present building exteriors, primarily houses. The students again address the structures in terms of design elements. Point out that the qualities of the house in the image are *not* the same as the qualities of the photograph itself. Ask the students to go deeper into detail and explore how their observations dovetail with assumptions, stereotypes, and preconceptions.

- Who lives here?
- What is it about the character of the building that informs the character of the possible inhabitants?

Ask the class to come up with a brief narrative about a house's inhabitant based on their perceptions of the exterior. Be sure that they consider specific details and qualities of the house when determining socio-economic status, how many people reside there, marital status, possible occupation, and status within the community. If a student decides, for example, that a house belongs to a retired professor (as was the case for the house in Figure 6.6), explore the stereotype of the retired professor and the cultural assumptions that link the image of the person to the expectations for their dwelling. Be sure the conversation travels in both directions: from character to house and from house to character.

"And yet a stage setting holds a curious kind of suspense. Go, for instance, into an ordinary empty drawing room as it exists normally. There is no particular suspense about this room. It is just – empty. Now imagine the same drawing room arranged and decorated for a particular function – a Christmas party for children, let us say. It is not completed as a room, now, until the children are in it. And if we wish to visualize for ourselves how important a part the sense of expectancy plays in such a room, let us imagine that there is a storm and that the children cannot come. A scene on the stage is filled with the same feeling of expectancy. It is like a mixture of chemical elements held in solution. The actor adds the one element that releases the hidden energy of the whole . . . to create this suspense, this tension, is the essence of the problem of stage designing."[3]

Robert Edmond Jones, *The Dramatic Imagination*

Discussion: Detail Informs Character

From exteriors, we turn to some selected interiors, again asking the students to consider design elements first, and then decorative details that might speak to the qualities of the inhabitants. Rooms, by their very natures, tend to have been arranged – whether by a single personality or by a group of people. Even the messiest of rooms are messy because someone has caused or allowed the mess. See Figures 6.7 and 6.8 for sample living rooms.

- What do the details/arrangement tell us about the inhabitants?
- What is the main function of this space?
- How is it set up to facilitate/inform that function?

- What could happen in this space?
- How does the space support that potential action?

Figure 6.7 Who Lives in This Room? How Do They Use this Space? Why?

Figure 6.8 Who Lives in This Room? How Do They Use This Space? Why? (Photo by Don Smith)

More useful vocabulary terms can arise at this point: whether a space is formal or informal, for example, and what compositional qualities create a sense of formality or informality. If a student stumbles over the name of a piece of furniture or decorative detail, be sure to supply it and point it out if it recurs in another image.

TEACHING TIP

Starting a photo library for use in class is relatively easy, and with the advent of smart phones and computer storage, certainly easier than it was not too long ago. If you're looking for a variety of fabric textures, take some articles of clothing outside and snap some close-ups. Stroll around your neighborhood collecting a variety of home styles. When you travel, be sure to photograph interesting buildings and places – as a whole and with attention to details. Ask friends to send you a picture of their living or dining rooms. Try to avoid including people in these photos, as they tend to give away the function or atmosphere. Of course, there is always the internet, but you have less control over content, intent, and resolution.

energies of the scenic environment are only unlocked once it is inhabited by the actors. Before the entrance of the first character, it's unknown what will happen in these theatrical spaces, but because an audience brings cultural, visual, and personal expectations the designer can use those expectations to create environments that hint at what is to come. Depending on the play, the designer might subvert expectations in order to create suspense and interest. It can be argued that a monster popping out of a closet in a mundane suburban ranch-style house is much scarier than meeting one in a creaky old gothic mansion.

TEACHING TIP

It is better to use photographs of unfamiliar plays by unfamiliar designers; you, as instructor, don't even have to know the play. If you use your own work, or the work of others in your department, pick productions that were mounted before the current group of students enrolled. Again, for these exercises, including people in scenic design images tends to give too much information away. If possible, photos featuring scenery under stage lighting is preferable to worklight. See Figures 6.9 and 6.10 for examples drawn from our department's production work.

Discussion: The Intentional Environment

Finally, we examine photographs of scenery. The point of this phase of the exercise is to determine *what kinds of actions are supported by the environment.*

This series of observation exercises also draws attention to what Robert Edmond Jones, in his book *The Dramatic Imagination,* calls "high potential." He believes that the dramatic

"Given circumstances are anything set forth by the writer or director that must be adhered to by the actor. The location of the action of the play and everything that this suggests – for example, dialects, costumes, or scenery – is a given circumstance. Any physicality specified

Figure 6.9 *A Scrap of Paper,* Produced by UW–Whitewater, set design by Eric Appleton

for a character by the playwright – a limp or a hunchback, for example – is also a given circumstance. Finally, anything asked for by the director, from specific blocking to crying or yelling at a certain moment, is a given circumstance and must be respected by the actor as such."[4]

Bruder, Cohn, Olnek, Pollack, Previto, Zigler, *A Practical Handbook for the Actor*

Figure 6.10 *Suds,* Produced by UW–Whitewater, set design by Eric Appleton

Discussion: Script Analysis for Scenic Designers

Since we have already analyzed a script for metaphor and imagery in the costume section, this portion of script analysis considers the details a scenic designer seeks in order to determine the parameters and logic of the world to be built. These parameters contribute to the visual creation of what actors and directors call **the given circumstances**, which frame and inform the choices available to an actor at any given moment of the play. Having to knock on a door is a basic example of an actor responding to a given circumstance: there is a door in the way and the character, via the actor, must decide what to do about it.

The above quote points out that there are layers as to how designers contribute to creating this set of given circumstances. The playwright indicates location; the scenic designer interprets the location as a physical environment; the director then works with the actors to inhabit that physicalized interpretation in a manner logical to the inner workings of the play.

While we sought many of the same details while working toward the costume design, this time we look more closely at the environment itself and how it collectively impacts the characters.

For example, if characters must knock on a door to be allowed into a room, the designer is alerted to the physical presence of a door, the actions required of characters to pass through the door, and the idea of the door as a barrier or gate through which passage must be negotiated. Each character may respond to the door differently, and the differences in these interactions may help the designer determine the door's details.

We begin by asking the students if they are aware of the basic questions journalists ask when investigating a story, writing the list on the board as they are called out.

- Where

  - Can the location/s of the actions taking place be determined? Nation, region, interior/exterior?

- When

  - Historical period, time of day, season

- Who

  - What are the characters' socio-economic statuses, relationships, religious backgrounds, etc.? What relationships bring the characters together for the events of this play?
  - Who is the protagonist? Who is the antagonist?

- What

  - What is the nature of the protagonist's journey? What is the inciting incident that gets the plot rolling? What choices are made by the protagonist and what are the results?

- Why

  - What motivates the characters to act as they do? What do they want? What do they hope will be the end result of their choices?

- How

  - How do the events of the play unfold? Is it through a quick, rapid-fire series of actions and reactions? Is there intricately plotted, slow moving intrigue? What strategies do the characters employ to achieve their goals?

Even questions as seemingly basic as "Where?" and "When?" require application of broader dramaturgical research. *A Raisin in the Sun*, for instance, notes that "The action of the play is set in Chicago's Southside, sometime between World War II and the present."[5] However, the South Side of Chicago is a big place. The Woodlawn neighborhood is not the same as Bridgeport, Pilsen, or The Back of the Yards. If a street address is not given in the course of the play the designer must look into the ethnic make-up of Chicago's post-World War II South Side neighborhoods to inform the architecture and style of the Younger family's apartment, especially since aspects of the apartment are important to the motivation and actions of each character.

"Sometime between World War II and the present" presents similar difficulties. The end of World War II is pretty firm, but what does "the present" mean? For *A Raisin in the Sun* the time period remains the late 1950s or early 1960s because of something that has not happened *yet*: The Civil Rights Movement. While urban slum dwelling and housing discrimination are demonstrable facts well beyond the 1960s, the cultural references made by the family do not reflect knowledge of the events of the mid-to-late 1960s. If the play is pushed later in the century, at what point do the cultural referents in the text start posing problems?

This is not to say a designer should have a slavish dedication to the facts of period detail. Having a solid base of research enables choices to be made. If a stripped-down environment is employed for *A Raisin in the Sun*, it's still necessary to know what elements will provide the most meaning with the fewest paint strokes.

TEACHING TIP

Searching for short plays and scenes that can be readily applied to the requirements of particular design exercises can be difficult. If you have an amenable playwriting colleague or student, consider requesting a short script tailored to a specific design exercise. *The Return of the Living* (Appendix C) requires a certain amount of research that follows up necessary directorial decisions. *That Horrible Human Condition* (also Appendix C) was originally written as a blocking notation and prop movement exercise.

Exercise: Searching for Scenic Clues

- A short play is distributed. The students are instructed to read it and note anything in the text that speaks to the physical environment. We use *The Return of the Living* (Appendix C).

Begin by identifying the given circumstances of the world of the play. Write the checklist of journalists' questions (who, what, where, why, when, how) on the board and start populating these lists with clues that can be supported by evidence in the text. For example, can the events of the play be pinned to a specific year, area, season, or day of the week? While no characters may comment on the year, if someone flips on an electric light switch the time frame has instantly been bounded by the advent of electricity. Economic status can be inferred through the style of language spoken by the characters as well as whether this suggested a particular level of education or social class. The size of the house can be inferred by how long and how far away someone must travel between leaving the room and returning. The size of house can then be used to infer the apparent wealth of the inhabitants.

- Ask the students to suggest a design metaphor for the short play, and as a group create a list of design elements suggested by the metaphor.

Use the metaphor to explore the parameters discovered through the given circumstance lists. If the words connected with 'line' are *sharp, angular, jagged, uncontrolled*, how might the features of the room reflect these qualities? You can also flip things around, considering an item on the given circumstance list and then discussing which design elements can be used to bring out the object's purpose and meaning. For example, in *The Return of the Living*, Devon is discovered sitting in a chair as the play begins. Determining the appearance of that chair can first follow the chain of given circumstances:

- Whose house is it?
- Who decorated the room?
- Who bought the chair?
- When does the play take place?
- How old is the chair?

The design metaphor and elements derived from it can begin to fill in details about the function of the chair. *Sharp, angular, jagged, uncontrolled* might suggest a very uncomfortable chair, or one that is encrusted with over-the-top gothic decoration. Depending on who bought the chair, this is an expression of character – Devon may be sitting in a very uncomfortable, ornate chair purchased by his father. Not only is his father's taste revealed, but the fact that Devon has chosen to sit in the room's most uncomfortable chair speaks to their relationship as well as Devon's character.

TEACHING TIP

We have found that for many young designers, making decisions that they feel are the domain of the director throws up a variety of walls and stalls progress. Whether or not a director is at hand, designers must make decisions. They may not be decisions that the director may agree with down the line, but unless the designer commits to a course of action the director will have nothing to respond to, positively or negatively. Students will not always instantly jump to fill the void left by missing production personnel and the instructor may have to explicitly enable the student designer to go ahead and think like a director.

Discussion: External Influences on the Scenic Environment

Style and genre are germane to discussion of any play, and students will be faced with making some directorial choices, especially for classroom projects without an actual director.

For *The Return of the Living*, there are directorial decisions that need to be made that will steer the overall appearance of the scenery. Is the play funny? Is it scary? Is it both? If it is scary, what makes it scary? If it's funny, where does the source of humor lie? Degrees of realism can emerge from this discussion: if funny, is the play funnier if the environment is exaggerated, or does the humor emerge from the juxtaposition of the extraordinary with the mundane? The same question applies to whether the play is scary: again, is it scarier if a monster shows up in a suburban tract home or in a decaying gothic mansion? In which do we *expect* the events of the play to unfold, and is the action undercut if the audience, through the environment, is led to expect certain things to happen? How can the environment contribute to the creation of suspense and surprise? Should it?

Determining the production's overall style and genre can guide subsequent design choices. A director might choose to produce *The Return of the Living* in the manner of a 1930s Hollywood monster movie. The designer must now align their working metaphor with this directorial concept. While examining the visuals of 1930s Hollywood monster films – both the films themselves and auxiliary materials like poster art – the design element terms suggested by the metaphor statement can be further distilled through the narrowed range of research images.

Exercise: Connecting Style/Genre to Metaphor

Depending on the short play you are using, select an external visual that connects to genre and/or style. For *The Return of the Living*, a good example would be a selection of posters for the 1932 film *The Mummy*, featuring Boris Karloff.

- What are the prominent design elements used in the posters?
- Compare these design elements with those suggested by the metaphor already developed for the short play. Are there similarities? Are there insurmountable differences?
- Is it useful to have a metaphor *before* looking at genre/style images, or do the students feel looking at the images first would have helped them develop a useful metaphor?

Homework: Exteriors Informing Interiors

Students are instructed to find an image of the building exterior they feel best fits the inhabitants of the house and the action described in *The Return of the Living*.

When presenting the image at the start of the next class session, the student should:

- Describe prominent design elements
- Explain how these elements contribute to a mood or atmosphere

- Connect their choice of building to the action and requirements of the play
- In general terms, apply the design elements to be found on the exterior to an interior space (tall, spacious, cramped, cluttered, dark, etc.).

Even if students bring in similar buildings (stress going beyond the first page of internet search hits), it's worth exploring even minor differences, or the path that led students to related structures. Discuss the pros and cons of various keyword searches and what descriptive terms led the student to find this particular image. For example, the keyword "mansion" implies that the student is already looking for a house commensurate with a high degree of wealth and status. Ask the student why he or she thinks a mansion is appropriate, and be sure they support it with evidence from the text. What is it about the play that has led half the class to use "mansion" as a keyword on their first search? Discuss strategies for refining keyword searches to not only make them more intentional, but to make students more aware of the thoughts behind seemingly intuitive keywords.

'Exteriors Informing Interiors' is a discussion exercise, and we do not grade it. However, if a sizeable number of students fail to bring in an image to talk about, it can become a pass/fail project with a low percentage value.

Session Break: End of Week 6, Day 1.

Scenic Design Vocabulary

Groundplan a drawing generated by the scenic designer to show where all items of the set are to be placed; a map of the stage

Scale ratios of measurement used to describe real objects at reduced sizes

Proportion the comparison of size, small to large. Scenic design drawings are small in proportion to reality, but the use of scale provides accuracy in measurement

Footprint of an Object The perimeter of an object; the outline of an object when placed on the floor

Straightedge Any drawing tool used to draw straight lines on a technical drawing, such as a T-square or drafting triangles

TEACHING TIP

Upcoming projects and exercises will require students to bring a variety of tools and materials. We distribute a list of tools and materials with the syllabus (see Appendix B), and alert students as to what tools will be needed at the next session. Be prepared for the student who will invariably come unprepared. Since sharing drawing equipment will inconvenience and slow down everyone, decide ahead of time whether the unprepared student gets to observe rather than participate, or if you will magically produce one-time-only spare equipment after admonishing their forgetfulness.

Discussion: Minimum Necessary Physical Requirements

The wealth of information derived from digging into "who, what, where, when, why, and how" can present a designer with almost too much information. Editing is required.

> "... if, in our particular play, the cafeteria means a place where the hero is always open to surveillance, the designer can build a set which reflects the idea: inability to hide. If the meaning of the cafeteria is a place where reflection and rest are possible, the designer's work can reflect *these* ideas. In neither case is the designer's first question: 'What does a cafeteria look like?' His first question is: 'What does a cafeteria mean *in this instance*?' This is a concern for scenic truth."[6]
> David Mamet, "Realism," *Writing in Restaurants*

In the quote above, David Mamet urges the designer to seek for scenic truth through the action taking place in the locale (also remember Mordecai Gorelik's *Three Sisters* example in Chapter 1). While in this instance, the larger, more important question is the meaning of the cafeteria, the designer still has to select the items and spatial qualities that will illustrate this meaning. If a character invites another to "take a seat," and the other character *does*, some sort of sittable is required. If that character invites another character to take the most comfortable chair available, the designer must also determine the apparent and/or relevant level of that chair's comfort. On the other hand, simply because a character enters a room does not mean that a door or even a doorway is automatically required. If that character pounds on a door until it is opened, the need for that physical element is much more urgent. If characters simply walk into a space, the designer has the choice of whether that door is real or implied.

This editing process is related to the creation of 'given circumstance' lists, but instead of looking at the world of the play as a whole, we are zeroing in on only essential physical items. This helps students focus on what is truly important in a scene. When asked why an item appears on the stage a student should be able to respond with a rationale that links it to the requirements of the action via the design metaphor. For example, all of the other, empty cafeteria booths and tables are there because the action calls for a vast space that gives a sense of all the people who are *not* there.

Exercise: What is Essential?

In class, ask the students to reread the short play, making a list of every physical item they think is necessary for the story to progress. A good rule of thumb is to include everything with which a character physically interacts.

On the board, three categories are offered:

- Absolutely Essential
- Extremely Useful
- Very Nice to Have

'Absolutely Essential' refers to all items (scenic or prop) that would cause major logistical problems were they not to appear on stage. For *The Return of the Living*, the poker falls into this category, as does the chair. Both are specifically noted in the script to be used by specific characters to particular ends.

'Extremely Useful' contains those items which aid clarity but would not stop the action through their absence. The fireplace could fall into this group. It is referred to, and provides a handy location for leaning, as well as being a possible focal point for other furnishings. The lighting designer may later determine the fireplace as the room's main source of illumination. Still, the fireplace can be suggested simply by placing the implement stand containing the poker at a specific spot and having the actors walk up to that space and rub their hands together as though warming them. The audience's imagination will do the rest.

'Very Nice to Have' are all those things that add flavor and complexity to the environment, speak to character and relationship, but would not impede the mechanics of the play in their absence. A mummy case in the corner of the room would suggest that the space is the father's trophy room and the children are interlopers in his sanctuary, but the action can progress without its presence. These items generally speak to and support the psychology of the scene.

There will be items that do not fall cleanly into these categories. We ask students to argue their case. Even seemingly small items can have large ramifications. For instance, it is noted in *The Return of the Living* that Devon drinks whiskey – but does he use a glass or drink directly from the bottle? Drinking the wedding scotch out of the bottle might underscore disrespect for all his father holds dear. Calmly pouring himself a tumbler while his sister battles a mummy in the other room can speak to *that* relationship.

> "A chair is not *per se* truthful or untruthful. That one may say, 'Yes, but it is a chair, an actual chair, people sit on it and I found it in a cafeteria, therefore it belongs in this play about a cafeteria,' is beside the point. Why was that *particular* chair chosen? Just as that particular chair said something about the cafeteria *in* the cafeteria (its concern for looks over comfort, for economy over durability, etc.), so that chair, on stage, will say something *about the play*, so the question is: What, do you, the theatrical director, wish to say *about the play*?"[7]
> David Mamet, "Realism," *Writing in Restaurants*

By clearing away gut-reaction generalities, a shortlist of essentials is created and students are forced to reflect on *why*

that item is on the stage. If walls are deemed absolutely necessary, there must be a deeper rationale than simply, "because rooms have walls" or "the playwright said so." What are the walls *for*? What do the walls represent? How do the walls shape the actions of the characters?

As attention is turned to why an item is on stage, the qualities of that item begin to be revealed. In *The Return of the Living*, the son drinks his whiskey slumped in a chair. It's the only sittable the script appears to require. By revisiting the text, the designer is forced to consider the meaning of this chair: why is *this* chair in *that* room, and what does the son experience while sitting in it? Some of these meanings may have already been discovered in the earlier given circumstances list. However, by thinking about the chair as not only the only chair in the room, but the only piece of furniture in the room, the designer gains a heightened awareness of this item and everything it must contribute to the play. If this room is the father's sanctuary, full of his prizes and relics, then the chair becomes the father's chair. Does Devon *belong* in his father's chair? The chair is a metaphor for the relationship between father and son, and the designer now goes in search of a chair that was once the father's favorite and makes the son look small and lost.

Discussion: Learning to Read and Draw in Scale

Now that we've thought about *what* we wish to put into an environment, it's time to begin thinking about *how* to put it into the environment. Scenic designers generate many drawings, and must be able to express real objects on two-dimensional surfaces (paper), as well as in models. They need to know how big items are so that they can represent them as truthfully as possible.

Our first step toward that end is consideration of proportion and size, and how they are described through the use of scale measurements.

To say that something is in *scale* is to use measurement ratios to produce a reduced-size drawing or model of a real object. A measurement of a feature of the real object is proportional to the measurement of the same feature on the drawing or model. A scale ratio of ½" = 1'-0" means that a line that is one half-inch long on a drawing represents something that is one foot zero inches long in reality. Scale is consistent throughout a technical drawing so that a true measurement can be made of any feature of the object (though there are exceptions, such as when describing very small, detailed items).

Two scales are typical for American theatrical usage: ½" = 1'-0", and ¼" = 1'-0". Traditionally, light plots were most often drawn in half-inch scale, while scenic designers most often used quarter-inch scale. This has become more fluid with the advent of computer-aided drafting and various graphics programs.

Exercise: Reading a Scale Rule

1. Find the side of the scale with real inches. The end of the scale will read "16" (this means that one inch has been expressed in sixteen one-sixteenths). This number tells you what scale is being read *from that end of the ruler.* See Figure 6.11.
2. Ask the students to look at the opposite side (not the opposite *end*) of the scale and find "3/16" (it should be there,

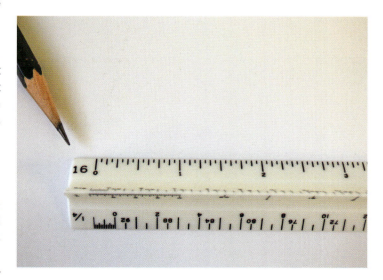

Figure 6.11 Locating One Inch Equals One Inch Scale

though some manufacturers arrange things slightly differently. The important thing is finding the end that reads "3/16." See Figure 6.12. Ask the students what scale that is: three-sixteenths of an inch equals one foot.

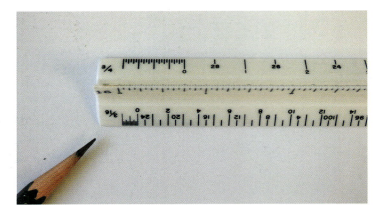

Figure 6.12 Locating 3/16 Inch Equals One Foot Scale

3. Ask the students to find the end of the scale with "1." See Figure 6.13. Ask what scale it is: one inch equals one foot.

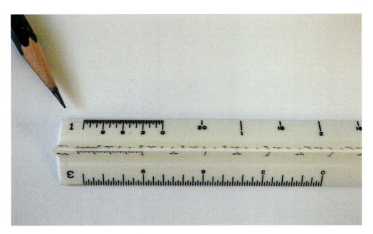

Figure 6.13 Locating One Inch Equals One Foot Scale

4. While still in 1" = 1'-0" scale, point out that the smaller increments at the end (see Figure 6.14) correspond to inches – but read backwards from the zero. The inch increment section is divided by longer lines first: 3", 6", 9". Those sections are then divided into thirds with shorter lines. On smaller scales (like ½" = 1'-0"), these divisions will be increasingly smaller and increasingly difficult to read, and will not include reference numbers.

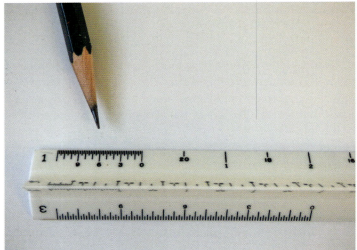

Figure 6.14 Locating Inch Increments in One Inch Equals One Foot Scale

5. While still in 1" = 1'-0" scale, point out that feet are read by reading *away* from the zero, and since it is one inch equals one foot scale, each foot increment will be, in reality, one inch apart. See Figure 6.15. They will notice the higher numbers on the shorter marks – 20, 18, and so on. This is the time to ask them to look at the other end of the scale and find "1/2."
6. If you are reading in ½" = 1'-0" scale, you read from *that* marked end of the ruler, and the smaller marks correspond to feet in half-inch scale. Reading from the half-inch end, the

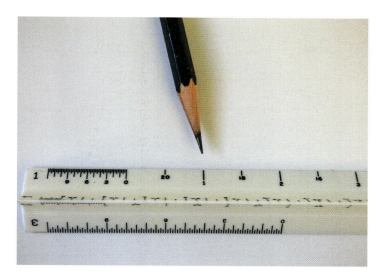

Figure 6.15 Reading a Measurement in One Inch Equals One Foot Scale

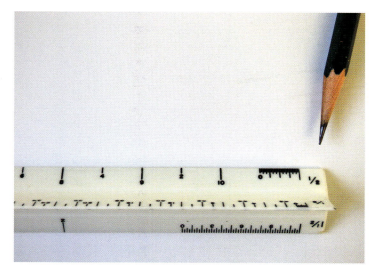

Figure 6.16 Locating One Half-Inch Equals One Foot Scale

numbers on the marks go 0, 10, 2, 9, 4, 8, etc. Since the 10, 9, and 8 on the longer marks are foot marks from the one-inch scale end of the ruler, when read from the half-inch end, 10 is really 1, 9 is really 3, etc.

It's time to measure some lines.

Exercise: Measuring in Scale

Prepare a worksheet with a number of lines to be measured in a variety of scales. See Figure 6.17 for a partial example. We use a hand-drawn version so that line weight can be mentioned.

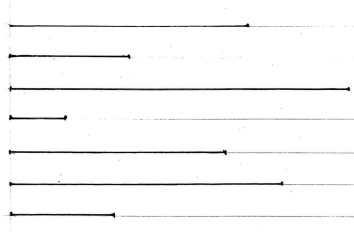

Figure 6.17 Line Measurement Worksheet Sample

There are a variety of types of lines used in traditional drafting, and the first two used in this class are *construction* lines and *visible* lines. Construction lines are light, thin, grey lines drawn with a hard pencil (4H to 6H) used to lay out an object; some can be seen on the worksheet sample (Figure 6.17). In hand drafting, a line is laid out *before* measurement occurs; there has to be something *to* measure. The thicker, black lines are visible lines, drawn with a softer pencil (H to 2H). Once the object has been completely laid out with construction lines and you are ready to mark the important outlines, visible lines are drawn directly over the construction lines that served as guides. If the construction lines are light enough, leftover lines will generally disappear in reproduction.

In 1″ = 1′-0″ scale, lay the ruler down so that the zero lines up with the left-hand start of the line, as in Figure 6.18. The right-hand end of the line is seen to fall somewhere between three feet and four feet, as noted in Figure 6.19.

In order to determine how many inches there are in addition to feet, slide the scale rule so that the 3′ mark lines up with the right-hand end of the line, as in Figure 6.20. Looking back to the left, the end of the line now falls within the inch increments. The line is read to be three foot three and one half inches long (3′-3½″).

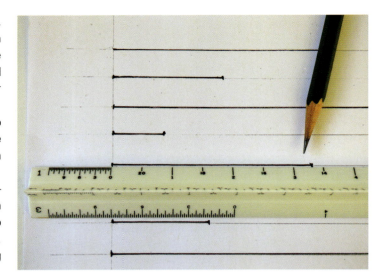

Figure 6.19 The End of the Line Falls Between Three and Four Feet

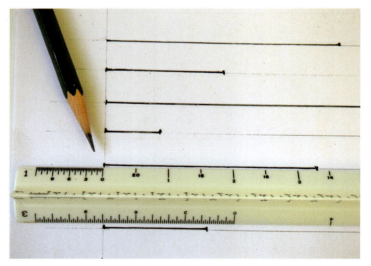

Figure 6.18 Measuring a Line, Part One

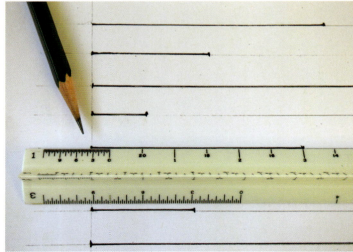

Figure 6.20 Slide the Rule so the Rounded Down Foot Mark Aligns with the End of the Line

Up to this point, this text has spelled out measurements in a variety of formats. Before students commence measuring lines on the worksheet (Figure 6.17), demonstrate standard measurement notation. Three foot three inches is notated as 3'-3". The dash is important, as it prevents this measurement from being read as 33". Three feet alone is notated as 3'-0" because without the 0" it could be thought something has been forgotten, or in a rush read as 3 inches. This is because dimensions shorter than one foot, such as four inches, are *not* notated as 0'-4" but as simply 4".

Have the students measure a group of lines in 1" = 1'-0" scale, the next set in ½" = 1'-0", and the final set in ¼" = 1'-0" scale. Compare the findings. There will be some minor variation, as hand drafting is not tremendously precise in small scales. This is why written dimensions are an important feature of any drawing.

Book Recommendation

For a discussion of how to choose the best scale for a drawing, as well as standard practices when noting dimensions, see Chapter 9 of *Designer Drafting and Visualizing for the Entertainment World*, by Patricia Woodbridge and Hal Tine (published by Focal Press).

Exercise: The Difference Between Proportion and Scale

Proportion is the comparison of size. A toy car is tiny in proportion to an actual automobile. Scale is the description of proportion as a measurement ratio. A toy car may be in 1/8" = 1'-0" scale, while the actual car is in 1" = 1" (or 1' = 1') scale.

One way to demonstrate this is to use a small cutout of a human figure that is about six feet tall in ½" = 1'-0" scale (we make these in Chapter 7) and a piece of 8½" x 11" cardstock (Figure 6.21).

- In portrait orientation, fold the cardstock.
- Ask the students how large the piece of cardstock appears to be. How have they determined the size? Through measurement, or by comparison with other objects?
- Place the folded cardstock on the table and place the human figure in front of it.
- Ask the students what this wall does to the figure; is the figure more or less prominent? Now how big does the piece of paper feel? How might it feel to be the person standing at its base? How might the audience feel when viewing a person in such an environment?
- Cut the cardstock in half so the wall is still quite tall in relation to the figure, but not nearly as massive.
- Ask the students the same questions about this wall.
- Finally, cut the cardstock down to a height that feels like a low ceiling in relation to the figure.
- Ask the students the same questions about this shortest wall.

Note that the human figure has not changed; in scale it remains about six feet tall. The walls, which can also be measured in ½" = 1'-0", have changed in *proportion* to the figure.

Figure 6.21 A Human Figure in Relation to Differently Sized Walls

Understanding that proportion does not automatically confer a standard scale of measurement such as 1/8″ = 1′-0″ or ½″ = 1′-0″ is important. If a stage manager is handed the groundplan of a set that has been reduced on a photocopier to fit onto an 8½″ x 11″ sheet of paper, the overall proportions of the smaller version set remain the same as the proportions of the larger, original drawing. However, the photocopier may have been set to reduce the drawing to 43 percent of the original size. It now becomes difficult to use a scale ruler to accurately measure anything on the reduced drawing because standard scale rulers do not offer a 1:86 scale to use. Written dimensions and the footprints of familiar objects, like a bed or dining room table, can help the reader get a sense of the overall space, but there's still no easy way to determine the exact placement of the bed through measurement.

To demonstrate the difference between proportion and scale, distribute reduced photocopies of a groundplan that does not include much in the way of furniture. Be sure the reduction is fairly random, and the whole of the groundplan fits onto an 8½″ x 11″ page (Figure 6.22).

- Using the visual cues of the plan, ask the students to draw the footprint of an object (sofa, couch, 4x8 platform) in the size they think it should appear on the drawing.
- Using their new ability to read a scale rule, ask the students to determine the actual size of the object they drew.
- Ask what information they need to make this determination.
- Offer the students the dimension of a line on the groundplan, such as noting that the front edge of a certain platform is 8′-0″ wide.
- With this information, ask them to use their scale rulers to determine the scale of the drawing.
- Once the scale has been determined (or has been determined as close as possible), re-measure the object. Was it the size students thought it was?
- Use a tape measure to lay out the size of the object on the classroom floor.

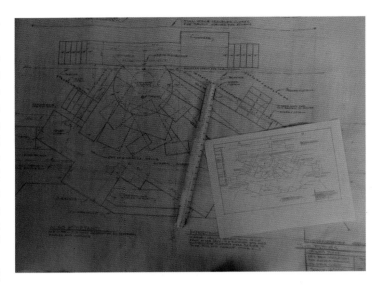

Figure 6.22 1/2″ = 1′-0″ Scale Groundplan with Version Shrunk to Fit 8½″ x 11″ Paper

- Compare reality to the drawn size.
- Is it possible to accurately measure anything else on the drawing?

Homework: The Sizes of Real Things

Since the next class session will explore the placement and arrangement of objects within the scenic environment, it's necessary to get students thinking about the measurements of real objects. Ask the students:

- What size bed do they sleep on?
- What are the dimensions of their mattress?
- How high off the ground is the top of the mattress?
- How high off the ground is the chair seat they are currently sitting on?

- What are the measurements of the classroom doorway?
- How high off the ground is the top of the desk at which they are sitting?

Chances are very good that few students will be able to answer any of these questions. Point out that since scenic designers often need to place items like couches and tables on a set, they need to know how large they are. This is not only to see how much can fit onto the stage but also to be sure enough space is allowed for the actors to move around in desired traffic patterns.

- Distribute tape measures and have the students measure some items in the room.

Now that the students are developing a general connection between the perceived size of objects and their measurements, distribute a list of furniture and building elements (such as front door and French doors). As homework, the students are to determine the overall sizes, especially the footprints, of these objects. They are free to consult whatever resources they expect will be useful, such as online catalogs or measuring actual items in their own homes. There is a purposeful generality to the objects in order to impress upon the students the range of measurements possible even within something seemingly as regular as a sofa. Our worksheet includes images of the following objects pulled from online sources:

- Queen-sized bed
- Twin bed
- Occasional table
- Coffee table
- Sofa
- Loveseat
- Sideboard (or buffet, or credenza)
- Front door
- French doors
- Wingback chair
- Recliner

This is a low-stakes, low percentage pass/fail grade. Completing the assignment with measurements well within reasonable allowances earns a passing grade.

Homework: Laying Out and Building the Small Stage House for 'Your First Set Design'

The mid-level project is to design a limited set for *The Return of the Living,* or whichever short play you have selected. This will be fitted into a small stage house constructed out of black foamcore in ½" = 1'-0" scale. A larger stage house will be constructed for the final project. The finished small stage house is due at the next class session, and the set itself the session after that (the project guidelines are found at the end of this chapter). The set is a good weekend project if the course schedule aligns accordingly.

Building the small stage house provides:

- Practice in reading a scale drawing
- Practice drawing in scale
- An introduction to basic model building
- Practice converting something from 2D to 3D

Since most of the students are unlikely to have previously built a model out of foamcore, we demonstrate cutting foamcore with an X-Acto knife. Emphasize that cuts should be made along a steel ruler or edge, NOT along their scale ruler or T-square. Measuring tools are for measuring, straightedges are for drawing, cutting edges are for cutting. Once a straightedge is nicked and shaved, it is useless as a drawing tool. The knife should be held vertically, and drawn along the metal ruler with light pressure. Use a series of passes to gradually cut through the material. Don't try to cut through the whole depth in one go, as this can produce ragged edges. Use a cutting mat to protect table surfaces.

The layout for the small stage house can be found in Figure 6.25, with instructional diagrams in Figure 6.23. A demonstration sheet of foamcore with all the parts laid out, including half-inch scale dimensions, remains in the classroom for reference purposes (Figure 6.24). A fresh sheet is used to demonstrate laying out the parts using the scale measurements found on the instructions, using a T-square and/or yardstick (this can gently introduce the T-square). Since this project has been repeated

Building the Stage House for Your First Set Design
Wait for each step to dry before moving to the next. Use pins and painter's tape to hold things in place as they dry.

Step One
Glue Deck Edges to underside of Deck

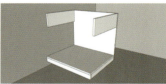
Step Two
Add Back Wall and Headers (Back wall sits on top of deck)

Step Three
Add Proscenium (glue to headers, upstage side of bottom is 17'-4" downstage of back wall)

Step Four
Add Legs (1st set is 5'-0" upstage of proscenium, 2nd set is 5'-0" upstage of first set)

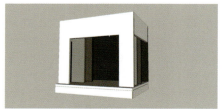
It should look like this when you are done

Figure 6.23 Small Stage House Parts Layout Handout

each year, a few finished models remain in the classroom, and are used to show the final product in three dimensions.

- Have the students lay out all the pieces in pencil on the full sheet of foamcore before cutting anything out. This will produce cleaner edges and corners, as well as a chance to correct errors without wasting material.
- To draw long lines that stretch completely across a piece, always measure end points from the same side of the foamcore. If the right-hand measurement is taken from the bottom of the sheet, measure the left-hand one from the bottom of the sheet.
- Label all parts, one by one, as they are laid out. This will prevent cutting through other pieces, or accidentally throwing away needed pieces.

Demonstrate assembling corners using tacky glue and straight pins. Low-adhesive painter's tape can also be used to hold joints together while glue dries. Note that patience and time are required. If an attempt is made to glue the whole thing

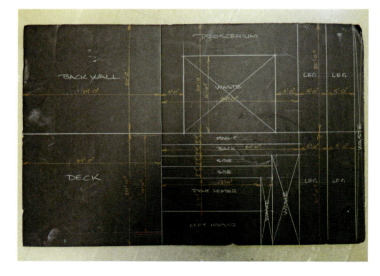

Figure 6.24 Demonstration Layout Sheet for Small Stage House

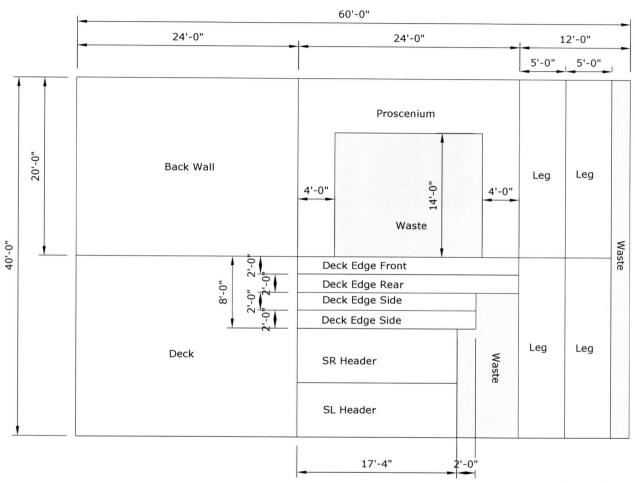

60'-0"
24'-0"
24'-0"
12'-0"
5'-0" 5'-0"
20'-0"
40'-0"

Proscenium

Back Wall

Leg   Leg

4'-0"   14'-0"   4'-0"

Waste

Waste

Deck Edge Front
2'-0" 2'-0"
Deck Edge Rear
2'-0" 2'-0"
Deck Edge Side
2'-0" 2'-0"
Deck Edge Side

8'-0"

Deck

SR Header

Waste

Leg   Leg

SL Header

17'-4"   2'-0"

Parts Layout for Small Stage House
Black Foamcore
Build 1/2" = 1'0"

Figure 6.25 Assembly Diagram for Small Stage House

Figure 6.26   Applying a Bead of Glue to an Edge of Foamcore

together all at once, frustration will result. Glue something, do some homework, come back, glue something else.

Evaluation of the 'Small Stage House' is rolled into the grade for 'Your First Set Design,' and will consider adherence to scale, accurate measurement, and the degree of craftsmanship. If necessary, it can be separately graded as a pass/fail depending on whether the project was completed. There are a number of things that can go wrong, but as long as the stage house is generally functional, a lot can be learned from engineering failures.

Homework: 'Your First Set Design'

'Your First Set Design' is a manageably-sized project to prepare students for the larger, more complex design they are expected to generate for their chosen play. By completing this project, students:

- Begin thinking in three dimensions
- Continue learning the use of scale
- Apply the lessons of reducing a design to its essentials
- Employ research in a set design
- Employ a design metaphor in the generation of a set design
- Continue practicing extraction of design elements from metaphor
- Continue applying design elements to physical elements
- And, the fear of model building is somewhat allayed so they can better focus on the content of their future design, rather than the mechanics of building it.

Your First Set Design

You have been invited to stage *The Return of the Living* as part of a ten minute play festival. You will have five minutes to get your scenery set up; therefore, you are limited to what you think you can successfully load in in **five** minutes (still, you are encouraged to be as ambitious as you can be within those five minutes). You may use backdrops and hanging pieces.

Considerations:

- How will your metaphor and design elements impact the items you choose or create?

- What physical elements are *absolutely essential* for this play to occur?

- How will the imagined exterior architecture of the house impact the interior space? If you went with a Victorian Gothic, does that mean lots of angles and eclecticism? If you went with a formal, rectilinear house, can we expect more straight lines and order?

- How will the actors move around the space? Is it wide open? Is it cluttered? Are there physical reasons for the actors to move anywhere? What does your metaphor suggest?

- What do things actually *look* like? What kind of fireplace might you chose? What does the chair look like? Are there curtains on the French door? Is the garden railing stone or iron or wood? Is there a chandelier? How fancy? What does an Egyptian sarcophagus look like? How do your choices support the meaning of the space?

You will present:

- A design metaphor for the play
- Paragraph of design elements drawn from the metaphor
- ½" = 1'0" scale model
- All furniture and scenic elements you require to tell this story is as high a degree of detail as you are capable of producing them (the expectation of detail will be high)

Be prepared to explain the need and function of every item you place on the stage, connecting it both to your metaphor and the action of the play.

Figure 6.27   Handout for 'Your First Set Design'

We also use the completed project to introduce ground-plans, both drawing them and as a 'plan of action' for the movement of actors around the environment.

Figure 6.27 presents the guidelines distributed for 'Your First Set Design.' It is handed out a week before it's due.

Evaluation parameters of this project will be discussed in next week's chapter.

Portfolio Development Projects

This week's work contributes toward projects that will reach completion in the coming sessions. While there is no formal portfolio project for this chapter, students should be alerted to those components which will feature on future project pages.

Exteriors Informing Interiors

This building image will be presented as part of the research for 'Your First Set Design.' Be sure that students have quality images that will print, scan, or project well. It is always useful if students know the name of the building or the source of the image.

The Small Stage House

The small stage house is a prominent visual element of 'Your First Set Design.' While we don't require redoing the stage house for the assignment, if portfolio presentation is playing a large role in your course, this would be the time to invite the student to learn from previous difficulties and build a new stage house that will show off their scenic design to its best advantage. For us, a running theme throughout student presentations is that sloppiness can undercut otherwise high quality content.

Notes

1. Lee Simonson, *The Stage is Set* (New York: Dover Publications, 1932), p. 11.
2. John Caird, *Theatre Craft: A Director's Practical Companion from A to Z* (London: Faber and Faber, 2010), p. 242–243.
3. Robert Edmond Jones, *The Dramatic Imagination* (New York: Theatre Arts Books, 1941), p. 71–72.
4. Melissa Bruder, Lee Michael Cohn, Madeleine Olnek, Nathaniel Pollack, Robert Previto, and Scott Zigler, *A Practical Handbook for the Actor* (New York: Vintage Books, 1986), p. 9.
5. Lorraine Hansberry, *A Raisin in the Sun* and *The Sign in Sidney Brustein's Window* (New York: New American Library, 1987), p. 22.
6. David Mamet, *Writing in Restaurants* (New York: Viking Penguin, Inc., 1986), p. 131–132.
7. Mamet, p. 131.

Chapter 7

Week 7

At this point, the students have been introduced to the use of scale and have embarked upon their first substantial scenic design project: the small stage house and the set that it will contain. This week, much discussion and activity is anchored by the fact the set designer is in constant communication with other members of the design team, particularly the director. Models and groundplans are not just generated to solidify the designer's thoughts or guide construction, but are important tools for a collaborative process.

This week's framing topics are:

- Research

  - Homework Follow-Up: The Real Sizes of Objects

- Design Mechanics

  - Homework Follow-up: The Small Stage House
  - Mid-Level Scenic Design Project: 'Your First Set Design'
  - The Human Figure as Baseline for Proportion
  - Discussing the Function of Models
  - The Groundplan is a Plan of Action

Supplies Needed

Instructor supplies:

- 'Human Figures' handout
- Handout of images of furniture, reduced to ½" = 1'-0"

Student supplies:

- Tacky glue
- Scissors
- Cardstock or Bristol board
- Rubber cement or glue sticks

- X-Acto knives
- Metal cutting edge
- Foamcore (scraps)
- Cutting mat
- Architectural scale ruler
- Toothpicks/bamboo skewers
- Drawing straightedge, such as a T-square or triangles

Scenic Design Vocabulary

Load-In the day or process of bringing the scenery from the shop into the performance space and setting it up

Blocking determining when, where, and how performers move around the stage environment

Drop large, flat, usually painted fabric scenic element; usually hangs laterally across the full stage space and is most often used in proscenium-style theatres

Homework Follow-Up: 'The Small Stage House'

We begin the week's first session checking in on homework. The small stage house is presented, and difficulties and discoveries are discussed. In general, we usually find a high level of relief and pride of accomplishment among the students (as with 'Twenty-One Black Dresses'). They've figured out a puzzle and built something substantial. Three to four hours appears to be the average amount of time required, from layout to final gluing.

TEACHING TIPS

Rather than beginning a response session by pointing out flaws and how to correct them, ask the students what was difficult and what was easy. They will usually point directly at their own model and explain what happened to cause ragged edges or tilted surfaces. Knowing that another student had the exact same problems can lighten any sense of failure.

Be prepared to demonstrate ways to correct technical problems students encountered during construction. Don't forget that issues can also lie in your instructions and dimensions; if an error occurs more than once (such as missing the apron) it may be an indication some part of the instructions require revision or clarification.

Tools are important. Students often purchase the least expensive option not realizing that their life will be a little easier, and their work will automatically be a small degree better, if they buy the decent watercolor set and good brush rather than the dollar tray with plastic brush included. While cost is always an issue and the quality of a tool is no replacement for skill, it's worth mentioning to students that cheap materials may hold them back from discovering what they are *really* capable of doing.

Figure 7.1 Completed Small Stage Houses

There *will* be engineering failures. We ask the students to pin their models to bulletin boards in the hallway, and a day or two later one usually exhibits a degree of collapse. The student may be distraught, but as long as they have the base and the scenic components they will be able to continue to the next step, which is developing a groundplan from their model. Hold a technical post-mortem with the student; we've had students who attempted to hold the model together with rubber cement rather than tacky glue, and others who tried to conserve glue by

using small dots rather than a continuous bead. Combine either with ragged foamcore edges, and the model is almost certain to fragment. Knowing what caused the structural failures in this instance will contribute toward making their Large Stage House (for the final project) more successful.

If the small stage house is to be graded, the answers to the following questions can guide their evaluation:

- Are all the elements of the stage house present?
- Is the stage house in the correct scale?
- Are the measurements correct?
- What is the degree of craftsmanship?

   - Straight cuts
   - Corners at right angles
   - Control of glue (lacking or overabundant)
   - Joints that hold together

After discussing the construction of the small stage house, we turn to making the objects that will be placed within it. The guidelines for the project (Figure 6.27) ask the students to limit themselves to only what they think they could load-in in five minutes. Each student will have a different idea as to how many items this span of time can accommodate; we find the total usually ends up around five. If the students have broken the script down to 'Essential,' 'Good to Have,' and 'Very Nice to Have' categories, they should all have the same basic group of items. When we evaluate the design, we don't worry too much about *how* items get on or off stage. We're more concerned with placement and appearance of each item, and how each item contributes to the action of the play.

Homework Follow-up: The Sizes of Real Things

The 'Sizes of Objects' homework is also discussed in this class session. The following questions will allow students to share their sources, as well as gauge the quality of information offered by that source. Since there are many variations of furniture types and styles, expect students to have a variety of answers that nonetheless are centered on an average.

- What sources were consulted?
- Why did you consult that source?
- How do you know that source was reliable?
- How wide a variety of dimensions were gathered?
- How easy or difficult was it to find an 'average' measurement?
- Why is it useful to have these measurements?

Share resources you frequently consult, be it catalog, website, or reference text.

Scenic designers must often choose items appropriate to the world of the play rather than reflective of their personal taste; the drawing room of the elderly Marchioness of Tewkesbury is unlikely to display the same tastes as a twenty-year-old Midwestern college student. This exercise can help students step away from their preconceptions of what is 'typical,' and acknowledge that what is normal for one person in one set of circumstances can be very different for someone else with a different standard of living.

- Is the sofa that a student grew up with truly a 'normal' piece of furniture?
- What physical attributes make it normal?
- Do they know what style or period influenced the appearance of the sofa?
- Who bought the sofa?
- When did they buy the sofa?
- From whom did they buy the sofa?
- Does personal experience influence what is perceived as normal?
- How do you *know* whether or not something is indeed typical?

Book Recommendation

Backstage Handbook: An Illustrated Almanac of Technical Information, by Paul Carter, with illustrations by George Chiang, is just about the handiest reference text a theatre technician, designer, or stage manager can possess. In this book the reader can find information regarding everything from the safe working loads of rope to how to bisect a line to fabric terms and definitions to hardware identification to how to fold soft goods.

Discussion: The Human Figure as Baseline of Proportion

One of the revolutionary ideas embraced by the New Stagecraft was that the scenic environment should be just as dimensional as the actor. Through the nineteenth and into the early twentieth

> "To [Adolphe] Appia the actor was *massgebend* – the unit of measurement. Unity could be created only by relating every part of a setting to him. He was three-dimensional, therefore the entire setting would have to be made consistently three-dimensional. . . . One began to set a stage not in mid-air or hanging back-drops, but on the stage floor where the actor moved and worked."[1]
>
> Lee Simonson, *The Stage is Set*

century, flat, painted drops were the usual major scenic component. This pictorial environment was one that an actor could not interact with. Adolphe Appia was one of the first theatrical thinkers to truly consider how to make the environment a more active participant in the drama, rather than merely a pretty vista in front of which acting took place. This meant thinking about human beings not as something to be added at the end, but as an integral factor from the very start of the design process.

Models should include at least one human figure to provide a sense of proportion. For example, if the set calls for extremely tall walls, it is useful to see what an actor looks like in comparison to them. What does creating an environment that dwarfs the characters within it add to the telling of the story? How do you feel when you walk into a stately mansion whose rooms have high ceilings, or when you enter a room in which you are constantly afraid of bumping your head? Including a human figure allows the viewer to get an instant sense of the relative size of its surroundings.

The figure's appearance should have relevance to the production. If the costume designer has line drawings or renderings in a state of completion, the set designer should ask if he or she can borrow a few to copy, scale, and use in the model environment. If appropriately styled human figures are unavailable, default to a simplified, generic line drawing. Since the students have already produced costume renderings, those should be used when presenting their final scenic design project.

Exercise: Measuring People and Making People

This exercise combines proportional human beings and reviewing scale measurement. Begin by asking the students what they perceive to be the height of the average person.

- How tall *are* average men and women?
- Is the size of an average person the same in every geographic region?
- How much of a variation in height is there in this class?

    - Is there anyone in the class we can point to as having an 'average' height?
    - Does everyone look more equal in height when they are seated?

- How can the environment in which we see a person change our perception of their height?
- What can be done to manipulate the perception or otherwise alter a person's height?

    - shoes
    - hats
    - coats and other outer garments
    - the background against which the person is seen

Hand out a worksheet presenting a number of human figures, both photographed and drawn. An example of drawn figures can be seen in Figure 7.2.

- Direct the students to measure the heights of each figure on the worksheet. They will have to determine for them-

Figure 7.2 Human Figure Handout: Figures to Be Measured in ½" = 1'-0" Scale

selves whether to include hats, and where along the figures' feet measurements should begin.

When complete, compare and discuss the findings. Everyone should have similar measurements. If not, find out why and discuss what happened. Review of scale ruler usage may be necessary.

After measuring the various human figures, have the students gather around a worktable and demonstrate cutting out a representative figure, affixing it to cardstock with rubber cement. When dry, cut out the figure and attach it to a small foamcore stand. Note that the students should use their X-Acto knives and cut cleanly to the outline of the figure. See Figure 7.3 for a rough, fast example.

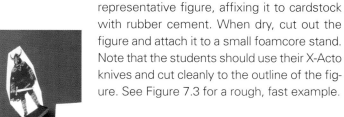

Figure 7.3 A Very Rough Reduced Scale Model Human Figure

Demonstration: Making Scale Things for the Model

The relatively simple task of making a 2D character cutout helps segue into the somewhat more involved task of making reduced-scale furniture for use in 'Your First Set Design.'

A selection of furniture and scenic model pieces are presented (see Figure 7.4). Have a variety of items, such as chairs, tables, books, carpets, doorways, and backdrops. Present pieces that use a variety of construction approaches. While three-dimensional objects are desirable, a scaled two-dimensional object is acceptable.

Allowing students to use a photo of a chair, stiffened with cardstock and made vertical with a brace or base, is more achievable at this point of the course, and still requires research and use of scale to implement. If you have a computer and printer in the room, you can demonstrate making a 2D reduced-scale chair by:

Figure 7.4 'Your First Set Design' Model Furniture Samples

- Using a list of design elements generated by the metaphor statement and list of given circumstances, do a quick internet search for an appropriate chair.
- Save the image and print it out at whatever size the file defaults to.
- The average chair seat is about 18" off the ground. On the printout of the chair, draw a box about 18" (in ½" = 1'-0" scale) high to gauge the relative proportions of the image to the desired scale.
- Import the image into the program of your choice, such as Paint or Photoshop.
- Reduce or enlarge the image. If the program allows measurement of the object, use it to help determine the correct reduction/enlargement percentage. If not, make an educated guess ("Let's try 25 percent of the starting size."). Print the image, check it against your 18" rectangle. Repeat reduction/enlargement as necessary.
- Once the chair has appropriate measurements in ½" = 1'-0" scale, paste the image to a piece of cardstock for stiffness.
- When dry, cut it out and attach to a stand:

- Foamcore base
- Triangular piece of cardstock attached to the back

Detail is not tc be discouraged, but what is possible within the time frame of the course and the skill level of the student should be kept in mind. Samples should include the bare minimal state of craftsmanship you are willing to allow on this assignment. Leave these samples in the classroom as reference.

TEACHING TIP

Demonstrate every crafty thing you expect your students to attempt. It may feel like your students should have picked up many of these skills earlier in life, but not only are students less and less likely to encounter craft-based art programs in secondary education, non-design students might not have hobbies that develop these skills. A wake-up call for us was discovering that most of our students had no idea rubber cement existed and had to be shown how to use it.

Exercise: Building a 2D Piece of Furniture

Prepare a number of scaled-down photocopies of average pieces of furniture: chairs, sofas, dressers, etc. Since the models will be in ½" = 1'-0" scale, reduce or enlarge the images as needed.

The students will need glue, scissors, cardstock, rubber cement or glue sticks, X-Acto knives, and a cutting mat. Scraps of foamcore can be used to create bases. Instruct the students to:

- Cut down each sheet of paper until the image is in a relatively tight box.

- Apply adhesive to the back of the image (and to cardstock if using rubber cement).
- Apply each image to cardstock, smoothing to eliminate bubbles.

  - Depending on adhesive, some drying time may be necessary.

- Once dry, use an X-Acto knife to cut the image along its outline, leaving enough on the bottom to both fit into a base and allow the image to stand upright.
- Slit a small rectangle of foamcore.
- After applying a bit of glue, slide the bottom of the image into the foamcore slit.

Figure 7.5 Demonstration of Building a 2D ½" = 1'-0" Scale Chair

Since these are pieces of furniture you have brought in for this exercise, be sure to warn students that this exercise is simply practice, and that the furniture they include in 'Your First Set Design' should be specific to *their* interpretation of the play. If one of these practice pieces is used, it should be accompanied by a thorough and persuasive argument for its presence.

Exercise: Building a 3D Piece of Furniture

Building a rough 3D element is more time consuming and requires a fair amount of patience. Rather than holding things together with their fingers, many designers have an array of clips and stands to hold parts as glue dries. A designer also needs to have an understanding of the parts required to assemble a piece of furniture, as well as the sizes of those parts.

Building a basic 4' x 4' square table is a good feet-wetting exercise, as most tables have two primary components: a top surface and legs that hold up that surface.

The students will need cardstock, round toothpicks or other narrow wooden rods (bamboo cooking skewers, for instance), tacky glue, X-Acto knives, cutting mat, scissors, and their scale ruler.

- Measure a ½" = 1'-0" scale square on the cardstock. Cut out.
- Determine the height of the table by looking it up online, measuring a table, or consulting a chart (average table height is 30").
- Cleanly cut four toothpicks or bamboo skewers to the correct height

  - When using cardstock for the table top, its thickness does not need to be subtracted from the height of the legs; when using a thicker material, like foamcore, subtract the thickness of the foamcore from the overall height of the table to determine the lengths of the legs. Otherwise your table will end up too tall.

- Apply a dab of tacky glue in each corner of the table top's underside.
- One by one place the toothpick legs in a dab of glue. It will be necessary to hold each leg in place until the glue thickens sufficiently. This will be tedious.
- Allow the legs to completely dry before turning over.

Using thicker rods (such as bamboo skewers) for legs will mean a little less time holding them in place.

While students hold drying legs in place, discuss how other items, such as chairs or sofas, might be constructed.

Discussion: The Function of Models

One of the conversations arising from presentation of the small stage house is the purpose of using models as part of the production process. While students are holding things together waiting for glue to dry, open a discussion by asking your students what purposes they think a model might serve.

The role that a model plays in the production process can vary greatly depending on the working habits of both the designer and the director. Models fall into two broad categories:

- The Experimental Model (helps work out design problems)

  - In this class, models are geared toward this first category: problem solving tools rather than finished products (Figures 7.6 and 7.7)

- The Exhibition Model (displays finished work to the rest of the production team and may even be used for publicity purposes). Exhibition models have two subcategories:

  - The White Model (no paint, might be built directly from drawings; Figure 7.8)
  - The Fully Rendered Model (paint, textures, high degree of detail; Figures 7.9 and 7.10)

Figure 7.6 1/4" = 1'-0" Scale Very Rough Experimental Model of the UW–Whitewater Production of *Sweeney Todd*, in the Theatre on the Director's Rehearsal Desk

TEACHING TIP

As instructors, we sometimes assign projects assuming students automatically understand why they're assigned and what we expect students to learn. Major, often unstated portions of the learning process are intentionality and reflection. When beginning a project, be sure students have a sense of what *can* be learned from the activity. When looking at completed work, grades and written responses may only tell students how *good* you think the product was, not *what* was actually learned. What you think they learned and what they think they learned can be quite different.

One way to approach this dilemma is simply to ask students what they got out of an assignment or project during the review session. What did they think was the point of the project? What did they feel they learned from it? ("Okay, what did we just do, and why do you think I had you do it that way?") A response such as, "I dunno, it's what you told us to do" means it's probably time to re-evaluate and re-structure the assignment. Don't wait for end-of-semester student evaluations; feedback given while the project is fresh in everyone's mind is usually far more valuable.

Figure 7.7 1/2″ = 1′-0″ Scale Experimental Model of the UW–Whitewater Production of *The Furies*

Figure 7.9 1/4″ = 1′-0″ Scale Presentation Model for the Milwaukee Chamber Theatre's Production of *Boeing Boeing* (Scenic Design and Model by Brandon Kirkham)

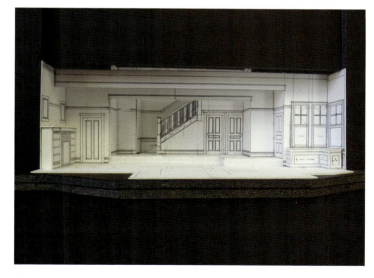

Figure 7.8 ¼″ = 1′-0″ Scale White Model for the UW–Whitewater Production of *Clybourne Park* (Scenic Design and Model by Keith Pitts)

Figure 7.10 1/4″ = 1′-0″ Scale Presentation Model for the Cincinnati Conservatory of Music's Production of *American Idiot* (Scenic Design by Thomas C. Umfrid, Model Built by Aaron Bridgman, Matt Hamel, and Olivia Leigh)

All types of models are to be shared with the director. The experimental type is shared as the show is being developed and the production team wishes to have concrete representation of those possibilities in three-dimensional space. Sketches and drawings are excellent communication tools, but details and proportions can be unconsciously (or consciously) adjusted for pictorial effect. There is a saying among scenic designers: Models don't lie.

The exhibition model can only be created after the design is substantially completed, the designer using dimensions from the finished drawings and sometimes copies of the finished drawings themselves to create the model (such as Figure 7.8). This model may also be painted, which, rather than 2D paint elevations, can serve as a reference tool for the scenic painters (Figures 7.9 and 7.10). As 3D printing technology advances, it may become possible to simply print out full models in scale with a high degree of detail. However, it must be noted that building the virtual model itself requires as much time as does building a physical model – possibly more.

If you or a colleague have documentation of an exploratory model from a recent departmental production, spend some time walking the students through the process.

- What kinds of models are made in your department?
- How are they integrated into the design process?
- How are they used by the design team?
- How are they used by your directors?
- Do they vary from director to director?
- How much time does fabrication require?
- How is the model used during rehearsals?
- What happens to the model after opening night?

Depending on the timeframe of the production and the needs of the director, a reasonably complete experimental model may be all that is required. The final project for the set design section is such a model. Figure 7.7 shows the final state of the model of the UW–Whitewater production of *The Furies*. Spatial relationships are evident, the overall look of the show is apparent, and scene shifts can be reviewed. Building a polished exhibition model was not necessary, nor did time allow. The experimental model for *Sweeney Todd* pictured in Figure 7.6 is even more rudimentary, and was built to guide discussion at an early production meeting. After its concepts were approved by the director, virtual modeling was used to create a more accurate and detailed depiction of the set.

TEACHING TIP

We've stressed that the instructor should model behavior he or she expects students to exhibit. This extends to your department as a whole. If production practices in which students see you engage are at wide variance to the ones you espouse in a class, you risk undercutting the value of the content of your course. You may need to have some difficult conversations with colleagues in order to chisel out time to create the drawings, renderings, and models you can then use as examples in class. Perhaps your department's production process simply needs more transparency. Explain to your students why the reality does not match the ideal and why knowing the ideal first might better prepare them to weather reality.

Discussion: Pros and Cons of Model Formats

For many students (and indeed, for some instructors) it will seem quaint and old-fashioned to emphasize hand-drafting and the building of physical models when powerful computer programs are available to make life easier. There are many pros and cons to virtual models. Any instructor who has graded a paper well knows that running a paper through a spellchecking program is not equivalent to actually proof-reading the content. Nor do spelling and grammar programs automatically help the student write *better*. They simply catch certain categories of error. The same is true for computer drafting and modeling programs. They can certainly help an experienced designer work more quickly and efficiently, but they do not necessarily make the design itself better.

Building a detailed and accurate virtual model also takes a considerable amount of time, since items need to be rendered *as they really are*. On the *Boeing Boeing* model in Figure 7.9, the designer used the heads of straight pins for doorknobs. On a virtual model, the designer would have to seek out and import someone else's model of the desired doorknob or take the time to model the correct doorknob. An approximation that looks fine on a physical model can make a virtual model look sloppy and unfinished.

On the other hand, since theatre production requires a lot of paperwork distributed among a production team sometimes communicating long-distance with each other, being able to instantly send electronic files rather than mailing bulky packages is preferable. Scenic designers can use a laptop or tablet during a production meeting to instantly revise a virtual model, rather than going back to their worktable and presenting those revisions a couple days later. Directors can have their own copy of the model for use wherever they happen to be. Technical directors are able to create their shop drawings directly from virtual models.

Many scenic designers work with both formats, developing concepts and providing accurate detail with a virtual model, but also building a physical version since, at present, a virtual model is still *viewed* as a 2D object on a monitor. In the not too distant future, 3D printing will likely enable full virtual models to move from the screen to real space. However, as with most things, cost and availability will determine what technology a beginning designer can access. Starting with cardboard, scissors, and glue means that when a student begins to work with

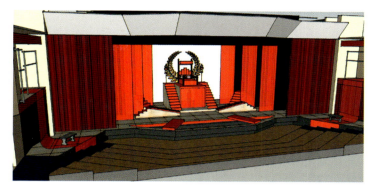

Figure 7.11   Virtual Model in SketchUp of UW–Whitewater's Production of *The Coronation of Poppea*

a virtual model they can focus on using the program to realize the design. The program becomes a tool rather than a crutch.

If you have access to examples of both physical models and virtual models, the following exercise can help students better understand not just their individual pros and cons, but how they can complement each other throughout the design process.

Exercise: Pros and Cons of Model Formats

Present the students with both the physical model and the virtual model. Take a few minutes to introduce the shows and walk through both models. The discussion can then be guided by asking such questions as:

- What kind of information can be gleaned from either model?
- Is the type of information different for each model?
- How useful is that information?
- What are the frustrations of each version?
- What are the obvious benefits of each version?
- How easy is it to use the model?

  - Can you easily understand spatial relationships between various components?

- Is it easy to understand how actors will move around the space?
- How easily can revisions to the model be made?
- Can the director use the model to help work out blocking?

Depending on the size of class and the number of models available, this can become a team exercise, with one group examining the physical model and the other examining the virtual model, and then presenting their group findings.

Book Recommendation

For introductory model building tips and approaches, consider Chapters 9 thorough 12 of Gary Thorne's *Stage Design: A Practical Guide*. More advanced students would be well served by reading the slightly dated but still highly relevant *Theory and Craft of the Scenographic Model*, by Darwin Reid Payne.

Session Break: End of Week 7, Day 1.

A scenic design is not a diorama. It needs to be inhabited by actors for it to become an active part of the play. The previous exercises and discussions were aimed at helping students realize that objects can be measured, their sizes can be proportionally reduced through the use of scale, and that there needs to be some standard object (such as a human being) in the environment to give the viewer an instant understanding of the *relative* proportions of the various scenic items.

We now start connecting this design mechanic groundwork back to the play. Characters move around their environment. The scenic designer, with the director, has to determine traffic patterns and how those patterns reinforce the action of the play. What does it say about the characters' relationships if there are many physical obstacles placed in their way? What do isolated groupings of chairs allow to happen? What if there is only one place to sit in the room – who gets to control it?

Furthermore, the scenic designer is in a position to give characters destinations on the stage. A small table with a candy dish downstage right may provide more of a motivation for a character breaking away from a conversation than turning and arbitrarily heading off to an empty corner of the stage. We find that many students, particularly performers, try to eliminate furniture and obstacles, or push it all upstage in an effort to 'make room for acting.' One of the goals of the following exercises is to present the idea that rather than being something in the way, scenic items can present actors with *more* choices and so aid character development and the explication of relationships.

Discussion: Using Footprints to Explore Space

Have the student pull out their completed 'Sizes of Objects' handouts. Direct them to:

- Select one of their pieces of furniture.
- In ½" = 1'-0" scale, lay out the footprint (perimeter) of the object on a piece of paper (Figure 7.12).
- Cut out the object *on the outline*, and label it clearly.
- Using one of the small stage houses and a reduced-scale human figure, use these footprints to demonstrate arranging items in a space (Figure 7.13).

Exercise: What is a 'Normal' Room Layout?

This exercise:

- Reinforces sense of proportion
- Recognizes the limitations and opportunities created by size
- Introduces the idea that a groundplan is developed through discovery and experimentation.

Figure 7.12 Abigail and Bridget Lay Out Footprints of Objects

Figure 7.13 Trying to Fit Two Sofas into the Playing Space while Bridget Looks on

Ask the students to consider what pieces are to be found in the average living room (some might call this a 'front room'). In many newer apartments and houses, the traditional living room may not be part of the design. To make sure that students understand the concept of a living room, the following questions can open the discussion:

- What is the purpose of a 'living room?'
- What activities take place in a 'living room?'
- Does every house have a 'living room?'
- What types of houses or apartments have living rooms?
- What pieces of furniture do you consider 'normal' for a living room?

After the brief discussion, direct the students to:

- Cut out those furniture footprints, using their sheet of measurements.
- Arrange the footprints on a piece of 8½" x 11" piece of paper to depict how they think the average living room is laid out.
- Share their layouts with the class and discuss the results:

  - Why did you place them in the room in the way you did?
  - How do people move around this room?
  - How does this arrangement reinforce the purpose of and activities taking place in this room?

Ask the students to rearrange their layouts to meet different goals or compositional qualities:

- Can you arrange the room in a more formal manner?
- A less formal manner?
- Can you make the room more cozy?
- Can you make the room more difficult for casual conversation?
- What happens if it becomes a TV room?
- What happens if you take the TV out of the room?

Figure 7.14 Exploring Room Layout with
Footprint Cut-outs

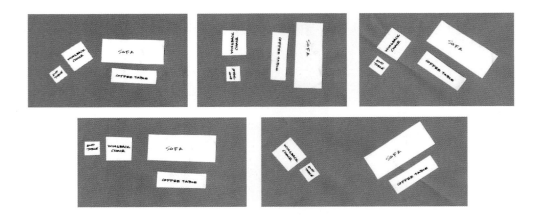

Offer the class a metaphor statement and/or series of design elements. Ask the students how the living room layouts can be arranged to reflect the ideas expressed.

- Is it the path of the characters or the items themselves that express the design elements?
- How can the shapes of the items change to better express the metaphor/design elements?
- How can the characters' use of the items express the metaphor/design elements?
- Are the furniture items alone enough to express the metaphor or is it necessary to know more about the space, such as the boundaries (walls?)?

Discussion: The Groundplan is a Plan of Action

After introducing the idea that the scenic designer must experiment to determine where essential items of the set will be placed, we scale up the exercise and use a short play to talk about how the placement of objects impacts the relationships of characters and the meaning of space.

"This is the moment for the ancient adage that all designers are frustrated directors. This could well be true, but why? Because the process of designing dictates the quasi-director role for the designer [sic]. His initial concept must project a scheme based on key action patterns. The set is the compass for the journey of the action. The proposed format of the actors' environment is a statement of the show's direction. This plotting of the movement flow is the designer's first chore — though it surely will be revised by the director."[2]
Howard Bay, *Stage Design*

As noted in Chapter 2, some scenic designers dive into the script and begin doodling diagrams of movement well before considering the overall appearance of the set. For this class, these diagrams of potential movement are noted to be visual expressions of the design metaphor. If the text of the play generates a metaphor that speaks to isolation and difficult communication, there should be evidence of this and expression of these qualities in the physical relationships of the characters as mapped into an environment. If a scene calls for two chairs, how are these chairs to be placed to reinforce isolation and separateness? Will substituting a sofa for the two chairs allow the same relationship qualities to be expressed by the characters? How do two twin beds speak to a marital relationship? The set is not just about creating an interesting picture on the stage, *but facilitating specific activities and types of movement that connect the performers to each other and the environment in a meaningful way.*

This is a good moment to review basic stage and scenic configurations, especially if the last time this was encountered was in a long past 'Introduction to Theatre' course. Ask the students for names and definitions of architectural configurations. Provide images to aid clarity.

- **Proscenium:** picture frame, audience on one side of playing space
- **Thrust**: audience on two or more adjacent sides of playing space
- **Arena:** playing space completely surrounded by audience
- **Stadium**: playing space as strip between halves of the audience
- **Black Box:** flexible space that can accommodate variety of configurations

Scenic configurations fit inside architectural configurations. Three basic scenic configurations can be seen in Figures 7.15 through 7.17.

Remember to note that these configurations are by no means exclusive or definitive, but rather broad categories that aid discussion. A set may have elements of both a box set and a unit set, and could be placed just as easily in a proscenium or thrust space regardless of style or period of play. As students develop components of their final project, remind them that

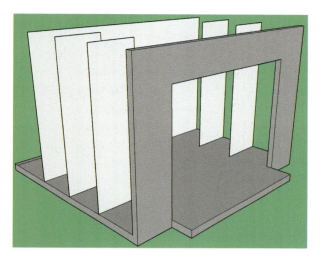

Figure 7.15 Wing and Drop: Typically Created by Flat Painted Surfaces, Such as Drops and Legs

Figure 7.16 Box Set: Removal of the 'Fourth Wall' to View the Space; Often Used for Interiors, Realistic or Otherwise

Figure 7.17 Unit Set: Generalized Architectural Structure Meant to Support Variety of Locales with only Minor Scenic Changes

while they're working in a proscenium space, design solutions may emerge from other stage configurations.

Exercise: Exploring the Groundplan as a Plan of Action

We use the short play *That Horrible Human Condition* for this exercise (see Appendix C for the script). Whatever play is used, be sure to have copies for everyone. Strip out everything but the absolute necessary stage directions so students don't leap to conclusions about what needs to be on the stage, or when and where characters move. A basic box set arrangement of three imaginary walls provides the starting parameters of the space. Since our classroom isn't large enough for this exercise we move into the costume shop.

The first point of discussion is placement of entrances. The generic box set features an upstage wall, and walls splayed right and left.

- How many entrances are required?
- What's beyond those entrances?
- Who uses those entrances?
- What do the characters do as they come through those entrances?

If time allows, periodically alter placement of the entrances to gauge the effect. Take votes if decision-making reaches an impasse.

Be sure to ask why students are inclined to place entrances where they do. Sometimes this is a manifestation of their experience in departmental productions, or what was discussed in acting and directing classes. If they have learned previously that up-center is the strongest point of entrance, ask why this is so and be sure to experiment with both up-center and off-to-the-side portals to see what advantages and disadvantages are to be found. If there are two entrances, which then is the more important portal that requires placement in the 'stronger' location? Is this importance determined by who enters, what's on the other side of the entrance, or by what happens upon a character's entrance?

Another point to consider is architectural logic versus dramatic logic. For a realistic play, constructing a stage space that at least *seems* architecturally feasible will support the realism of the world; in other words, the audience won't need to wonder why the door to the backyard is right next to the house's front door. In plays like farces, door placement might be determined less by straightforward architectural logic than by the need to have the requisite number of doors fit into the space close enough to keep the action rocketing along yet not so far apart that danger of discovery is diminished. For a more abstract play, it might even be advantageous to set up the incongruity of illogical door placement because the audience *should* question the reality of the environment.

For *That Horrible Human Condition*, our class chose to place the entrance to the hallway, and thus the house's interior, in the stage right wall. The French doors to the garden were on the stage left side of the upstage wall. The script asks for only one sittable, and that was placed just off-center in the middle of the space. A phone on a small table was also determined to be required, and that was placed in the upstage right corner. At that point, volunteers were requested to read and allowed to determine their own blocking as the scene began.

Stop frequently, change elements, and repeat. Ask for blocking suggestions as the configuration changes; what helps, what hinders? What do we learn about the characters as they physically interact within the space? In Figure 7.18, the single center chair was joined by a second chair and the phone table placed between them. If a character hovers upstage behind the chair occupied by the sister rather than crossing downstage of her or sitting in a chair across from her, what does that say about their personalities and relationship? Does having a choice in

Figure 7.19 What if the Phone is Right Next to the Sofa?

Figure 7.18 What About Two Chairs, the Phone Between Them, and a Bar Down Right?

movement and not using it mean the same as not having that choice in the first place? In Figure 7.19, chairs were lined up to create a sofa. After that, all the furniture was pushed against the walls, which meant that no character could sit next to anyone else, and conversations had to take place across distances.

Explore giving characters destinations. While the single chair and telephone table can be found on the 'absolutely essential' list, a small bar or drinks cart could be added to the 'very nice to have' list, as it gives the characters a place to go and things to do, as well as explicating which characters are perfectly at home with a mid-day cocktail. Placing the telephone next to the chair means that the sitting character does not need to move to answer it, and movement is delayed until she decides to retreat to the garden. If the phone is a short distance from the chair, she must rise and cross to answer it. Which action helps underscore her need to escape the room?

Explore metaphor and movement. Prepare a couple of metaphors that could be applied to the play, and ask the class to arrange the room's elements to express aspects of the metaphor. If the siblings "squabble like parakeets in a cage," using a sofa rather than chairs is a way to group the siblings like birds on a perch, and perhaps ratchet up the chattering quality of their dialogue.

The Scenic Design Final Project

Even though the students haven't yet presented the mid-level design project, at the end of this week we distribute the guidelines for the final scenic design project (due in Week 10). This is to help frame the discussions and exercises in the next two weeks and give students the chance to set their own timetables and goals in assembling the project's various components.

For this project we again use the KCACTF guidelines for format. Expectations for the oral presentation follow the same lines as those for the costume design project. The materials expected as part of the presentation include:

- A Title Block with show title, author, name of designer
- Metaphor Statement

  - It is expected that the statement has been revised to reflect adaptations to the scenic environment and includes discussion of design elements

- Central Image

  - This serves as a cohesive visual encapsulation of the metaphor, and the student is expected to explain how this image is used to inform subsequent design element choices

- Research Images

  - A wide range, both abstract and of physical detail, with notation regarding how various elements will be incorporated into the scenic environment

- Color Palette

  - This can either be a standalone color swatch page or indicated by notes on the research images. While the model does not include color, the student should be able to talk about how color is specifically used throughout the design

- White Model

  - ½" = 1'-0" scale
  - Presented in the appropriate black foamcore stage house
  - Appropriate human figure present
  - As much detail as possible: 3D standing furniture, drops, rugs, doors, artwork on walls, etc.
  - The student may include grayscale photocopied surfaces where texture or detail is important, or detail is beyond current drawing ability
  - Include masking (legs and borders)

- Rough Groundplan

  - This is drawn on the supplied ¼" = 1'-0" scale plan of the stage house
  - Center and Plaster lines included
  - Appropriate line type and symbols as required
  - Masking
  - Labels
  - If there are multiple arrangements, multiple plans may be needed

The end of this session is also a good time to remind students of the professional designer presentations that are also due in Week 10. The guidelines for those remain the same as those used for the costume designer presentations in Week 5.

Portfolio Development Project

Since designers cannot always present portfolio material in person, being able to include easily read process information will inform directors (and other readers) of how they might expect a collaboration to proceed. While the work of this week was largely geared toward preparation of next week's homework, a conflation of these exercises can be used to demonstrate how process, as opposed to end product, can be presented in the portfolio.

Portfolio Project: Illustrating Groundplan Development

Direct the students to:

- Develop a design metaphor for the short play used in the 'Plan of Action' exercise. Compile a list of associated design elements.
- Cut out the footprints of all the furniture they would like to use for the short play used in the 'The Groundplan is a Plan of Action' exercise.

- Lay out three to four possible furniture configurations using a basic three-wall groundplan. Their final configuration should be the one they feel will work the best.
- Write a brief statement of one or two sentences describing the intention of each arrangement. Be sure to state how the design metaphor informs each arrangement. Note how each configuration revises the one before it, and why the final step is considered to be the best.
- Lay out each configuration on the glass of a scanner (white paper cut-outs with a grey background works well). Scan each configuration.
- Depending on format, paper or electronic, arrange the images so they read from earliest to the most favored. Caption with the statements to one side.
- Create a title block noting that these images discuss the process of groundplan development.

Notes

1. Lee Simonson, *The Stage is Set* (New York: Dover Publications, 1932), pp. 356–357.
2. Howard Bay, *Stage Design* (New York: Drama Book Specialists/ Publishers, 1974), p. 93.

Chapter 8

Week 8

"Scenographic modelmaking is a more comprehensible skill for the beginning student to develop than that of illusory painting. This is not to suggest that drawing and painting are not necessary skills for the scenographer; indeed, their mastery is absolutely essential to him . . . . Modelmaking can, in fact, serve as a focus for pursuing more graphic skills; drawing from the scenographic model, in fact, can greatly enhance the student's appreciation of the particular kind of space with which he must deal."[1]

Darwin Reid Payne, *Theory and Craft of the Scenographic Model*

In the costume design section, the primary expression of the design was the costume rendering. For the scenic design section, the three-dimensional model will serve as the primary expression of the design. It can be argued that for costume designs, the structural considerations – figuring out *how* to build the costume – largely happen in the shop after the rendering is delivered. For set design, development of the model often goes hand-in-hand with the creation of base construction drawings such as the groundplan. The model expresses the three-dimensional qualities, but the groundplan is an important tool that both aids the creation of the model and then in a more finished version provides the shop, director, and stage manager with detail and information that cannot be easily included on the model. The activities of this week will continue development of model building, but also introduce the fundamental hand-drafting skills needed to draw a groundplan.

The framing topic for this week is:

- Design Mechanics

  - Homework Follow-up: 'Your First Set Design'
  - Introduction to Drafting
  - Drafting the Classroom Perimeter
  - Introduction to Graphics Standards
  - Drafting the Groundplan for 'Your First Set Design'

Supplies Needed

Instructor supplies:

- Tape measures

Student supplies:

- Architectural scale ruler
- Drafting tape or blue painter's tape
- 8½" x 11" paper
- 14" x 17" paper
- Pencil (No. 2 or 2H)
- 24" T-square
- Drafting triangles: 45 degree and 30/60 degree

Homework Follow-up: 'Your First Set Design'

The model for the short play (the mid-level project) is due this session. We have the students pin their models up on the bulletin boards in the hallway. If bulletin boards are not available, try to arrange some way to display the models at eye height. This allows the viewer to see the set from an audience's perspective.

Lead the group through the following discussion questions:

- What worked?
- What didn't work?
- What surprised them?
- What did the students like most about building the model?
- What did the students like least about building the model?

Since the degree of elaboration on the individual components is largely left up to the students themselves (though hopefully they have examined the sample pieces from the earlier session), there's usually a wide range represented, from three-dimensional chairs with applied photocopy detail, 2D images pasted onto cardstock, and furniture molded out of clay, to structural pieces made out of foamcore with no added detail at all. Sometimes students default to simply having the footprints of the elements rather than stand-up representations. We discuss what each of those items allows us to discuss. Even though stand-up pieces of furniture are preferable to footprints, footprints still allow discussion of placement and traffic patterns, especially if they are to the correct scale. Since we *do* explicitly ask for standing pieces, footprints alone will be noted on the written evaluation, adding that the final project requires the student to go further.

As students present their model, they are expected to discuss the following questions:

- What was your working metaphor, and how did it manifest through design elements?
- Was there a connection to the house image, and how was that connection expressed?
- Whose room is this, and what elements and features tell us that?
- Where are the entrances, and why are they placed where they are? How does this facilitate the action of the play?
- Why were particular textures, colors, shapes, etc., chosen for specific items? Are these choices supported by the design metaphor?

- How does your arrangement of items facilitate the action of the play?
- How do your items express the relationships between the characters?

If a student can't explain why they have chosen an item or placed an item in a particular way, lead them through an exploration of those gut-reactions. For intriguing, non-traditional looks this is an important discussion. In the model pictured in Figure 8.1, the student placed an armchair dead center, facing directly upstage toward the fireplace. By placing the chair in this position, the audience might not even know someone was in the chair until someone else spoke to that character. The audience would likely not see the character's face until, for whatever reason, he felt compelled to get out of the chair.

It's a bold, interesting choice, but in this case the student had difficulty expressing a text-based rationale as to *why* he'd made the choice. The possibilities offered by this upstage-

Figure 8.1 'Your First Set Design': *The Return of the Living* (Model by Eric Guenthner)

facing chair were discussed by the group: what does this chair position allow to happen, and how can it contribute to the action of the play? Because the character sitting in the chair is also the one in whom the other characters express disappointment, it might be intriguing *not* to reveal his face until later in the action. Perhaps the audience sees nothing but a hand hanging over the armrest with the glass of whiskey. At what point in the script could we expect that character to get out of the chair? *Why* would the character get out of the chair at that particular moment?

Especially for a scenic environment where the stage is stripped to essentials (for this assignment, only as much scenery as could be accommodated in a five-minute scene change), every item must be packed with purpose. Even pictures on walls contribute to the meaning of the space. For *The Return of the Living,* are pictures on the wall the son's watercolors, which would indicate he has made an attempt to make the room his own? Or are they pictures one would expect the father to have selected, thus making the children interlopers in their father's domain? Remind students that everything on the stage is there for a reason, and those reasons should have become clearer to them as they determined what items were absolutely essential to the action of the play. If the item on the set wasn't in the 'absolutely essential' category, the student has made a decision to include it. If the decision cannot be supported, it will be unclear what that item brings to the world of the play.

If there are elements that stand out or seem incongruous, ask the student to explain them. In Figure 8.1, the painting is supported by a bold blue vertical upright. Since the rest of the model features objects without color or detail, why does this one element have bold color? If it *is* just to support the picture, discuss less intrusive technical solutions to achieve the same end. If it *is* intentional, discuss both the perception of the viewer and the intention of the design and see where they do and don't align.

The following questions can lead to deeper examination of the work:

- What does clutter do for/to an actor?
- How does a particular element relate to a particular character?
- Which character has left the greatest impression upon the environment?
- What's the most visually important item in the space? Why?
- Is a particular item an aesthetic choice or a technical solution/issue?
- Was there an intentional use of period?
- Was there an intentional application of style?

The students are expected to include a human figure in the model, and there are likely to be a variety of images used for this purpose. This is an opportunity to discuss the appropriateness of *everything* that is being presented, and how the details contribute not just to the content, but to the perceived attitude of the designer toward the work. Figures such as the current U.S. President may be intended to inject some humor, but is that humor necessary, and how much will the presence of the President distract from the work? Remind students that not all collaborators will get or appreciate the joke, and may question whether the designer takes the project seriously. Figures dressed in a manner clearly contrary to the intentions of the environment should be reevaluated, as should figures engaged in activities that draw attention to themselves rather than integrate them into their surroundings. Since the students have already created appropriate figures for their costume design projects, these should be used in the final scenic project.

Figures 8.2 and 8.3 picture two more models well within the range of technical expectation for this project.

Grading and Evaluation of 'Your First Set Design' Homework

As 'Your First Set Design' is a mid-level project it forms a moderate percentage of the total grade. Evaluation is based on the points students are expected to touch upon during the presentation and how well the student addressed them. Notes are

Figure 8.2 'Your First Set Design': *The Return of the Living* (Model by Bridget Kelly)

Figure 8.3 'Your First Set Design': *The Return of the Living* (Model by Kelsey Smyth)

taken on the form by the instructor during the presentation, then typed up and returned to the student.

Questions for 'Your First Set Design' Evaluation

- Are all components (stage house, individual scenic elements) present and in a reasonably finished state?
- Are all pieces consistently in the correct scale?
- What is the degree of craftsmanship and attention to detail? Was it clear what objects were meant to be? How did you accomplish this clarity?
- Were the scenic objects presented both pictorially and spatially?
- Was there an appropriate human figure to provide a sense of proportion?
- Were you able to explain your choices: why items were chosen, why they look the way they do, and why they are placed where they are placed? Were you able to connect your choices back to the needs of the text?
- Did you consider entrances and exits and how they impact the action of the play?
- Were you able to explain how your choices connected to the action of the play as revealed through character relationships? (Whose room is this?)

Grade:

Discussion: Introduction to Drafting

In approaching drafting, our view is that the content should remain thoroughly introductory, the material should be considered in small, incremental steps, and those elements of drafting taught should be immediately put to use on assignments.

"Although there is really only a minimal place for hand-drawn or drafted work in the modern professional world, those skills remain necessary. . . . The brain to hand connection at every stage of the design process, especially at the beginning of the design process, is critical."[2]
Kevin Lee Allen, *Vectorworks for Entertainment Design*

Drafting helps students develop spatial knowledge, foster the ability to conceive and describe three-dimensional objects, and practice 3D objects clearly. We skip over freehand sketching because model building does the heavy lifting of representation, and getting students to sketch well enough to represent ideas to their satisfaction often takes much more time (and more frustration) than teaching them to draft at an adequate beginning level.

TEACHING TIP

Many students fear drawing because they cannot already draw well. Use of the croqui and garment templates in the costume section helps allay that fear. In scenic design, the method of overcoming that fear is drafting. If students can read a ruler and draw a line along a straightedge, they can draft.

We're not arguing that sketching ability is not an essential skill for designers (see the Darwin Reid Payne quote at the start of the chapter), only that in the time available for this course we have chosen to introduce and reinforce those skills that result in the most immediately achievable product; after all, the costume design final project was due after only eight class sessions. The decision to jettison freehand sketching and the fundamentals of perspective from this course was made after many, many attempts and are now saved for more advanced courses and independent studies.

Scenic Design Vocabulary

Line Weight the darkness, thickness, and pattern of a line on a drawing; the various types of lines indicate the purpose and importance of the object drawn

Vellum a high quality semi-transparent paper traditionally used in hand-drafting

CAD acronym for 'Computer Aided Drafting;' refers to any number of computer programs such as AutoCAD and Vectorworks

H, 2H, HB, etc. the grading scale of graphite hardness. 'H' denotes harder leads, 'B' denotes softer leads. The higher the number, the harder or softer the lead. The average No. 2 pencil is HB, which is a middle grade.

Square in drafting and scenic construction refers to whether an object or line is at a right angle (perpendicular – 90 degrees) to another object or line

Proscenium Arch the 'picture frame' through which an audience views the stage; depending on the venue, the proscenium arch may be a permanent architectural feature

These are the steps we follow to introduce the use of drafting in scenic design:

- Use of the scale ruler
- Introduction to line weight
- Measuring and drawing lines
- Use the tools to draw simple geometric shapes
- Use the tools to draw a room's perimeter
- Introduce basic graphic standards and symbols
- Draw the groundplan for 'Your First Set Design'

When approaching drafting, keep it basic and resist getting into nuances and details. At this stage, a No. 2 pencil will be adequate. Vellum is expensive overkill; a piece of 14" x 17" drawing paper will work fine. Line weight is important (more about that later in this chapter), but while pointing out where proper line weight is useful remember that the content of the drawing should receive the lion's share of evaluative consideration. The students will work at a variety of paces, so be prepared to move around the room to help those struggling. The slowest student will determine when you can move on to the next step, and that's okay. Check on and discuss discoveries with the faster students to add value to waiting.

We have found it more productive to uncouple early drafting attempts from theatrical goals. While the timeframe of an introductory course may suggest that it's desirable to kill the birds of basic drafting and groundplan layout with one stone, combining them muddies the goal of the immediate project and raises the stakes too high. Students will have more confidence in drawing the groundplan if they are relatively secure in the required drafting skills first.

Avoid asking students to draft something they do not know how to build or for which they have no mental or visual references. Simple geometric shapes and room perimeters work well for beginning exercises. When we finally introduce students to drafting a groundplan, they use the model they've built for 'Your First Set Design' so they can visualize the objects being represented and measure the model to determine exactly where they are placed on the stage. When the exercise is about drafting (even with CAD) try to eliminate extraneous moving parts so that the focus is on drafting, not design or engineering.

Exercise: Taping Down the Paper

For these first few steps (Taping, Borders, Drawing a Square), 8½" x 11" copier paper can be used. The next exercise, drafting the perimeter of the room, will require larger paper. 14" x 17" drawing paper is recommended. A No. 2 pencil (HB) works fine, but tends to smudge. We find a 2H pencil is more controllable. Students who are serious about scenic design can look into

Figure 8.4 From Left to Right: 2 mm 2H Drawing Leads, a 2 mm Lead Holder, a .2 mm Mechanical Pencil, a .9 mm Mechanical Pencil, Blue Painter's Tape, a 2H Drawing Pencil, a No. 2 (HB) Pencil, a White Vinyl Eraser

lead-holders and mechanical pencils for future use. We also recommend a white vinyl eraser as they tend to erase cleanly, without leaving colored residue on the drawing.

To tape paper down, use either drafting tape (or drafting dots) or blue painter's tape. Cellophane tape and regular mask-ing tape have too much adhesive and will rip up the corners of the paper when removing the drawing from the table. Drafting tape and drafting dots are meant for taping down drawings, but tend to be expensive.

It is difficult to introduce drafting without drawing tables. Eric has taught drafting in a make-up room by requiring the students to purchase drafting boards (a 24″ x 36″ wooden board that has a surface smooth enough for drawing); using drafting boards also allows students to transport their work, securely taped down, between home and classroom. Indeed, it means they *can* do the work at home. Depending on the size of class and type of room available, it might be beneficial for your department to look into the purchase of either drafting boards that can be handed down from year to year or basic drawing tables.

Students will have the very logical urge to center the paper on the table top. If the paper is taped down in the center of the average drawing table, a 24″ T-square will not reach the far side of the drawing. The seemingly sensible solution would be to move the T-square to the opposite side of the table as needed; this is undesirable, and will be explained in a bit.

- Butt the T-square firmly against one edge of the drawing table (for the right-handed, the left side; for the left-handed, the right side). Be sure there is enough space between draw-ing tables to allow the T-square free passage.

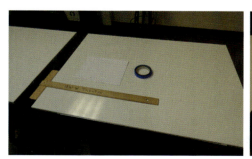
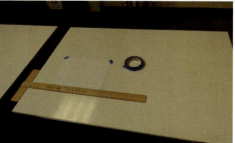

Figure 8.5 A Piece of Copier Paper Taped to a Drawing Table, with Space for a T-Square Between Tables

- In landscape orientation, line up the bottom edge of the paper along the top edge of the T-square, centering it along the length of the T-square.
- Using painter's tape, drafting tape, or drafting dots, tape the top two corners of the paper securely to the table.
- Move the T-square out of the way and tape the bottom corners down.

This begins the process of creating a consistently oriented drawing. We do not know for sure if all four edges of the table are square and parallel; therefore the T-square is used *only* along one edge – the right *or* the left, depending on the handed-ness of the student. Similarly, we only draw with the top edge of the T-square, since we do not know for sure that the top and bottom edges are indeed parallel. If the primary straightedge remains consistent, the drawing remains consistent and there is less opportunity for error.

Exercise: Drawing Borders

The next step is to designate the space on the paper that will enclose the drawing. This is done by creating a border. When a drawing is reproduced, the border assures the recipient that it is indeed the entire drawing that has been delivered; the full drawing is to be found within the borders. Missing portions of border are an alert that part of the drawing may be missing.

Before drawing begins, it is useful to review the two line weights we will use in this class and which were introduced in Chapter 6: **construction lines** and **visible lines**. Construction lines are light, grey lines that help the draftsperson arrange items on the paper. They can also be called guidelines. Visible lines are black, thick lines that are drawn on top of construction lines once the object has been completely laid out and the draftsperson wants to finalize the drawing.

Standard borders are ½" from the top, bottom, and right-hand side of the paper, and 1" from the left-hand side to allow for binding. To draw a border, first use construction lines (see Figure 8.6):

- Draw a vertical line intersecting the bottom and top horizontal edges of the paper.
- Measure up from the bottom edge ½".
- Measure down from the top edge ½".
- Draw a horizontal line at the each mark across the full width of the paper.
- Choose one of the horizontal lines and measure inward ½" from the right hand side, and 1" in from the left (the edge of the paper).
- Draw vertical lines through both marks the full height of the paper.

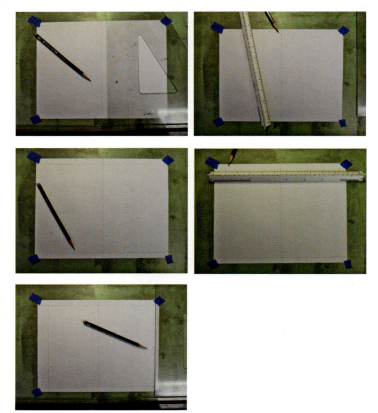

Figure 8.6 Laying Out Borders

- Erase the original vertical line if desired; leave the eraser crumbs on the paper to help tools slide over the surface and reduce smudging.

    Draw the border, step by step, on the chalkboard. When the students are done, they should each have a light grey box around the perimeter of the paper. If their paper is slightly angled, the box should still (because of the T-square) be correctly oriented to the side of the drawing table.

    The border, as the thickest line of the drawing, will be the *last* thing darkened up when the drawing is complete. This prevents undue smudging. Pre-bordered vellum is available, and computer drafting programs will usually take care of borders for you.

Exercise: Drawing a Square

Students now draw a 7'-0" square in ½" = 1'-0" scale. This is demonstrated, step by step, on the blackboard. See Figure 8.7 for the steps.

- Draw a line horizontally across the paper to place the bottom edge of the square (try to approximately center the future square on the paper). For an 8½" x 11" piece of paper this line is about a third of the way up the page.
- Make a tick mark along the line to place the left-hand edge of the square (#1). A tick mark is a small, dark mark placed on the line to indicate where a measured point lies. Examples can be seen in Figure 8.7.
- Draw a vertical line through the tick mark. Be sure to extend it *well past* the intended length (#2).
- Alert the students that from this point on, all measurements will be given in ½" = 1'-0" scale.
- Measure 7'-0" up the vertical line from the intersection with the horizontal. Make a tick mark (#3).
- Measure 7'-0" along the horizontal line from the intersection with the vertical. Make a tick mark (#3).

    The magic of drafting is that because of the consistency of tool placement (the T-square against the edge of the table)

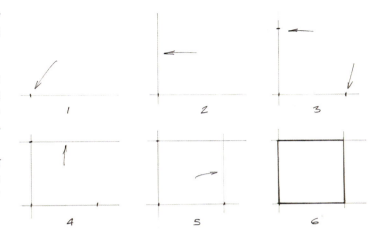

Figure 8.7 Steps in Drafting a Square

measurements can be transferred across the page *solely with the drawing tools*.

- Using the T-square, draw a horizontal line through the tick mark on the vertical line (#4).

Figure 8.8 Hand Drafting a Square

- Using a triangle butted against the T-square, draw a vertical line through the tick mark on the horizontal line (#5).

These two new lines should intersect to create a square. Once the square is laid out, darken the final shape with visible lines (#6). Only the square should be darkened.

Most of the basic principles of hand drafting have now been addressed:

- Scale
- Noting measurements
- Using tools to transfer measurements
- Line weight
- Layout

Circulate as the students work, keeping an eye out for free-floating tools or unsettled T-squares that will result in trapezoids and rhomboids rather than squares. Darkening the visible lines should be done along firmly oriented tools. There are exceptions when tools are used without orientation against the table edge, but it's best to start with the rules and break them as need dictates. Don't let students use their scale ruler as a straightedge (it wears down and muddles the markings). Measuring tools are measuring tools, drawing tools are drawing tools. Note which students have managed to center their square on the page and which have been less successful. For those whose squares are not centered, ask what approach they imagine might help them better center a drawing next time.

Exercise: Drafting the Perimeter of the Classroom

This exercise:

- Helps students develop a sense of the actual sizes of real objects
- Applies the use of scale to real-world objects
- Develops a sense of logic in laying out objects

In order to apply their new drafting skills to a practical end, students measure the classroom's perimeter and then draft it in

scale. After laying out a fresh piece of larger paper (14″ x 17″) and laying out the border with construction lines, the concepts of the **center line** and **plaster line** are discussed.

Scenic Design Vocabulary

Center Line the axis of the stage, from downstage to upstage, splitting the playing space equally in half right and left (the Y axis)

Plaster Line a line through the proscenium arch that denotes the plane of the upstage side of the architectural proscenium (the X axis)

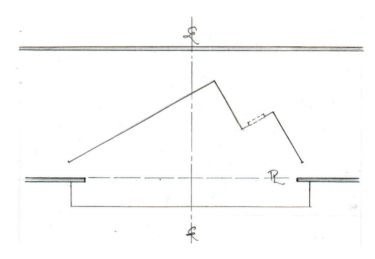

Figure 8.9 Simplified Scenic Groundplan with Center and Plaster Lines

These two lines are the primary reference lines on any groundplan, providing the basis of a single system of measurement coordinates throughout the playing space, just like using an X/Y set of axes to map out a graph or chart. On a drawing, to find the placement of a sofa upstage left a line can be drawn from a corner of the sofa horizontally to the center line. The distance between that intersection and the plaster line creates the coordinates of that sofa corner which can then be located with tape measures on the actual stage floor (i.e., 10'-6" upstage and 3'-5" toward stage left).

As seen in Figure 8.9, the center line is denoted with a specific line type – short dash, very long dash, short dash, etc. – and the interlocking CL symbol, which is placed at both the top and bottom of the drawing. The center line is drawn through (on top of) all items in its path.

As also seen in Figure 8.9, the plaster line is also denoted with a specific line type – uniform long dashes – and an interlocking PL symbol, which is usually placed to the right or left side of the proscenium arch, and appears only once. Not all theatres have proscenium arches, and therefore the plaster line may not be a meaningful reference in your theatre space (particularly in black boxes).

While the center line of the plan or object being drawn may not coincide with the center line of the piece of paper, we conflate the two in this exercise in order to center the drawing on the page. This also introduces the idea that a drawing is *laid out*, rather than haphazardly situated on a page. Centering a drawing allows sufficient white space around the object for the addition of dimensions and notes (which, beyond labeling, we do not include in this course).

- Measure the distance between the left and right borders along either the top or bottom border. This is a moment to reinforce the no-floating-scale rule dictum as some students will lay their scales across the middle of the paper rather than along an already drawn line.
- Divide the measurement in half. Make a tick mark along the horizontal border that was measured.
- Draw a vertical construction line from the top of the page to the bottom.
- Lightly label with a CL as a reminder of the line's purpose.

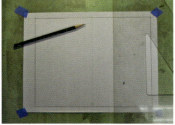

Figure 8.10 Steps in Laying Out the Center Line of a Page

After locating the page's center line, distribute tape measures and have teams of two collect the room's measurements. Measure the base of walls wherever possible. Cinderblock walls usually have reasonably level horizontal mortar lines that can be used if the floor is inaccessible in places; be sure the tape doesn't sag and add inches to the dimension.

Placement of doors, windows, and other openings should be noted with tick-marks and labels. The drafting conventions for these elements will be discussed later.

Figure 8.11 Lilliana Measures the Classroom

Figure 8.12   Centering a Generic Room Perimeter on the Page

When most of the teams have gathered their measurements, call the students back to their tables and demonstrate how to center the groundplan on the page using the center line. See Figure 8.12.

- Measure halfway up the center line. Make a tick mark.
- Draw a horizontal construction line across the paper through the mark.
- Ask for the overall length of the room.
- Divide the distance in half.
- Mark this half measurement on the horizontal line *outward from the center line*; there will be a tick mark to the right and a mark to the left. The distance between the marks should equal the overall width of the room.
- Draw vertical construction lines through the tick marks.
- Ask for the overall depth of the room.
- Divide the distance in half.
- Mark this half measurement along the center line above the horizontal line, and again below the horizontal line. The distance between the marks should equal the overall depth of the room.
- Draw horizontal construction lines through the tick marks.
- A rectangle centered in the middle of the paper should be the result. If the room has no indentations, alcoves, or notches, except for openings, the plan is done.
- Depending on the irregularities of the room's perimeter, have the students pick a corner of the rectangle and work their way around it, measuring, marking, drawing, measuring, marking, drawing. The original rectangle was a tool to center the drawing, and depending on the room's details, the perimeter being drawn may deviate from it. Trust the measurements.

Homework: Perimeter of the Room

For the next session, students are to bring in a finished drawing of the room's perimeter. The border and all required visible lines should be darkened. The center line should be included with the correct line type and symbol. Depending on the size of the room and the size of the paper used, this will be in either ¼" = 1'-0" or ½" = 1'-0" scale.

Exercise: Perimeter of Your Bedroom

An alternate version of this project calls for the student to measure and draw the perimeter of his or her bedroom. If everyone completes the plan of the classroom within the session, this can be a good follow-up homework exercise.

Session Break: End of Week 8, Day 1.

TEACHING TIP

Design Elements Everywhere

The more often the instructor connects classroom content to the students' everyday lives, the more likely the students will retain concepts and understand the relevance of those concepts. Keep an eye out for everyday occurrences and encounters that can be turned into exercises.

One such exercise emerged when Tracey came across an online catalog for decorative false fingernails. The patterns on offer were divided into categories with titles such as 'trendy' and 'classic.' We used this as a quick review of the design elements at the start of the next session.

The catalog images were projected and the students were asked to use the vocabulary of design elements to analyze the decorative patterns and match a category title to each set of images. They were asked to argue their case, and when the category titles were revealed, discuss why they thought the manufacturer chose that category title.

Homework Follow-Up: Classroom Perimeters

At the beginning of the next session, the classroom perimeter drawings are discussed. We bring them all together and spread them out on a table, gathering the students around so all the work can be seen side by side. Students are asked what they had trouble with, what was easy, and where, if anyplace, confusion occurred. The following questions address what we find to be the most common issues:

- Are there discrepancies between measurements and reality?

  - Since the room is right there around you, it's easy to point out where things went awry. Remind students to trust their measurements rather than rely on what they *think* the room looks like.

- Are the drawings in appropriate scale?

  - If students are still unsure how to read a scale ruler, review it, using one of the drawings.

- Are the visible lines solid and black?

  - Point out the most solid, black, consistent line on the page as a goal for next time

- How were doors, windows, and other openings depicted? (This can serve as a segue into graphics standards and symbols.)

TEACHING TIP

For some students presenting work before the class is a terrifying experience, as they believe not only that all their weaknesses and deficiencies are on display but that they are being personally singled out and used as an example of poor work. Some of this can be mitigated by the following pedagogical strategies:

- Keep comments within the single piece of work being discussed, rather than overtly comparing different students' work ("if you look at this one, here's how you *should* have done it").
- On any project, note the good things, however small, first.
- Even on the best projects, note something that can be worked on (there usually is).
- Keep comments technically based.
- Note that this is a single step, and the next time will be better.
- If a project is particularly disastrous and you know the student to be fragile, don't get to it. Pick a handful of examples, make your point, and move onto the next class activity. Speak with the remaining students individually during the following work sessions, or collect them for a written response.

Once a student becomes defensive or combative, behavior rather than work becomes the focus of the class. If a student appears on the edge of an emotional reaction, it may be best to move on to the next project and have a quiet one-on-one conversation after class to determine what was going on.

Scenic Design Vocabulary

Masking refers to the various curtains (soft-goods) and flats used to hide the backstage and overhead equipment from the audience

Leg a vertical curtain used to hide the offstage (wings) from the audience

Border a horizontal curtain used to hide overhead equipment and pipes from the audience

Sightlines designers will use the extreme seats in the audience to determine if offstage and overhead spaces are masked properly; if someone sitting in those seats cannot see the backstage, the rest of the audience can't either

Practical most often refers to lighting fixtures that are part of the scenic environment, such as sconces and chandeliers. Can also refer to appliances and other electrical devices

Flats refers to the temporary walls built for theatrical production; these can range from fabric-covered wooden frames to plywood-covered steel frames

Wagon a wheeled scenic unit, usually large enough to accommodate actors

Deck the bare stage floor

Discussion: What Exactly IS a Groundplan?

The groundplan is more than a drawing of a space's perimeter, or the simple placement of objects within that perimeter. The groundplan views the stage floor from above, but is more than an aerial snapshot. It is a "conventionalized horizontal offset section."[3] This means that the theatre and scenery are sliced horizontally (a cutting plane) somewhere around shoulder height above the stage floor (see Figure 8.13). Any vertical element sitting on the stage floor that is taller than the cutting plane will be cut through, revealing its interior or

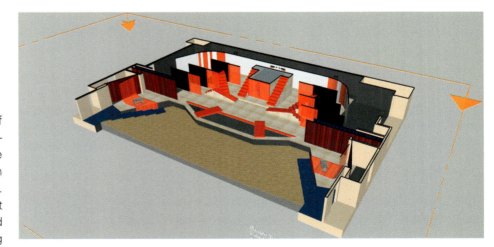

Figure 8.13 Horizontal Section of Virtual Model of Set for *The Coronation of Poppea*, UW–Whitewater, Scenic Designer Eric Appleton

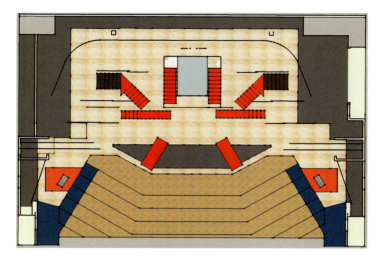

Figure 8.14 Top View of *The Coronation of Poppea*'s Horizontal Section

thickness. There are, of course, exceptions (such as staircases, platforms), and graphics standards and conventions supply a variety of symbols and diagrams to provide maximum logic and clarity.

Figure 8.14 shows the section of the model of *The Coronation of Poppea* oriented to approximate a standard groundplan; however, this is just a top view of the horizontal section, and there is a fair amount of necessary information missing.

After explaining the overall concept of the groundplan, show examples to the class, both from department productions and other sources, such as textbooks (see the earlier book recommendations). If possible, bring out a couple of sets of drawings (whether hand-drafted or drafted with a CAD program). We find that students are usually wowed by the sheer amount of information that must be generated to move a show into and through a scene shop; up to this point, most of them, even those regularly working in the scene shop, have never seen all the drawings for a single show in one package. Students also tend to exhibit a bit of relief that they are not being asked to conquer the whole mountain, but rather a single, low foothill.

This is also an opportunity to model behavior for those students pursuing design, showing what will be expected of them when they commence their first realized designs. If your experience is not in scenic design, this is a good moment to invite a colleague or guest to present materials to the class.

Guide the students through an exploration of a groundplan by pointing out features like:

- The center line
- The plaster line (if extant)
- Walls and flats
- Platforming
- Masking
- Architectural features
- Furniture and set dressing placement
- General notation methods (dimensioning, platform heights, labeling)
- Border and title block
- Sightlines
- Practicals (lighting fixtures, both hanging and mounted)
- Movement of elements, like wagons (denoted with phantom lines)

If you have scenic groundplans for theatres in different configurations (proscenium versus thrust), note the similarities and differences between the drawings. If you have the complete set of drawings for a production, note how the other drawings all connect back to the groundplan, expanding upon the information first encountered on this drawing. We prepare a handout of groundplans culled from a variety of sources for the students to use as a reference when preparing their final project's plan.

Exercise: Quick Coordinate Demonstration

Use a sample regularly scaled groundplan (either ½" = 1'-0" or ¼" = 1'-0") to demonstrate the use of the center line/plaster line coordinate system.

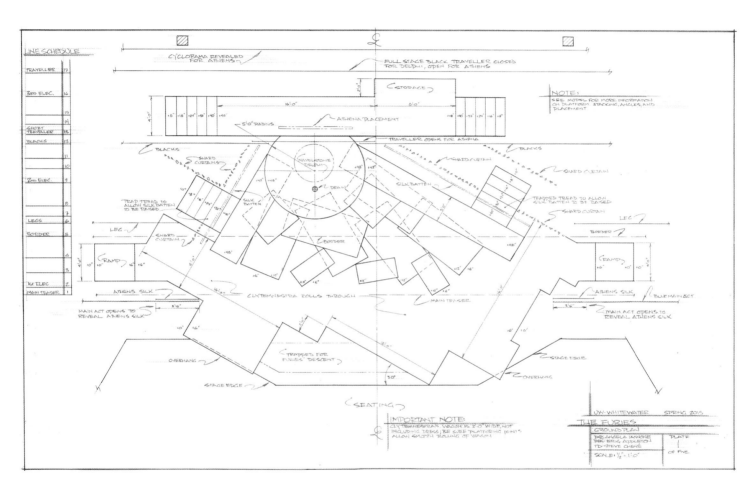

Figure 8.15 Hand-Drafted Groundplan, *The Furies*, UW–Whitewater, Scenic Design by Eric Appleton. The UW–Whitewater's Barnett Theatre Does Not Have an Architectural Proscenium; Therefore There is No Plaster Line

- Identify an item on the groundplan.
- Using the center line and plaster line as axes, ask students to measure the coordinates of various items or locations on the groundplan.

If time and space allow, take some of these coordinates into your theatre and place them on the stage. This reinforces the real-world application of the measurements, and helps students develop a mental sense of distance and proportion.

Discussion: Graphics Standards

There are two basic ways to provide much of that information missing from the pictorial groundplan (such as Figure 8.12): symbols and labels.

On the classroom perimeter project we find that some students will attempt to draw doors or add dimensions. This leads to a discussion of drafting graphics standards that are used to depict elements like doors, windows, platforming, and stairs. Some of these have been pointed out on the sample groundplans presented to the class; now a handout is distributed and the most common symbols are discussed. See Figure 8.16 for a small selection of the United States Institute for Theatre Technology (USITT) standard symbols most useful at this stage. Dimensioning, while important, is beyond the goals of this class. Inclusion of non-standard format dimensioning tends to confuse drawings, so we instruct students to refrain from adding it.

Be sure to use the board to demonstrate the most used symbols, such as doors, windows, and archways.

There are also a few more drafting conventions and line weight issues that are brought up at this time:

- Hidden lines
- Phantom lines
- Cross hatching (or shading) cut-through elements

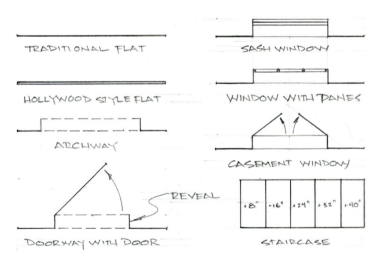

Figure 8.16 A Small Selection of Useful USITT Standard Graphic Symbols

- Soft goods (with and without fullness)
- Heights of decking, stairs, and platforms
- Practicals

A **hidden line** shows an object behind, above, underneath, or otherwise obscured by another object. It is a series of short, equally sized and equally spaced dashes:

Figure 8.17 Line Type for Hidden Line

There are conventions for how hidden lines intersect other types of lines, but at this point the introduction of the line type is usually enough (consult the recommended drafting books for this advanced information).

A **phantom line** is generally used to note the position or movement of items that change in the course of the show, such as a wagon that is moved into position only for scene three. This line is two short dashes followed by a longer dash (longer than the dashes of the hidden line):

Figure 8.18 Line Type for Phantom Line

To emphasize elements with architectural meaning (whether a column on the stage or the walls of the theatre itself), the interior of the object is **cross-hatched** to show that it has been cut through by the horizontal section plan and extends well above it. These are black lines at a 45 degree angle, and are thinner than the visible lines outlining the object itself. Since this is a tedious process for large items, we also allow shading. A piece of masking tape 1/8″ from the edge of a triangle can make this task somewhat easier and more uniform.

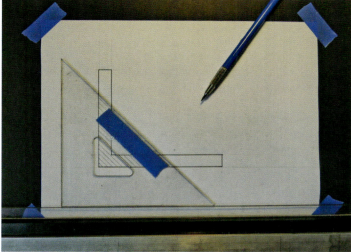

Figure 8.19 Tape on a Triangle Makes Cross-Hatching Easier

Soft goods include legs, borders, drops, and cycloramas. There is some variation on drawing these, depending on the source. Most agree that fabric with fullness (pleats and folds) is to be shown by a wavy line. However, most students are unlikely to possess a template that allows uniformity, and sketching folds freehand is seldom satisfactory. We use USITT graphic standards, which call for solid lines for drapes (legs) regardless of fullness, and dashed lines for borders (because they are hanging *over* the stage), also regardless of fullness.[5]

Figure 8.20 Lines for Soft Goods Without Fullness

A **practical** is any lighting or electrical device that appears on stage as part of the scenery. Depending on the item, scenic designers vary in how they depict these. We turn to the standard symbol used by lighting designers to denote practicals: a triangle drawn with a simple geometric shapes template available from most office supply stores.

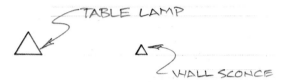

Figure 8.21 Labeled Triangles Denoting Practicals

While symbols get most of the message across, labeling is still essential, and pretty much everything except the architecture of the theatre itself can benefit from the clarity a label provides. There are two basic placements for a label:

1. Within the object itself
2. Using a **leader line** to connect the label to the object

A label should be placed within an object only if there is ample room to do so. Curved, mirrored lines like the arms of a galaxy with dots on their ends can be used to denote the object itself or a treatment of the object's surface.

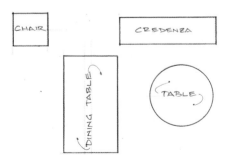

Figure 8.22 Examples of Labels Within Objects

A label placed cutside of the object it refers to is connected to the object with a **leader line**. The leader line may be straight or curved – choose one style and be consistent. If using curves, be simple and unobtrusive. Leader lines always start from either the beginning or the end of the words comprising the label. If indicating the perimeter of an object, the leader line ends in an arrowhead. If indicating a feature or quality in the interior of the object's outline, the line ends with a dot.

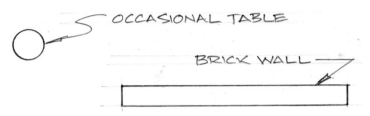

Figure 8.23 Examples of Labels with Leader Lines with Arrowheads

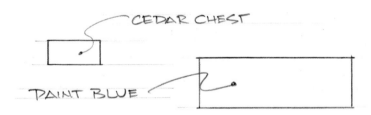

Figure 8.24 Examples of Labels with Leader Lines with Dots

Finally, the one dimension we do ask students to include is that of deck and stair heights. This measurement breaks with the convention of noting measurements in feet and inches, using *only* inches. A platform that is six feet above the permanent stage floor is noted as being + 72". The stage floor itself is noted as being at + 0". Every flat surface upon which actors are expected to tread must have a height notation.

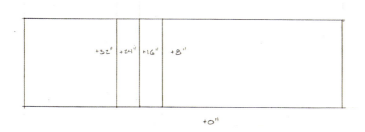

Figure 8.25 Noting Heights of Platforms and Steps

Homework: Drafted Groundplan of 'Your First Set Design'

Begin this project in class. Be sure students have paper large enough to draft their 'Your First Set Design' in ½" = 1'-0" scale (14" x 17" is usually adequate). They will need their models. The handout of furniture footprint sizes will also be useful.

- Lay out the paper's borders with construction lines.
- Lay out the paper's center line, labeled lightly for reference.
- Center the footprint of the model on the page. This can be done as per the centering instructions in the earlier exercise. Since the model is already in ½" = 1'-0" scale, it can be placed on the paper and eyeballed for centering up and down the page (see Figure 8.26). Make a tick mark on the center line at the bottom of the paper where the apron crosses. Everything else can then be measured using this mark as the initial reference point.
- Using their models, measure the placement of all items and transfer those measurements to the groundplan.

  - Scale rulers don't always fit into models, and have space at their ends to note the scale being used. To transfer measurements in awkward places, lay a strip of paper down and mark the two ends of the measurement. Use

Figure 8.26 Centering the Plan by Eyeballing the Model

Figure 8.27 Abigail Works on Her Groundplan with Measurements Taken from the Model

the scale ruler to measure the distance marked on the strip of paper.

- Lay everything out in construction lines. Darken visible lines *only* when everything is placed.
- Include legs and architecture
- Include the center line and plaster line in correct line type
- Label appropriately

This is unlikely to be completed during the session, and is due at the start of the next session.

Homework: Prep for Final Scenic Project

The due date for the final scenic project is approaching (see the end of Chapter 7 for the full project guidelines). To ensure that students are on track, the following items are also due the next class session. We list them on a handout so that students know exactly what is expected.

- Revised Metaphor Statement

  - If the metaphor used in the costume section still works well for the student they do not have to change it. This statement should, however, open up the discussion of the design elements to address the overall environment of the play.

- Central Image

  - If the central color image used for costume design works it can be retained. However, for scenery we do ask the students to go a bit further and try to connect the image with the metaphor and in some way speak to the whole of the play. The student should be able to pull a selected number of design elements from the image, such as color palette, use of line, space, shape, etc.

- Twenty research images

  - These can be specific detail or general atmosphere. Notes are to be included on how each image is to be used.

- List of locales with essential items

  - This is a list of all the locales traveled to in the course of the play, with a list of the absolutely essential physical elements required for each. Much of this information can be gleaned from the earlier French Scene Breakdown exercise.

Homework: The Large Stage House for Final Scenic Project

The final scenic project will be housed in a slightly larger stage house than the one used for the 'Your First Set Design' assignment. Since the students have already built one stage house, we do not review or work on this one in class. The students are given a handout with the parts layout and assembly instructions (Figures 8.28 through 8.30). We suggest they complete the stage house by the in-class work session in Week 9 so it can be used to inform visuals and proportions. It is not due, however, until the final scenic project is due.

Portfolio Development Projects

'Your First Set Design' can be the centerpiece of a portfolio entry that brings together process and final product.

Your First Set Design

Photograph the model from the front. You may need to provide more illumination, which can be done with desk lamps or in your department's light lab. Avoid camera flashes, as they flatten everything and wash out color.

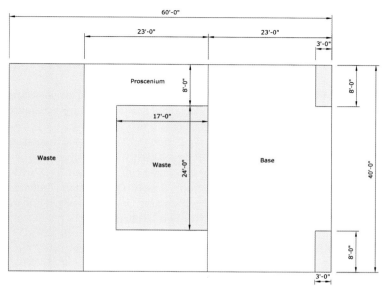

60'-0"

23'-0"   23'-0"

3'-0"

Proscenium   8'-0"   8'-0"

17'-0"

Waste   40'-0"

Waste   24'-0"   Base

8'-0"

3'-0"

Large Stage House for Final Project
Parts Layout Sheet One
Black Foamcore
Build in 1/2" = 1'0" Scale

Figure 8.28 Layout for Sheet One of the Large Stage House

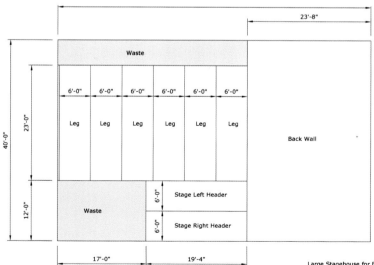

23'-8"

Waste

6'-0" 6'-0" 6'-0" 6'-0" 6'-0" 6'-0"

23'-0"

40'-0"

Leg   Leg   Leg   Leg   Leg   Leg

Back Wall

6'-0"   Stage Left Header

12'-0"

Waste

6'-0"   Stage Right Header

17'-0"   19'-4"

Large Stagehouse for Final Project
Parts Layout for Sheet Two
Black Foamcore
Build 1/2" = 1'0"

Figure 8.29 Layout for Sheet Two of the Large Stage House

Assembly of the Large Stage House (for final scenic design project)

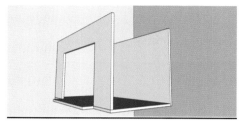

Step One: Attach the back wall to deck. Note that back wall does *not* sit on the deck, but attaches to the back edge of the deck.

Step Two: Attach the proscenium to the deck. The proscenium sits on the deck, flush with the notch cut from the apron.

Step Three: Attach wing headers on right and left flush to the tops of the proscenium and back wall.

Step Four: (not shown) *After your scenic design is complete*, place masking (legs) where necessary.

Figure 8.30 Assembly Instructions for the Large Stage House

On the portfolio page, include:

- Prominent photograph of the model from the front, labeled
- The drafted groundplan of the model, labeled
- Title of play, with author and name of scenic designer
- Statement of working metaphor, with explanation of design elements
- Image of house exterior, labeled, with usage notation
- Other research images, labeled, with usage notation

Arrange the elements in a way that illustrates the process. Present the model's front view first, then lead the reader to the statement, through the research images, and finally to the groundplan.

Notes

1. Darwin Reid Payne, *Theory and Craft of the Scenographic Model* (Carbondale: Southern Illinois University Press, revised edition, 1985), p. xvii.
2. Kevin Lee Allen, *Vectorworks for Entertainment Design: Using Vectorworks to Design and Document Scenery, Lighting, and Sound* (New York: Focal Press, 2015), p. 1.
3. Dennis Dorn and Mark Shanda, *Drafting for the Theatre* (Carbondale: Southern Illinois University Press, 1992), p. 165.
4. USITT website, http://www.usitt.org/about/, accessed 3/17/2016.
5. USITT Education Committee, *Scenic Design and Technical Production Graphic Standards* (Syracuse: United States Institute for Theatre Technology, 1992, reissued 1999), p. 9.

Chapter 9

Week 9

Since the scenic design final project and the professional designer presentation are due in Week 10, this week is about synthesizing the previous weeks' material and guiding student progress on groundplans and models for the final project.

> "Obviously a director is not going to wax enthusiastic over an embryonic sketch, even if you are confident of the beauty that still resides in your cranium . . . A bold, simplified ground plan should accompany same . . . First, all structural boundaries, such as proscenium, back and side walls, are marked in with heavy lines. The center and curtain lines are added, the opaque walls of the set itself drawn in solid line, openings (windows, doors, arches) in dotted lines, elevations indicated with the heights noted (+2'-0", for instance) and the important features added in outline."[1]
>
> Howard Bay, *Stage Design*

The framing topics for this week are:

- Research

  - Using Essential Gesture Exercises to Analyze Research Imagery
  - Incorporation of Research Imagery in Model Construction

- Design Mechanics

  - Homework Follow-up: Groundplans and Final Project Items

- Development of Groundplan for Final Project
- In-Class Model Work Sessions

Supplies Needed

Instructor supplies:

- Collage materials (such as magazine and newspaper clippings)
- Handout of blank Large Stage House groundplan
- 3 x 5 cards

Student supplies:

- Charcoal
- Cardstock or Bristol board
- Scissors
- Glue sticks
- Cellophane tape

Homework Follow-Up: Drafted Groundplan of 'Your First Set Design'

The first activity of this session is a review of the drafted ground-plans for 'Your First Set Design.' We spread them out so everyone can see them side by side, then ask the students what they discovered: what was easy; what was hard; what, if anything, surprised them one way or another. After a brief discussion, the work is collected for evaluation.

This project is a low-percentage grade. Evaluation is based on answers to the following questions, with written responses to each.

- Is the drawing in consistent ½" = 1'-0" scale?
- Are center and plaster lines present with correct line types?

- Are architectural elements, like the back wall and proscenium, crosshatched or shaded?
- Are soft goods like legs shown with correct line type?
- Are furniture and other items placed as reflected by the model?
- Are the furniture and other items drawn in the correct size/proportion?
- Are all scenic components, including masking, labeled?
- Are visible lines consistently thick and black?
- Is there a border?
- Notes on general neatness.
- Other:

Comments on dramatic mechanics and aesthetics can be placed in 'other,' but since the project is about drafting, be sure that the grade is based on drafting. If the component is present and in an acceptable state, "*yes*" is all the response required for that question.

Homework Follow-Up: Central Metaphor Image, Research, List of Locales

After reviewing the groundplans we move to the other homework that was due today.

Because this homework keeps the students on track as they approach the due date for the scenic design final project, this is also a low-percentage grade. Since we discuss the items in class, we base a pass/fail grade solely on whether all four components are present.

- Revised Metaphor
- Central Metaphor Image
- 20 Research Images
- List of Locales with Essential Items

Ask each student to:

- Share their metaphor statement and specifically address how they expect to apply the selected design elements to the environment they are about to build

Figure 9.1   Abigail Presents Her Central Metaphor Image to the Class

- Present their central metaphor image, connecting it to the metaphor and discussing the design elements they intend to extract
- Present three to six of their research images and explain how they expect to use them
- Select one of the play's locales and explain what physical elements are absolutely required by the action of the play, as well as how the appearance of those items is influenced by research and design element choices.

Thumbnails and Essential Gestures

At this point, some students may even have begun doodling. If possible, ask students to share their thumbnail sketches with the class and talk about what they were exploring through the drawing.

Figure 9.2 Mason Works on Thumbnail Sketches

Exercise: Quick Thumbnail Sketches

At this point, the students have a lot of raw material and some of them are just now starting to mentally picture their play's scenic environment. This brief exercise can help them firm up some of their ideas and express them visually. Direct the students to:

- Take out their metaphor statement and list of associated design elements
- Select the single research image that they feel best applies to the whole of the play
- Spend a few minutes considering which desired design elements are most evident in the image
- Use the 3 x 5 notecard to represent the proscenium arch of the theatre space
- Use charcoal to interpret the lines, shapes, textures, etc., of the image into the imagined theatre space.

  - Avoid representation of details and objects; don't try to draw a set.

If the student's play has multiple locales or settings, direct them to select those images that best represent the feeling of each. Use charcoal to create a series of cards, one for each major change of locale.

When discussing the cards, ask the students:

- Are there areas of light and dark?

  - Where are they located?
  - How might they translate into components of the realized stage environment?

- What shapes were used?

  - Where are they located?
  - How might they translate into components of the realized stage environment?

- If a series of cards were produced, what similarities track through them?

  - What are their differences?

- Does anything on the card suggest particular scenic components, such as hanging pieces, walls, or tall platforms?
- Rather than presenting an image of the stage from the audience's view, could one of the cards suggest shapes that could be used in a groundplan?

Exercise: Essential Gestures in Three Dimensions

The following is a quick three-dimensional project to help nudge students away from literal thinking and explore the possibilities a more abstracted approach can offer. It's also a good exercise to jumpstart stalled design thinking and continues linking the stage space with the design elements generated by the metaphor statement.

Supply the students with one sheet of cardstock, scissors, glue sticks and transparent tape.

Direct each student to:

- Distill their chosen play into two adjectives
- Choose one geometric shape that somehow speaks to the play
- Write these three words down. The instructor then collects and redistributes the lists at random
- Using *only* variations of that geometric shape, each student builds a three-dimensional object that attempts to evoke the two descriptive terms
- A time limit of about ten minutes is adequate.

There should be no additional drawing on the objects. Transparent cellophane tape is preferable as it doesn't add color or shading to surfaces.

See Figures 9.3 and 9.4 for examples.

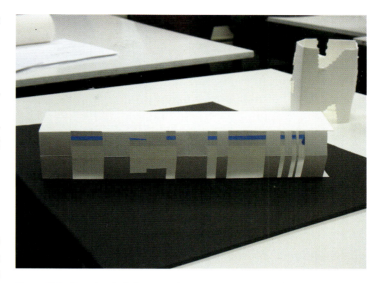

Figure 9.3   Completed 3D Essential Gesture Exercise Project (Eric Guenthner)

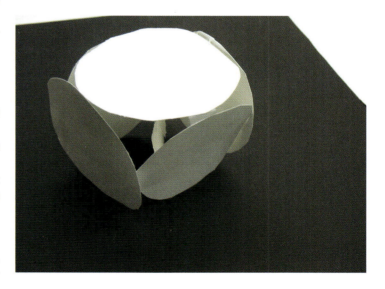

Figure 9.4   Completed 3D Essential Gesture Exercise Project (Mason Ronan)

Bring the objects together and discuss them one by one using the following prompts:

- What do you see? Describe each object using design element vocabulary.
- How do the elements work together?
- Guess the shape used, supporting with observation.
- Guess the adjectives used, supporting them with observation.
- What play is the object most likely to be associated with, and why?
- Ask the student who built the object to reveal the words used.

    - How close did the viewers get?

- Ask the student who generated the words if they think there is anything about the object that might be of use as they develop their design.

Exercise: Essential Gestures in Color and Texture

This exercise can use descriptive words related to the full-length plays used for the final projects, or can be a stand-alone in-class project using short alternative texts, such as poetry. Rather than having a different text for each student, shuffle three or four so that multiple students receive the same text. This underscores how different conclusions can be drawn from identical sources.

Provide each student with a 3 x 5 notecard, scissors, glue sticks, and collage materials. We like to plunk a random handful of images on each table, limiting what visual materials are available. Students may only use images from the closest pile. This prevents overthinking, and fosters improvisation. Do not include images with text or faces, as those allow students to tell rather than evoke.

Instruct the students to:

- Read the short text
- Distill the *feeling* of the text to two adjectives (if students have trouble with this, direct them to select two descriptive words from the text itself)

- Choose a design element (texture, shape, form, line, etc.) that is somehow evoked by the text
- Write the three words down on the back of the notecard.

The instructor collects the notecards and randomly redistributes them.

- Each student creates a collage using only the materials available to evoke the qualities of the descriptive words.

    - The collage does not have to fill the whole card.
    - The collage may exceed the boundaries of the card.
    - Materials can be rumpled, curled, or otherwise manipulated to create texture of dimension.

- A time limit of about ten minutes is adequate.

When the stopping point has been reached, collect all the collages and spread them out on a table. Select a collage and:

- Ask the class what emotive qualities are suggested by the collage, and how they believe the collage evokes them (color, shape, textures, composition, etc.)
- Reveal the words used
- Discuss whether the words suggested by the class came close to the words used. If there was variance, explore why it occurred
- Once the words are known, ask the class what text they believe was used to generate the words

    - What was it about that text that suggests those words? Images? Use of language?

- Ask the student who wrote the words to reveal the text, and explain why they chose those words.
- After a number of collages are presented and discussed, display those using the same text together. Discuss their similarities and differences.

The following is a variation of the exercise that can be used as a follow-up. This version asks the students to focus on the use of language in the text.

- Write one word that describes the use of language.
- Does the writer use short, clipped sentences? Long, complicated words? Run-on sentences?
- Choose one geometric shape that seems appropriate to the use of language. Write it on the card.
- Trade cards.
- Create collages that use only that geometric shape to evoke the language description word.
- Discuss.

These exercises can serve as a stepping stone in the creation of collages that speak to the plays used in the final projects, whether costume, scenic, or lighting. When considering the play, ask the students to start with a distillation of qualities, or the list of design elements suggested by the metaphor. Direct use of the metaphor can lead to collages that present visuals in a literal manner. For example, if the metaphor references board games the collage might end up featuring straightforward pictures of board games rather than presenting an exploration of the *qualities* of board games. Unless the intention is to create a giant board game on the stage (which is not out of the question), the qualities of board games will likely be more applicable to shaping the environment.

For plays with multiple locales it can be a useful project to build collages that reflect design elements and research images appropriate to each scene, thus creating a storyboard of visual impressions. This storyboard can reveal progression, rhythms, and cycles of the play, as well as commonalities and differences between the scenes. To unify the series, try using the same base collage materials with one or two desired design element variations per scene.

TEACHING TIP

Throughout this course, we attempt to strike a balance between presentation of the work and letting work speak for itself. Few theatre designers (or artists in general, for that matter) have the opportunity to stand before an audience and explain what it was they were attempting to convey. Indeed, if a piece of work cannot stand without the artist there to prop it up the work is of limited value to the viewer. On most smaller projects, we first ask the audience – the class – to describe what they see so that the student designer can begin to understand that what may be self-evident to the designer is not always self-evident to the viewer. This means that while personal experience remains a vital component of design, the designer must also have the ability to step outside of his or her head to determine whether the intention not only *is* being heard, but *can* be heard.

Scenic Design Vocabulary

Batten a pipe hung horizontally and laterally across the stage, used to suspend scenery or lighting equipment; in a proscenium stage, usually attached to ropes and pulleys to allow the pipe vertical movement

Lineset refers to a single complete arrangement of ropes, pulleys and batten

Fly Rail the fly rail is the area in which manual linesets are operated; normally located against either the stage left or stage right wall of the stage area

Flying/Flown refers to the act of raising and lowering items; to fly something out is to raise it up off the stage

The Flies in the proscenium theatre, the portion of the building over the stage where the battens are located when flown all the way out

Line Schedule a diagram included on a groundplan to show the placement of linesets; placed on the drawing where the fly rail is found in the venue

Turntable a large, rotating platform

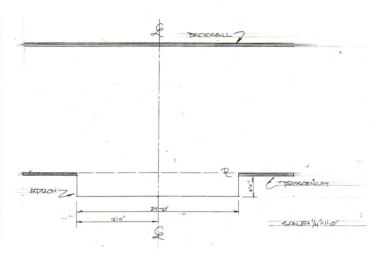

Figure 9.5 Large Stage House Floor Plan

Work Session: Rough Groundplan for the Scenic Final Project

While 'Your First Set Design' was constructed as a model first and then used to draw a groundplan, we now ask students to flip the order and work up a rough groundplan as the foundation of their model building efforts. This changes the emphasis (for a time) from aesthetics to logistics.

To help students focus on the content of the groundplan rather than the drafting of it, provide multiple photocopies per student of a scale floor plan corresponding to the dimensions of the Large Stage House handout (see Figure 9.5). Encourage the students to work in pencil, sketch freehand, and refrain from erasing, keeping the early attempts intact to inform subsequent iterations. They may make as many extra copies of the plan as needed.

For the work session, students should have with them all the materials generated thus far for this final project: metaphor statement, central research image, general research, French Scene breakdown, and locale list with essential elements. The worksheet of furniture footprints sizes is useful, and any sketches, doodles, and collages should also be present. The script should also be available for reference.

The rough groundplan is developed by trying out all the permutations that seem feasible and preferable regarding the placement of necessary items on the stage. For any play there are a number of solutions that can present themselves through experimentation. Remind students about the three basic stage configurations discussed earlier. A wing and drop arrangement can support multiple locales through a series of drops and wagons. A unit set can support multiple locales through minimal scenic elements being moved on and off as needed. A turntable might present itself as a logical solution. And of course, there are myriad hybrid solutions. Darwin Reid Payne, in *Theory and Craft of the Scenographic Model*, offers a brief list of "influences the scenographer exercises in a production" in the order he feels they are likely to be discussed. Wherever the student is heading, as you circulate, the following questions based on Payne's list can help the student clarify their thinking:

- What are the essential physical requirements for each locale?
- What approach, connected to the play through the metaphor, seems to be the best way to get from locale to locale?

  - Do actors announce location through dialogue?
  - Has the playwright offered a device for establishing location, such as signage?
  - Does the metaphor offer a mechanical suggestion, such as circles and swirls leading to the use of a turntable?

- How is the basic perimeter of the playing space established?

  - Does your metaphor suggest a shape or configuration?
  - Do you need to change the overall shape frequently?
  - Do items come on and off from the wings, or fly in and out?
  - What does the shape say about what can happen within it?

- Is it necessary to break the stage up into portions that serve as sub-locales?

  - Is it better to have every locale required by the play on stage at the same time?
  - Is it better to completely change the stage space for each locale?
  - How much detail is required in each locale?

    - If it's a realistic play taking place in three different rooms, do you require three different and complete realistically depicted rooms?

  - Does the basic space need to be broken up to accommodate locales or sub-locales?
  - What actions occur in the sub-locales?
  - How do these smaller areas relate to each other as well as to the overall space?
  - Will it be a good idea to separate these areas by height (levels) or through other means?

- How do actors access these separate areas?
- How is the space contained by scenic elements?

  - Does the play require walls or the suggestion of walls?
  - Are there stairs and ramps?
  - Are there other vertical or hung elements that can help define the space?

    - Drops, legs, borders, signage, ceilings, columns, etc.

  - How do actors pass through or among vertical elements?
  - What is the proportion of the vertical elements in relation to a human figure?[2]

We note that this design project has no budget limitations. Nor do we ask that students figure out the mechanical details of scene changes. At this point, it is more important to clearly depict the different required looks rather than worry too much about *how* the changes between looks occur unless the scene change methodology emerges logically from the design metaphor. For example, a carousel used as a central visual image can lead to the use of a turntable; a flat, pictorial approach might suggest the flying in and out of a number of painted drops.

How to depict multiple locales on the groundplan depends on the scope and nature of the changes. A unit set with relatively simple moveable items can usually be contained on a single plan, the items drawn with phantom lines and labels noting when they appear. A more complex set with objects whose placements overlap on the plan as the play progresses may require multiple drawings to provide clarity. We suggest a large primary groundplan supplemented by smaller (postcard sized) groundplans noting the various scenic arrangements, and presented chronologically. If a number of linesets for flown scenery (such as drops) are required, demonstrate how to draw a rudimentary line schedule along the side of the page (see Figure 9.6). As you circulate during the work session, ask students with multiple looks what they think to be the clearest graphic solution, and make suggestions accordingly.

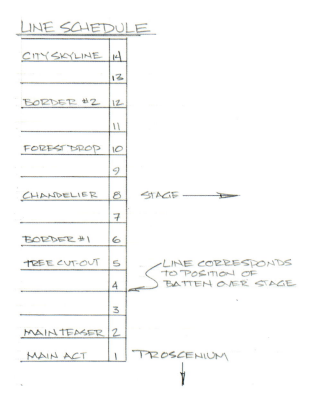

LINE SCHEDULE

CITY SKYLINE	14
	13
BORDER #2	12
	11
FOREST DROP	10
	9
CHANDELIER	8	STAGE ⟶ ▷
	7
BORDER #1	6
TREE CUT-OUT	5	LINE CORRESPONDS TO POSITION OF BATTEN OVER STAGE
	4
	3
MAIN TEASER	2
MAIN ACT	1	PROSCENIUM

Figure 9.6 Rudimentary Line Schedule

Figure 9.7 Mason Works out Measurements for Staircases on His Rough Groundplan

TEACHING TIP

Some students will approach their design from a purely logistical standpoint, settling for getting everything on and off the stage in as expedient a fashion as possible. This approach is a particular danger for plays with short, swift scenes and many, many locales. While some of these mechanical solutions will be rather ingenious (and the scenic designer *does* have to be concerned with logistics), the evaluation of the finished product relies primarily on whether the arc of the story has been explored through design metaphor and how design elements suggested by the metaphor manifest on the stage. If the technical contrivances are clearly developed through the application of the metaphor, lovely. If metaphor and design elements have been scrapped in favor of logistics, regardless of how efficient, we commend the effort but remark that the goal of the project is to present an integrated design process with design metaphor as its foundation. Evaluation will be done with that process in the forefront. In short, deliver what was promised.

Homework: The Rough Groundplan

To facilitate the best use of time during the next class's work session, students are instructed to bring in the version of the rough groundplan that they feel to be their most effective attempt. This is by no means the finished groundplan, but a start at planning the space. They are to use one of the photocopied floorplans and, while items may be drawn freehand, proportion and consistent scale must be evident.

Session Break: End of Week 9, Day 1.

Homework Follow-up: Rough Groundplans

At the start of the next session, students are asked to present their rough plans. We spread them out on a table and gather around them. Each student is asked to briefly describe their intentions and choices, once again explaining how these link back to the text through the design metaphor and selected design elements. They should also be able to discuss where and how the various locales of the play are to be accommodated. If items on the groundplan are unclear or confusing, ask the student to clarify; often the content is sound but the required graphic expression is beyond what has been covered in class. We try to keep instructor comments technically based; how better to represent something graphically, or asking the student whether they have considered a particular aspect of the play ("I'm not sure where the tavern scene is played; can you tell me more about your plans for that scene?"). Larger, graver issues are addressed individually as the instructor circulates during the work session.

Scenic Design Vocabulary

Scenographer a person who is in charge of all design aspects of the production: scenery, costumes, *and* lights. It is more common to find scenographers coming out of European practice

TEACHING TIP

It might seem old-fashioned in this age of electronic teaching software and the administrative desire for the paperless classroom, but Eric still firmly believes in paper handouts. Not all students remember to look up assignments online (not to mention those students who may not have reliable internet access), and information hidden away in a folder on a website can easily be forgotten, despite any degree of electronic savvy claimed by the student. Data out of sight is often data out of mind. By handing the students a sheet of paper and then going through the content in class, students are made more accountable for missing work, or for work that clearly does not fall within a project's parameters.

"Even when designing settings where furniture and set dressing have little part, he [the designer] is expected to understand the visual language that results from the juxtaposition of objects and performers. For the fact of the matter is, that objects — singularly and in groups — can and do speak. The language, of course, is different from that of words, but it is no less eloquent or exact than that of the actor. It is, in fact, often part of the scenographer's function to send to an audience complex and meaningful signals by the use of an object or configuration of objects . . . they can amplify an actor's role or clarify a director's point of view in a situation where words would be inadequate."[3]
Darwin Reid Payne, *Theory and Craft of the Scenographic Model*

In-Class Work Day

This day recalls the plate-spinning moment at the end of the costume design section, when metaphor, research, and mechanics all came together as students began expressing their designs on croqui. For this session, the students should once again have their metaphor statement, their central metaphor image, their research, sketches and doodles, and rough groundplan on their worktable as they sit down to start expressing their thoughts as a three-dimensional environment. If they have finished the large stage house, they should bring it along so they can gauge size and proportion of objects in the space.

Before work begins, go around the room and ask the students to restate:

- The design metaphor for the play
- The design elements suggested by the metaphor
- How the student expects to use the design elements
- How they intend to use specific research images

Ask each student what specific things they intend to do with the work period. Be sure to ask to see research and other materials, especially if a student doesn't at first seem to have anything with them.

Be specific and clear regarding your expectations for a work session. It's unlikely, given the variety of plays being worked on, that a blanket goal as specific as "work on platforming," or "work on walls" will be possible. Instead, consider proposing process-based goals such as:

- "By the end of the session I would like you to explain how you will accommodate each locale of the play."
- "For those of you working on the farce, I would like to see how you intend to fit in the required number of doors."
- "By the end of class, show me how you plan to accommodate the staircase."
- "This play notes exactly what types and how many pieces of furniture are in the drawing room. By the end of the session I would like to see your research on each piece of furniture and a plan of how you intend to arrange them in the room."

This session is a time for demonstration and problem solving. In the costume section, the blank croqui provided a solid base from which to launch work, if for no other reason that the immediate task was to clothe an already existing line drawing. For the scenic project, students are faced with an empty stage house that they must somehow fill. The rough groundplan should help students overcome the paralysis of the blank stage, but some students will still believe they don't know where to begin. Patiently posing a series of questions that review what the student already knows about the environment can help break the logjam.

We have found it a good use of time to introduce the session with a few general techniques, like building up a platform to the desired height and facing it (Figure 9.8), or cutting a piece of Bristol board to create a hinged door (Figure 9.9). More specific construction needs are demonstrated as we circulate. If an item is required by multiple students, have them pause and gather around. While students are expected to experiment on their own, giving them construction tips and tricks will allow them to focus more on the content of their environment – what the chair looks like – than on wondering how they are to build that chair. Demonstrations may even free the students to

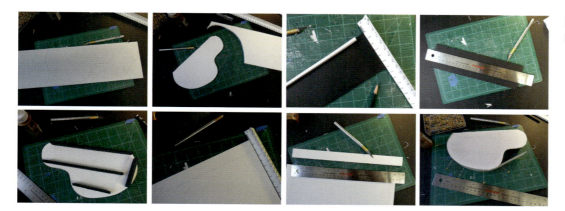

Figure 9.8 Building Up and Facing a Platform

Figure 9.9 Cutting Out a Hinged Door

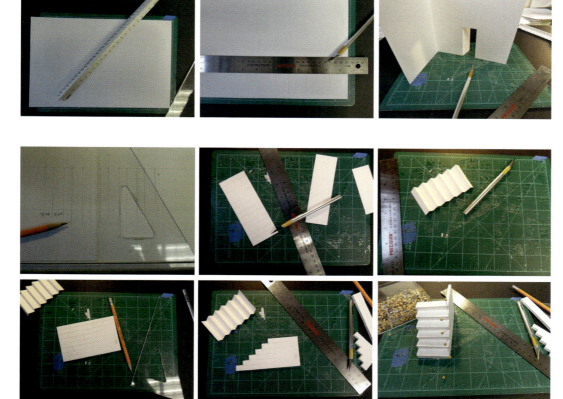

Figure 9.10 One Way to Build a Straight Staircase

explore objects and elements they hadn't before considered possible.

Ask questions that require the students to justify their choices. If one scene of the play takes place in a unique location, how does having a dedicated space on the stage for that scene contribute to the whole? Is it useful for the audience to *always see that location* as the action travels to other places? If the student can offer a compelling, script-based rationale, let them continue with that idea and see where it leads. They may come up with an interesting, workable solution. Or, they may hit a wall and need to backtrack. The path they attempted now serves as a learning experience.

For those students who have moved past the initial list of space-planning questions (the ones based on Darwin Reid Payne's list), try to keep your questions and suggestions technically-based, such as:

- How do you plan to fit in all the required doors?
- What parts of your central metaphor image are being used and how?
- Are you planning to differentiate the playing spaces with levels or by painted floor treatment?
- How does an actor access this raised area?
- Do you want the audience to see the living room while the bar-room wagon is on stage? Why?
- What's happening upstage to prevent the audience from seeing the theatre's back wall? Will there be a cyclorama, a drop, something else? Do you want the audience to see the naked back wall?
- What shapes are suggested by your metaphor statement and how do you think you'll use them?
- How are these curved walls informed by your design element choices?
- How does this turntable connect to your metaphor statement?

Figure 9.11   Eric Applies Facing to His Platforming

TEACHING TIP

This work session is not the point at which to engage in aesthetic debate and whether you, as a designer, agree or disagree with particular design choices – after all, it's not about how *you* would design the set, or even sharing what you know to be more effective and interesting choices, but rather about introducing design *process* to the uninitiated. Engaging in aesthetics can be explosively counterproductive, as students might feel it necessary to begin all over again in order to please the instructor (time will not be on their side), as well as undermine tentatively budding confidence. Some students thrive on this kind of ferment and upheaval, but unless the impetus for wholesale revision comes from the student's own dissatisfaction, we prefer to let them see how far their chosen path will take them. For our class it's always useful to keep in mind that most of the students have had only three weeks of experience learning the fundamentals of scenic design; just the fact that models are happening can be cause for celebration.

Figure 9.12 Abigail Checks Out the Proportions of a Periaktoi in Her Stagehouse

At the end of the work session:

- Comment on exciting and interesting work accomplished
- Review upcoming sessions and assignments

  - 'Professional Designer Presentations'
  - 'Presentation of Final Scenic Design Project'

- Ask if the students have any questions or concerns
- Remind the students that you are available to answer questions outside of class, and that asking questions sooner rather than later will help avoid panic
- Tell the students you look forward to seeing their finished work.

Portfolio Development Projects

Portfolio Project: Essential Gestures

The 'Essential Gesture' exercises can serve as standalone portfolio layout exercises, or, if linked to the chosen plays, can be included in the portfolio pages presenting the full scenic design project. The portfolio page should contain:

- A photo of 3D object or collage
- Explanation of project's goals

Portfolio Project: Rough Groundplan

If a drafting sample is desired, have the students redraw the rough groundplan, incorporating all the comments made during its review and evaluation, including correct graphic symbols and standards. This can be done by hand, or can serve as an early introduction to computer drafting programs. The portfolio page should contain:

- The rough groundplan, redrafted on standard sized drafting paper or vellum
- Title of show, with the name of the draftsperson
- Any visuals that help support the groundplan, such as thumbnail sketches and research images. Include labels that explain how these items contribute to the development of the groundplan.

Notes

1. Howard Bay, *Stage Design* (New York: Drama Book Specialists, 1974), pp. 104–105.
2. Darwin Reid Payne, *Theory and Craft of the Scenographic Model* (Carbondale: Southern Illinois University Press, 1985), pp. 94–95.
3. Payne, pp. 115–116.

Chapter 10

Week 10

Within the two projects of this week, we will address all of the framing topics:

- Formal Presentation of a Professional Scenic Designer

  - Metaphor
  - Design Principles
  - Script Analysis
  - Research
  - Design Mechanics

- Formal Presentation of Student's Final Scenic Design Project

  - Metaphor
  - Design Principles
  - Script Analysis
  - Research
  - Design Mechanics

As with the costume section, the scenic section culminates in the presentation of two big projects. In this week, those students who were assigned a scenic designer in the first week of class will make their presentations. *All* of the students will present their final scenic design projects. This chapter is primarily about the evaluation of these projects.

Scenic Designer Presentations

The guidelines for this presentation can be found at the end of Chapter 2. The overall expectations for the presentations remain the same, whether for costume, scenery, or lighting. Since students have much longer to prepare this presentation and have also been through the first round, this second round should be even stronger.

It was noted earlier that Tracey prefers rubrics for evaluation while Eric prefers a long-form question-based evaluation. In this format the same basic questions from the rubric are posed,

but without a numeric score. Notes are taken for each question as the presentation progresses. If the presenter does not address an issue, this is noted. If the student offers a rationale for not addressing an issue, such as lack of usable images, this is also noted. Afterwards, we compare notes and the evaluation with full notes is typed up and given to the student. No grade is released without the receipt of a bibliography. If the listed resources are particularly weak, Eric will include a detailed response to the bibliography, including additional sources the student might have considered or a more in-depth look at ones the student *did* cite.

Designer Presentation Evaluation Format

Student's Name:

Professional Designer:

1. What does your designer feel is the role of design in a production?
2. Do they have a particular design approach or philosophy, and what is it?
3. What do they hope to add to a production through their design?
4. Give examples of the designer's use of metaphor and visual research.
5. Does the designer talk about how they use the elements of design (interviews, quotes, video)?
6. What characterizes their work? Does the designer have a particular style recognizable from show to show?
7. Show and discuss no fewer than two but no more than four examples (an example is the whole of a single work, not a single photo of a work) of their production work.
8. Discuss the designer's use of line, shape, form, space, texture, color.

   - How do the design elements contribute to creating an effective/meaningful environment?

9. With how much depth and detail are the images discussed?
10. How was the overall quality of the presentation?

- Was it organized?
- How credible were the sources?
- General neatness and oral presentation skills

Other Notes:

Grade:

The Scenic Design Final Project

For this project we again use the KCACTF guidelines for format. Expectations for the oral presentation follow the same lines as those for the costume design project. The materials expected as part of the presentation include:

- A Title Block with show title, author, name of designer
- Metaphor Statement

  - The statement should have been revised to reflect adaptations to the scenic environment and include discussion of design elements.

- Central Metaphor Image

  - This serves as a cohesive visual encapsulation of the metaphor, and the student is expected to explain how this image is used to inform subsequent design element choices.

- Research Images

  - A wide range, both abstract and of physical detail, with notation regarding how various elements will be incorporated into the scenic environment.

- Color Palette

  - This can either be a stand-alone color swatch page or indicated by notes on the research images. While the model does not include color, the student should be able to talk about how they intend to use color throughout the environment.

- White Model

  - In ½" = 1'-0" scale
  - Presented in the appropriate black foamcore stagehouse
  - Appropriate human figure present
  - As much detail as possible: 3D standing furniture, drops, rugs, doors, artwork on walls, etc.
  - The student may include grayscale photocopied surfaces where texture or detail is important, or detail is beyond current drawing ability
  - Include masking (legs and borders)

Figure 10.1   Abigail Presents Her Final Project for *She Stoops to Conquer*

Figure 10.2   Mason Presents His Final Project for *Boeing Boeing*

Figure 10.3   Bridget Presents Her Final Project for *Boeing Boeing*

- Rough Groundplan

  - This is drawn on the supplied ¼″ = 1′-0″ scale plan of the stage house
  - Center and plaster lines included
  - Appropriate line type and symbols as required
  - Masking
  - Labels
  - If there are multiple arrangements, multiple plans may be needed

Evaluating the Scenic Design Final Project

Once again, we compare notes on the oral and visual presentation. Examine each project individually and write up the evaluation, including content from the oral presentations. The following is the format Eric uses to evaluate these projects:

Final Scenic Design Project Evaluation

Name:

Title of Play:

1. Are all the elements (*metaphor statement, supporting research, model, color representation, groundplan*) present and in the most presentable state possible? Did you pay attention to craftsmanship in your model and presentation materials?
2. Can you clearly articulate the action and relationships of the play and how your design metaphor connects to them? Are your design ideas clearly rooted in the world of the play?
3. Have you done adequate visual research not only to inform mood and atmosphere, but also for real items and locations? Can you clearly articulate the path this material took from page to stage?

4. Have you made a credible attempt toward the style (realism, abstract, period, etc.) you have chosen for your play?
5. Is your model in the correct scale throughout? Is there an appropriate human figure?
6. If you have multiple looks, does your model allow for these changes?
7. Does the groundplan reflect decisions presented in the model? Is it in scale (on the scale template that was handed out)? Are elements present and labeled? Have you used the correct symbols and conventions to represent items such as doors, stairs, and windows?
8. Have you made color/texture choices, and can you articulate how they are drawn from your visual research and design metaphor?

Other Notes:

Grade:

Wherever possible and appropriate, go beyond simple "yes" or "no" responses to provide substantive affirmation of good practice or constructive and actionable criticism for issues and problems.

Presentation by a Guest Artist

When class size is small, the designer presentations do not take up the entirety of our one hour and forty-five minute session. The extra time can be designated as a work session for the upcoming final project, or can be used to gently segue into the next section with a relevant video or film. The American Theatre Wing's website (www.americantheatrewing.org) offers a number of excellent videos of designers talking about their work.

Other times, we are able to invite someone to speak to the class. Our institution is about an hour's drive from Milwaukee, WI, and we work hard to maintain ties with the professional community there. Depending on the year's budget there is sometimes funding for small stipends to entice local designers into spending a morning on our campus. If the location of your institution is not conducive to reaching out to professional designers, consider asking a member of another department to speak on media techniques or a period of art history relevant to one of the texts.

Guests can make a number of important contributions to the learning environment of the class:

- Alternate, yet equally viable approaches
- Corroboration of class content and methods
- Introduction to professional networking
- Familiarization with local or regional companies
- Information (and proof) on making a career in the field

Figure 10.4 Milwaukee-Based Scenic Designer Brandon Kirkham Presents His Work to the Class

Portfolio Development

This is the pinnacle of the scenic design work and like the costume design should be prominently displayed in the expanding portfolio. As before, process is an important feature of the layout. The intent of the design should be clear and the application of that intent to the design will be the litmus test by which success is gauged.

Depending on the preferred format, convert materials into a size dictated by the paper portfolio, or digitize elements for electronic presentation.

Condense the material so it can be displayed on either two facing paper portfolio pages (24″ x 18″ is a good size) or two sequential PowerPoint (or equivalent) pages. Depending on the size and complexity of the design more pages may be desired. Unless it's a particularly show-stopping project whose detail and complexity must be wholly displayed for comprehension of the work's totality, keep in mind that a portfolio is also meant to show a designer's *breadth* of work.

Regardless of delivery system, the portfolio pages for the scenic design should include:

- A Title Block

  - Name and Author of play
  - Name of Designer
  - Date of Design
  - Name of Director (if extant)
  - Name of Venue (if extant)

- Metaphor Statement (condensed to a single paragraph)
- Research Images, labeled and attributed
- A Photo of the Finished Model, from the front

  - If multiple locales are required, include photos of each. The most interesting or spirit-capturing one should be most prominent; others can be of reduced size.

- A Reduced Size Groundplan

  - Shrunk to fit on the page, yet readable. Be sure that other content, such as research, can also fit on the page
  - Include required information regarding major scene changes

- Sketches that contributed to the development of the final design

  - Display only the most important and evocative development sketches. These can be laid out to show progression of development or placed in proximity to what they informed.

When displaying photographs make sure the photo looks as good as the content it displays. If the portfolio is expected to go beyond the classroom, print images on photo paper or have them printed at a photo developer. Be sure that date and time watermarks sometimes automatically inserted by the camera do not make their way into the final presentation.

Section III

Lighting Design

Chapter 11

Week 11

> "The fundamental lighting of a production is outlined by the playwright's manuscript. The indications of place and time of day, demanding specific details such as lamp-light, sunlight, moonlight, etc. (which are called motivating sources) are unconsciously or consciously dictated by the playwright."[1]
>
> Stanley McCandless, *A Method of Lighting the Stage*

Instructor Supplies Needed

- Photos/images for observation and analysis
- Standard Angles of Light handout
- Camera to photograph scenic models
- Light lab materials:

  - Figure (doll)
  - Four to six moveable lighting units
  - Way to control intensity of individual lighting units
  - Black background
  - White background
  - Objects to place in background of light lab

The framing topics for this week are:

- Research

  - Observation and Analysis of Light in Images

- Design Mechanics

  - Stage Lighting Vocabulary
  - The Functions of Light
  - The Controllable Properties of Light
  - The Standard Angles of Light

Our Approach to Lighting Design

We focus on naturalistic, motivated lighting as the foundation of meaningful theatrical light. One reason is because motivated lighting can be demonstrated by doing something as simple as turning the room's overhead fluorescent lights on and off. The concept of naturalistic, motivated light is one that's easy for students to grasp: e.g., a scene taking place in a yard on a sunny day is lit by the sun. Once that source of light is acknowledged, the complexity then lies in creating the appropriate sunlight with available lighting equipment.

Depending on the style of the production, of course, the role of lighting can vary greatly and naturalism may not always be a goal of the designer. In some cases light becomes a more abstract tool as in dance, where the dimensional revelation of the dancer's body is a primary concern and there is often no expectation of knowing what 'real' source (like the sun) is emitting the light. For rock concerts, spectacle created by the shape and movement of beams of light through haze is a major visual element, and in many cases replaces physical scenery. A production attempting to recreate the look of an eighteenth-century drama may go so far as to replicate the footlight-driven illumination of the period. However, even these applications of light can be discussed and planned using the steps and language introduced in the following chapters.

Lighting design and technology use a lot of jargon which is very difficult to avoid. As terms are introduced to the class, be sure to define them, use them consistently, and review them as often as possible. The vocabulary boxes included in this

Book Recommendation

If you are new to and a bit frightened by stage lighting, David Hays' *Light on the Subject: Stage Lighting for Directors and Actors – and the Rest of Us* is a pleasant, short, yet thorough introduction. Full of anecdotes and gentle instruction, Hayes leads the reader through then-current equipment into conceptual tools and the working relationships between the lighting designer and other members of the production team. "Stage lighting is not a black art. It can be practiced openly."[2]

Incandescent Light source with a filament enclosed in a glass bulb; light is produced by the wire's resistance to the electricity sent through it

Conventional A lighting unit that uses an incandescent light source and has no in-built motorized movement

Lamp Non-theatre people call this a lightbulb

Light Plot A drawing that shows where each and every lighting unit is to be placed in the venue

Lighting Vocabulary Terms

Motivated light on the stage that appears to come from an identifiable source such as a sconce, chandelier, window, or the sun

Light, Unit, Fixture, Luminaire generally interchangeable terms that refer to the piece of theatrical stage equipment that emits light

Dimmer the piece of equipment which controls how much electricity is sent out to an incandescent unit, and therefore determines how bright is the light that is emitted

Console or light board, also called a desk; the piece of equipment that tells the dimmers how much electricity (or data) to send to the units

LED Light Emitting Diode; electronic light source that is fast replacing incandescent light sources due to color changing capability and reduced energy usage. Requires a high degree of electronic control

chapter are less memorization lists for the students than to help the instructor provide a definition when the need arises.

Technology plays an intimate role in lighting design and some textbooks feel that it is useful to introduce the arcana of equipment first – lay out the tools, then learn how best to use them. In our class, the first concern is to decide what the lighting should look like, and *then* worry about equipment. Learning the difference between communication tools (such as a storyboard), and execution tools (such as a light plot) is critical. Some student lighting designers conflate the completed light plot with the completed design, forgetting that the light plot is a drawing that is only one step (though admittedly a major step) in the implementation of the design. If, in a portfolio, a plot takes more precedence than photographs of the populated lit stage, it's evidence that the student designer does not yet understand this. Storyboards and research images are not only essential phases of the design process but speak a language with which directors (and the other members of the design team) are familiar.

On the other hand, for scenery and costumes physical objects manifest the design. A costume is built in the shop and worn by the actor. While it can be argued that the costume does not 'live' while hanging on a garment rack, it can still be seen and touched. Lighting, however, does not make its way to the stage in the same way. When the equipment is turned off, there is no light. Looking at the lighting units hung around the venue does not give a viewer a sense of the light that will be seen during the play. Looking at the numbers displayed on a lighting console's monitor does little to reveal the movement of light through time that will be experienced by the audience. This is one of the reasons the light plot becomes a stand-in for the lighting design as a whole; it's a physical artifact condensing all of the designer's thought about the show into a single technical drawing.

In an introductory class it remains necessary to not only talk about the light the designer intends to put on the stage, but *how* that light will eventually be put on the stage. This doesn't mean in-depth discussion of equipment, but rather, discussing factors like angles, intensity, and direction. These factors are controllable properties of light that will, down the road, help a designer figure out *where* the appropriate lighting units will be placed and how they will be controlled.

The chapters of this section will shuttle back and forth between these aspects of lighting design. The first session introduces several layers of vocabulary that will help the class discuss light more precisely. Later sessions will use script analysis and research to determine the desired light for a scene. Sketching will aid communication of those intentions. Finally, we'll develop diagrams of how that light might be created in a theatrical venue. Along the way there will be frequent trips to the light lab to try it all out.

A light lab of some sort will be extremely useful. Whereas in the scenic section, the instructor could fold a piece of cardstock and instantly have a wall, to demonstrate stage lighting you need to have equipment that produces light. Trying to teach introductory lighting in the theatre itself tends to mean spending a lot of time running from catwalk to ladder to booth for even the simplest set-up. If you do not have the resources to set up a classroom light lab, use three flashlights and a doll to demonstrate the standard angles of light (later in this chapter) and bring in more images of both the natural world and realized stage lighting to analyze. When you get to the portions of Chapters 12 and 13 that spend time building a scene in the light lab, focus instead on the half of that extended exercise that diagrams the lighting on the chalkboard. Then use Chapter 16 to explore breaking the stage into areas of control and the development of the preliminary channel hook-up.

> "I am constantly being asked, 'What kind of spotlight do you need to give afternoon sunlight?' and my only answer can be, 'Where and when do you need this sunlight?' To answer this in any other way it would be necessary to explain that for the whole approach to this subject one must have first, a credo, then an understanding of the tools, and finally, the ability to apply them."[3]
> Abe Feder, "Lighting the Play" from *Producing the Play*

Discussion: Thinking About Light

The first discussion point is how to become *aware* of light, and recognize that we can talk about light just as we can talk about the materials scenic or costume designers use to implement their designs.

We see light when it hits and is reflected by an object. This can be easily demonstrated by clapping an eraser in a beam of light from a projector or a window – before particles are introduced into the beam of light, we do not see the light as it travels through the clear air. Certain wavelengths of light (color) are absorbed by the object it hits, and others are reflected. Our eye sees the reflected light, and therefore the object appears to have the color of the reflected light (for example, plants appear green because they reflect most of the green to be found in sunlight). Color will be discussed in more depth in Chapter 13.

By manipulating the qualities of the light hitting objects, the lighting designer can manipulate the perception of those objects by changing factors like color, depth, and delineation of fore- and background. When you shine a flashlight upward from beneath your chin you change the arrangement of facial shadows we are used to seeing; the face becomes spooky because *the shadows are in the wrong places*. Since we all unconsciously carry a large assortment of mental preconceptions about the lit environments around us, the lighting designer can impart psychological meaning by adjusting the qualities of light to fit with or undermine the audience's expectations.

Naturalistic theatrical lighting design is the illusion that the light on the stage is coming from a light source logical to the world of the play, rather than from theatrical lighting equipment. In other words, if the text calls for a scene lit by a table lamp, the lighting designer is tasked with creating a look on stage that serves the psychology of the moment and appears *as though* it is being lit by the table lamp, whether or not the actors are actually illuminated by it.

Exercise: Observation and Analysis of the Light around You

Once again the classroom can serve as a laboratory of direct experience. If you teach in a room without windows, ask the students what the light was like outside the building, as they came to class. The first responses are usually weather related – sunny, cold, rainy. Use these questions to help the students to dig deeper and describe the *light*:

- How bright is the light?
- If it's overcast, where exactly is the light coming from?
- What's the angle of the light and how does it relate to the time of day?
- What color is the light?

Book Recommendation

Stanley McCandless, an instructor at Yale, developed the first systematic approach to lighting the stage. In 1932, he outlined this system in *A Method of Lighting the Stage*. His method has since influenced not just American lighting design, but theatrical American architecture throughout the twentieth century. Despite the fact that the equipment he discusses is quite out of date, the method itself remains easily understandable and is the basis of the three point lighting system discussed later in this chapter. Remember, though, that McCandless' book does not present design dogma. It is a logical, ordered system that produces naturalistic light distributed evenly across the stage. McCandless himself acknowledges as much: "Moreover the plan does not solve all the problems of lighting; it is in fact simply an effort to clear the ground for actual expression and experimentation."[4]

- Is it the light that's hot/cold or the air temperature that's hot/cold?
- Is there a relationship between light and the perception of temperature?
- How sharp are the shadows?
- Where is the light coming from that allows you to see *into the shadows*?

Use these questions to help the students examine the light in the classroom:

- How bright is the light?
- How dark are the dark places in the room?
- What color is the light?
- Does the light appear to be a different color or intensity if you look directly into the source, rather than at what the light hits?
- How many light sources are in the room? What are their differences?

- How well distributed is the light throughout the room?
- What direction do shadows fall?
- What color are the shadows?
- Do the shadows have sharp or fuzzy edges?
- How many shadows does a single object cast? If multiple shadows are cast, why?

Look at physical objects in the room, particularly white ones like table tops or painted walls.

- Are white objects uniformly white no matter where the light hits them?
- Are all the white objects the *same* white?
- Can you determine the color of shadows better on white surfaces?
- Does the shadow have its own color or is the shadow the color of the object?
- Are white objects perceived as white because we *know* they are white or because we actually *see* them as white?

Discussion: The Functions of Stage Lighting

Begin this discussion by asking the students what they think lighting provides, or does for a show. The first function offered is usually visibility – just being able to see things on the stage, especially when the performance is indoors. Make a list on the board of what the students come up with before consolidating items into the categories below.

Stage lighting serves several very specific functions through the course of a production. Most lighting textbooks are in general agreement about this list:

- **Visibility:** how well the audience can or cannot see things on the stage
- **Focus:** attention will be drawn to where the stage is brightest; the lighting designer tells the audience where to look

- **Environment**: weather conditions, time of day, season, etc.
- **Mood/Atmosphere:** linking the environment to the psychology of the moment
- **Depth/Dimension**: reveals the three-dimensional actor in a three-dimensional environment
- **Style and Genre**: helps to underscore the style of the production, such as realism, abstraction, period, comedy, tragedy, etc.

Exercise: Looking at and Describing Light using the Functions of Light

Prepare a number of images to share with the class. See Figures 11.1 and 11.2 for examples. Ask the students to describe how light functions within them. Direct them to describe the light hitting the physica objects rather than the physical objects themselves. Work your way down the list of functions, beginning with visibility. The following questions can guide the discussion:

- How well can we see objects in the image? How bright or dim is the light?
- Where does the light draw the eye first? How bright are the bright areas, how dark are the dark areas? How well distributed is the light?
- What can be determined about the atmospheric conditions and why? What time of day or season it is? How can we tell?
- Is a mood created by the light? How?
- How do objects relate to each other in the image through the placement of light? Is there a distinct difference between foreground and background? Do objects exhibit a degree of dimensionality? How are these effects created by the light?
- Is there any stylistic quality created by the light? Is the image naturalistic? Carefully staged? Is the photo manipulated through camera filters or effects?

All light is natural. Because we spend most of our time in sunlight, the effect of sunlight on the world around us has become what we are used to and any light source created by humans has been deemed artificial. The *source* of light may be 'un-natural' but the light itself is not. When a student describes light as 'natural' or 'artificial' ask them to provide specifics – the visible qualities that cause the light to seem natural or artificial. An office fluorescent fixture is no less artificial than a bonfire. However, the light emitted from a fluorescent may be described as cold, antiseptic, steady, and bright whereas the light from a bonfire might be described as warm, flickering, and intense.

Figure 11.1   Functions of Light Discussion Image #1

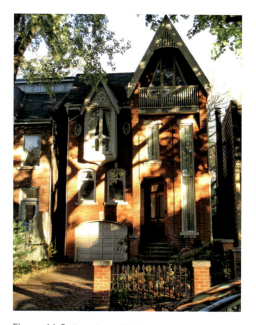

Figure 11.2   Functions of Light Discussion Image #2

Lighting Vocabulary Terms: Common Acronyms

LD Lighting Designer

ME Master Electrician. The person in charge of executing the technical aspects of the design, such as hanging the lighting units

ALD Assistant Lighting Designer

FOH 'front of house,' or the seating area of the theatre

Discussion: Standard Lighting Angles

Most theatre venues have standard places, or **positions**, where lighting equipment can be hung (see Appendix E for a list of standard lighting positions). This means that lighting designers will often use a standard vocabulary of directionality to describe their choices: for example, "the main source of light for this scene is afternoon sunlight, which will be accomplished by using **frontlight**." The term 'frontlight' means that an actor, standing on stage and looking out at the audience, is being lit by light that comes from lighting positions in front of the actor.

While the following list presents basic categories of angles, keep in mind that these are by no means the *only* angles allowable or preferable. If the lighting designer feels that a particular direction of light will create the desired effect, and can place a lighting unit where it needs to go, then it's a valid angle. By framing directions with this vocabulary the designer can describe most angles with reasonable accuracy, such as 'steep frontlight,' 'low stage left sidelight,' and 'stage right diagonal back uplight.'

Figure 11.3 presents the diagrammatic representation of standard basic lighting angles.

- **Frontlight:** illumination from the front of the performer, applying to the full range of angles possible from in front of the stage
- **Downlight:** illumination from directly above the performer
- **Backlight:** illumination from behind (upstage) the performer
- **Diagonal Backlight**: illumination from behind the performer but off to the side
- **Uplight**: illumination from below the performer, such as from footlights
- **Sidelight:** illumination from the side of the performer, ranging from floor units ('shinbusters') to those hung above the performer

After drawing the angles on the blackboard and discussing them, we distribute a handout version of Figure 11.3. This will be of use later when we begin to diagram stage lighting. The angles will also be revisited in the next class session through a light lab exercise.

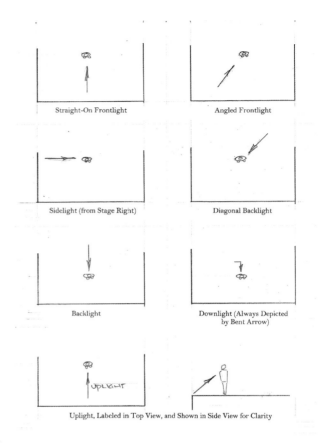

Figure 11.3 Diagrams of Standard Lighting Angles, as Seen from Above

Exercise: Using the Standard Angles to Describe Light

Prepare a number of images with a clearly directional main source of light. See Figures 11.4 through 11.6 for examples. Ask the students to describe the light using the standard angles of light vocabulary.

We tend to take shadows for granted, until they're missing or in the 'wrong' places. As demonstrated in the 'Observing

Figure 11.4 Angles of Light Discussion Image #1

Figure 11.6 Angles of Light Discussion Image #3

Figure 11.5 Angles of Light Discussion Image #2

the Light around You' exercise, shadows are an important clue in determining the direction of light. The above exercise helps students begin looking for and *seeing* shadows, since they not only indicate directionality, but provide dimensionality.

A good rule of thumb is that the light that casts the shadow is coming from the exact opposite direction to where the shadow lies.

Discussion: The Controllable Properties of Light

To achieve any of the functions of stage lighting, there are attributes of light that the designer can control:

- **Direction**: the angle of the light source relative to the part of the stage being lit (where the light comes from); the standard angles of light

- **Distribution:** how much of the stage is lit – remember, the lighting designer not only controls the light, *but also controls the darkness*
- **Intensity**: how bright the light is, how dark the dark is
- **Color:** can be used to enhance and create mood, atmosphere, etc.; can change the color qualities of scenery, costumes, and actors' complexions and should always be considered with those in mind
- **Diffuseness**: how soft or sharp is the light as revealed by shadows and beam edges
- **Shape**: beam outlines, textures, definition of objects; also the beam itself as revealed by passage through haze and dust
- **Movement**: the physical movement of a beam of light (such as a followspot or automated fixture) as well as any change in the lighting from moment to moment (cuing)

The controllable properties can also be used to more accurately analyze the light on stage or in an image. The audience's attention may be directed to an actor in a small pool of bright light that shines down from above; this focus is created through distribution (a small pool), direction (from above the actor), and intensity (bright).

Review the design elements at this point and connect the controllable properties to them. Light doesn't quite play by the same rules that scenery and costumes do; for instance, it's harder to express 'line' with lighting unless beams are revealed with the use of haze or fog. While the design elements continue to frame discussion of the overall stage environment, the controllable properties will provide a higher degree of clarity when describing light itself.

Exercise: Using the Controllable Properties to Analyze Light, Part One

The controllable properties of light provide a working language to discuss light from now on. Revisit the light in the classroom and ask the students to speak to its specific, controllable properties.

Lighting Vocabulary Terms: Color

Warm refers to colors of light that are, or contain, red, orange, and/or yellow. A warm blue, for example, is a blue that contains red, but not so much red that the color becomes violet or magenta

Cool refers to colors of light that are, or contain, blue. A cool green is a green that contains more blue than yellow, but not so much it becomes cyan

Gel transparent color media, also called simply 'color' (as in "go drop color into those units"). Commonly called gel because it was once made from gelatins and lacquers. Color media is now made from plastic

- From what direction does the main source of light come?
- How evenly spread is the light throughout the room?
- How bright is the light? Are there places where the intensity is different?
- What color is the light? If 'white' what *kind* of white? Cool, warm? Does the light seem to be bluish (cool) or amber-y (warm)?
- How soft or sharp is the light? Are shadows well defined? Are faces evenly visible?
- Does the light create any shapes – shadows on walls created by light fixtures, sunlight passing through windows or trees?
- If you are standing near light switches or curtain controls, change the illumination to demonstrate movement. Discuss the new look.

Exercise: Using the Controllable Properties to Analyze Light, Part Two

Prepare a number of photos that feature light. See Figures 11.7 and 11.8 for examples.

- Ask the students to describe the light in the photos. Don't let them jump to feelings or general atmosphere, but stick with the controllable properties.
- Start with the direction of light and go down the list of controllable properties.
- Be sure that students attempt to first describe the light in the image rather than the objects being lit.
- When the controllable properties have been thoroughly exhausted, ask the students questions connected to the **functions** of light.

  - Where is the eye directed and why?
  - Has a mood or atmosphere been created?
  - How do the controllable properties serve the function being addressed?
  - What could happen in a stage environment lit with these qualities?

Figure 11.8 Controllable Properties Discussion Image #2

Figure 11.7 Controllable Properties Discussion Image #1

Lighting Vocabulary Terms

Purpose refers to the effect a particular direction of light is intended to accomplish on stage, such as 'afternoon daylight,' 'light through window,' 'moonlight,' or 'light spilling in through open kitchen door.' A purpose can also be generalized to describe *only* the direction of light (where it comes from in the theatre), such as 'frontlight' or 'downlight.' It may also be linked to a specific part of the stage, such as 'frontlight downstage left.' However, once you stop describing the *quality* of the light it becomes less a **purpose** and more simply a note on where the lighting unit is to be focused

Practical any powered light source on the stage that is part of the scenic environment (chandeliers, table lamps, refrigerators, etc.). A chandelier is both a practical and the main source of light, though its purpose is simply noted as 'chandelier'

Review Moment

At the end of the class session, it is useful to review the vocabulary introduced so far.

First, the Functions of Stage Lighting. Lighting provides:

- Visibility
- Focus
- Clues to the environment
- Mood/atmosphere
- Depth and dimension
- Helps to establish the style and genre of the production

There are Standard Angles that help describe the direction (oriented as though standing on the stage) from which the light is coming:

- Frontlight
- Downlight
- Backlight
- Sidelight
- Uplight

The Functions of Stage Lighting can be achieved by using the Controllable Properties of Light:

- Direction
- Distribution
- Intensity
- Color
- Diffuseness
- Shape
- Movement

Homework: Line Drawings of Sets

Each student will eventually create a storyboard for the play assigned as the lighting final project. To facilitate that project, they are asked to make line drawings of their scenic designs to give to their lighting designers.

Bring the students' models into the light lab, and with some added illumination photograph each set from the front. If the set has multiple looks, each set-up is photographed.

Each student is to create a line drawing of their set, using whatever media the student is most comfortable with. They may print out the image and trace it or use a computer graphics program to draw over the photograph. The line drawings should focus on the outlines of objects and avoid shading. Human figures should *not* be included as the lighting designer will add those later. The proscenium and apron are to be included.

The line drawings should be about 3″ x 5″, as this allows a good number of sketches to be mounted on a display board. The smaller size also nudges the students away from trying to create detailed art rather than simplified lighting gestures.

This is a low percentage pass/fail grade based on completion. See Figures 11.9 and 11.10 for sample line drawings traced from photos of scenic models.

Figure 11.9 *Boeing Boeing* Line Drawing Traced from Set Photo (Bridget Kelly)

Figure 11.10   *Boeing Boeing* Line Drawing Traced from Set Photo (Mason Ronan)

Session Break: End of Week 11, Day 1.

"Lighting is not a mechanical process; it is neither simply a matter of illumination nor of making effects. The art of creative lighting is to create an IDEA based upon a play, and upon the concept of the director and the set designer. This idea is of light and shade and SPACE which enfold the actor and help him project his story to his audience. Therefore the designer must have a mental image of the overall visual effect of the stage, filled with actors and scenery. This image must be in three dimensions, and in the fourth too – in time – as the lighting ebbs and flows and changes with the drama."[5]
Richard Pilbrow, *Stage Lighting*

Review and Homework Follow-Up

The introduction of so many new terms and concepts from the previous session means that we begin the next class period with a review of the Functions of Light, Standard Angles, Controllable Properties. Rather than listing them on the board and presenting definitions, try to get the students to call out the items on each list, either from memory or by referring to their notes. Constant and active use of the terms means they are more likely to be retained.

TEACHING TIP

We find that in a hands-on class, students often forget to take notes, and when they do, forget that they have actually written down the information and can refer back to it. While our goal is learning by doing and we would rather have students be actively present rather than furiously transcribing content, there are times things should be written down. You may have to gently remind students that they might want to take some notes just before you present some conceptual material.

The line drawings of sets are collected. We find that any adjustments required can usually be completed right then and there. If it's a mess, we ask the student to touch base with us after the class session and then expect the revision before the end of the day.

The line drawings are photocopied (also reduced, enlarged, and darkened as needed). About ten copies per drawing allows for experimentation and re-dos. These are distributed at the next class session. Students are instructed to make more copies on their own as needed.

Assignment of the Play for the Final Lighting Design Project

Because we want to reinforce collaboration as part of the process, the students are assigned their new play. If possible, students should not light the same text used for their own scenic design.

If students have failed to produce the required line drawings, we warn that they are now impacting a fellow student's work, that responsibility and collaboration is an important part of the production process, and give them until the next session to get the work done. Since storyboard sketching will not begin in earnest until then, this does not precipitate a crisis. Sometimes, though, it is necessary to reluctantly assign the same set of line drawings to more than one student.

Demonstration: Standard Angles in the Light Lab

After assigning plays, we move to the light lab to illustrate the standard angles of light. The angles of light are building blocks used to create a composition of light across the whole of the stage. Seeing them realized in the light lab is a bit like choosing swatches of fabric; the designer has the idea of what is wanted, and now the actual fabric is selected. As various materials (or angles) are experienced and remembered, the designer becomes more accomplished in using them.

Of the controllable properties of light, this demonstration focuses upon:

- Direction
- Distribution
- Intensity

Depending on the time available, either pre-hang the lighting units or have the students use what they learned in their stagecraft class to hang units as part of the exercise.

First, present frontlight, at full intensity, directly from the front with a wide distribution. At each step, ask the students what they see, describing it through the controllable properties.

Ask the students to observe the shadows on the face of the figure used as a light lab subject.

Figure 11.11 Flat Frontal Light with Wide Distribution

Figure 11.12   Flat Frontal Light with Tighter Distribution

- Where are the shadows?
- How easy is it to see the doll's facial features?

Replace the dead-on frontlight with an angled frontlight about 45 degrees up and about 45 degrees to the side, also at full intensity. Ask the students how well they can see the features of the doll, the location of the shadows, and the degree of contrast between light and dark. As we are going to attempt to create a naturalistic, sunny scene, this direction is now labeled as the main source – the sun.

Figure 11.13   Angled Frontlight from Stage Right

Introduce a second light from house left. Slowly bring up the intensity until the students feel they can see the other side of the doll's face well enough but it still appears that the first unit remains the primary source of light. This new unit becomes the shadow fill – the sky.

Figure 11.14   Adding Angled Shadow Fill from Stage Left

Lighting Vocabulary Terms

Look   or, 'lighting look.' Refers to how the light looks on stage at a given moment. Usually used to describe the light of a scene before the actual cue is written: "In this look I plan to have the sunlight stream through stage left window."

Cue   both a moment in the show when the light on stage changes, and the appearance of the light on stage at a given moment as programmed into the lighting console. 'Cue Six' refers to both the moment the stage manager calls the change ("Cue Six Go") and the look that that change establishes ("Are we in Cue Six?")

Two shadows will be cast by the doll, one darker, one less so. Students often express concern about the number of shadows created by the number of lighting units used to build a look. Remind them that it is the effect on the performer's face that tells the truth about the lighting, not the number of shadows on the floor. Most stage lighting is created by a large number of lighting units, and multiple shadows will necessarily be created. However, the shadows created by the units representing the main source of light will usually provide the dominant shadow because those lighting units will be at a higher intensity than everything else.

Take out both frontlight angles in order to demonstrate back- and downlight, one after the other. Ask the students about effects on the figure:

- What is visible?
- What is not visible?
- Which angle isolates the figure more?
- How well can you see facial features?
- Is a mood created?

Figure 11.16 Backlight

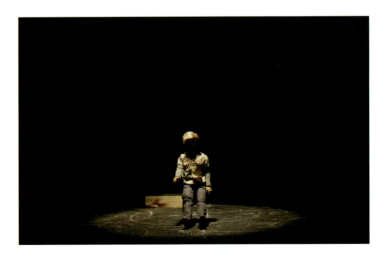

Figure 11.15 Downlight

While both back- and downlight serve to add dimension to the performer and separate the figure from the background, it is usually the scenic environment which determines which angle can be used. regardless of the designer's preference. If a set has walls, downlight is likely to be the choice available; for more open spaces without vertical barriers, backlight is possible.

Look at all three angles as they relate to each other:

- Bring up the main source to a high intensity.
- Slowly add the shadow fill until the students feel that features are visible and the main source remains the more apparent light source.
- Slowly add the back- or downlight until it is just evident on the figure but does not overwhelm the front light. After reaching the desired level, it may be necessary to flick the back/down light on and off so students can see the effect better.

  - What happens if the back- or downlight is brought up to full?

Figure 11.17 Main Source, Shadow Fill, and Downlight

qualities of the sidelight. Together with back- or downlight, this approach is known as **four point lighting** and is most often found in productions that require more stylized lighting, such as dance or in musical numbers, or in older theatres where the architecture limits available angles.

Figure 11.19 Diagram of Four Point Lighting Seen from Above

Using these three standard directions to provide plasticity and visibility is commonly called **three point lighting.**

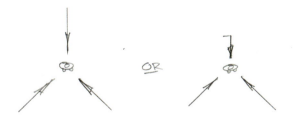

Figure 11.18 Diagram of Three Point Lighting Seen from Above

Light from the side creates deep shadows on the opposite side of the face. The addition of sidelight from the other side can help fill in features somewhat; however, while the overall body is sharply defined and given heightened dimensional qualities, there tends to remain a zone of shadow down the center of the face and figure. If better visibility of facial features is desired, a dead-on frontlight can be gently eased in so as to soften the zone of shadow without obliterating the dimensional

Finally, demonstrate how depth and separation of background from foreground can be created by layering light. In our light lab, we place a black cloth behind the stage area; light is now smeared across this from the side (a secondary source). A line of white columns are placed upstage and are also lit from

Figure 11.20 Layering Light to Create Depth

the side (another secondary source). Excess light is shuttered so that the beam is narrowly focused on the columns. Light on the doll is then added, and distribution is contained by shuttering to focus the light into a small pool (see Figure 11.20). At this point, the students are asked what kind of atmosphere or mood has been created. What is expected to occur in a scene lit like this? This is not a naturalistic stage picture, but serves to illustrate how light can be used for heightened dramatic or psychological effect.

Exercise: Analyzing the Lit Environment

This exercise attempts to consolidate the vocabulary of the previous session with the just completed demonstration of the standard angles of light by analyzing images.

Present the students with photos of lit stage environments. Avoid shows that are familiar or whose titles can be easily guessed, as it is the light evident in the image that is to be analyzed and knowledge of the show can cause students to jump to conclusions. Look for a variety of lit environments, from the naturalistic to the highly stylized. Performers can be included in this set of images, though be aware that students will look to them for the first clues about what can occur in this scene rather than the environment itself.

This time, rather than looking at the individual controllable properties of light, ask the students to begin with the result created by them:

- What is the mood/atmosphere created by the light?
- What can be expected to take place in this environment?
- How does light contribute to the meaning of those actions? How do the observed properties fulfill the functions of light?
- From what direction do various lights come?
- Where is there light? Where is there dark? What is the proportion of light to dark? What is the degree of contrast between light and dark?

- What range of intensities can be seen? Where is the eye drawn first?
- What colors are used and where do they appear? Why have those colors been chosen?
- How soft or sharp is the light? Are shadows well defined? Are faces evenly visible?
- Does the light create any shapes – textures on walls, sunlight passing through windows or trees, abstract shapes, small defined pools?
- Is a time of day, season, or weather condition evident?
- Does the light contribute to definition of style or genre?
- How do the various lit areas and surfaces work together to create an integrated look for the *whole* of the stage?

Homework: Metaphor and Scene Breakdown for Lighting Final Project Play

For the next class session, each student is to:

- Bring in a metaphor statement for their assigned play. They may choose to work with the metaphor developed by the scenic designer, but the statement must be revised to reflect lighting needs.
- A breakdown of the first three scenes of their assigned play. For each scene, they should list every clue about lighting that can be found in the text.

Portfolio Development

In most instances, the lighting designer will present his or her work to a director rather than another designer; therefore, it's important to present information, such as a cue synopsis or storyboard, that speaks to process and collaboration before presenting technical nuts and bolts such as the light plot.

While many of the upcoming exercises are group work, students can still use them as components in displaying design process. Bring a camera to class to snap photos of looks created in the light lab.

Notes

1. Stanley McCandless, *A Method of Lighting the Stage* (New York: Theatre Arts, Inc., 1932), p. 12.

2. David Hays, *Light on the Subject: Stage Lighting for Directors and Actors – and the Rest of Us* (New York: Limelight Editions, 5th edition, 1998), p. 3.

3. Abe Feder, "Lighting the Play," in *Producing the Play* by John Gassner (New York: The Dryden Press, 1941), p. 354.

4. McCandless, p. 4.

5. Richard Pilbrow, *Stage Lighting* (New York: Drama Book Publishers, 1991 edition), p. 30.

Chapter 12

Week 12

"The basic concern in theatre lighting is with the *dramatic intention* of a particular moment. The visibility, or the kind of light, in which you see the actors and the scenery, the place, must have a logic. The logic is based on tying all of these in with the idea of being there, in the scene, in the first place."[1]
Jean Rosenthal, *The Magic of Light*

This week, we connect the design mechanics learned last week with metaphor and research, and begin expressing light through sketching, diagramming, and creating a look in the light lab.

The framing topics for this week are:

- Design Metaphor
- Script Analysis

  - Scene Analysis for Lighting Designers

- Research

  - Research Images for Lighting
  - Using Research Images to Inform Sketches

- Design Mechanics

  - Creating a Look in the Light Lab
  - Six Categories of Purposes

Supplies Needed

Instructor supplies:

- Sketching handouts (postcard-sized box centered on white paper)
- Cue Synopsis Sample handout
- Light lab materials:

  - Figure (doll)
  - Six to ten lighting units
  - A way to control the intensity of individual lighting units (dimmers)
  - A reduced scale set to accommodate the short play used in exercises

Student supplies:

- Drawing charcoal

Homework Follow-up: Metaphor Statements and Scene Breakdowns

As the students share their homework, ask them to connect the design elements suggested by their metaphors to the clues about lighting discovered in the script.

- What specific things did the script reveal about the lighting?

  - Time of day, weather conditions, season, brightness of the room, etc.

- Can they speculate on how the chosen design elements will affect the appearance of a specific lighting requirement?

  - For instance, if the design elements suggest *grey, soft, puffy, quiet*, can they reconcile those descriptive words with a scene that calls for a bright, sunny day?

"Never think of a cue as a mere change from one setting to another. No matter how fast the change, a motive or even a convention lurks in it, and that should be in your thinking as you work out the pace and organization of the shift . . . Never let your stage become ugly or drab through carelessness."[2]
David Hays, *Light on the Subject*

Discussion:
The Cue Synopsis

As the costume designer uses a French Scene breakdown to generate a costume plot, the lighting designer begins to organize script information into a preliminary **cue synopsis.** The cue synopsis is a spreadsheet noting at which moments the light changes, how the light changes, and what the new light looks like. The cue synopsis will ultimately become a document shared with the stage manager and director to aid in cuing the show at the first technical rehearsals.

The play's text contains information about what the light in each scene will look like, and how the light changes from moment to moment. Some of this information is overt, as with blackouts at the ends of scenes, or when someone turns the light in a room on or off. There are also inferred changes, such as whether a slight shift is desired to aid focus during a monologue. Any and all lighting changes that the script suggests should be noted and compiled. Revision *will* occur throughout the rehearsal period, but revision can't occur unless there is something to revise.

Distribute examples of cue synopses (see Appendix D for some samples) and review them. Columns formatted in Word, a Word table, spreadsheet in Excel, or other simple database program can be used. Aim for ease of information entry and revision. We use five columns:

1. **Page Number:** The page of the script upon which the change occurs. The lighting designer *must* use the same text pagination as the stage manager
2. **Cue Number:** The numeric designation of the lighting change, with 'one' being whatever the audience sees upon entering the theatre
3. **Count:** The number in seconds that it will take for the change in looks to occur (duration of the change). At this preliminary stage counts can, at best, be estimated; however, there will be clues in the text and educated guesses can be made. If a comic scene ends on a double-take, perhaps a zero count snap to black should follow immediately upon completion of the double-take. Perhaps the shift of focus for a monologue should be subtle and slow – ten seconds – and the character's return to reality swift and jarring – two seconds. Considering counts at this preliminary stage can help the lighting designer learn the rhythms of the show
4. **On:** When the change occurs and where the designer thinks the stage manager might place the 'Go' to execute the change. Stage directions might indicate a blackout, or a character may flip a light switch. A long sunset may begin on a certain line of dialogue. The exact moment of execution will change as determined by watching rehearsals and the calling practices of the stage manager. If a line or action is repeated in the course of single page, be sure to note which occurrence prompts the cue (the fourth time Jean says "Hello")
5. **What:** Includes both the action of the cue and a description of the look being moved into. Students are encouraged to be as descriptive as possible as a high level of description at this point will reinforce and organize subsequent choices.

Q	Page	Cnt	On	What
1	7			preset and house
2	7	3	house closes	house to half (announcement?)
3	7	3	house out	
4	7	3	preset out	
5	7	7	actors in place	reveal stage; morning, breakfast, crisp – Internationally romantic. . . (with kitchen for Berthe) Morning light through windows (you can see all Paris on page 16); tableau?
6	7	9		open tableau
7	10	7	"I'll go and get dressed"	#1 light up for Gloria's exit (up before exit?)

Figure 12.1 Cue Synopsis Headings

"Lights Up Scene One" does not contain as much useful information as "Slow Fade into Warm Evening Living Room/ Sunset through Curtains"

Exercise: Developing the Preliminary Cue Synopsis

After introducing the concept of the cue synopsis launch right into creating one. We use the stage version of Lucille Fletcher's *Sorry, Wrong Number* for this exercise because of the high number of clearly delineated changes in the first few pages. The script is distributed to the students along with a blank cue synopsis chart (see the end of Appendix D for a sample chart).

Instruct the students to scour the first few pages for any and all lighting changes and in pencil both mark the script and write the salient information in the chart. Direct them to note the changes but not yet number them.

Lighting Vocabulary Terms: Cuing

Preset the lighting look that the audience sees as they enter the theatre

Curtain Warmer for proscenium theatres, the preset illuminating the act or show curtain as the audience enters the theatre

Bows or, curtain call. A look for the performers' bows at the end of the show

Postset the lighting cue that the audience sees after the performers have left the stage, and as the house is cleared

House Lights auditorium lighting for the audience, usually up during the preset, intermission, and postset

House to Half the lighting cue that partially dims the house lights in preparation for the start of the show

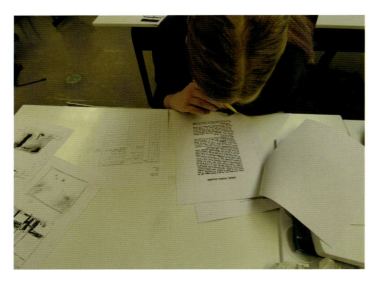

Figure 12.2 Abigail Combs through the Script to Build a Cue Synopsis

Before sharing what lighting changes have been discovered in the short play, cuing terms from the above text box are introduced. Just as the lighting designer controls the darkness on the stage, he or she is also responsible for introducing the show to the audience, what the stage looks like during intermission, and providing the final look as the audience departs. None of these cues should be afterthoughts.

A standard opening sequence of lighting cues runs as follows:

1   Houselights and Preset Up
2   House to Half (Preset Remains Up)
3   House Out (Preset Remains Up)
4   Preset Out (Stage to Black)
5   Reveal Scene One

Each cue serves a specific purpose. House to Half alerts the audience that the show is about to begin and allows people still in the aisles a chance to safely find their seats. House Out darkens the auditorium and directs the audience's attention to the lit stage. Finally, Preset Out darkens the stage and signals a full break from the real world beyond the theatre and the world about to be presented on the stage. There are, of course, exceptions depending on how the playwright and the director choose to structure the audience's initial engagement with the play.

An intermission sequence might look like this:

30 Fade to Black
31 Intermission Look with House to Full
32 House to Half (Intermission Look Remains Up)
33 House Out (Intermission Look Remains Up)
34 Intermission Lock Out (Stage to Black)
35 Reveal Stage for Act Two

At the end of the show, a cue sequence such as the following is fairly standard:

67 Fade to Black
68 Bows (Curtain Call)
69 Postset with House Lights to Full (as actors exit after bows)

Lighting Vocabulary Terms: Cuing

Crossfade a smooth transition from one look into another; generally, the first look is gone by the time the second look is fully established

Fade to Black a smooth crossfade into no light on stage, usually three to four seconds in duration

Blackout (snap to black) a zero-second crossfade into no light on stage

Transition Light a very low intensity look that allows stagehands to reset the stage or actors to get into place between scenes; the audience will see them, but the low level of light is a signal that this activity is not part of the action of the play

Button in comedies and musicals, there may be a tag-line or final beat to a song or gag that requires a quick pop in the lighting as a finale; often this entails brightening the performer, letting applause begin, and then fading into the next look

After the pre- and post-show sequences are introduced, the class shares each change of lighting they have discovered in the first pages of the script. Cues are listed on the board as they are suggested, along with the cue's pertinent information:

- What occurred
- How fast it occurred
- How it moves the action of the play along

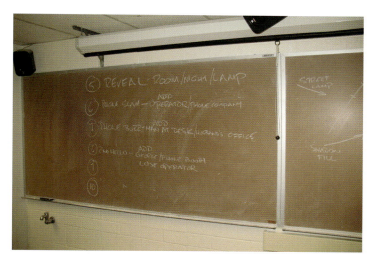

Figure 12.3 Listing Cues for *Sorry, Wrong Number* on the Board

- How it contributes to the pace of the action
- Any descriptive terms related to the change itself or the look moved into.

After accumulating cues for the first few pages and making sure that students understand the process, we assign homework and introduce lighting storyboards.

Homework: Cue Synopsis for the Final Project Play

Develop a preliminary cue synopsis for the play assigned for the final project:

- Format as illustrated by the sample synopses in Appendix D
- For shows with many short scenes, only the first act is required, though the full synopsis will be reviewed at a later date and will be due as part of the final project.

This is collected at the next class session.

This is a low-percentage grade and a stepping stone that contributes to the final project. Evaluation is based upon evidence of a close reading of the text and inclusion of detailed descriptions of the light in each look. Revision is expected.

Book Recommendation

While Stanley McCandless was the first to systematize stage lighting practice, Jean Rosenthal can arguably be considered the first American designer who made lighting alone her professional focus. Her work was seen on Broadway throughout the 1950s and 1960s. She also worked extensively in dance, particularly with Martha Graham. Her book (written with Lael Wertenbaker), *The Magic of Light*, is an excellent introduction not only to the basics of design, but to the spirit of collaboration. She should be amongst any lighting designer's heroes.

Discussion: Storyboarding a Lighting Design

One way that lighting designers can solidify their thoughts and communicate their ideas to the rest of the design team is through a **storyboard**. This is a chronological series of quick sketches, either greyscale or in color, that map out the gist of the lighting for each major look of the play. By mapping out the lighting in this manner the designer can begin to see rhythms and cycles in the lighting, or purposefully work toward particular rhythms and cycles as suggested by the text or design metaphor. The cue synopsis will help the student determine how many different lighting looks the play requires.

We assign a greyscale storyboard for the lighting final project, done in charcoal. Because of varied levels of drawing abilities, we direct the students to focus on the distribution, intensity, and direction of light in each look.

Exercise: Essential Gesture Drawing Exercise for Interpreting Light in an Image

Having begun the process of verbally describing light, we now begin introducing the visual interpretation and communication of light. The following is an observation exercise to help students overcome the fear of sketching light.

Prepare three or four photos that have been converted to greyscale. This allows students to focus attention on distribution, intensity, diffusion, and direction. See Figures 12.5 and 12.6 for examples.

Distribute photocopies of a postcard-sized rectangle on white paper and pieces of charcoal.

After briefly discussing each image, direct the students to interpret the light, focusing on distribution, intensity, and diffusion. They do not need to replicate the light, but rather catch the gist of it.

- Where is there light?
- Where is there darkness?
- Does the light or darkness create shapes?

Figure 12.4 Lighting Storyboard for *Rashomon* (Allison Lozar)

Figure 12.5 Greyscale Sample Lighting Image #1

Figure 12.6 Greyscale Sample Lighting Image #2

- Is the boundary between light and dark sharp, fuzzy, or somewhere in between?
- How bright is the light; how dark is the dark?

Figure 12.7 Eric Works on a Charcoal Sketch

The first sketch should be completed in about five minutes. Ask the students to share any tips or tricks to using charcoal discovered on the first sketch.

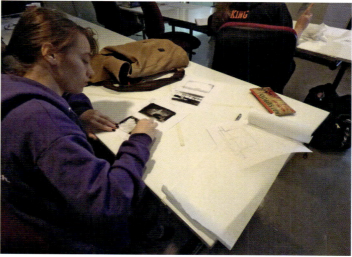

Figure 12.8 Bridget Works on a Charcoal Sketch

After two or three essential gesture sketches are done a photocopy of a proscenium stage with a human figure is distributed. The students are asked to interpolate a grayscale photo image into this stage space, focusing on distribution and intensity. Keep this photo fairly simple.

Figure 12.9 Image and Interpretation, Figure on Stage

Finally, a photocopy of a simple box set on a proscenium stage is distributed. Students are again asked to interpolate the light of a grayscale photo into the space. They will have to make decisions; the important thing is that the sketch has a similar feeling to that of the photograph.

Figure 12.10 Image and Interpretation, Box Set on Stage

Any stage of this exercise can be used as a quick review activity in subsequent sessions.

Use aerosol hair spray or workable fixative to fix the charcoal drawings as they are completed.

TEACHING TIP

One method of catching the essential gesture of light in an image is the **squint test**. Squinting at an image blurs the detail and allows the viewer to get a better sense of the generalities – where is there light, where is there not light? As a sketch develops, squinting at the image and then at the sketch is an instant way to determine if it's on the right track.

Session Break: End of Week 12, Day 1.

The following session is an effort to link together the whole process, in order – developing a design metaphor, looking for textual clues, research and sketching, and then creating a look in the light lab. Since the first portion of this session is dedicated to script analysis and sketching, we typically only get part way through the light lab work before having to end the session. The light lab work continues in the next class period.

Homework Follow-up: Cue Synopses

Collect the cue synopses for the play assigned for the final project. Ask about problems and discoveries. This is a low-percentage assignment and we grade this simply on the basis of whether it was completed and turned in.

After checking that the student has addressed the whole of the play and made notes (our most common comment is for the student to have more elaborate cue descriptions), we return the synopses the following class session with the expectation of seeing a revised version as part of the final project.

Exercise: Research Images and Gesture Sketches for the Short Play

Using the short play that introduced cue synopses (in our case, *Sorry, Wrong Number*), direct the students to comb through the first scene for any and all clues to the lighting, both physical and psychological. They should write down everything they find including:

- Time of day
- Geographic location
- Season
- Evident light sources
- Action/dialogue that determines mood and atmosphere
- Stylistic/genre influences (for *Sorry, Wrong Number*, a genre like film noir may influence the lighting design)
- Historical referents that might inform the lighting (New York, the 1940s, . . .)

Direct the students to come up with a working design metaphor for the play, and discuss the design elements suggested by the metaphor. Once a list has been created, give the students about ten minutes to find two applicable research images. They may use online sources or art books you've supplied.

Have the students present their research images, addressing the following questions:

- How are the design elements suggested by the metaphor reflected in the research images?
- Why/how does a particular research image support or reinforce the action of the play?
- Is there a particular mood or style the research images suggest?
- What are the primary controllable properties of light as seen in the image that you feel are most applicable to the play's first scene?
- How do you think those controllable properties can be used to create your intended mood/style/support of action?

Select two of the research images presented. Direct the students to use charcoal and 3 x 5 cards to create quick gesture sketches of the light found in the images. Discuss commonalities and differences among the sketches. For instance, if most students have sketches containing sharp angles and dark, bold lines, ask them to translate these visuals into controllable properties and consider how they might be manifested on the stage.

Exercise: Interpolating Lighting Research Images into a Scenic Line Drawing

A play like *Sorry, Wrong Number* is useful for the sheer number of cues that occur in the first five pages. It's also useful because the central setting is limited (a woman in her bedroom who never leaves her bed), and that central locale is lit with a prominent motivated source (a bedside lamp).

Figure 12.11   Light Lab Set for *Sorry, Wrong Number*

We have a small bedroom set for *Sorry, Wrong Number* that has served us well for a number of years (Figure 12.11), and use it to help demonstrate the path from textual clues to a realized light lab look. A simple line drawing of that set is now distributed to the students. They are directed to:

- Sketch a greyscale look with charcoal for the first scene of the play, incorporating information from the research images and the quick gesture sketch.

Discuss the sketches, especially which design elements from the research images were incorporated and why.

"Light in nature may, broadly speaking, be divided into two categories: general indirect light (skylight or the light of an overcast sky), and specific direction light (sunlight). By filling the space of the stage within which the actor moves with an appropriate balance of these two kinds of illumination, the lighting designer creates a living space around the actor. This links him to his surroundings and completes the process of making a living environment within which he can perform, thus emphasizing to the audience the full meaning and emotion of the play."[3]

Richard Pilbrow, *Stage Lighting*

Lighting Vocabulary: Purposes

Special   usually refers to a single lighting unit that serves a highly specialized purpose, such as providing a small pool of stationary light for a monologue or song; typically, a special picks a performer or object out of the overall stage lighting to attract the audience's attention

Discussion: Six Categories of Purposes

We now step away from the research images and sketches for the short play to introduce one final set of terms. These are categories of **purposes**, or, what effect the designer plans to accomplish with a particular direction of light. Purposes are building blocks that use the controllable properties of light to accomplish the functions of light. Each purpose should be specific and unique, such as 'light from chandelier,' 'afternoon direct sunlight,' or 'Joe's monologue special.' Keep in mind that the chandelier itself may be one purpose, but the light it supposedly emits may be a second purpose. By thinking in purposes, the designer creates the overall design by adding unique components one by one.

As we diagram the lighting look for the short play on the blackboard, we discuss each purpose category as it arises. Once we complete a basic look for the scene, we will use the research images and sketches to revise it.

The six basic categories of purposes are:

1. Main Source of Light
2. Shadow Fill
3. Support of the Main Source
4. Sculpting Angles
5. Secondary Sources
6. Tonalities

The above Richard Pilbrow quote breaks light into two broad categories based on how we as human beings experience sunlight: the direct light from the sun and the indirect light from the sky (which is also sunlight, but whose qualities are transformed by refraction through the Earth's atmosphere). The sun

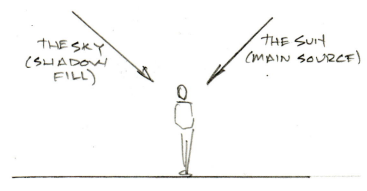

Figure 12.12 Sun as Main Source and Sky as Shadow Fill

and the sky correspond to the first two categories of purposes. The direct sunlight is the **main source** of light. The indirect sky light allows us to see into the shadows, and can be called **shadow fill** (because it fills in, or allows us to see into, the shadows created by the main source). Thinking about light on stage as being composed of a main source and a shadow fill is the first step in creating a naturalistic, motivated lighting environment.

For an interior space a table lamp may be the main source. One side of a person is directly lit by the lamp when standing in close proximity to it. The rest of the light emitted by the table lamp bounces off the various surfaces of the room – walls, ceiling, floor, furnishings – and at a subsequently reduced intensity provides reflected illumination that allows the viewer to see into the shadows created by the direct beams of the table lamp itself. Further, if the walls of the room are, say, violet, the bounced light will pick up that tonality and the shadow fill will have a violet cast to it. Not only does the lighting designer choose the color of the main source of light, the lighting designer *also chooses the color of the shadows*.

Establishing the Main Source of Light

Ask the students what the main source of light is for the first scene of the short play. For *Sorry, Wrong Number*, it's the bedside lamp. Since the main character of the play is in the bed next to the lamp, on the blackboard we draw an arrow pointing at the head of the bed from the lamp's location. For other plays in

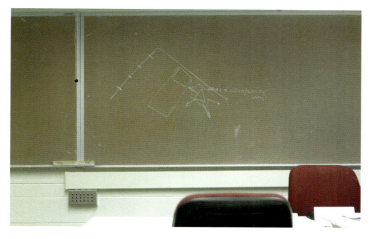
Figure 12.14   Arrow Indicating the Main Source of Light

other sets, place the footprint of a figure in the middle of the stage. Performers do move around, but at this point all we are concerned with are broad purposes, not coverage of the stage. For the time being, assume that each purpose will cover as much of the stage as necessary.

Be sure to label the arrow descriptively, such as 'Main Source Bedside Lamp.'

Figure 12.13   Table Lamp as Main Source and Reflected Light as Shadow Fill

TEACHING TIP

Nomenclature

For our class we prefer labels to be as descriptive as possible. The names for what we call 'main source' and 'shadow fill' can change across photography, television, film, era of lighting text, and geographic region of designer. Whatever the name, though, the base purpose remains the same. We feel that for intro students 'main source' is a pedagogically clearer term than, for example, 'key light.' This also helps avoid confusion when discussing later items, such as 'color keys.'

We now begin shuttling back and forth between the blackboard and the light lab. Have the set for the short play ready. Allow the students to place the lighting units as each is discussed. For *Sorry, Wrong Number*, we turn on the bedside lamp at full intensity and ask some questions:

- Is this enough light to allow the audience to see everything they need to?
- How well can we see the face of the actor in the bed?
- What happens if the actor turns away from the lamp (main source)?
- How much of the room does the lamp illuminate?
- What color is the lamp light?
- What can we do to help the audience see what they need to but still make it seem as though the bedside lamp is providing all the required light?

Figure 12.15 The Bedside Lamp (Main Source)

Adding Support to the Main Source

When lighting a scene requiring sunlight, such as a yard in mid-day, the frontlight angles used to represent the main source (the sun) and the shadow fill (the sky) also provide adequate visibility. With bright, even distribution of light across the stage, the audience should have little problem believing that the light is coming from the sun, or that it is mid-day. These two purposes, 'sun main source frontlight' and 'sky shadow fill frontlight,' do not need to be supported by other angles of light to allow the audience to see everything that needs to be seen.

However, in the case of an interior scene where the main source is a table lamp or chandelier, it may be necessary to add lighting units to complement the main source of light and provide sufficient visibility for the action taking place. If a scene is illuminated solely by a single table lamp set on a table center stage, any time an actor crosses downstage of it the audience will not be able to see the actor's face. In many cases, this is not desirable. The designer can **support** the table lamp by adding frontlight that will light the actor's face but through color and intensity create the sense that the actor's face is still being lit by the table lamp. The purpose of this additional frontlight becomes 'downstage table lamp support.'

Figure 12.16   Adding Frontlight Support to a Table Lamp (Main Source)

Ask the students to consider whether the main source and shadow fill for the short play will allow the performer to have adequate visibility should movement be required. For *Sorry, Wrong Number*, if the character leans forward in the bed,

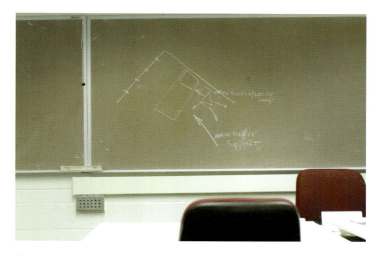

Figure 12.17   Adding Support to the Diagram

or turns toward the lamp, will the audience be able to see what they need to see? Usually, the students agree support is necessary.

Send a student back to the chalkboard to add an arrow to represent the support. Since it should mimic the main source, it should come from a direction similar to that of the main source. Remember that the idea of the support is to create the *illusion* that the bedside lamp is providing all the necessary illumination.

Have the students determine the corresponding positions for the support in the light lamp. When this unit is placed, slowly bring it up until the students feel that the doll's face is better lit, but still feels as though the light comes primarily from the lamp. If the students have placed the support in a more frontal position (rather than off to the side), look at the doll's features and consider whether they have been flattened or accentuated by the angle of light and if adjustment of position is necessary. Since the bedside lamp is only at about shoulder height in the room, the students might consider a low frontlight, or frontal uplight.

Adding the Shadow Fill

Once the need for a **shadow fill** is determined, ask the students what angle they think will be the best for it. Have one of the students go back to the blackboard and draw an arrow to indicate the direction of the shadow fill. Next, have the students determine the corresponding angle in the light lab and position a light there.

Take the main source out (to zero percent intensity), and slowly bring it up again until the students feel that it is at the right level for the scene. Then, slowly bring up the intensity of the shadow fill unit until the opposite side of the figure's face is visible, but preserves a sense of shadow – that the main source remains the bedside lamp. At this point, it may be necessary to adjust the intensity of the main source. If the shadow fill seems to obliterate the directionality of the bedside lamp, it may have to be moved to another position. Experiment until it feels right.

Figure 12.18 Adding Shadow Fill to the Main Source and Support

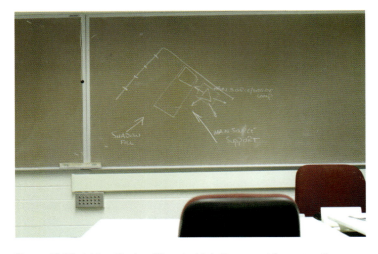

Figure 12.19 Adding Shadow Fill to the Main Source and Support on the Blackboard

This is about as far as we usually get in this session. If you have more time take a look at Chapter 13 for the next steps in this exercise. If you weren't able to advance this far, keep in mind that the final day of the lighting section is planned to be a workday. If you fall a session (or part of a session) behind, it just means there's a little less time for the students to work on their storyboards in class.

Before assigning homework, we review the categories of purposes covered so far:

- Main Source
- Shadow Fill
- Support of the Main Source

Homework: Metaphor, Research, and Script Analysis

For the next session, we expect a number of items that will contribute toward progress on the lighting design final project:

1. Revised Metaphor Statement

    - This may be an adaptation of the scenic design metaphor
    - The statement must include discussion of design elements and how controllable properties of light can be used to implement them

2. Central Metaphor Image

    - A single visual image that speaks to the whole of the play
    - Brief statement detailing the design elements/controllable properties suggested by the image

3. Ten research images

    - These can expand upon the central image or speak to different looks/moments of the play; preferably a combination of both

4. Choose one French Scene of the assigned play and:

- Write a paragraph explaining what happens in that scene (action of the characters).
- Write a paragraph noting all the clues as to the qualities and sources of light that can be found, from dialogue, stage directions, both overt and inferred.
- Considering the action and the textual clues, describe the mood/atmosphere that suggests the quality of lighting for that scene.
- Using the Controllable Properties of Light and the Purpose Categories checklist, write another paragraph discussing how you might go about creating the stage light as called for by the textual clues. The paragraph should address questions such as:

  - What is the main source of light?
  - What direction is it coming from?
  - What color is the main source of light?
  - Do you think the main source of light will need support?
  - What colors do you expect the various purposes to be?
  - Based upon the set you are working with, what secondary sources might be expected (cyc, accents, rooms visible through doorways)?

The Lighting Design Final Project

Finally, a handout containing the guidelines for the final lighting design project is distributed.

For this project we again use the KCACTF format. Expectations for the oral presentation follow the same lines as those for the costume and scenic design projects. The materials expected as part of the presentation include:

- A Title Block with Title, Author, name of Designer
- Metaphor Statement

  - It is expected that the statement has been revised to reflect adaptations to the lighting environment and includes discussion of design elements

- Central Metaphor Image

  - This serves as a cohesive visual encapsulation of the metaphor, and the student is expected to explain how this image is used to inform subsequent design element choices

- Research Images

  - A wide range, both abstract and of physical detail, with notation regarding how various elements will be incorporated into the lighting environment

- Storyboard

  - A charcoal sketch (about 3″ × 5″) for each and every major look of the show, labeled with act and scene number, and ordered chronologically from the start of the show to the end.
  - If a look repeats (i.e., every two scenes Mary has a short monologue in a tight special), the sketch should repeat. This is important to illustrate the rhythm and flow of the show. Do not label a single sketch as representative of scenes 3, 7, 12, and 16, as that does not contribute clarity to the throughline.
  - The research image informing each look should be in close proximity for easy reference. If the sketch repeats, the research image repeats. The research image must be in color.

- Two Color Sketches

  - Select two of the charcoal images and create color versions. For layout reasons, these may be placed in their own section of the presentation boards.
  - Label with act and scene number.

- Two Magic Sheets

  - For each of the two color sketches, develop a magic sheet that develops the lighting choices. These should be drawn on the reduced groundplan provided by the scenic designer and should be about 3″ x 5″ unless labeling requires a larger size for clarity.
  - Label each arrow with purpose and color, as well as any other important details.

- Two Preliminary Purpose Lists

  - From each magic sheet, generate a purpose list.
  - Select specific gel color for each purpose and notate appropriately.

Portfolio Development

Realized Lighting Look from Research to Light Lab

Whether or not they realized it, the class designed some realized lighting this week. For the short play they've prepared:

- A cue synopsis
- Research
- Made a list of lighting cues for a scene
- Developed a magic sheet
- Selected color
- Hung the show in the light lab

These materials can readily be used to create lighting design portfolio pages.

The portfolio layout should include:

- Metaphor Statement
- Research Images (color)
- Cue Synopsis (at least for the first chunk of the play)
- Gel names as selected in the light lab
- Photos of all completed light lab looks (color)

  - Be sure to photograph the *whole* stage, not close-ups of the actors. Since the LD is responsible for composing the entire stage environment, close-ups are of limited use in a portfolio.

Photos should have prominence of place. Experiment with one- and two-page layouts, arranging the materials to present the finished product at the beginning, and then walking the viewer through the process to arrive once again at a production photo as a closing item.

Notes

1. Jean Rosenthal and Lael Wertenbaker, *The Magic of Light: The Craft of Jean Rosenthal, Pioneer in Stage Lighting* (Boston: Little, Brown, and Company, 1972), p. 8.
2. David Hayes, *Light on the Subject: Stage Lighting for Directors and Actors – and the Rest of Us* (New York: Limelight Editions, 5th edition 1998), p. 61.
3. Richard Pilbrow, *Stage Lighting* (New York: Drama Book Publishers, 1991 edition), p. 12.

Chapter 13

Week 13

This week connects diagramming standard angles of light with the creation of the light lab scene through the development of the magic sheet. Communication of a design is explored by adding color to storyboard sketches.

The framing topic for this week is:

- Design Mechanics

  - Building a Look in the Light Lab
  - Introduction of Magic Sheets
  - Color in Lighting
  - Colored Lighting Sketches

Supplies Needed

Instructor supplies:

- Light lab materials:

  - Six to ten lighting units
  - Ability to individually control the intensity of each lighting unit
  - Figure (doll)
  - Reduced scale set for the short play
  - Selection of gel

- A prism
- Gel swatchbooks (enough to give each student their own)
- Magic Sheet handout

Student supplies:

- Cellophane tape
- Scissors

Homework Review: Metaphor, Research, and Script Analysis

The students were asked to bring in:

1. A Revised Metaphor Statement
2. A Central Metaphor Image
3. Ten research images
4. Paragraphs on a chosen French Scene that include:

   - Actions of the characters in the scene
   - All the clues as to the qualities and sources of light that can be found
   - Description of the mood/atmosphere
   - How the student might go about creating the stage light as called for by the textual clues and using the controllable properties of light

We collect the written portion for comment and return it at the start of the next class session. Evaluation focuses on whether the student has offered a reasonably detailed consideration linking the action of the scene to the described lighting choices.

In class, we ask a few students to share their work. They are directed to:

- Connect the metaphor statement to the central visual image using design element vocabulary
- Present a few of their research images and explain how these images inform or connect with the world of the play

Exercise: Building a Look in the Light Lab

We pick up this week from where we left off last week in building a look in the light lab. During the last session, using the short play (for us, *Sorry, Wrong Number*), we placed lighting units to fulfill the following purpose categories:

- Main Source (bedside lamp)
- Shadow Fill (the light bouncing around the room that fills in the side of the performer's face on the opposite side of the main source)
- Support for the Main Source (since the bedside lamp itself doesn't provide enough illumination if the performer moves around)

Review those purposes, and be sure to redraw the rough groundplan diagram on the board with labeled arrows indicating the directions of the already established purposes.

The remaining purpose categories are:

- Sculpting Angles
- Secondary Sources
- Tonality

Each will be presented and explored in turn. After this initial basic look for the scene is built, we'll return to the metaphor and research images generated for this project and see how they can provide more dramatic meaning to the look.

Adding Sculpting Angles

Frontlight, when it shines on the performer from an angle, can provide a fair amount of dimensionality. Still, a higher degree of sculpting is usually desirable as this will help separate the performer from the background. **Downlight** and **backlight** are often employed for adding dimension, though **sidelight** is also an option (especially in dance). These angles impart a degree of liveliness to the environment, just as the eyes of a painted portrait can seem dead until a minute highlight is added to the pupils.

To choose between back and downlight, ask the students how much space there is behind the performer. In our *Sorry, Wrong Number* set, the bed butts against the wall. This means backlight is not possible since the wall would block it. Have a student go to the blackboard and add an arrow for downlight, directly over the head of the bed.

Figure 13.1 Addition of Bed Downlight

Have the students position a downlight. If possible, try to cut the beam of light to keep it tight to the doll's upper body (aluminum foil flaps can work well to shape the beam of the light on non-standard lighting units like clip-lights).

Slowly bring up the intensity of the downlight until the students feel it is balanced with the rest of the already established light. Ask if the downlight helps pull the doll away from the wall. Again, intensity adjustments to the other purposes may need to occur.

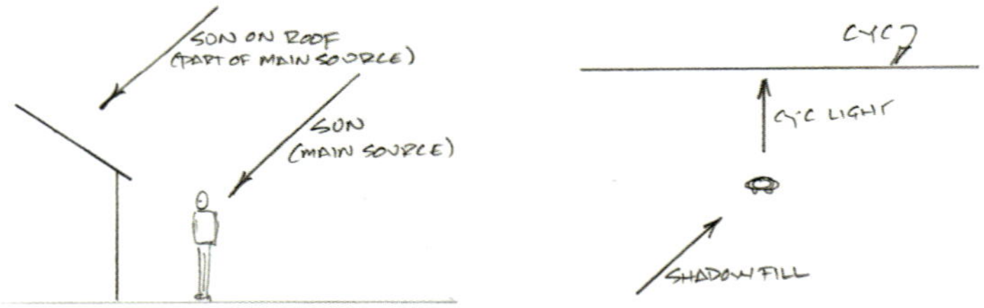

Figure 13.2 Lit Roof and Main Source (side view); Lit Cyc and Shadow Fill (top view)

Adding Secondary Sources

The next item on the list of purpose categories is **secondary sources.** Secondary sources are those that illuminate the stage but do not provide immediate visibility of the performers. They can often be thought of as accents.

Light can also paint scenery into the stage picture; it is up to the designer to determine if these scenic purposes are truly secondary sources or are expansions of other purposes, such as the main source or shadow fill. For example, sunlight hitting a roof piece may not illuminate the performers, but it *is* part of the main source of light (the sun) and helps create the illusion that sunlight is evenly distributed through the environment. On the other hand, a cyclorama (cyc) might be linked to the color of

the shadow fill and thus represent the sky itself, but since lighting a cyc does not normally employ angles duplicating those of the shadow fill, it can be considered a secondary source.

Secondary sources may also have their own directional purpose breakdown. For example, a night scene might include a kitchen partially viewed through a doorway with an over-sink fluorescent fixture (a practical) perceived to be the secondary source for the kitchen. The designer might choose to add support for the practical, as well as shadow fill and an overall color tonality provided by the down- or backlight.

For *Sorry, Wrong Number*, we ask the students where the apartment is located. It is an urban location, most likely New York.

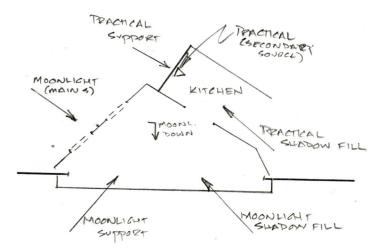

Figure 13.3 Secondary Source and Additional Purposes for a Night Kitchen

ally seeing what is beyond the windows. The students are asked what kind of light source might be outside the apartment; in our case the students usually respond with light from a streetlamp.

Send a student back to the chalkboard to add an arrow to indicate the secondary source (streetlamp). Then direct the students to hang a lighting unit in the appropriate light lab position.

For a streetlamp, angle is important in the logic of this purpose. After placing a unit above the set students often feel that this doesn't quite work – a streetlight would likely be *below* the apartment's windows. Move the unit and try it out.

After placing all the units, wipe the intensity levels already set and rebuild the look from scratch, starting with the main source and slowly adding each purpose in turn.

The bedroom has windows, and the character can hear the elevated train pass by. It appears likely that the room is on an upper floor. Since it is evening in the city, the students are then asked what kind of light might be shining through the windows, or maybe visible on objects *beyond* the windows. On our set, the scenic designer has supplied sheer curtains, which means that light can be projected onto them from outside without the audience actu-

Lighting Vocabulary

Gobo in theatrical usage also called a 'pattern' or 'template.' Traditionally, it is a stamped piece of thin metal placed in an ERS to project textures and shapes. They can also be made of glass or plastic imprinted with photographic images.

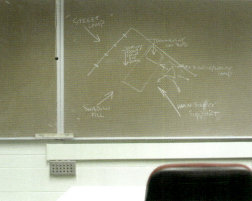

Figure 13.4 Completed Look with Exterior Streetlamp Light

Adding Tonality

Tonality refers to color and texture added to a look that is not already part of one of the other purposes. For instance, a research image might call for adding an overall blue quality to the set so that the color is seen in shadows and corners but does not alter the color of light seen on performers' faces. Similarly, texture through the use of gobos can be laid across the stage to add interest and dimensionality.

Downlight is an excellent way to provide tonality to the shadows and nooks of the entire stage environment. Frontal tonality carries the risk of adding more light to the performer's faces and flattening features. In our look for *Sorry, Wrong Number* the downlight on the doll provides sculpting that pulls the performer out of the background. The addition of downlight over the rest of the room can not only create interesting shadows, but give the designer more control over the contrast between light and dark throughout the room. If there are available dimmers,

suggest experimenting with this concept. If another downlight is added, add it to the magic sheet and label appropriately; for instance, change the first to 'bed sculpting downlight' and the new unit 'room tonality downlight.' This is already included in the diagram pictured in Figure 13.3.

As the class incorporates research images into this look, a range of tonality choices will likely arise.

Exercise: Applying Research Image Information to the Light Lab Look

In the time remaining, select one of the working metaphors and accompanying research images.

Setting color aside, what changes to distribution, diffusion, direction, and intensity can be made to incorporate them into the look of the scene? For example, if a film noir image is selected, explore high contrast and sharp delineation of light and dark often found in that genre. This might be expressed in the light lab through sharpening beam edges, scraping light across walls (shape), and keeping a tight focus on the woman in the bed.

It is important that students understand that this stage of the process is one of experimentation. If an angle doesn't seem right, try something different. If the relative intensities of the various purposes don't seem to work, adjust them. If another purpose seems called for, add it. Eliminate the extraneous. Try out overkill. Unless variations are explored, the student lighting designer does not build up a mental library of those possibilities. Keep the research images handy and refer to them often.

Always remember to ask the students what they *see* and how that compares to what they expected to see, or want to see. Resist offering solutions. Instead, try to lead students to their own alternatives by analyzing their observations (whether research image or light lab look) through the controllable properties of light. If they're stymied, suggest directed inquiry: "The research image has sharp, crisp delineation between light and dark – how can we get more of that into this look?"

As the students explore applying the information from the research images into the light lab look, start using color. We have a box of gel filed by color that we keep in the classroom. As students identify color in images they would like to use, have them go through the box until they find a piece of gel that seems to match the image. Don't worry about the names of colors at this point; that will be discussed in the next session. If you know how your box of gel is organized, suggest what section contains the blues or the reds and let the student take it from there.

Figure 13.5 Our Box of Gel

As you continue describing light and planning lit stage environments, this checklist of purpose categories helps structure exploration and should be repeated frequently:

- Main Source
- Possible Support of the Main Source
- Shadow Fill
- Sculpting Angles
- Secondary Sources
- Tonality

Discussion: Magic Sheets (or, Lighting Diagrams)

A **magic sheet** is a diagram laying out the purposes the designer intends to use to build a scene's look. The diagram the class drew on the board as each purpose in the light lab was determined and discussed is an example of a magic sheet. These help the designer organize thoughts and keep track of what will eventually become a proliferation of purposes.

As each magic sheet is created, the designer makes a list of all the purposes that appear on it. This is the preliminary **purpose list** for that scene. In most cases this is simply a listing of all the arrows drawn on the diagram. It is, though, a chance for revision and ordering in preparation for the oncoming compromises brought on by inventory and architectural realities. Lighting design information regularly shifts format back and forth between lists like the purpose list and graphics such as the magic sheet.

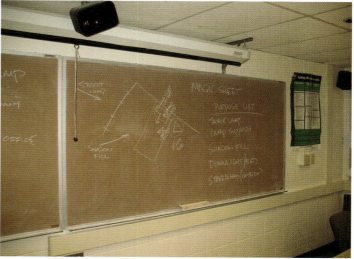

Figure 13.6 Magic Sheet and Purpose List for *Sorry, Wrong Number*

For a student design a magic sheet should be completed for each and every look of the show to demonstrate thorough analysis of the play. This means that a purpose list for each look will also be generated. By comparing and collating the various purpose lists, the designer can more easily see what purposes are duplicated in various scenes as well as what purposes are unique. More accomplished designers may compress this roster of magic sheets into script margin doodles and use memory and experience to seemingly skip this step of the process – they're still doing it, just in a more advanced manner.

The collated revised purpose list is used to develop the **channel hook-up**. The channel hook-up is a spreadsheet that contains all the information about all the lighting units that will be used to implement the lighting design, organized by channel. A **channel** is a number assigned by the control console to the dimmer or electronic device controlling a lighting unit. The assignment of channels allows the designer to organize the control information in a manner logical to how the designer likes to cue a show. This means that if a designer would like to bring the daytime sunlight focused upstage right (currently at fifty percent intensity) up ten percent in intensity, the light board operator might be instructed to "take channel fifteen to sixty percent." The hook-up will be discussed in Chapter 17.

Homework: Reduced Size Groundplans

The lighting design project includes creating a magic sheet for two looks of the play. To facilitate this, students are directed to photocopy the groundplans of their scenic designs and reduce them until they are about the size of a note card, 3" x 5". They should make at least five copies, to allow for mistakes and revision.

At the next class session, they are to turn these copies over to the student lighting their set.

Session Break: End of Week 13, Day 1.

TEACHING TIP:

Nomenclature

The term 'magic sheet' is also used by some designers to refer to a sheet used during the cue writing process. This sheet contains a compression of all the lighting paperwork's channel information onto a single piece of paper for ease of reference. This way, if a designer wants to bring the daytime sunlight focused upstage right up ten percent, they don't have to page through long documents to locate the channel number that that light is assigned to. Some designers, instead of calling this cuing reference aid a 'magic sheet,' refer to it as a 'cheat sheet.' On the other hand, the diagram used to lay out purposes during the design process may also be called a 'lighting key,' or a 'color key.' Be aware that there is a variety of nomenclature across textbooks, as well as generations of lighting designers.

"When thinking about how much or how little colour to use, the choice may seem to be between stark Brechtian whiteness, a psychedelic morass of multi-coloured sensation, or an attempted distillation of the colours of nature. The guide line [sic] seems to lie in the simple rules that we have tried to follow throughout this book: first, what does the playwright call for, and second, how does the director intend to re-create his work on the stage?"[1]

Richard Pilbrow, *Stage Lighting*

Discussion: Color

In many lighting texts, the use of color is prefaced by a fair amount of scientific discussion. We try to limit our class to the points that help with basic color selection and general explanation of what is observed in the light lab. When the Physics Department offers their 'Physics of Light' course we urge students interested in lighting to take it as an elective. Even still, because stage lighting is so tied to the technology that produces it, a certain amount of review is useful.

In our light lab, we use incandescent theatrical lighting units and gel. LED lighting units are becoming more popular and more available, but are not as easy to use in light lab situations because of their more complex technology. Still, if you have access to LED units and have a console in the light lab able to control them, it is useful to compare the color they produce against that of traditional plastic color media. Some of the following exercises include an LED component.

Discussion: The Visible Light Spectrum

The color wheel was introduced earlier in the semester but is now discussed with an eye toward lighting. First, we introduce the mnemonic ROY G BIV to help students remember the colors of the rainbow, or, more properly, the **visible light spectrum**. ROY G BIV stands for: Red, Orange, Yellow, Green, Blue, Indigo, and Violet. Each color is produced by a certain wavelength of energy.

Purples and blues are shorter wavelengths; red and ambers are longer wavelengths. Invisible wavelengths just beyond red are called infrared (heat lamps). Invisible wavelengths just beyond violet are called ultraviolet (sunburn and blacklights). Radiowaves, microwaves, and cosmic rays are also on the spectrum, but far beyond the range visible to the human eye. ROY G BIV represents the wavelengths of electromagnetic energy that human beings have evolved to perceive with their eyes, and is a tiny portion of the complete electromagnetic spectrum. Sunlight contains them all. A prism held in sunlight will break the white light of the sun into the spectrum of colors.

Discussion: Subtractive and Additive Mixing

Objects have color because they reflect certain wavelengths of light. Red objects are red because they bounce back the red and absorb most everything else. Objects are black because they absorb almost all of the wavelengths and reflect little back. If you shine blue light on a red object, the object will appear black because there is little red in the light for the object to reflect (see Figure 13.7). This is why fabrics should be tested in the light lab during the design process.

Figure 13.7 Objects are the Color of Light They Reflect

The process of mixing opaque or translucent pigments to create other colors, such as mixing red and blue to create violet, is called **subtractive** mixing. The number of wavelengths reflected is steadily reduced with the addition of each pigment. Red does not bounce much blue back to the observer; blue does not bounce much red. Mixing red and blue together results in not much red and not much blue being reflected; therefore the resulting violet is darker than either original color. In a spectrally pure world, mixing together yellow, red, and blue paint results in black.

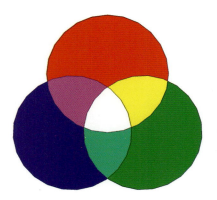

Figure 13.9 Mixing the Primary Colors of Light

LED fixtures also work through additive mixing. Since a single light-emitting diode produces a single color, most of these units feature an array of colored diodes. The intensity of each diode in the array is then electronically controlled to create the palette of available colors.

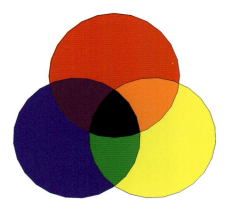

Figure 13.8 Subtractive Mixing of Primary Colors

In paint, the primary colors are red, blue, and yellow. For lighting, the primary colors are red, blue, and green. Mixing colors of light to produce a new color is called **additive** mixing, because the number of wavelengths increases with each additional light; instead of the mixed color being darker, it's brighter than either of the original colors. Quite simply, the mixed color is brighter because there's more light. Green light and red light produce yellow light. While orange, green, and magenta are the secondary colors of paint, yellow, cyan (blue/green), and magenta are the secondary colors of light. In a spectrally pure situation, mixing together red, blue, and green light creates white light. Essentially, you're pushing the rainbow back through the prism.

Demonstration: How Light Sources Can Change Gel Color

At this point we pass out gel swatchbooks to the class, which are the students' to keep. There are currently four major manufacturers of gel serving North America: Rosco (R or Rx), Lee (L), Great American Market (Gam), and Apollo (AP). If you live in or near a city with a lighting rental house, there are usually free swatchbooks at the counter to keep designers current on that year's new colors. Have a couple of brands handy for class. You can go to the manufacturers' websites to locate distributors in your area.

- Rosco: www.rosco.com
- Great American Market: www.gamonline.com
- Apollo: www.apollodesign.net
- Lee: www.leefilters.com

Rosco 59, Indigo, works best for this demonstration but other dark, warm violet/blues will show some degree of change. This demonstration requires both a fluorescent and an incandescent light source. Turn on an incandescent light source and ask the students to:

- Find Rosco 59 in their swatchbooks
- Look at the light through the gel swatch and describe the color
- Switch the light source to a fluorescent
- Describe how the color changed

The color should become more blue under fluorescent light. Rosco 59 allows red to pass through, which makes it a warmer color. Since fluorescent lights (even warm fluorescents) don't emit as much red light as incandescent lights, there's less red in the first place to pass through the gel. The color becomes cooler and bluer.

As time allows, ask the students to select a few other colors to observe under different light sources. Discuss observed differences. Is there a range of colors that retain their color better regardless of light source?

This exercise is a reminder to always select gel color by looking at it in the same type of light source (be it incandescent, fluorescent, sodium discharge, sunlight, or even LED) that will be used for performance.

Discussion: How Gel Works

Placing a piece of gel in front of a light is a subtractive action. Blending together the light from two differently colored fixtures is an additive action.

Gel allows a certain amount of light to pass through it. A blue piece of gel allows mostly blue light though. The rest of the light is either reflected or absorbed by the gel itself, creating heat. This is why saturated colors burn out so quickly.

When light passed through different gels blends on a surface, additive mixing occurs and we see the result of the combined wavelengths.

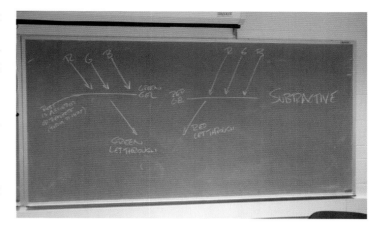

Figure 13.10   Gel Lets Selected Wavelengths through to Color Light

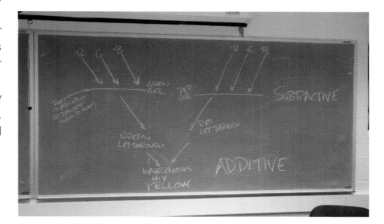

Figure 13.11   Light from Multiple Sources Mixing Color Additively

For incandescent sources, there's also the factor of **amber drift**. The lower the intensity of the lamp, the redder the light emitted by it becomes. This can be demonstrated by bringing an un-gelled lighting unit to full and then slowly decreasing its intensity. Blues and lavenders will change color, becoming warmer and muddier the lower the intensity of the incandescent light shining through it. Amber drift is another reason LED fixtures are so exciting; colors remain true regardless of their intensity level.

Discussion: Using the Swatchbook

The gel swatchbook can be a daunting tool. However, there's no need to memorize the colors and their numbers. With use and experience, designers and electricians automatically become more familiar with the designations of various colors; if you keep a swatchbook handy, there's no *need* to memorize it.

Figure 13.13 Which Bastard Amber Will You Choose?

Figure 13.12 Swatch Books from Four Major Brands

Each gel manufacturer produces their own thick, chunky swatchbook of color. Because of the sheer number of colors available, gels are not called by their descriptive names.

Gel color is referred to by the manufacturer's name and the **number** assigned to that color by the manufacturer, such as R 56 and Gam 105.

Figure 13.14 Some Antique Gel Books, Some from Defunct Gel Product Lines

Figure 13.15 Swatchbook Transmission Charts

There are two more useful pieces of information provided in the swatchbook for each color regardless of brand: **transmission** and **spectral distribution**.

Transmission refers to how much light passes through the gel and is expressed as a percentage. A very saturated color may have a transmission of 2 percent. This means 98 percent of the light is either reflected or turned into heat, so this color may not read on the stage unless the channel plays at a high intensity.

Spectral distribution refers to how much of each wavelength is allowed through the gel. A small chart provides information on which spectral wavelengths are transmitted by the gel. If you're unsure just how warm a blue might be or must take an educated guess on how it will affect a piece of fabric, check the chart to see how much red, yellow, and orange will be allowed through.

When white light is desired and no gel is placed in a unit, that light is called **no-color**. It is abbreviated on light plots as NC or N/C. A unit drawn on a plot without color notation is not de facto white light – the designer may have forgotten to note color for that unit, is using a unit with internal color changing capabilities, or has located all color information in the hook-up.

knowledge of skilled designers and technicians, for a student who is serious about lighting, the personal exploration of color will impart lessons and methodologies that will be of great use when they venture into territory the charts do not cover.

Demonstration: The Primary Colors of Light

Set up three units in the light lab, all focused at a white cloth. Overlap the beams so that students can see both the color of the gel and the color produced by mixing with the other units (Figure 13.16).

Depending on which brand of swatchbook you've distributed, have the students search for the colors designated as primary blue, primary red, and primary green. Not all manufacturers label colors as primary, so the darkest (most **saturated)** blue, red, and green can be used. Even if the color is named as a primary, the media is not spectrally pure and will let other

wavelengths through. This is one of the factors to be explored in this demonstration.

- Project each color individually. Observe and discuss the relative warmth or coolness of the color.
- Bring up two colors to full intensity.

  - What color is created?
  - Does the intensity of one of the colors need to be adjusted to make the created secondary more 'truthful?'

- Switch pairs. Repeat discussion and adjustments.
- Switch pairs again.
- Bring up all three colors and adjust intensities to create as white a light as possible.

Depending on the units used, you might not be able to get to a clean white. Adjust the levels of the three primaries to get as close to white as possible. Discuss why it's hard to get to white with those units and these gel colors.

Hold an object several inches away from the projection surface.

- What color is the object, and what color is its shadow?
- As you move the object from color to color, how many shadows are created in each zone of color? What colors are the shadows?

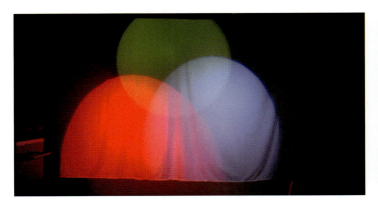

Figure 13.16 Color Mixing in the Light Lab

Figure 13.17 Placing White Objects in Multiple Saturated Colors

Blending saturated colors on a flat surface can give the appearance of naturalistic acting light colors (that adjust atmosphere and mood but do not greatly change skin tone). But since actors are three-dimensional, shadows are created not just on the floor but on their faces and bodies. Unless the context of the production calls for this kind of intense color-work, highly colored shadows on actors' faces tend to be distracting. This is why less saturated **tints** (color plus white) are generally used for acting areas and deeper colors used for the surrounding environment. There are, of course, always exceptions.

Exercise: Gels Are Not Spectrally Pure

Unexpected colors allowed through by individual gel colors can be demonstrated by doubling saturated colors in a single unit. Dark blues and dark greens work well for this.

- Point a unit at a red object.
- Add a saturated blue or green filter. The object is likely to remain red.
- Ask the students what's going on. What wavelengths are allowed through the gel?
- Ask the students what *should* happen if a second piece of the same color is added.
- Add the gel and ask the students to observe and describe.

Placing a dark blue and a dark red together in the same unit *should* cancel each other out, since each gel stops the wavelengths the other allows through. Try it and see what happens.

Exercise: Colored Light and Its Effect on Fabric, Part One

This exercise stresses that young designers should work together early in the process to avoid unpleasant surprises involving time and labor that may not be readily available. Gather a wide range of fabric samples: various colors, textures, and patterns. Find at least one heavily patterned, highly colored fabric, such as the one pictured in Figure 13.18.

Figure 13.18 A Highly Patterned Fabric Used for Color Demonstration

Direct the students to:

- Hang three lighting units side by side. Be able to control them separately
- Aim all three units at the same spot in the light lab, where the fabric samples will be draped
- Select primary colors – red, green, and blue. Place the gel in two of the units, leaving the third no-color for the start of the exercise.

Starting with the highly patterned, highly colored fabric, project no-color light at full intensity onto it. Ask the student :

- What colors do they see?
- Do any colors seem more dominant than others?

Take the no-color light to zero intensity and add the last piece of gel to it. Cover the patterned fabric with a piece of white cloth. Bring up all three units and mix the best white light possible on the white fabric. Once a reasonable white has been achieved, whisk away the white fabric to reveal the colored fabric below. Ask the students:

- Does the fabric look as it did under no-color light?
- How have the colors shifted?
- Is the most dominant color still the one that was noted earlier?

Take out two of the units and look at the fabric under a single primary color. Once again, ask the students:

- What colors do they see?
- Is there a dominant color?
- Which colors are being reflected and which are being absorbed?

Repeat these steps for each of the other two primary colors.

Choose a color on the fabric and ask the students what gel color will either make it pop or make it turn muddy and brown.

- How easy is it to kill the blues? The reds? The greens?
- Are there any colors that refuse to die regardless of gel color?
- Are there colors that seem more sensitive to colored light than others?

Look at a selection of fabric samples under the primary colors. Have the students describe what they see, and explain the results in terms of what colors are reflected and which are absorbed. Throw some curveballs in, such as iridescent and shiny fabrics.

Exercise: Colored Light and Its Effect on Fabric, Part Two

Select a range of less saturated colors from throughout the swatchbook. Include some of the more traditional acting light colors such as no-color blue, no-color pink, light straw, and pale lavender. The 'no-color' colors are named as such because they create a light that reads as white but is tipped ever-so-slightly toward the warm or the cool. Surprise Pink is good to have on the list, as the gel itself appears lavender but the light created is a pleasant pink.

Look at the effect of tints and mid-saturated colors on various fabrics. Observe and discuss.

As time allows, have students suggest colors to try.

Exercise: Incandescent and LED Color Matching

LED units present amazing color mixing capabilities, but due to the specific and narrow wavelengths produced by the diodes, their light can have very different effects on fabric and painted scenery than colored light produced through gels.

If you have access to both LED and incandescent fixtures, hang both types of units as frontlights aimed at two different spots with no overlap.

- Place a piece of the same highly patterned fabric in both spots.
- Have the students find colors closest to primaries in the swatchbook, as well as a few other colors that seem interesting. Aim for about ten colors.
- Start with white light (no-color) from the incandescent unit at full intensity. Match the white with the LED unit. Are the whites similar? What needs to be done to the LED to match the incandescent white light? What needs to be done to the incandescent to match the LED white light?
- See what happens when both units are brought down to 75 percent intensity, then 50 percent, then 25 percent.
- Look at the primary colors first. Try to match the LED fixture color to the gel color by sight. If the console you are using has one, use its electronic catalog of colors to match the gel color. Discuss differences.

Exercise: Colored Light on Skin Tones

Lighting designers do not just light fabric and scenery but also actors, and actors have a range of skin tones.

If the cast of a production has a fairly narrow range of complexion colors, the lighting designer can select color for the desired effect and be reasonably sure that all the performers will have the same general appearance. The caveat is that the color range that helps Northern European skin look robust and healthy is not necessarily the same range that will make African, Latin, Native American, or Asian skin look robust and healthy. Certainly, the designer is not trying to average out or cancel skin pigmentation differences, but if everyone is supposed to look healthy and the main character's complexion turns chalky and pale under the light, there's a problem to be solved.

- Select a range of gel colors, making it a mix of both more saturated colors and standard acting area tints. Be sure to include light greens and saturated yellows.
- Ask the two students with the widest variation of skin tone if they are willing to volunteer. As this exercise progresses, be sure to regularly swap out students so that everyone has an opportunity to observe. This avoids singling out a particular student for having the most unique skin tone in the class. Be sure to be sensitive – this exercise is about skin tone and how it changes under light, not about ethnicity or stereotyping. If you're the only person in the room with a particular skin tone, jump in.
- Use a unit with a wide enough throw to cover both subjects sitting side by side (or two units – just have doubles of all gel selections).
- As each color is projected on to the subjects' faces, observe and describe differences and similarities.

  - Which colors make which skin tones appear healthy?
  - Which colors make which skin tones appear sickly?
  - Are there colors that don't show a marked difference regardless of skin tone?

Exercise: Choosing the Color of Back- and Downlight

While down- and backlight provides sculpting and dimension, it's a color choice that isn't always made clear from research images. One way to approach this decision is to connect the color to either the main source or the shadow fill depending on which one the designer wishes to emphasize, and on which provides the desired level of separation of performer from background. Intensity, of course, plays a role, and nothing says down- or backlight *must* be related to either the main source or shadow fill. This exercise explores the possibilities of color used in sculpting angles.

- Hang three lights in the light lab: two angled frontlights from house left and house right, and a downlight (three point lighting).
- Point all three units at your figures (dolls).
- Focus all three lights at them. If you have the ability to change between a white and black background, start with white.
- Select two cuts of each pair of gels from your selection, regardless of brand. Either pre-select them or have the students choose likely candidates from their swatchbooks. Some suggested combinations include:

  - No-color blue and a slightly more saturated blue
  - A light straw and a slightly more saturated straw
  - No-color blue and No-color pink
  - No-color blue and a light straw
  - Light lavender and a slightly more saturated blue
  - Light straw and light lavender
  - Light straw and a medium amber
  - Medium amber and medium lavender
  - Light blue and dark blue

- For each pair, drop one color in one unit and the other in the other unit. Designate one unit as the main source (the sun), and the other as shadow fill (the sky). Adjust intensities so the main source of light is prominent.

- Ask the students what time of day and season it feels like.

  - Is there an emotional quality to the light?
  - What might the performers be discussing in this atmosphere?
  - Can the atmosphere be changed by changing the intensities of the lights?

- Leaving the downlight as no-color, add it to the composition, having the students stop the intensity at a level that provides definition but doesn't overwhelm the other sources.

  - Does the no-color downlight contribute to or change the feeling of the look?

- Add a piece of the main source color to the downlight and adjust the intensity as desired.

  - Does the main source color downlight contribute to or change the feeling of the look?

- Change the downlight to the shadow fill color.

  - Does the shadow fill color downlight contribute to or change the feeling of the look?
  - Which of the three color choices contributes most to the atmosphere established at the beginning of the exercise?

Exercise: Notating a Color Palette on a Magic Sheet

Swatchbooks are tools. Since manufacturers will usually distribute them free to encourage designers to buy their products and update them as new colors are developed, designers often cut samples out of swatchbooks to get a better sense of how colors will work together.

Prepare a magic sheet handout for the short play, as it was diagrammed on the chalkboard. Present the students with one or two research images connected with the short play; these may be either new images, or ones the students brought in for the previous light lab session.

Instruct the students to:

- Go through the gel swatch book(s) and find colors they think will work best for each purpose
- Note the gel name on the magic sheet at the appropriate arrow
- Using a pair of scissors, cut a 1/4″ strip of gel from the swatches selected
- Using clear cellophane tape, tape the gel strip at the appropriate arrow

Homework: Research, Sketching, and Magic Sheets

For the next class sessions, students should bring in:

- Research images informing the light for three scenes of the their final project play
- A grayscale sketch for each of those three scenes, incorporating design elements from the research
- A magic sheet for one of the selected scenes. The magic sheet should:

  - Be drawn on a copy of the reduced groundplan provided by the set designer
  - Include all the purposes they can determine necessary through script analysis and research
  - Include complete descriptive labels for each purpose
  - Include gel choices for each purpose, with both the name of the color and a gel snippet accompanying each purpose arrow

Portfolio Development

Whether or not they realized it, the students have completed their first lighting design with the creation of a light lab look for the short play. If you intend to use the light lab exercise as a portfolio project, be sure to photograph the final looks. A sample portfolio entry should include:

- Metaphor Statement with Suggested Design Elements
- A Cue Synopsis

  - A single page is adequate; reduce the size of the page by half so that it is readable, yet does not take up too much space on the page

- Research Images

  - Accompany images with brief descriptions of how, via design elements, they are to be applied to the lighting

- A Magic Sheet

  - If the student has not copied the group diagram from the chalkboard, use the magic sheet handout in the last exercise. Include all purposes, with appropriate labels and gel choices

- A Photo of the Corresponding Light Lab Look

It is important to stress that the photo of the final product should display the evidence of the thinking that led to it. If the research features a specific palette of colors, those colors should appear in the look photographed. If the design elements suggested by the metaphor statement lead the reader to expect a moody, claustrophobic space, then the lighting can be expected to be tight and controlled, with a high degree of contrast between light and dark. It does not speak well of the designer's process if one thing is stated, but something else entirely is delivered.

Note

1. Richard Pilbrow, *Stage Lighting* (New York: Drama Book Publishers, 1991 edition), p. 82.

Chapter 14

Week 14

Students have been introduced to sketching in greyscale, and have explored some of the color relationships common to stage lighting. In this final week, they will attempt to integrate color into their sketches to more fully express their intentions.

The framing topic for this week is:

- Design Mechanics

  - Developing Color Sketches
  - In-Class Work Day

Supplies Needed

Instructor supplies:

- Color Sketching Template handouts
- Reference images
- Light lab equipment/materials

Student supplies:

- Watercolors
- Brushes
- Water and container

Homework Follow-Up: Research, Sketching, and Magic Sheets

This session begins with sharing the research, sketches, and magic sheets that were created as homework. We ask the students to spread their work out so everyone can see what was produced.

The students then:

- Share their metaphor statement and design elements suggested by it.
- Share and discuss their central metaphor image; how it connects to the play through the metaphor.
- Talk about their research images and what design elements/controllable properties they intend to extract from them.
- Talk about what scenes they sketched:

  - The action of that scene and how the lighting supports it
  - How the research images and design elements inform the sketch
  - How the controllable properties will express the design elements

Explain the purposes shown on the magic sheet and how they will create the intended effect.

- What is the main source of light and where does it come from?
- Did the main source need any support?
- Where does the shadow fill come from and what color is it?
- Is there down- or backlight? Is the color of this sculpting angle related to the main source of the shadow fill?
- Are there secondary sources?
- Are there any tonality purposes?

Point out the basics of what you, as the instructor, see in the sketches. Focus on distribution, intensity, and color. Use the squint test. If the student has stated that the sketch is meant to depict a candlelit scene the expectation is to see fairly tight distribution of light around the source, darkness at the perimeters, and a certain amount of gradation between the light and the darkness.

whole, and how the paint itself incorporates those qualities. This is relatively easy to see in a medium like charcoal, but watercolor poses new complexities. We try to address those issues one by one and step by step.

Prepare some paintable templates. These can be on copy paper (though cardstock will be easier to work with), and each image should be about 3" x 5". We place two line drawings on each page in portrait orientation. See Figures 14.1 and 14.2 for examples. Distribute multiple copies of each page to allow for mistakes, exploration, and re-dos.

A photo such as Figure 14.3 can be used as a research image to help derive the color palette and intensities.

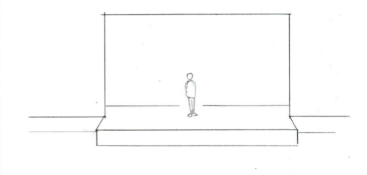

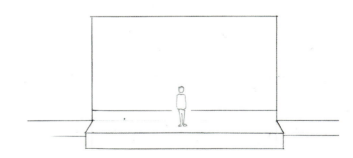

Exercise: Sketching Light in Color

We use simple line drawings as the basis for color lighting sketches to keep students from worrying overmuch about the colors and textures of the set. These color sketches differ from the charcoal sketches as we are now asking the students to provide a higher degree of intentional detail as they fill a stage space with light.

Using color to build a lighting sketch requires thinking about the controllable properties of light in the sketch as a

Figure 14.1 Human Figure on an Empty Stage Template

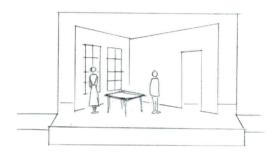

Figure 14.2 Leafy Cut-Outs and Box Set Template

Figure 14.3 Research Image for Painting Reference

Exercise: Sketching Direction in Light

Shadows are important indicators of direction, both the shadowed side of the object itself and the **cast shadow**. If the shadow falls on the floor behind a person, the light automatically appears as though it's coming from in front of the person. Using this principle, select a direction for the main source, such as from the front and to house left, and then lightly shade the opposite side of the human figure with pencil. Add a cast shadow that falls behind at an angle (Figure 14.4).

Instruct the students to do the same on their templates. Ask:

- How much light does there appear to be on the stage?
- From what direction does it appear to come?
- How bright does the light appear to be?

Even though no paint was added to portray the main source, it has been *implied* by the application of a shadow.

The perceived brightness of the stage light can be increased by adding contrast. Have the students darken in the proscenium and ask how the perception of light changes (Figure 14.5).

Figure 14.4 Shadow Cast by Human Figure, Drawn in Pencil

Figure 14.5 Making the Light on Stage Pop on Stage by Darkening the Proscenium

Figure 14.6 Layering Light by Shading the Cyc

On the page's second template, have the students:

- Again use pencil to lay in the figure's shadow and cast shadow
- Lightly shade in the cyc behind the figure, being careful not to go over the figure
- Darken the proscenium

Ask what effect has been created, and whether the qualities of light have changed. They have now layered light. The foreground, where the figure stands, is lit by one purpose (frontal sunlight, for instance), while the cyc is lit by another (cyc light color related to that of the shadow fill).

Exercise: Sketching Directional Light in Color

Using a second copy of the same line drawing template, demonstrate the same steps, but with watercolor.

- Select the angle of light.
- Using a pale blue, shade in one side of the figure (use blue because it is a naturalistic shadow color; see the reference photo in Figure 14.3).
- Using the same blue, add a cast shadow.
- Using black, darken the proscenium.

Do not paint the cyc. Ask if the cyc is related to the color of the main source, or to the color of the shadow fill.

- Repeat the steps on the next line drawing, *this* time laying in pale blue on the cyc.
- Avoid going over the figure so that the light on the figure pops against the background.
- Have the students paint both of these steps.

Which source is the cyc color related to now?

Figure 14.7 All of the Templates Laid Out for the Demonstration

Watercolor Reminders

- The white of the paper serves as the light in the image.

  - Adding paint not only adds color, but diminishes intensity.

- The more pigment in the paint, the darker the light becomes.

  - Color alone does not make something bright; it's quite possible to apply enough yellow pigment that it becomes darker than blue.

- Wait for one application of paint to dry before moving to the next.
- It's useful to have multiple sketches going at once to avoid impatient painting.

Exercise: Sketching Light in Color – Side Trip to the Light Lab #1

Recreate the look just painted in the light lab. This demonstrates that decisions made while sketching can be explicated as magic sheets and then developed as actual lighting looks.

- Create a magic sheet/color key for the look (see Figure 14.8).
- Go to the light lab:

  - Hang a main source
  - Hang a shadow fill

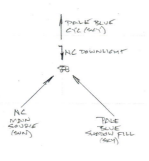

Figure 14.8 Sketch, Magic Sheet, and Light Lab Look

Figure 14.9 Adding Color to the Main Source of Light

- Balance their intensities
- Hang a cyc light
- Balance the cyc's intensity
- Add a down- or backlight if desired

Exercise: Sketching Light in Color Step #3

Using the same line drawing template, paint for the main source is now added. Keeping in mind that the light becomes less intense as color becomes more saturated, lightly wash the whole of the upper line drawing with a light pale yellow (straw), going over the cyc and the human figure. On the bottom template, apply the straw wash only to the lit side of the human figure and the stage floor. The stage has now been flooded with a pale straw, non-directional light.

Depending on time, either ignore the guideline about waiting for paint to dry or have the students do this step before demonstrating the next.

On both templates, using the same light blue as earlier, add shadow and cast shadow to the figure. Both drawings now depict a directional pale straw light with a light blue shadow fill. On the upper line drawing, the cyc is the same color as the main source.

On the bottom line drawing template, wash the as-yet-unpainted cyc with the pale blue, connecting it to the shadow fill. Note and discuss the differences in light quality between the top and bottom sketches.

Finally, wash the cyc on the top sketch with the light blue. It will not end up a pure blue, but if the straw is pale enough, it should read reasonably blue (rather than green).

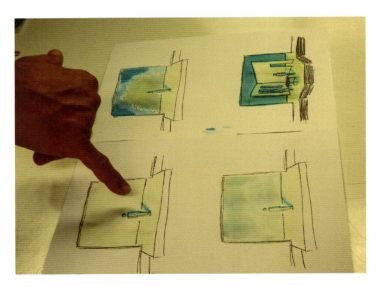

Figure 14.10 Progression of Sketches Demonstrated

These two sketches demonstrate two basic approaches to quick lighting sketches. The top illustrates washing the main source of light across the whole of the stage and then chiseling out space and depth by adding darker pigmented shadow on top of it. The second uses more selective layering, placing the preferred light only on the surface it hits.

Exercise: Sketching Light in Color Step #4

Now that establishing direction and intensity have been practiced, creation of fore- and background are further explored. We continue using blue for shadow and straw for sunlight because these are common colors for naturalistic sunlight. The following steps use the foliage cut-out template.

- Wash the whole space with a pale straw sunlight color.
- Add pale blue shadow and cast shadow to the figure.
- Wash the cyc and all the layers of foliage with the same light blue.
- Allowing drying time between, add layers of blue to the subsequent foliage cut-outs so that the downstagemost cut-out ends up the darkest.
- Darken the proscenium with black.

Exercise: Sketching Light in Color Step #5

Using the approaches just explored, direct the students to create light in the box set sketch. Have them pay attention to fore- and background, and use only the two colors of straw and light blue. Direct the students to make some decisions before they begin painting:

- What is the main source and its direction?
- In which direction are shadows cast?
- Depending on the direction of the main source, are all surfaces equally well-lit?
- What happens in the background?

Figure 14.11 Foliage Cut-outs and the Box Set (Lilliana Gonzalez)

Exercise: Using Research to Develop a Lighting Sketch

Since the students are likely to paint at different speeds, have extra templates of the box set ready. Have those who are ready to move ahead:

- Use a research image to make a list of its qualities/controllable properties of light.
- Determine a main source direction.
- Select and mix colors drawn from the research image.
- Create a look for the box set that relates to the research image.

Too many variables can stall a student as they try to figure out just where to start. Have students reduce the goal of the sketch by selecting one or two controllable properties, such as direction and distribution or distribution and color.

Exercise: Sketching Light in Color – Side Trip to the Light Lab #2

If time allows, and everyone has completed at least one research-inspired sketch, select one to build in the light lab. We have a variety of walls and shapes that can be arranged to create many basic scenic configurations.

Develop a magic sheet for the sketch, this time noting intended color for each purpose (don't worry about gel numbers – descriptive names are all that is needed at this point). When the class moves to the light lab, instruct the students as to where in the gel box to look for colors.

A certain amount of seemingly arbitrary decision making will need to be made as the sketch is interpreted. Start with what the student thinks is the main source of light and work your way down the purpose checklist. Ask the students to choose angles of light that they think will do the job, knowing that once you get to the light lab a different direction may prove to be more effective.

Figure 14.12 Casey Discusses Interpreting Some Research Images

Figure 14.13 A Selection of Our Basic Set Configuration Blocks and Walls

As the class hangs, circuits, and patches, have the student who made the sketch select color from your gel assortment by comparing available gel to the colors of the sketch.

Try it all out and revise as deemed necessary until you get as close as possible to the feeling of the sketch.

Homework: Making Progress on the Lighting Design Final Project

For the next session students are directed to:

- Draw grayscale charcoal sketches of three different looks from the assigned final project play (these may be the same as those presented for previous homework, revised versions, or wholly new ones)
- Create color sketches for two of those looks
- Bring in the research images that inform the sketches.

Session Break: End of Week 14, Day 1.

Homework Review: Research, and Charcoal and Color Sketches

We have the students lay out all their sketches so that discussion can move down the table at a good pace. The students discuss how the design elements seen in their research images are reflected in the sketches. Ask the students what they found easy and difficult about using watercolor. Have them share both useful discoveries and approaches to avoid.

Use the accompanying charcoal sketch to gauge the success of the color rendering. Do the same areas of the sketch exhibit the same levels of brightness or darkness? Is the distribution of light similar? When you squint at the sketch, is it easy to tell where you are supposed to be looking?

One of the most common hiccups in using watercolor to depict light is the over-application of pigments like yellow and orange. The assumption is that, since yellow is an inherently brighter color than blue, more pigment makes it even brighter. There is usually at least one sketch where candle- or table

Book Recommendation

Not every student interested in lighting plans to pursue theatre as a career. Lighting designers also have careers in film, television, trade shows, events, and concerts. *Bullet Proof I Wish I Was: The Lighting & Stage Design of Andi Watson*, by Christopher Scoates, is a good book to hand a student interested in rock concert lighting. Not only is Watson's work with bands like Radiohead and Oasis examined, but his work is presented in the context of both stage lighting and light as used in visual studio arts.

Figure 14.14 Looking at Research Images, Charcoal and Color Sketches

lamplight is depicted with a heavy use of yellow that ends up being darker than the light blue tonality used to represent darkness. Have a set of watercolors handy to demonstrate technical fixes.

The Final Session Before Presentations

For us, the final lighting session before presentations can take any number of shapes, depending on the progress of the class as a whole.

It is good to remind students of the components comprising the final project (the full list can be found in Chapter 12):

- A Title Block
- Metaphor Statement
- Central Image
- Research Images
- Greyscale Storyboard
- Two Color Sketches
- Two Magic Sheets
- Two Preliminary Purpose Lists

An important point to reiterate is that the greyscale storyboard must include an image for *each and every major look of the play*, labeled by act and scene, and arranged in chronological order. If a look repeats, it should be copied or scanned so that it is placed throughout the storyboard every time it occurs. This is important to get a sense of the overall rhythm of the show.

The storyboard should also be laid out so that the research image that informs each charcoal sketch is placed in immediate proximity to the sketch, rather than clumped off to the side. The research images should also repeat as required.

The color sketch can be placed in a separate portion of the presentation board, and should be in close proximity to the magic sheet and preliminary purpose lists for ease of reference.

We find that the generation of the storyboard and other final project content does not usually require an in-class work session unless the students specifically request one. If no work session is necessary the final day might be used for review, or using a student's sketch and research to build a look in the light lab. Or, depending on interest, we might forge a bit further ahead with lighting, moving onto the preliminary channel hook-up (see Chapter 16).

If the content of the course has moved more slowly than expected, this session can also be used to ensure that all of the materials required for the final project have indeed been introduced and explored through in-class exercises.

Portfolio Development

Targeted Portfolio Pages

We've noted before that in most instances the designer presents his or her portfolio to directors and other non-designers. For these viewers, the way the work is presented should speak to end product, collaboration, and process, with less emphasis on the technical nuts and bolts. On the other hand, if a student designer is on an interview for an assistant designer or other more technically-based job, the portfolio should be able to speak to those aspects of the work. Electronic formatting allows a designer to more easily build targeted portfolios.

- Discuss what different reviewers hope to learn from a designer's portfolio.
- Using the materials from the same extended project (this could be any of the final design projects), lay out a portfolio presentation aimed at a director.
- Lay out a second portfolio presentation aimed at another designer or technician.
- After completion, present the pages and explain why choices were made; are there any items missing, or yet to be generated, that would be useful?

Chapter 15

Week 15

Within the two projects of this week, we will address all of the framing topics:

- Formal Presentation of a Professional Lighting Designer

  - Metaphor
  - Design Principles
  - Script Analysis
  - Research
  - Design Mechanics

- Formal Presentation of Student's Final Lighting Design Project

  - Metaphor
  - Design Principles
  - Script Analysis
  - Research
  - Design Mechanics

As with the costume and scenic sections, the lighting section culminates in the presentation of two big projects. Those students who were assigned a lighting designer in the first week of class will present their research (and since they have had three months to prepare, expectations are accordingly higher). All of the students will present their final lighting design projects.

We use the semester's scheduled final exam period for the presentation of the final project. This gives us an extra day of class time.

Lighting Designer Presentations

For evaluation, the same basic process questions are asked. Afterwards, the full notes are typed up and given to the student. No grade is released without the receipt of a hardcopy bibliography.

The rubric can be found in Chapter 5; the long form question-based response version can be found in Chapter 10.

On the lighting evaluation, you may find it useful to replace:

8. Discuss the designer's use of line, shape, form, space, texture, color.

   - How do the design elements contribute to creating an effective/meaningful environment?

With:

8. Discuss the designer's use of distribution, diffusion, direction, color, texture, shape, intensity, and movement.

   - How do the controllable properties of light contribute to creating an effective/meaningful environment?

It is more difficult to find good visuals of lighting designs than of scenery or costume. When choosing lighting designers to assign, be sure to check to see if they have websites with full stage portfolio images or that recent major designs are photographically well-represented in articles and reviews. Close-ups and stage detail can be useful for close analysis of direction, intensity, color, and angle but don't speak to the whole of the composition. If close-ups of actors or partial stage images are used, be sure the student can connect them to the larger picture. Since lighting usually changes through the course of the show, looks from several different moments of the show are desirable.

Every so often a student will ask if it's okay to contact a designer. We're delighted that they've realized these are living, working people who exist beyond a website, but remind the student that these are living, working people with lives beyond a website. If a student chooses to contact a designer via the information found on his or her website, there are some things we tell them to keep in mind:

- Do not rely on an interview for the full content; contact with a designer is lovely, but should be the icing, not the cake itself.

Book Recommendations

USITT is in the midst of producing books and monographs on major designers. Some of these were noted in the costume section as sources for sample costume renderings. Student lighting designers should consider these titles:

- *The Designs of Tharon Musser*, by Delbert Unruh, with Marilyn Rennagel and Jeff Davis
- *Late and Great: American Designers 1960–2010*, edited by Bobbi Owen
- *The Designs of Jules Fisher*, by Delbert Unruh

- There may be no response, not even a "no." A polite second inquiry two to three weeks later is fine, but don't be a pest. Know when to drop it and move on.
- Do the work *first*. Have a list of specific questions that demonstrate your knowledge of the designer's work. Anything asked should be a follow-up to information gathered elsewhere. Don't expect them to write the presentation for you. "Where did you go to school," is a poor question; "What's the single most important thing about design that you learned from your teachers?" is a better one.
- Keep it short. A handful of specific, intelligent, probing questions that can be discussed in a half-hour or less.
- Do not send the designer a written list of questions unless they ask for it.
- The designer is doing you a courtesy. If you are offered a half-hour of phone conversation at 8:30 Sunday morning, you take it and you are prompt and present. *Do not stand them up.*
- This is an aspect of networking. Present yourself as someone serious about not only the field, but your own education. It's a small world, and the student not only represents him or herself, but the program and the institution.

- We ask to review emails and material before they are sent out. We have found that many of our students have not yet written a business letter and that texting has had a truly negative impact on formal written communication. No one seems to have told them not to send a missive to a potential employer that begins "Yo," or "Hey, Jennifer." You don't want to receive an email (and this has happened to us) from a designer explaining that she or he received a confusing, poorly spelled email from a student in the program and that a talk about grammar and personal presentation might be important before this student heads out into the industry.

With a third of the students presenting, and a thirty- to forty-minute presentation from a guest designer, this concludes the first half of Week 5.

The Lighting Design Final Project

For this project we again use the KCACTF guidelines for format. Expectations for the oral presentation follow the same lines as those for the costume and scenic design projects.

Figure 15.1 Lilliana Presents Her Lighting Project

Figure 15.2 Mason Presents His Lighting Project

Added Advanced Material

If the class is small enough and time allows, have each student select one of their looks and build it in the light lab.

Remember that hanging, focusing, and setting the intensities for each look will eat up time. Depending on the number of students, it may be necessary to have strict time limits on presentations to accommodate light-lab set-ups, or work out a way in which the light-lab set-up incorporates a discussion of process. A repertory plot of standard angles can be hung and employed for all looks, but we feel this can undercut the emphasis of generating direction from text and research.

Evaluating the Lighting Design Final Project

Once again, we compare notes on the oral presentation. Eric then examines each project individually and writes up his notes, including content from the oral presentations. The following is the format Eric uses to evaluate these projects:

Name:

Title:

1. Are all the elements present and in the most presentable state possible?

   - Design metaphor statement
   - Central visual image
   - Cue synopsis
   - Grayscale storyboard with sketch for each major look
   - Visual research informing each storyboard sketch
   - Two color sketches
   - Two magic sheets
   - Two purpose lists with gel choices

2. Was the design metaphor clearly articulated and connected to the ideas/themes of the play? How well does the central image connect to the design metaphor?
3. Does the cue synopsis note and describe as many cues as could be reasonably assumed from the text and the design metaphor? Is there an adequate amount of description of the look of the light in the cues? Has preshow, intermission, and post-show been considered?
4. Does the storyboard include a sketch for each major look of the show? Are they labeled? Are they chronologically presented? Do looks repeat as required?
5. Does it appear that the visual research for each look informs the sketches created for those scenes?
6. Can a main source of light be determined for each sketch? Considering the skill level of the student, do the sketches offer a reasonable representation of light based on the information noted in the cue synopsis and suggested by the research?
7. Do the magic sheets indicate all the sources/directions that seem to be present in the sketch/research? Are there labels? Has the background also been addressed? Has color been selected? How descriptive are the purposes?
8. Do the purpose lists note all the angles, labels, and color created on the magic sheet? Has specific gel color been selected?

Other notes:

Grade:

Again, except for the initial checklist of present materials, Eric refrains from simple "yes" or "no" responses, as those don't provide substantive affirmation of good practice or constructive and actionable criticism for issues and problems. Since this project is turned in during finals week, the full written evaluations are emailed to the students as they are completed.

Our university schedule has regularly slotted our final exam period into the first part of finals week, which gives us a good seven or eight days to evaluate projects before grades must be turned in to the registrar. If you don't think that you'll have enough time to adequately review and evaluate each project, some compression of the lighting section may be required. Adjust the components of the final project to reflect what cannot be covered.

Figure 15.3 Kelsey Presents Her Lighting Project

Portfolio Development

This is the pinnacle of the lighting design work for the semester and, like the costume and scenic designs, should be prominently displayed in the portfolio. As before, process is an important feature of the layout. The intent of the design should be clear and the application of that intent into the design will be the litmus by which success is gauged.

Depending on the preferred format, convert materials into a size dictated by the paper portfolio, or digitize elements for electronic presentation.

Condense the material to be displayed on either two facing paper portfolio pages (24" x 18" is a good size) or two sequential PowerPoint (or equivalent) pages.

Regardless of delivery system, the portfolio pages for the lighting design should include:

- A Title Block

  - Name and Author of play
  - Name of Designer
  - Date of Design
  - Name of Director (if extant)
  - Name of Venue (if extant)

- Design Statement (condensed to a single paragraph)
- Central Research Image, labeled and attributed
- A selection of storyboard images in order to give the viewer a sense of progression
- Research images that inform storyboard sketches
- Color sketches
- One charcoal image that was expanded through color sketching, magic sheet, and purpose list

  - Arrange this material to show progression of development

- Photographs of light lab looks

- If multiple looks were realized, start the page with the most interesting look
- Label with act, scene, and action

The emphasis should be on storytelling and progression; technical items like a plot are useful, but in most cases should not take up so much space that photos of realized looks or storyboard elements are crowded out.

Figure 15.4 The Corridor of Completed Projects

Chapter 16

An Extra Chapter of Introductory Steps in Developing a Lighting Design

"Theoretically the whole acting area might be lighted with one powerful instrument directing its beams to the stage from a distance, at an angle which would light up the face of the actor somewhat as the rays from the sun make objects visible on a sunny day. But we have neither such an instrument nor the physical position from which it can direct its rays to the rather restricted acting area within the setting. It is more practical to use a number of instruments in available positions."[1]
Stanley McCandless, *A Method of Lighting the Stage*

The framing topic of this chapter is:

- Design Mechanics

  - Breaking the Stage into Areas of Control
  - Making Beam Throw Templates to Help Select Instrumentation
  - Consolidation of Preliminary Purpose Lists
  - The Preliminary Channel Hook-up

Supplies Needed

Instructor supplies:

- Cardstock
- Sample drawings (such as a scenic section)
- Lighting units from your theatre's inventory
- Area of Control Stage Configuration handouts
- A way to plug in the lighting units
- Tape measures
- Specification sheets for lighting units
- Magic Sheet handouts
- A groundplan

Student supplies:

- T-square
- Architectural scale ruler
- Scissors
- Pencil
- 30/60- and 90-degree drafting triangles
- Circle template
- Protractor

The content in this chapter goes beyond what we normally cover in our Introduction to Design course. As mentioned in Chapter 14, if the class has moved ahead steadily and the students are able to tackle the next step, we'll discuss breaking the stage into areas of control. If your class is unable to do much light lab work, you may find that omitting those activities has left you with empty spaces in your syllabus. The following discussions and exercises are mostly paper-based, and continue helping student designers organize their thoughts as a design takes shape. If you have student lighting designers who are embarking on their first realized designs and your own knowledge of lighting practice is limited, these are also the steps that lead up to creating a plot and deciding how to assign channels at the lighting console.

Discussion: Why We Break the Stage into Areas of Control

Lighting designers *should* be control freaks. If the area upstage of an actor is too bright, the LD should be able to reduce its intensity without changing that of the light on the actor. If a subtle shift of focus is required there should be enough precision in the design that a single unit, focused where the actor is standing, can be brightened a few points. This precision and flexibility requires first breaking the stage down into **areas of control.**

The area of control is the amount of the stage that a single lighting unit covers with light of adequate intensity. The larger the area of the stage lit by a single unit, the less intense the light will be overall, like spreading a teaspoon of jam over a table top rather than a single slice of bread.

In general, each area of control should be about six to eight feet across. It's easiest to think of these as circles on the stage floor, though since light will usually be striking the stage from an angle (except in the case of direct downlight) the shape made on the floor will be a lopsided oval. The important part of the light is what hits the actors' faces five or so feet above the stage floor.

"On *Children of a Lesser God*, Ostermann witnessed her [Musser] doing something extraordinary . . . As Musser was focusing the show, Ostermann noticed that she was setting the hot spots of the lamps about a foot lower than normal. When he asked her why she was doing that, she responded, 'They speak with their hands in the show.'"[4]

Delbert Unruh (with Marilyn Rennagel and Jeff Davis), *The Designs of Tharon Musser*

Lighting Vocabulary Terms: Instrumentation

ERS refers to an ellipsoidal reflector spotlight, also commonly called a 'Leko' or 'Lekolight.' Lekolight is a brand name. The reflector of the unit is ellipsoidally shaped, which allows the beam of light to be shaped by features like shutters or accessories like gobos. The edge of the beam can be sharpened or softened. ERS units come in a variety of beam angles

Beam Throw the beam of light emitted by lighting units will have a certain diameter at specific distances. The angle of the beam's cone of light can be expressed in degrees. Standard beam angles for ERSs include 50 degrees, 36 degrees, 26 degrees, and 19 degrees

Fresnel refers to a type of unit with a Fresnel lens. This is a lens with concentric rings and stippling on one side. This unit emits a soft-edge beam of light that can be made larger (flood) or smaller (spot)

PARcan acronym for Parabolic Aluminized Reflector (in a can). The parabolic reflector of these units provides a beam of light that does not spread out like a Fresnel or ERS. To change the beam angle of a PARcan involves either swapping out a lens or the lamp, depending on the model

In North America, the unit most often used for frontlight is the Ellipsoidal Reflector Spotlight (ERS). There are different brand names, as well as manufacturer variants. One commonality is that ERSs are designed to have **beam throws** of defined angles. This means the beam is a certain width at a certain distance from the unit. Conveniently, in most cases the beam angle can be known by the name of the unit. It is relatively easy to figure out how wide the beam of a 26 degree ERS will be twenty feet or forty feet away from the unit. **Zoom** ERS units have lenses that can be adjusted to vary the diameter of the beam. These units tend to be used in smaller venues where having a certain amount of flexibility in a limited inventory is desirable. Knowing that the optimum area of control should be six to eight feet in diameter regardless of the hanging position's distance from the stage will help the designer choose the best unit from the available inventory for an intended purpose.

Exercise: Laying Out Areas of Control

Copy and reduce the groundplan of a box set in a proscenium space. Include an 8'-0" diameter circle to one side of the drawing to provide a visual baseline of the appropriate area of control size. Be sure that the circle is in the same scale as the rest of the drawing. Circle templates make this exercise a little neater.

- Distribute the groundplan. Draw it on the board. Include a center line. Because downstage center tends to be a place that finds a lot of use throughout a show, it's usually a good

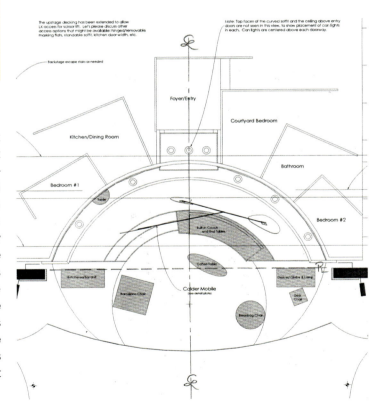

Figure 16.1 Groundplan of *Boeing Boeing* Used for Demonstration (Set Design and Drawing by Brandon Kirkham, Used by Permission)

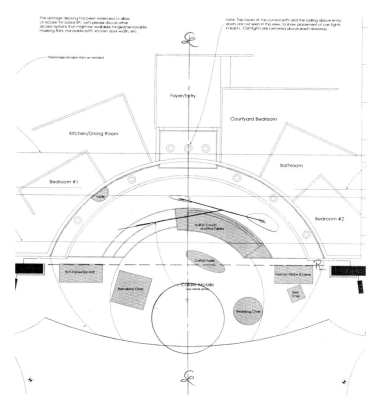

Figure 16.2 Add DC Area of Control to Groundplan (Set/Base Drawing by Brandon Kirkham)

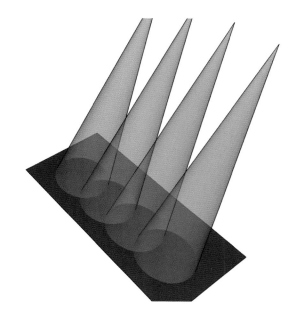

Figure 16.3 Overlapping Beams of Light

idea to be able to draw focus to it. Therefore, the first area to delineate is down center (DC), directly over the center line. Since actors may come right to the lip of the stage, accommodate that possibility by letting some of the circle hang over the front edge.

If you know that actors will be sitting on the floor or even on the lip of the stage, this area of control should slide even further downstage so that there's more assurance of providing adequate illumination for faces lower down.

As actors move across the stage, we usually want them to be evenly lit – in other words, there should be no dips in intensity as they move from one beam to another. This is very important in creating the illusion of a space lit by a single moti-vated source; therefore the beams overlap. In older fixtures, the center was the brightest part of the beam (the 'hot spot') with the intensity decreasing the closer one came to the outer edge of the beam. Through overlapping, the designer increases the intensity at a beam's perimeter.

In newer units, the beams have less difference between the center and the edges. Regardless of the light source, ERS beams remain conical, and it's still necessary to overlap the beams so that actors are less likely to walk into a dark spot.

Overlapping the circles, add areas of control immediately adjacent to down center: down center right (DCR) and down center left (DCL).

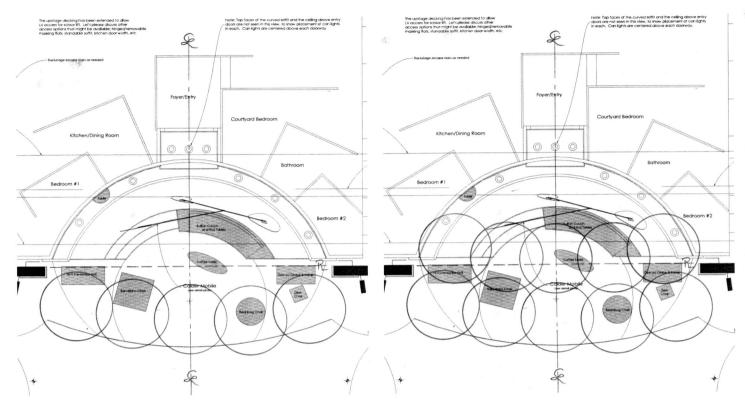

Figure 16.4 The Downstage Broken Up Into Five Areas of Control (Set/Base Drawing by Brandon Kirkham)

Figure 16.5 The Midstage Broken Up Into Five Areas of Control (Set/Base Drawing by Brandon Kirkham)

Continue mapping out the downstage areas of control by overlapping circles stage right (SR) and stage left (SL) until the edges of the playing space have been reached. Be sure that the edge is adequately covered; if you expect actors to linger at the fringes of the space, you might need to add a circle that falls mostly off the stage but still picks up the boundary in its hot spot. There will be consolidation and adjustment later.

In Figure 16.4, the five areas of control across the downstage means that it will take five units (beam throw to be determined later) to provide coverage and flexibility. The five areas are DR, DRC, DC, DLC, and DL. The number of areas will vary depending on the width of the playing space.

Starting center again, map out the midstage areas, overlapping them with the downstage row of circles. These are MR, MRC, MC, MLC, ML.

Depending on how deep the set is, an upstage and possibly a far upstage row of circles may be needed. These are UR, URC, UC, ULC, UL. At this point, the walls and boundaries of the set may start requiring adjustment to rows and columns. On the *Boeing Boeing* set used in these diagrams, the walls curve and only three areas fit in the upstage.

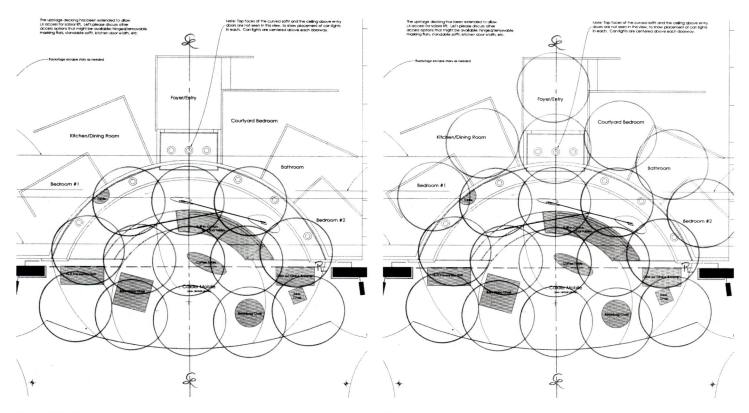

Figure 16.6 The Upstage Broken Up Into Three Areas of Control (Set/Base Drawing by Brandon Kirkham)

Figure 16.7 Areas of Control for Auxiliary Spaces (Set/Base Drawing by Brandon Kirkham)

There may yet remain other parts of the stage that are not part of the central playing space but still need to be lit. On the *Boeing Boeing* set, for example, there are a number of rooms that will be seen whenever someone opens and passes through a door, including the foyer beyond the upstage double doors. Each room is small enough that it can be considered a single area of control.

The script gives each room a specific name, so each area of control is given the name of that room; i.e., Bedroom #1, Kitchen, Hallway, Court Bedroom, Bathroom, and Bedroom #2.

TEACHING TIP

Nomenclature

Many LDs letter or number their areas, starting with 'A' or '1' downstage right. Eric prefers to name, as much as possible, areas with their actual geographic location. This means less

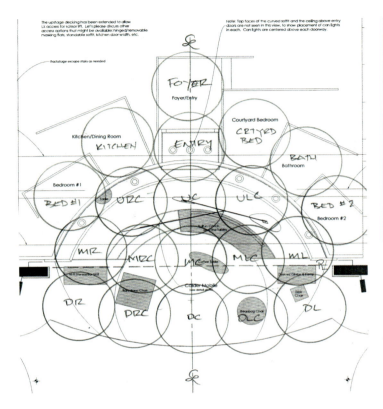

Figure 16.8 Labeling the Areas of Control Descriptively (Set/Base Drawing by Brandon Kirkham)

effort remembering where area 'K' or '11' is and ties into our general attempt to make the purposes as descriptive as possible. Much of the time electricians don't care what the designer names the areas as long as there's clarity, consistency, a map with a key, no jokes, and the designer knows where to stand during focus. In technical rehearsals, the director is also less likely to know what you mean when you note that you'll hit that actor standing in Area 'G' with a special. 'Up Right Center' or 'Kitchen Platform' is terminology the director *will* understand.

each of the show's units (focus points). Units from multiple systems are likely to be focused on each area; a sticky-note or piece of gaffer's tape (depending on the state of the floor at the time of focus) placed in the center of each area of control will allow the designer to be consistent as the electricians move across each hanging position.

The main playing space should now be covered in relatively orderly rows of control areas labeled in a logical fashion. For *Boeing Boeing* a purpose with a uniform distribution across the stage such as a daytime sun frontlight would, in an ideal venue with an ideal inventory, be implemented by thirteen units – one unit per area of control. The type of unit with the best beam throw would be determined by how far away the available hanging positions are from the part of the stage to be covered.

In addition, by laying out areas of control the designer has now determined where to stand on the stage when focusing

Lighting Vocabulary Terms

Circuit the path electricity takes from the dimmer to the lighting unit. This is usually numbered or lettered in order to keep track of them in the paperwork

Patch the act of assigning a circuit to a dimmer: "circuit 6 is patched into dimmer 12." This can also refer to the spreadsheet containing this information

Channel each dimmer is assigned to a channel in the lighting console so that the designer can control the lighting units in a manner that is logical and consistent. Channel 18 may control Dimmer 12, to which Circuit 6 is patched. The unit at the end of Circuit 6 is controlled by Channel 18

Softpatch in a computerized lighting console, the act of assigning dimmers to channels is called softpatch. The spreadsheet containing this information is also called the softpatch, or simply, the patch

System a group of units that serve the same purpose; for example, all of the units that provide the mid-afternoon sun frontlight comprise a system. The channels of systems are usually grouped together for ease of reference: the channels for the mid-afternoon sun frontlight system are channels 30 through 45

Figure 16.9 Steps on the Board: Groundplan Broken Up Into Areas of Control, the Magic Sheet Applied to it, the Generated Purpose List, the Start of the Rough Hook-Up Applying Areas of Control to Purposes, and the Hook-Up Used to Build the Look in the Light Lab

All of the lighting units that implement a single purpose are called a **system**; for example, a system of daytime sun frontlight, or a system of night blue downlight. The individual units creating this system may be controlled by individual channels, but all this means is that the daytime sun frontlight system will consist of Channels X through Z on the channel hook-up. The designer can now bring all of those channels up to the same level for uniform distribution, and then make adjustments to tweak the focus as desired but maintain the illusion that the stage is lit by the daytime sunlight.

For example, we've determined that the daytime sun front light for *Boeing Boeing* will be produced by thirteen units. We can start the assignment of channels with DR as Channel 1, DCR as Channel 2, and so on, from stage left to stage right, row by row, until we get to Channel 13 controlling UCL. Channels 1 through 13 comprise the daytime sunlight system. See Figure 16.9.

When cuing the show, the designer can ask to see Channels 1 through 13 at an intensity of 75 percent. The actors

for this moment are all clustered down center so the upstage areas don't need to be quite as bright. The designer then asks for Channels 6 through 13 to be lowered to 65 percent intensity. Perhaps the far upstage is still a little too bright and more focus on the actors is needed. The designer asks for Channels 11 through 13 to be lowered still further in intensity to 45 percent. This would, theoretically, provide focus downstage where the actors are, but still give a sense that the *whole stage* is lit by the sunlight.

Of course, there will likely be several systems (one for each purpose) on at the same time – daytime sun shadow fill and daytime sun downlight, perhaps – and those will also be broken up into an array of channels that can also be adjusted to provide focus where it is needed on the stage. There are a lot of numbers that need to be kept track of, and the LD's paperwork needs to be accurate and up to date.

Exercise: Laying Out Areas of Control

Distribute groundplans of two differently configured sets, perhaps a thrust and an arena. The same guidelines as for laying out areas of control in a proscenium space apply, though in the case of an arena the designer may have to choose which axis determines the 'front' of the stage.

Direct the students to:

- Break each stage into 6' to 8' areas of control
- Label the areas in a logical fashion, whether with letters or by geographical name
- Compare and discuss.

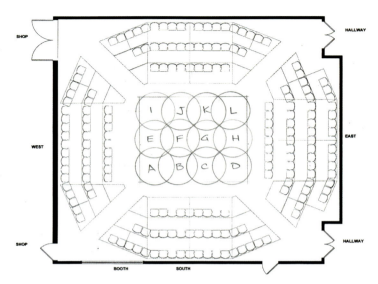

Figure 16.11 An Arena Stage Broken Up Into Areas of Control

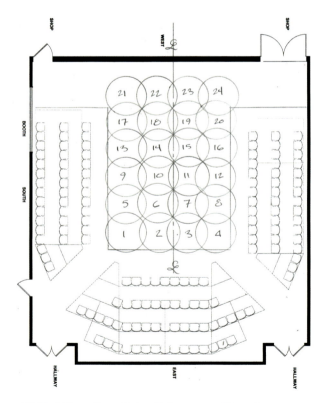

Figure 16.10 A Thrust Stage Broken Up Into Areas of Control

Lighting Vocabulary

Section this is a drawing of the set, stage, and auditorium as viewed from the side. Most often this side view is a 'center-line' section, meaning that the theatre has been cut in half along the center line. For the lighting designer, it is important that this drawing includes all the lighting positions in the theatre, as well as all hanging scenery and soft goods (like legs and borders)

Trim Height the distance an item hangs above the stage floor

Electric any batten on which a lighting unit has been hung becomes an electric. Electrics are typically numbered from the proscenium toward the upstage; the electric closest to the upstage side of the proscenium arch is Electric #1, or, the 1st Electric

Discussion: The Section

Ideally, the scenic designer will have drawn a **center line section** of the set and given a copy to the LD. This is a drawing that cuts the theatre space along the stage's center line (from down to upstage) and then looks either stage left or stage right, depending on which direction provides the most important information. It should be noted that *after* the lighting designer has used the scenic designer's section to work out hanging positions, the LD will then draft his or her *own* section (as a companion drawing to the light plot) showing the venue's hanging positions, the set, borders and legs, electrics at their designated trim heights, as well as any other pertinent lighting information that is best expressed from a side view. See Appendix E for a list of standard hanging positions.

This drawing includes the heights and **trim heights** of all objects above the stage floor, as well as the lateral placement of the battens that will be used as **electrics**. An electric is any batten (pipe) upon which a lighting unit has been hung. Some theatres have battens with permanent wiring; these are called **dedicated electrics**. In many cases, though, the lighting designer will choose from among the battens that the scenic designer hasn't already reserved for scenic use; another reason the LD will want to be present at early production meetings.

The set designer is generally less concerned with the front of house architecture unless the scenery extends out into the audience. Lighting designers may have to obtain drawings from the venue management or technical director in order to draw their own section that includes the placement of auditorium hanging positions such as coves, balcony rails, and box booms.

The section helps the LD determine the distance from any lighting position to the stage, and is therefore a great aid in the selection of units.

Figure 16.12 Center Line Section of the Virtual Model of *The Coronation of Poppea*

Figure 16.13 Section Including Front of House Positions

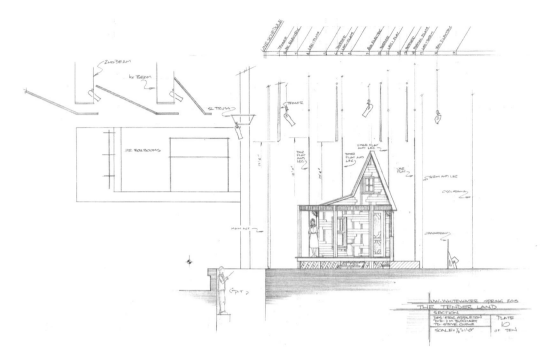

Exercise: Creating Beam Throw Templates

With the stage broken up into areas of control, it's now time to think about which units will best accommodate the areas of control. For students unfamiliar with the types of units available, creating beam throw templates is a good introduction to the characteristics of the basic categories of lighting unit (ERS, Fresnel, PAR). The beam throw template is then used with the section to see how large a beam of light a particular unit will cast on the stage from any available lighting position.

Part One, Version One

If you have time, space, and access to the equipment, bring in various types and brands of units, such as ERS, Fresnels, and PARs (or your inventory equivalent). Create teams and hand out tape measures. Assign each team to a certain number of units. Direct the teams to:

- Hang the lights so they point at a flat surface about ten feet away
- Measure the distance from the unit to the projection surface
- Turn on the unit (for ERSs, sharpen the edge of the beam)
- Measure the diameter of the beam
- Write down the distance and diameter measurements for each type of unit

After all the beam diameters have been measured have the students exchange information so everyone has all the measurements for all the units.

Part One, Version Two

If time and equipment do not allow, bring in the specification sheets for a variety of the more common units found in your inventory. Most manufacturers post these on their websites.

Unit Type	Dia. at 10'	Dia. at 20'	Dia. at 30'	Dia. at 40'	Dia. at 50'
50 degree ERS	9'–3"	18'–6"	27'–9"		
36 degree ERS	6'–0"	12'–3"	18'–6"	24'–6"	30'–6"
26 degree ERS	4'–6"	9'–0"	13'–6"	18'–0"	22'–6"
19 degree ERS	3'–6"	6'–6"	9'–6"	12'–6"	15'–6"
6" Fresnel full flood	2'–7"	5'–7"	8'–4"		
6" Fresnel full spot	14'	28'	42'		

Figure 16.14
Sample Beam Throw
Spread Sheet

Your local lighting equipment supply house may also have copies.

Either procure enough copies so that each student has a copy of each, or create a spreadsheet that contains the name of the unit and the relevant beam throw information. Be sure that the diameter measurement is accompanied by the distance at which that diameter is to be found.

Part Two

Be sure students have their T-squares, triangles, scale rulers, paper, tape, and scissors. For units that have beam throws measured in degrees, be sure that students have protractors.

Have the students draw a line down the center of a piece of paper, landscape orientation. Make a tick close to one end to represent the lens of the unit.

If measurements were taken, use a ratio to figure out how wide the beam will be at ten feet and at twenty feet:

Width/Distance = Width/Distance

If the beam is 6'-6" at twelve feet, find the width at ten feet by solving for X. This is easier if feet and inches are converted to inches: 6'-6" equals 78".

$78/144 = x/120$
144 times x = 78 times 120
144 times x = 9360
65 inches, or 5'-5" = 9360/144
The beam would be 5'-5" wide at 10'-0" from the unit.

If the unit's throw is already described in degrees, set the protractor on the line and measure an angle of 36 degrees, centered on the line (18 degrees to either side). Draw lines that extend from the lens tick through each degree mark to create a triangle.

Depending on whether the section you're about to use for demonstration is in ½" = 1'-0" scale or ¼" = 1'-0" scale, have the students measure down the center line and make ticks at ten feet and twenty feet. Draw horizontal lines at those ticks

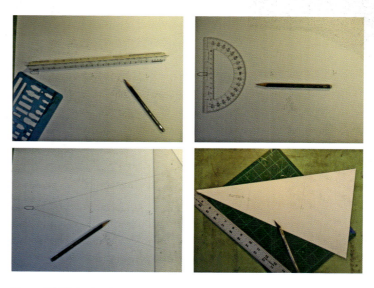

Figure 16.15 Laying Out the Beam Throw of a 36 degree ERS Unit

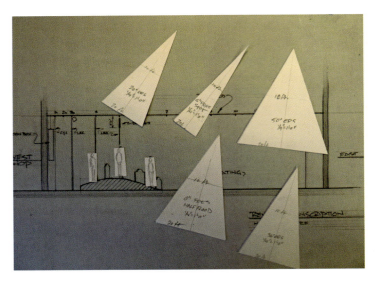

Figure 16.16 Cut Out Beam Throw Templates

across the width of the triangle. Cut out the triangle and label with the unit type.

Have the student create templates for a number of units, especially the standard variations of ERS types:

- 36 degree (6x9)
- 26 degree (6x12)
- 19 degree (6x16)

Since Fresnels have a widely variable beam throw, include two Fresnel templates:

- Full Flood
- Spot

Again, be sure to label each template with the type and brand of the unit, as well as the scale. While the angle of the throw won't change from scale to scale, the diameter of the beam will be very different at ten feet in ¼"= 1'-0" scale as opposed to ten feet in ½" = 1'-0" scale.

Exercise: Using Beam Templates to Guide Instrument Choices

Bring in the sections of a couple of productions. Be sure that the scale used by the students in creating their beam templates allows their use on the drawings. A ¼" = 1'-0" scale template used on a ½" = 1'-0" scale drawing will be problematic when looking at lighting positions a fair distance from the stage.

- Place a cut-out of a scaled human figure on the stage three or so feet from the front edge.
- Using the 36 degree template, place the point at the mark for the closest position above the seating (this works more clearly for proscenium theatres), with the axis of the triangle pointing at the figure's head.
- Ask the students how much of the stage they can expect this beam to cover.
- Does it seem as though it's large or small enough for the desired area of control size?
- Remember that it's the head level of the actor that is most important.
- Try all three sizes of beam throws.
- Which is optimum for that lighting position?
- Move to the next lighting position away from the stage.
- Repeat the process to determine the unit with the optimum size of beam spread.

Note that the further toward the rear of the auditorium you go, the shallower (less steep) the vertical angle of the beam becomes on the figure standing downstage. From a balcony rail position, units essentially shoot their light into the stage from a dead-front angle, which is not the best for maintaining plasticity and will throw just as much light onto the scenery behind the actor as on the actor. Remember too, that the desire is to create systems that should have a generally consistent (as far as that is possible) angle for each instrument serving that purpose. If an actor moves across the stage in the morning sunlight, shadows should not swing widely across her face every few steps. Next:

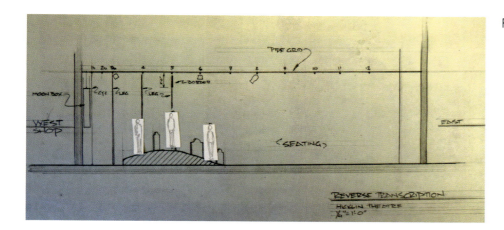

Figure 16.17 Three Figures on the Stage

- Move the figure about six feet upstage.
- Which front of house lighting position comes closest to providing a beam whose axis is around 45 degrees from horizontal (use a drafting triangle to check)?
- Move the figure another six feet upstage.
- Now which position provides a 45-degree beam of light?

Forty-five degrees is an angle that provides good plasticity and good visibility. It's solid and practical and a young designer should not be faulted for using a basic three point lighting approach – unless, of course, the text, the research, and the experimentation in the light lab suggest a goal other than adequate naturalistic illumination.

Place three human figures on the section: one at the lip, one six feet upstage of it, and another six feet upstage of the second one.

- What beam throw of units in which positions will provide the vertical angle closest to 45 degrees for each figure?

Because this is a center line section, the figures are standing in areas DC, MC, and UC. This means that as an actor moves upstage along the center line the direction of light indicated by the placement of shadows on her or his face will not shift noticeably. Depending on the placement of lighting positions in the auditorium of the theatre, the positions closest to the stage will be the best ones for the light falling furthest upstage.

If the height of the proscenium opening or trim height of a border blocks the nearest auditorium ceiling position (often called beams or coves) from lighting the upstage areas, it may be necessary to jump to the first electric. Check the angle with a beam template. Here is one of the places lighting designers often face compromise – the upstage can't be reached by a front of house position, and the first electric provides an angle steeper than that of the rest of the system. Does the designer live with this, or seek another solution? Encourage the student to experiment and re-think.

Exercise: Not all Types of Units Require the Same Size Areas of Control

Fresnels and PAR units are often used over the stage for down- and backlight as they tend to have wider beams than the ERSs used to enable finesse of front light purposes. This does not mean they cannot be used for frontal purposes, just that controlling the beam spread tends to be a little more problematic. The following demonstrates that the number and size of areas of control can be connected to the type of unit expected to implement them.

- On the center line section diagram, place one of the figures downstage, a couple feet up from the downstage edge of the deck.
- Note the height of the proscenium opening; it's helpful to draw a horizontal line across the upstage to keep this reference height visible.
- Select the first electric, or first available batten. Draw another line from the drawing's line schedule (if the designer has not drawn in battens) down to the horizontal proscenium height line. For the purposes of this exercise, we will consider this intersection to be the electric's trim height.
- Select the Fresnel cut-out that shows the beam at spot. Place the point at the trim height for the electric.

  - How large is the beam at face level?

- Select the Fresnel cut-out for full flood. Place the point at the trim height.

  - How large is this beam at face level?

  - How many Fresnels at full flood would it take to cover the full depth of the set?
  - How many Fresnels at spot would it take?

- Is the number of Fresnels needed to cover the stage the same number as the areas of control mapped out earlier?

- Select the 36-degree ERS cutout. Place the point at the trim height.

  - How large is this beam at face height?
  - How many 36-degree ERSs would it take to cover the fell depth of the set?

Distribute three fresh scale groundplans to each student and ask them to break the stage up into areas of control appropriate to:

- Fresnels at spot
- Fresnels at full flood
- Fresnels at half spot (or half flood).

How many Fresnels are needed to cover the stage if they are focused at half spot?

Whether a designer chooses to use Fresnels, PARs or ERSs for systems like down- or backlight depends upon the purpose of the system as well as available inventory and

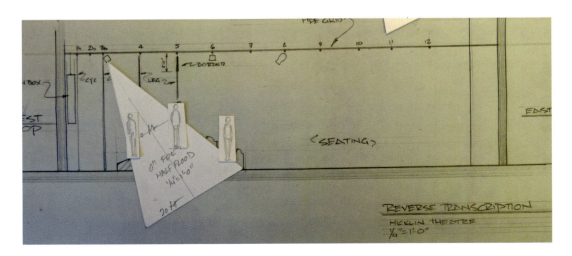

Figure 16.18 Fresnel Beam Throw Cut-out on a Section

number of lighting positions over the stage. If the designer wishes the downlight to have texture created by gobos, the unit choice is going to be an ERS, since Fresnels and PARs are not designed to accommodate gobos. If the designer wants soft, diffuse coverage, then Fresnels would likely be the better choice.

Exercise: Using a Groundplan to Explore Beam Angles

A more three-dimensional way of using beam throw templates is by using a groundplan. Be sure the groundplan has the venue's lighting positions noted.

On the groundplan, place a figure midstage center, preferably directly under an electric.

- Using a section, measure from the deck to the electric's trim height.
- Measure this height onto a strip of Bristol board and cut it out.
- Hold the measured strip vertically, touching the groundplan at the base of the human figure.
- Hold the beam throw template for a full flood Frensel with the point at the top of the strip.
- How much of the stage does it cover?
- If the unit is moved to an upstage electric and tipped to focus on the figure, how much of the stage will *now* be covered?

If you can determine the height of the position from the deck of the stage (assuming that the groundplan in this case represents deck height rather than a shoulder-height section), you can use this method to get a good sense of how much of the stage a particular unit will cover.

There are, or course, software programs that help the designer see beam throws through virtual modeling. As with modeling of scenery, a balance must be struck between the time needed to learn the program itself and the time the program can save once it is mastered.

Figure 16.19   Using a Groundplan to Demonstrate a Beam Throw

Discussion: The Preliminary Hook-Up

A **Hook-Up** is a spreadsheet of almost all of the non-graphically expressed information required to execute a lighting design. There are a few different ways to organize this spreadsheet. A Channel Hook-Up organizes the information numerically by channel. A Dimmer Hook-Up organizes it numerically by dimmer. Programs like Lightwright allow the designer and electricians to break out and organize information in myriad ways: by gel color, by instrument type, by lamp wattage, by position, by circuit, etc. If access to lighting specific programs is not available, a photocopy of a formatted table will work (and was what designers used until the advent of personal computing, anyway).

For the designer, the channel hook-up is the conceptual ordering of data that is most important earliest in the process. Different designers have favorite ways of organizing their

Boeing Boeing   CHANNEL HOOKUP   Page 1 of 9

Untitled.lw5   2/4/2016

LD: Eric Appleton   August 2015

Milwaukee Chamber Theatre   director: Michael Cotey

Cabot Theatre   ME: Phil Warren

Channel	Dm	Position	U#	Purpose	Type & Acc & W	Color	Gobo
(1)		2nd Electric	9	Amber Diag Back > SR	PAR 64 MFL 1kw	L103	
(2)		2nd Electric	10	Amber Diag Back > SRC	PAR 64 MFL 1kw	L103	
(3)		2nd Electric	11	Amber Diag Back > SLC	PAR 64 MFL 1kw	L103	
(4)		2nd Electric	12	Amber Diag Back > SL	PAR 64 MFL 1kw	L103	
(5)		2nd Electric	8	Blue Back SR	PAR 64 MFL 1kw	R381	
(6)		2nd Electric	7	Blue Back SRC	PAR 64 MFL 1kw	R381	
(7)		2nd Electric	6	Blue Back SLC	PAR 64 MFL 1kw	R381	
(8)		2nd Electric	5	Blue Back SL	PAR 64 MFL 1kw	R381	
(9)		2nd Electric	1	Lav Diag Back < SR	PAR 64 MFL 1kw	Gam 101	
(10)		2nd Electric	2	Lav Diag Back < SRC	PAR 64 MFL 1kw	Gam 101	
(11)		2nd Electric	3	Lav Diag Back < SLC	PAR 64 MFL 1kw	Gam 101	
(12)		2nd Electric	4	Lav Diag Back < SL	PAR 64 MFL 1kw	Gam 101	
(13)		1st Electric	12	Lav Down > SR	PAR 64 MFL 1kw	Gam 106	
(14)		1st Electric	11	Lav Down > SRC	PAR 64 MFL 1kw	Gam 106	
(15)		1st Electric	10	Lav Down > SLC	PAR 64 MFL 1kw	Gam 106	
(16)		1st Electric	9	Lav Down > SL	PAR 64 MFL 1kw	Gam 106	
(17)		1st Electric	5	Pale Blue Down < SR	PAR 64 MFL 1kw	R364	
(18)		1st Electric	4	Pale Blue Down < SRC	PAR 64 MFL 1kw	R364	

University of Wisconsin-Whitewater / Lightwright 5   (1) thru (18)

Figure 16.20 Sample Channel Hook-up Page Generated by Lightwright

Show Title: Date of Paperwork:

Lighting Designer: Page: of

Producer: Director:

Venue: Master Electrician:

Chn	Dim	Ckt	Position	Unit #	Purpose	Type & Acc & W.	Color	Gobo

Figure 16.21 Sample Blank Channel Hook-up Table

channel hook-up and sometimes the nature of the show will determine how channels are grouped. The channel hook-up should feature the most *logical* ordering of purposes possible as the designer will have a very intimate relationship with this document.

In order to build a preliminary hook-up, the designer should have first created a magic sheet for each major look of the show. Each magic sheet generates its own short preliminary purpose list. The purpose lists are then consolidated, looking for purposes that repeat in multiple scenes, or purposes that can be merged together for the sake of expediency (such as a limited equipment inventory).

For example, here are three purpose lists for a show with three major looks:

Scene One	Scene Two	Scene Three
Morning Sun Main Source Frontlight <	Afternoon Sun Main Source Frontlight >	Moonlight Frontlight >
Morning Sun Shadow Fill Frontlight >	Afternoon Sun Shadow Fill <	Moonlight Frontlight Support <
Morning Sun Downlight	Afternoon Sun Downlight	Moonlight Downlight
Morning Light Blue Cyc	Afternoon Mid Blue Cyc	Table Lamp in Frontroom
Morning Sun Cloud Templates (on cyc)	Joe's Porch Step Special	Frontroom Downlight
Joe's Porch Step Special	Table Lamp in Frontroom Window	Joe's Porch Step Special
Lizzie's Front Walk Special	Tabitha's Porch Special	Lizzie's Front Walk Special

Figure 16.22
Three Purpose Lists

Once the individual purpose lists have been collated to create a single purpose list, the next step is to re-order them in a manner conducive to the designer's working habits. This order will become the organizing structure of the channel hook-up. A good way to order purposes is by general direction and/or function. The categories might look like this:

- Frontlight
- Sidelight
- Specials and Practicals
- Back- and Downlight
- Cycs and Drops

If the show is short enough and each scene is different enough, organization by scene or order of use might be desirable. Most designers, though, will find themselves using bits planned for one look to augment the looks of other scenes; for instance, adding the downlight color from the night scene to the afternoon scene to add some tonality to shadows. If all the downlight systems are kept together in the hook-up, it's easier to find them. This is why we ask students to organize their hook-ups by broad directional qualities. In the following list, the first two purposes are downlight systems; the next four are frontlight systems even though they come from house right and house left; the third group are cyclorama colors; the final three are all specials.

- Day Straw Downlight
- Evening Purple Downlight
- Daytime Warm Sun (light straw) <
- Daytime Warm Sun Shadow Fill (lavender) >
- Evening Silvery Moonlight (pale blue) >
- Evening Moonlight Shadow Fill (deep blue) <
- Daytime Cyc (pale blue)
- Evening Cyc (violet)
- Shirley's SL special
- Dexter's UC special
- Lonny's Kitchen special

While every show is different, LDs are generally consistent in how they personally organize their hook-ups. Eric likes to start his hook-ups with cyc purposes, then down- and backlight systems, then frontlight systems, with practicals and specials at the end.

Exercise: Expanding the Purpose List into a Preliminary Hook-up

This exercise can be done with two or three pre-prepared magic sheets. Each student will need diagrams breaking the stage used as the basis for the magic sheet into areas of control for both ERS units and for Fresnels. Have the students:

- Create a purpose list for each magic sheet
- Consolidate the purpose lists into a single list, edited for duplication

- Order the consolidated purpose list to group broad directional purposes together
- Discuss why they have chosen to order their groups as they did
- Using the areas of control diagrams, determine how many units it would take for each purpose to cover the requisite amount of the stage.
- On lined paper, make a column of numbers along the left hand side, starting at 1.
- For the first purpose on the list, begin at 1. Write down the name of the purpose, the area of control where it will be focused, the suggested type of unit, the color, and a small arrow for direction. Many designers consistently begin the numbering of each system DL, going stage right, then going back to start the midstage areas with ML (like reading a book).

1 Warm Morning Sun DL, 26 degree ERS, R08 <
2 Warm Morning Sun DCL, 26 degree ERS, R08 <

- Once all of the areas of control for the first system have been numbered, start the next system at the next available number:

13 Warm Morning Sun UR, 26 degree ERS, R08 <
14 Warm Morning Shadow Fill DL, 26 degree ERS, > R52
15 Warm Morning Shadow Fill DCL, 26 degree ERS, > R52

- Repeat until all purposes have been broken into areas of control and each area of control has been assigned to a channel number.

The preliminary channel hook-up just generated is a wish-list. The venue's inventory and number of dimmers are vital pieces of information necessary to incorporate into the finished hook-up. Some designers start with the physical parameters; some create the wish-list and whittle things down to fit.

Exercise: Revising the Hook-up to Accommodate Number and Capacity of Dimmers

Using two or three magic sheets and accompanying area of control diagrams, give the students a limited number of dimmers just shy of the number necessary to assign every area of control its own channel. Most dimmer racks come in packs of 12, so allow 36, 48, 60, etc. available dimmers.

Instruct the students to write a column of numbers representing available dimmers down the left-hand side of a page.

The students will then have to determine how to consolidate, merge, or even eliminate purposes in order to create a hook-up that gets them as close as possible to the wish-list.

Exercise: Revising the Hook-up to Accommodate Number and Capacity of Dimmers, Variation

One way the compromise of variant one can be done is by **ganging** areas of control; in other words, Channel 1 controls both DL and DCL areas, Channel 2 DC, and Channel 3 DRC and DR. As long as the combined wattage of the units is less than the load limit of the dimmer, this will work fine (which means that LDs need to know how much power various dimmers can handle). A 1.2kW dimmer can handle two 575 watt units; it cannot handle two 750 watt units.

Give the students a limited number of dimmers, this time providing a load in watts, either 1.2kW (1200 watts) or 2.4kW (2400 watts). Also provide a list of instruments with typical wattages, i.e., 36-degree ERS lamped at 575 watts and 6" Fresnels lamped at 500 watts. Wattage information can be found on most unit manufacturers' specification sheets.

Direct students to once again work through compromises to the wish-list, using wattage and dimmer load information to guide their decisions.

For LED fixtures, power is less of an issue since those fixtures are lower in wattage than conventional units (30 to 120 watts depending on how many LEDs in the fixtures contribute to the color created, as opposed to 575, 750, or 1000 watts for conventional units at 100 percent intensity). LED fixtures require simple AC (like being plugged into a wall) because the dimming is controlled electronically rather than electrically. They will get circuited into the dimmer rack's **non-dim** dimmers (dimmers that are either at 100 percent or at 0 percent – they do not fade).

LED fixtures, because they *are* electronically controlled, require more channels than conventional fixtures. A basic LED unit might require four channels: one for overall intensity, one for the level of the red LEDs, one for the blue, and one for the green. These four channels are then used to select the color and intensity of that single unit. Brand of unit and type of console will determine how LED units (and other moving lights) are controlled.

Exercise: Revising the Hook-Up to Accommodate a Venue's Inventory

Dimming capacity is not the only technical compromise facing the lighting designer. The instruments available for use can vary greatly depending on the venue's in-house stock and the available budget for rental.

Up to this point, the students have been working off a wish-list of units, letting the areas of control and the desired quality of light guide their choices. Now comes the time to make decisions based on what is actually available.

Part One

- Allow the students the total number of dimmers suggested by the expansion of the purpose list via areas of control. However, note the capacity of each dimmer, either 1.2kW or 2.4kW.
- Distribute an inventory that provides more than enough units (ERSs, Fresnels, PARs, Far Cycs, etc.) of each type likely to be needed, each with wattage noted.
- Direct the students revise their hook-up by including the preferred unit type for each channel, but keeping an eye on the dimmer capacity.

Part Two

Distribute an inventory that has enough overall units but is short in the two or three types that are likely to be heavily relied upon, such as 36-degree ERSs and 6″ Fresnels.

- Direct the students to revise their hook-ups and make the necessary compromises to accommodate the shortages.

  - Will they split up unit types within systems, or convert a system to a less desirable but still reasonable fixture?
  - What other solutions can be discovered?

Part Three

- Distribute an inventory that does *not* have enough overall units to accommodate all the channels of the expanded purpose list.
- Direct the students to revise their hook-ups and make the necessary compromises to get as close as possible to their design wish-list. They might not only have to use less-preferred fixtures for some systems, but may have to gang units or consolidate areas of control to achieve their ends.
- Discuss obstacles and solutions.

  - How compromised was the wish-list?
  - Does the student feel the design has radically changed?

> "The process of lighting is a strange contradiction. In performance we are dealing with a totally insubstantial medium: light is so difficult to contain, describe, or confine. Yet when we employ it in the theatre, it is essential that every detail be precisely planned in advance. Every single part of the lighting can be calculated and considered on paper. Only by preparing all the physical aspects of the lighting, i.e. the equipment, in great detail, can we get sufficient creative freedom on the stage itself."[5]
>
> Richard Pilbrow, *Stage Lighting*

- Will the looks created on the stage greatly suffer, or was this just a different route to the same destination?

Notes

1. Stanley McCandless, *A Method of Lighting the Stage* (New York: Theatre Arts, Inc., 1932), p. 13.
2. J. Michael Gilette, *Designing with Light: An Introduction to Stage Lighting* (New York: McGraw-Hill Higher Education, 4th edition, 2003), p. 192.
3. Linda Essig, *Lighting and the Design Idea* (Belmont, CA: Thomson Wadsworth, 2005), p. 169.
4. Delbert Unruh, *The Designs of Tharon Musser* (Syracuse, NY: United States Institute for Theatre Technology, Inc., 2007), p. 78.
5. Richard Pilbrow, *Stage Lighting* (New York: Drama Book Publishers, 1991), p. 37.

Section IV

Sound Design

Chapter 17

Introduction to Sound Design

> "There is the distant sound of a string breaking, as if in the sky, a dying, melancholy sound. Silence falls, and the only thing to be heard is a tree being struck by an axe far off in the orchard."[1]
> Anton Chekhov, Final Stage Direction from *The Cherry Orchard*

Instructor Supplies Needed

- 3 x 5 notecards
- Playback system
- Numerous recordings of music and sound effects
- Microphone connected to playback system
- Object that produces sound, such as a music box
- Blank Sound Plot handout

In many small theatre departments and programs, sound is a subject that can easily fall through the cracks due to lack of instructors and the small number of students professing interest in the field. Communication Departments often offer the technical side of sound production through television and radio work, but those experiences seldom have the dramaturgical component found in theatre production – unless, perhaps, the Communication Department supports radio drama and television serials. Sound is important to the theatrical environment (witness the Chekhov quote above) but at the undergraduate level students are not often presented with a systematic approach to developing a design that is meaningfully integrated with all the other design components of the production. As we've developed our course through the years, we've realized that our general approach also works as an introduction to sound design. This chapter is for those instructors unfamiliar with sound who seek a structured introduction to the field.

There are fundamental parts to building a sound design that can be addressed through the process previously used for costumes, scenery, and lighting. This chapter will consider the foundations of sound design through learning about:

- How to Talk About Sound
- Categories of Theatrical Sound
- Script Analysis for Sound Design
  - The Sound Plot
- Research for Sound Design

Sound, like lighting, has a technical aspect that can be daunting to the newcomer. The technological progress of the field has been rapid throughout the past century, from live Foley-style sound to reel-to-reel tape recorders, though DAT, compact discs, and into MP3s and software editing programs. A sound designer can now walk into a theatre, plug a laptop into the house sound system and not only play all the cues and adjust their levels, but even edit on the spot. Just as a lighting designer needs to account for inventory and dimmer capacity, at a certain point the sound designer must also take the venue's available equipment into consideration. The equipment *is* necessary for the realization of the sound design and deep knowledge of the technology will make a sound designer more nimble. However, it must always be remembered that the design is in service to the story, not the equipment.

There is a difference between sound designing, sound engineering, and sound operation, and depending on the size and scope of the production the duties of any one of these can vary greatly. Still, even if the director has determined the production only requires the sound effects listed in the text, someone has to interpret those sound effects as revealed by the text, the style of the production, and the technical systems available for use. The procurement of the best sound for a show involves thorough script analysis, historical and theatrical

Sound Vocabulary Terms

Foley A Foley artist is someone who creates the sound effects and background noises that are added in post-production to film and video. Foley can also refer to the craft of creating sound effects in a live theatrical environment

DAT Digital Audio Tape

MP3 A common digital recording format used in many consumer audio players

> "Imagining sounds in the context of a production is the first step in designing sound for the theatre. You must hear sound not as a single entity, but as an interaction of parts making up a whole. Many individual sounds may comprise one effect; many effects used together constitute a design. The sound designer is asked to produce a whole from the parts, so the separate sounds that make up the whole are the essence of your design."[2]
> Kaye and Lebrecht, *Sound and Music for the Theatre*

knowledge, communication skills, and technical savvy. The script may call for a doorbell, but there are many doorbells to choose from. The designer must determine where the sound originates on the stage (speaker placement) and set volume levels appropriate to the sound, the action, and the acoustics of the auditorium (both when filled with an audience and empty).

Like lighting, some specific equipment will be necessary to explore sound in the classroom; namely, a playback system. Fortunately, in this digital age tablets, laptops, and smart phones not only have their own speakers but can also be connected to classroom systems. Currently, a few common sound design software programs are QLab, Sound Forge and Audacity; check their websites to see if they work with your computing platform and if there are free or low-cost educational versions. Still, a lot can be done – however rudimentary it feels – with the media player installed on your classroom computer or personal tablet.

Discussion: Learning to Talk About Sound

How we talk about sound is often highly subjective, both in taste and in descriptive terms. A sound is often first described as pleasant or not pleasant, and when asked *why* it is unpleasant, vocabulary falters. We feel that, as with light, the first task is to get the students more proficient in talking about sound, both when describing what is heard and in explaining what is proposed.

To develop ways to talk about sound it's sometimes useful to translate sound into visuals. A sound can be described as smooth and rolling, sharp and spiky, suggestive of colors, textures, etc. A director might ask for a piece of music that sounds like "waves on the ocean," which is very different from the actual sound of waves. The designer needs to ask the director what are the expected *qualities* of "waves on the ocean," which can, in turn, be explored through design element vocabulary.

Exercise: Describing Sound

Select four distinctly different sounds: for example, Irish folk music, a current rap song, whale vocalizations, and ambient forest noises. Try to have at least one of the pieces be highly organized and one be somewhat random. Each piece should be no more than one minute in duration.

As time allows, repeat with different sounds and a different design element (Version Three).

Version One

Distribute 3x5 cards to the class. Have the students number the cards on the reverse side, one through four. Direct the students to write down up to three words describing the *emotional* quality of the sound; what feeling that sound evokes. Collect the cards. Collate them by number.

Select three or four from each set and without revealing the number lay them out in groups. Ask the students:

- Which set do they think belongs to which sound? (Request that students not comment if their card is in a group.)
- What is the rationale for the match?
- Did each sound evoke the same emotions in everyone? Why or why not?
- Are there cultural aspects of particular sounds that come into play?
- Did the reaction come from engagement with the sound as heard, or from previous personal familiarity with the sound?
- Are there words that were used for multiple sounds? What are the similar qualities of these sounds?

Version Two

Distribute 3x5 cards to the class. Have the students number the cards on the reverse side, one through four. Use the same four sounds used in Version One, only this time direct the students to use three descriptive statements drawn from design element vocabulary (wavy lines, nubbly texture, etc.). Collect the cards.

Collate them by number. Select three or four from each number, and without revealing the number, lay them out in sets. Ask the students:

- Which set belongs to which sound? (Request that students not comment if their card is in a set.) Explain their rationale for the match.
- Did the same words pop up for particular sounds?
- Does this mean that if a word is used by *anyone* to describe a sound, this particular sound will come to mind?

Compare these descriptive cards to the earlier emotive cards. Discuss similarities and differences between the words offered in both exercises.

Version Three

Distribute 3x5 cards to the class. Have the students number the cards on the reverse side, one through four. In pencil, and using *only* the design element of 'line,' direct the students to draw their response to each of the four sounds previously used. Collect the cards. Collate them by number. Select three or four from each number, and without revealing the number, lay them out in sets. Ask the students:

- Which set belongs to which sound? (Request that students not comment if their card is in a set.) Explain their rationale for the match.
- What are the commonalities and differences as to how line was used to express the sound?

Discussion: Vocabulary for Sound

Conversation about sound can become more effective if it is broken down into controllable properties. The first four basic properties of sound can be simply demonstrated vocally by the instructor:

- **Pitch** (frequency of sound waves): How high or low the sound is – the slower the vibration, the lower the note
- **Duration**: How long the sound lasts – a quick ping or a sustained drone
- **Intensity**, or **Volume**: How loud or soft it is; does it fade into the background or overwhelm all other sounds?
- **Direction** (have students close their eyes as you move about the room): Where does it seem as though the sound is originating from?

Exercise: Describing Sound through Controllable Properties

Select a number of recorded sounds: for example, a period telephone ring, an alarm clock buzzer, a piece of music by Mozart, and industrial factory noises. For each sound, ask the students to determine how high or low the pitch of the sound was, how long the various sounds were held for, and the volume of the sound compared to both the previous sound and to the overall sound level of the room. The following questions can direct the discussion:

- Does a sound have the same impact at different volumes?

  - Does something played nearby at a lower volume sound closer in proximity than one played further away at a higher volume? Or vice versa?
  - Can a different emotional impact be created through volume?
  - Is a loud phone ring more or less urgent than a soft one?
  - Can a character's response be altered through a sound's volume?

- If technically possible, play the same sounds but with pitch and duration changed; for example, slow down a piece of music.

  - How does changing those properties alter the perception of the sound?

- If your classroom has a controllable speaker set-up, play a piece of music that has been recorded in both mono and stereo. What does having different parts of the composition emerge from different locations do to the listening experience?
- If you have a microphone, set the classroom speakers so that the sound coming from all of them is equally balanced. Have the students close their eyes. Speak softly into the microphone so that the sound of your actual voice cannot be heard above the sound of your transmitted voice. Quietly move around the room. Ask the students if they can locate you. Have them open their eyes but continue to speak quietly as you move.

  - Is it easier to follow a performer visually, or aurally?

- Reset the balance so that your voice comes out of a speaker across the room.

  - What happens when a sound you expect to come from one locale (the person) originates from elsewhere (the speaker across the room)?

> "Sound design doesn't work if the speaker placement isn't properly worked into the initial design. Most of my musical collaborators have said to me that I never used to look at where speakers were going to go in the original design of the set, and I have taken that to heart. In the last several years, I have striven to rectify that omission."[3]
> Jack O'Brien, quoted in *Sound and Music for the Theatre*

Discussion: More Controllable Properties of Sound

The next three controllable properties address more complex aspects of sound:

- **Tone Quality** or **Timbre**: How the item (musical instrument, speaker) that creates the sound imparts a quality to the sound
- **Rhythm**: Does the sound have a beat, or tempo? Is it regular, irregular? Fast, slow?
- **Dynamics**: Overall changes as the sound progresses; does it speed up, slow down, become louder or softer? How are changes organized throughout the sound as a whole?

Exercise: Exploring Tone Quality through Design Element Vocabulary

Musicians are well-aware that a note played on a flute has very different tonal qualities than the same note played on an oboe. The structure and material of the instrument impart distinct resonances to the note.

Select a piece of music that has been adapted for three different types of instruments. Try to find solo performances. Bach works well for this, as many of his pieces have been adapted for a variety of instruments; recordings of his brief *Prelude in D Minor (BWV 999)*, for instance, can be found performed on piano, guitar, and lute.

Distribute 3x5 cards to the students; have them number the backs as one, two, and three. Instruct them to write down up to three descriptive words drawn from design element vocabulary for each piece of music; don't tell them they will be listening to the same piece three times. Play each version of the selection in turn. Collect the cards, collate, display arranged by number. Ask the students:

- For each piece, how similar or different were the descriptive terms?
- What were the differences from piece to piece?
- At what point did students realize they were listening to the same piece of music?
- Can they identify the instrument used to play the music?
- Was there a quality to the music that seemed specific to the instrument?
- Were differences in quality tied more to the performers' interpretations of the piece?
- Did the different instruments *allow* or support the different emotive interpretations?

Exercise: Comparing Tone Quality #1

Computers and synthesizers have come a long way in duplicating the tonal qualities of physical musical instruments, but there remain major differences as well as the fact that electronics can generate sounds that *cannot* be duplicated by musical instruments.

Select a piece of music performed by traditional musical instruments and also performed wholly electronically. Bach is still a good candidate (*Switched-on Bach*); William Orbit's *Pieces in a Modern Style* offers a selection of classical pieces performed via wholly electronic means. Play the two versions for the class. Have the students use design element vocabulary to describe and compare the pieces. Ask them:

- Is it easy to tell which one is the traditional version and which is the electronic version?
- What kind of tonal qualities are apparent in each piece? Is one 'warmer' and one 'colder'?
- What makes a recording warm or cold?
- Which piece has more aural complexity? Is every note perfect and clean, or is there fuzziness and layering?
- Which piece, if any, seems to have more *emotional* complexity?
- Are there differences in what kind of scene the two pieces might be used to preface or underscore?

This exercise can be further linked to design elements by distributing cards and asking each student for a graphic response using line, texture, etc.

Exercise: Comparing Tone Quality #2

Bring in a real sound-making item, such as a music box or musical instrument, and a recording of that item's sound. If possible, set up a microphone to reinforce the real item's sound and play it through the system. Have the class close their eyes and play all three versions of sound for the class. Afterwards, ask the students:

- Were there differences between the three versions?
- What were the differences?
- Did one sound more 'real' than the other? What made the sound more 'real?'
- What can affect the quality of a recording's playback?
- Is the reinforcement of the sound closer to the unamplified sound or the recording?
- Does the reinforced sound have a completely different quality?
- What is the nature of those differences, if any?

> "I hate miking actors. If it is a must, I try to use PCC-160s as foot microphones and replace what is missing acoustically in the theatre. I never want microphone levels in a play to sound electronic or reinforced. I believe in separate bussing. I play music through one system, voice reinforcement through another, sound effects from a third. I never cross streams."[4]
> Tom Mardikes, quoted in *Sound and Music for the Theatre*

Exercise: Exploring Dynamics, Part One

Select a poem or short piece of dialogue. Prepare two pieces of music to underscore the reading; they should be thematically appropriate, but one should be faster and one should be slower. Ask for volunteers and direct the students to read the piece aloud without underscoring. After the reading is finished, ask the readers:

- How did they determine what pace to read it? What pace do they think is required for the piece?
- What did they feel is the overall mood/atmosphere of the piece?

Have the volunteers read the piece again, this time with the first piece of music underscoring it.

- Ask the rest of the class if the addition of the music had an effect on the reading.
- Ask the readers if the music changed anything for them.

Read the piece again, with the second piece of music.

- Again, ask the class if their perception of the piece changed.
- Ask the readers if the new music changed anything for them.
- Which was most preferred by the class: no music, the first, or the second piece of music? Why?

Exercise: Exploring Dynamics, Part Two

Select a short piece of dialogue (preferably something at night on a porch) and ask for volunteer readers. Prepare a long recording of crickets chirping. Start the recording of crickets. Play at a reasonable speaking volume. After about ten seconds, instruct the readers to begin. Allow the crickets to play at the same volume throughout the reading. Ask the audience what impact the sound of the crickets had on the scene.

- Did the readers compete with the sound?
- Did the audience get used to the sound and tune it out after a while?

- How could the crickets be better integrated into the reading?

Start the recording again at the same volume. After about ten seconds, instruct the readers to begin. After a line or two, slowly fade the volume of the crickets until barely perceptible. After the reading is over, ask the audience:

- Did they notice when the crickets were turned down?
- Did they miss the crickets through the rest of the scene?
- What does establishing the crickets at the beginning and then fading them out do for or against the clarity of the dialogue?

Start the recording a third time, at the same initial volume. After about ten seconds, instruct the readers to begin. After a line or two, slowly fade the crickets until barely perceptible. Every so often, adjust the volume of the crickets so a chirp or two can be heard within pauses or under a line of dialogue. During the final lines of the scene, slowly bring the volume back up to the starting level and allow to play for about five seconds after the last line. Slowly fade the crickets out. Discuss whether these changes contributed to or detracted from the scene, and why.

"However you deliver your storm, think too about the actor. What sounds are going to help the actor? He may appreciate a bit of competition, but you don't want to drown him out. He has to play the part again tomorrow and he needs his voice. Work it out with him. How much is helpful and how much is too much? And so it goes with every sound effect you ever consider. How do you deliver it? What's your style? Do you really need it?"[5]

John Caird, *Theatre Craft*

Homework: Evocative Listening

We've noted before that what the designer thinks will be apparent may not always be so to the viewer or listener. The following homework exercises explore intention and perception via the selection of sound.

Version One

Prepare slips of paper for each member of the class that contain three related descriptive terms. Use the same terms for all the students, but do not tell them they are all receiving the same words. As you distribute the slips, tell the students that when they present their sound samples, the class will be asked to determine the associative words; therefore the words should be kept secret from classmates. Instruct the students to select two pieces of sound, each no longer than one minute (they can be excerpts from longer work), that best fit with the words on their slip of paper:

1. a non-vocal piece of music
2. a non-vocal ambient sound

Be sure to have the students find a recording in a file or playback format supported by the classroom's equipment. Smartphones and tablets alone may not have consistent or desired speaker quality. At the next class session, listen to as many tracks as time allows. Following each listening:

- Ask the students to describe the properties of each piece using both design element vocabulary and controllable properties.
- Discuss the emotive qualities of the piece.
- Ask the class for descriptive words the student might have had as their starting point.

Don't reveal the fact that everyone had the same words until all pieces have been listened to. After the reveal, ask students to comment on the variety of pieces brought in:

- Why *is* there a variety of pieces?
- Why did they select the specific pieces they brought in?

  - Where did they look? What factors led their search approach?

- Were there pieces brought in that they were unfamiliar with, either by specific piece or by genre?
- What was the most unexpected piece, and why?
- Were there any duplicates? How did those students arrive at the same piece?

Version Two

Distribute a list of design metaphors. The number should be slightly less than the total students so that some duplication is likely. Instruct the students to:

- Select a design metaphor from the list
- Extract a list of design elements from the selected metaphor
- Decide which one or two design elements will provide the focus for their research
- Locate a piece of non-vocal sound, no longer than one minute, that best fits the selected design elements

After each piece is played to the class:

- Ask the students to use design element vocabulary to describe the selection
- Determine which of the design metaphors the sound best fits, and explain why
- Ask the presenter if the class came close, and if they did not, what might account for the distance

This exercise can also be assigned with a more specific sound, such as a telephone ring, dog bark, or alarm clock to introduce the idea that even individual, mundane sounds can be informed by a design metaphor.

Version Three

Give each student a copy of a costume rendering, either generated from the class or from a departmental production. Each student will:

- Write a paragraph using design element vocabulary to analyze the character
- Write a second paragraph explaining what kind of music or sound that analysis will lead the student to explore
- Select a piece of music or sound that, via the design elements noted, best expresses the character depicted.

In class, review the students' choices. One way to open discussion is to display the costume renderings and play the sound selections one after the other, asking students to write down which image they feel best fits the music being played (much like the discussion of the 'Twenty One Black Dresses' project). Compare and discuss the results.

Discussion:
Categories of Sound Cues

"When I did *Mr. Roberts,* I had a mental picture of an onion in regards to the various sounds on that show. The outer layer was the reality of the theater and the audience. We had some lobby displays of period material, but they were museum-like; our perspective was that of the time and place the audience existed in. Within the auditorium, I was in period, but not specific to a time or place; my pre-show selection was music and vocal material presented as if we were listening to short-wave broadcasts. When the lights went up on stage, all the sounds there were within the reality of the ship; they were 'Source,' also known as **diagetic**; if we heard music, it was because 'Sparks' had turned on the short-wave and hooked it to the ship's PA."[6]

Mike Sweeney, *brian-the-techie.blogspot.com*

Theatrical sound effects can be broken down into several categories, depending on their relationship to the script and the style of performance. The following list is largely drawn from Kaye and Lebrecht's *Sound and Music for the Theatre: The Art and Technique of Design* (published by Focal Press):

- Framing
  - Preshow, intermission, post-show, lobby
- Underscoring
  - During action as a kind of subtext; heard by the audience, not by the characters
- Transitional Sounds or Music
  - To help move the play through scenic transitions, both geographic and chronological
- Specific Cues
  - Required Music
    - Indicated by the script to support action

- Spot Effects
  - Specific sounds indicated by the script, and required for/by character action and reaction
- Ambience
  - Provides atmosphere and setting; heard by the characters
- Progression of Effects
  - A dynamic series of sounds that is a mixture of ambience and spot effects, playing through a substantial period of time; e.g., a thunderstorm
- Voiceovers
  - Disembodied speech presenting information or thoughts, as indicated by the text[7]
- Reinforcement
  - Instruments and Vocalists; primarily for musicals and other productions with live music[8]

Discussion: The Sound Plot and Script Analysis

A preliminary **sound plot** is a spreadsheet containing all the information about sound that the designer has gathered from the script. Like the costume plot and the lighting cue synopsis, the sound plot serves as a framework for subsequent research and analysis. The sound designer now knows what to go in search of – a doorbell, for example – but it's the design metaphor and further research into the world of the play that will inform the specific aural qualities of that doorbell.

The quote heading this chapter is Chekhov's stage direction for the end of *The Cherry Orchard*. Different translations may phrase it differently, but there are two basic parts to the author's request: a mysterious, melancholy sound that somehow both manifests and comments upon everything that has gone before, and the distant chopping of the trees.

The sound of chopping wood at first appears relatively easy. Making it sound as though it is occurring at a distance will utilize volume and direction. But what about the actual content of the sound? Who is doing the chopping and how far away is the orchard? This might tell us more about the pace and intensity of the chops. Who exactly is listening to the chopping? Is the sound meant for characters or for the audience? If it's for the characters, does this ground it more in their reality? If for the audience, does it become a more heightened sound?

The sound of a string breaking, as if in the sky, can only be determined with thorough knowledge of the text and what, ultimately, this sound *means* for both the characters and for the audience. Every production of the play is likely to come to different conclusions as to the nature of this sound depending on what the directorial approach for the piece has been.

Similarly in *Death of a Salesman*, Arthur Miller asks for a framing sound before anything else happens: "The theatre is dark and silent. As though out of the air itself a melody is heard, played on a flute; it is a song, small and fine, telling of grass and trees and the horizon. The curtain rises."[9] This is no mere pre-show, but music that truly sets the tone for everything else to come. It sets the audience in direct contact with Willy Loman's soul. As Willy stands in the kitchen, Miller adds:

> . . . and he flows back into the present. It was so with the music we heard as the curtain rose and which only now is fading away entirely. It was a song Willy has been remembering more and more often in recent weeks, a distant, clean melody that plays in his mind, a sound from somewhere beyond his remembering, but a sound that draws a sense of longing out of him and undefined sadness.[10]

Unless the sound designer understands the character of Willy Loman, this framing sound is in danger of being a meaningless frippery. Worse, it will be a meaningless frippery that is the audience's first encounter with the play.

Exercise: The Preliminary Sound Plot

A short play like *Sorry, Wrong Number* (used earlier for a number of lighting exercises) is good for the following exercise, as the opening sequence requires a number of obvious sound cues. Being a period genre play, it can also point to more specific eras and styles of music for use in framing and underscoring.

Distribute a handout containing a blank table. The columns of the table should contain the headings 'Page,' 'On,' 'Effect,' 'Notes,' and for this exercise, 'Category.' This is a preliminary sound plot.

Instruct the students to examine the first few pages of the text and list every sound mentioned, either by stage directions or by dialogue. 'On' is when the sound cue occurs, and may need to be separated as to when the sound begins and when the sound ends. In the 'Effect' column, students should name

Preliminary Sound Plot

Show:

Designer:

Date:

Page #	On (execution)	Effect	Notes	Category (Type of Effect)

Figure 17.1 Sample Rough Sound Plot Headings

the sound; "door buzzer," or "rain pattering on window." 'Notes' should include all other qualities of the sound as described or implied by the text. On later iterations of the sound plot, 'Notes' will include manipulation, editing, and speaker location information.

Discuss what sounds have been found in the text:

- What is known about these sounds from evidence in the text?
- What category does each sound fall into?
- If they are spot effects, how does the sound impact the action of the play? What happens because of the sound?
- What other sounds, not specified in the text, would be useful to help establish time or locale (ambience)? Why?
- What other sounds, not specified in the text, would be useful to help establish mood, atmosphere or production style (underscoring)?

Ask the students if they have suggestions for preshow framing sound:

- Does the author suggest a framing sound?
- Is music appropriate?
- What is the function of the music? For example, will it suggest what is to come or misdirect the audience to heighten later surprises?
- What styles or pieces of music would fit best?
- If not music, what other sound could create an effective preshow?
- The director has decided to go to black to start the show. Does the preshow sound fade out with the light fading to black, or play through the black into the start of the scene? What are the pros and cons of either decision?
- Where might you go to *find* the most suitable music/sound for the preshow?

"As far as I am concerned, sound is a design element. With *A Walk in the Woods*, I thought of the sound as a major element in terms of bringing the forest to life. Michael Roth was with me for the whole journey. We always thought of the forest as the third character in Lee Blessing's two-character play."[11]
Des McAnuff, quoted in *Sound and Music for the Theater*

Exercise: In-Class Analysis/Research Project

Select a short play (we'll use *Sorry, Wrong Number* as an example) and prepare a design metaphor for use by the class. If this is a new play, have the class create a preliminary sound plot before moving on.

- Discuss the design metaphor and the design elements suggested by it.
- Consulting the sound plot, have each student select a sound and outline how they feel the design elements can inform their research.
- Discuss the category of sound effect their selection falls into; will this have an effect on their research direction?
- Have the students consult a sound library (whether departmental or online) to locate a sound they feel most appropriate. Allow about ten to fifteen minutes. Headphones may be required.

"I often have lots of feelings and images that I want a piece of music to fulfill. I hate it when a designer says, 'Just tell me what piece you want.' If I really am certain, fine. But most of the time, I'm not. I don't have all the answers. That's why I hired a sound designer."[12]
Roger T. Danforth, quoted in *Sound and Music for the Theatre*

Exercise: Script Analysis – Digging Deeper

The sound plot notes the placement of effects, and we have begun exploring how to fit sound to metaphor and design elements. To continue linking this conceptual work to evidence from the text, have the students engage in a close reading of a script for sound. Select a scene or short play that contains a fair amount of textually required sound.

Instruct the students to comb through the text and note everything that might have some impact on the aural environment. This will include stage directions as well as dialogue, overtly stated as well as inferred.

Contributing factors might include:

- Location/Proximity
- Time of Day/Season
- Period/Era
- Weather Conditions
- Production Style

Compare and discuss findings. What sounds are most likely to be influenced by which factors, and why? How might those factors influence research or manipulation/alteration of a particular sound?

"The age of recording has brought with it a limitless menu of sound effects. We can, if we wish, fill our plays with a continuous soundscape of recorded sound. But we should be careful how much we wish it. However naturalistically our plays are written, the characters within them do not speak exactly as they do in real life. They come in on cue, take turns to speak, and use heightened language. They do not exist in a real aural landscape, so if you surround them with one, they may not survive the experience."[13]
John Caird, *Theatre Craft*

Homework: Sound Research

For homework, narrow the range of research and instruct students to bring in the applicable sound. Provide a few sound library sources as a starting point and be sure to let students know what recording format the classroom supports. Assign three to five specific sounds. Try to keep the sounds relatively simple and singular; for example:

- a 1930 American telephone ring
- tires pulling away on a gravel driveway
- a ticker tape machine

When reviewing the projects, start by asking how the student *knows* that the sound is appropriate (especially in the case of period sounds like phones or ticker tape machines); where did the recording come from and how does the student know it's period authentic (or at least reliably duplicates appropriate period qualities)?

Listen to samples one after the other. Ask the class to note variations between recordings and how those variations can be described using the properties of sound.

Of the sounds obtained, is there one that:

* Has the best overall sound quality?
* Feels more 'authentic' than the others?
* Has a unique emotive quality?

To tie the assignment more closely to script analysis, use a script excerpt with well-defined sound requirements. Include a design metaphor to further inform the students' research directions.

"Your Sound Designer should be at all production meetings, but you may need additional meetings to discuss new ideas that come up in rehearsal. Better still, the Sound Designer should attend rehearsals after, say, the second week, or at least two weeks before technical rehearsals start. That way he can play you the cues as he has imagined them and you can start working them into the scenes as they're being rehearsed."[14]
John Caird, *Theatre Craft*

Large Project: Assembling a Preliminary Sound Design

Depending on the time and scope of the treatment of sound in the course, either select a fresh short play or have the students use the play they were assigned for the lighting design final project. Direct them to:

* Develop a design metaphor for the play
* Write a statement that outlines how design elements informed by the metaphor can be applied to sound for the play
* Develop a preliminary sound plot including:

   * All sounds noted and inferred by the text
   * Sounds suggested by the designer for preshow, transitions, etc.

* Choose three to four specific sounds from the plot and write a paragraph outlining how those sounds can be informed by the metaphor and design elements
* Choose two or three of the sounds and outline research avenues to locate the most appropriate sound
* Using whatever playback program is best suited for classroom use (this could be as basic as iTunes or Windows Media Player), each student should assemble a recording of all sounds listed on the preliminary sound plot

   * Track numbers should be added to the sound plot for ease of reference
   * Recordings do not have to be edited or manipulated; the raw track is adequate

* Choose two to three of the tracks recorded and write a paragraph explaining how the track connects to the design metaphor and contributes to the action of the play.

Large Project Addendum

For sound designers, copyright plays a role in gathering the raw material for a production, particularly where music is concerned. When playwrights request a specific piece of music, they usually include a caveat that permission to perform the play *does not* include permission to use the music – the rights must be obtained from whoever holds that particular copyright or license. Neither are all sound libraries free, and even with subscriptions there might be rules limiting public use of that material. No theatre wants to receive a cease and desist letter partway through a run and face legal consequences for improperly using protected material.

For whatever sound/music is obtained for the large project, have the students include royalty/copyright information on the sound plot:

- What does the site/source of the item say about using the material?
- Are there fees and royalties involved? How much do they cost?
- Is there a difference in quality from sources that require royalty payment and sources that are free, with no restrictions?
- Is it possible to access material from sites/sources that require royalties or fees?
- For recorded music (whether LP or mp3 format), how do you figure out who to ask for permission for use?

Portfolio Development

Student sound designers can break their portfolio materials into two categories: visual and auditory. A CD or flashdrive of examples should be provided. These should be carefully selected and recorded so that it is apparent that the designer can do more than pull unaltered items from a sound library. Highlight interesting built effects, music/sounds composed by the designer, and items unique to a particular production. In presenting portfolio materials in person, the designer should also bring along a compatible system that will provide good quality playback.

Visual materials include speaker location in the set and auditorium, speaker diagrams, equipment lists, sound plots/cue lists, and other relevant paperwork.[15] KCACTF guidelines ask student designers to "include a moment from the play and communicate how sound supported that moment" keeping the focus on how the sound supports the story rather than a detailed discussion of the technology.[16] This can be aided by including a production photo of a particular moment and providing a statement of how the sound for that moment contributed to the action, as well as the analysis, research, and editing necessary to make the sound appropriate and effective.

As a portfolio project, use the components generated for the large sound design project at the end of the chapter to lay out a presentation.

Notes

1. Anton Chekhov, *The Cherry Orchard* from: *Anton Chekhov: Plays*, trans. by Peter Carlson (London: Penguin, 2002), p. 346.
2. Deena Kaye and James Lebrecht, *Sound and Music for the Theatre: The Art and Technique of Design* (Burlington: Focal Press, 2009, 2013 ed.), p. 12.
3. Kaye and Lebrecht, p. 205.
4. Kaye and Lebrecht, p. 225.
5. John Caird, *Theatre Craft: A Director's Practical Companion from A to Z* (London: Faber and Faber, 2010), p. 685.
6. http://brian-the-techie.blogspot.com/2010/12/basics-of-sound-design.html, accessed 2/1/2016.
7. Kaye and Lebrecht, pp. 23–30.
8. J. Michael Gilette, *Theatrical Design and Production: An Introduction to Scenic Design and Construction, Lighting, Sound, Costume, and Makeup* (New York: McGraw-Hill, 2008, 6th edition), p. 513.
9. Arthur Miller, *Death of a Salesman* (New York: Bantam Books, 1951), p. 1.
10. Miller, p. 7.
11. Kaye and Lebrecht, p. 211.
12. Kaye and Lebrecht, p. 204.

13. Caird, p. 682.

14. Caird, p. 679.

15. Rafael Jean, *Developing and Maintaining a Design-Tech Portfolio* (Burlington: Focal Press, 2006), p. 50.

16. http://www.kcactf3.org/exhibit.html, accessed 2/1/2016

Our Current Syllabus

The following is our current syllabus, which was used to organize the structure of this book. Day-to-day homework assignments have been deleted so that the reader can better see how the topics flow one to next. Our course meets twice a week; each session is an hour and forty-five minutes long.

THTR 252-01 Introduction to Theatrical Design

Required Texts

Play A
Play B
Play C

Catalog Course Description

An examination of the basic principles of scenic, costume, and lighting design for the theatre. Topics covered include the design process, research, design elements, and practical considerations. Studio labs include instruction and practice in sketching, drafting, and rendering.

Goals

Upon completion of this course, students should be able to demonstrate:

- The ability to analyze a script for meaning, functionality, and to distill a design metaphor.
- Knowledge of the design elements and the application of that vocabulary when considering a metaphor and script.
- Agility with research techniques in order to research a script or metaphor from new and differing perspectives.
- Graphic techniques that are traditional to the communication of ideas in the field of theatrical design.
- A self-critical eye needed to let go of some ideas with the willingness to engage new ones.

Theatre is a collaborative art, and as you develop your ideas you will receive criticism and advice from your instructors in what works, what might work better, and what is unlikely to work. Carefully consider the criticism and advice of your instructors as this feedback is intended to help you recognize and explore ways to improve your product, not squelch your creativity or deny you ownership of ideas.

Grading

Reading Quizzes	5%
Script Analysis/Scene Breakdown	5%
Costume Design	26% (15% final project)
Scenic Design	26% (15% final project)
Lighting Design	26% (15% final project)
Designer Class Presentation	12%

There may also be a number of other assignments that will arise as the semester progresses; some will be done in class, some will be homework. At the discretion of the instructor, a letter grade or points may be given for these projects, which will then be tabulated into the course grading as a whole. This may mean that the Scenic portion ends up with five additional smaller projects as well as the final scenic design project; the cumulative total for all six of these grades will remain 26% of the course grade.

Proposed Schedule

Below is the proposed schedule for the course. Changes may be made at the discretion of the instructor due to valid topic digression, unavoidable current events, illness, or weather emergencies.

All readings should be done for the dates listed so you are prepared to discuss the content of the reading in class that day.

Part One: Costume Design

Week 1

Read: Play A
Play B
Play C

T   Housekeeping, Syllabus, etc.; Design Elements; All plays must be read before the next class!
Th Reading Comprehension Quiz; Discussion of all three plays; Design Metaphor, Script Analysis

Week 2

T   Final Project Explained; Metaphor Statement; French Scene Breakdowns; The Costume Plot; Script Analysis by Character
Th Costume Rendering Techniques; Drawing Clothing Items; Discuss/Demo homework project: Twenty-One Black Dresses

Week 3

T   Costume Rendering Techniques; Costume Computer Aided Techniques; Color and Watercolor
Th Color and Watercolor; Twenty-One Black Dresses; Research – What to Research and Where to Go; Library Resources; Transitioning research and character analysis, through metaphor, into designs

Week 4

T   Swatching; Depicting Fabric with Paint; Exploring Color Palettes
Th In-Class Work Day; Work on renderings, swatching, items for Final Project

Week 5

T   Costume Designer Presentations (guest designer afterward)
Th Presentation of Final Costume Design Project; Metaphor Statement, Visual Research Materials, Renderings, Swatches. You will be expected to present and discuss your project.

Part Two: Scenic Design

Week 6

T   The Purpose of Scenery; Describing Environments; Environmental Detail and Clues to Character; Script Analysis for Scenic Design
Th What is Essential?; Scale and Proportion; Learning to Draw and Read in Scale; The Sizes of Real Things; Building a Stage House for 'Your First Set Design'

Week 7

T   The Real Sizes of Objects; The Human Figure in an Environment; Making Model Furniture; The Function of Models
Th 'Normal' Rooms; Introduction to Groundplans; The Groundplan is a Plan of Action – Using a Short Play to Develop the Environment

Week 8

T   Presenting 'Your First Set Design;' Introduction to Drafting; Center and Plaster Lines; Drafting a Room's Plan
Th Groundplans, continued; Drafting Line Types and Symbols

Week 9

T   Present groundplan of 'Your First Set Design;' Thumbnails and 3D Gesture Exercises
Th In-Class Work Day; work on models and final project items

Week 10

T   Scenic Designer Presentations (guest designer afterward)
Th Presentation of Scenic Design Final Project: metaphor statement, core metaphor image, visual research, rough groundplan, white cardstock model, color/texture choices

Part Three: Lighting Design

You will swap plays at this point; your lighting design will be done for another student's scenic design. It may not be the same play you worked on, so this is a good time to review all the plays.

Week 11

T   Describing/Talking About Light; Functions of Stage Light: Standard Lighting Angles; The Controllable Properties of Light

Th Demonstrate Standard Angles in Light Lab; Analysis of Lit Environments;

Week 12

T   Script Analysis; The Cue Synopsis; Introduction to Storyboards; Interpreting Light in an Image

Th Sketching Light; Six Categories of Purposes (the Main Source of Light, etc.); Building a Look in the Light Lab

Week 13

T   Purposes, continued; finish Building Look in Light Lab; Applying Research Image Information to Purposes; Magic Sheets

Th Color for Lighting; Gel and the Swatchbook; Mixing Color in the Light Lab

Week 14

T   Sketching Light in Color

Th In-Class Work Day; Storyboards and other Items for the Final Project

Week 15

T   Lighting Designer Presentations (guest designer afterward)

Final Exam

Presentation of Lighting Design Final Project. This will include the metaphor statement, core metaphor image, visual research, charcoal sketch storyboard, cue synopsis, and two color sketches with magic sheets, gel choices, and purpose lists for those two sketches.

Materials for Introduction to Design

This appendix contains lists for both the instructor and the students. The instructor's list does not include all of the various handouts and discussion images noted throughout the book.

We have tried to be sensitive to the cost of materials for this class. However, in order to do the projects, there are items that must be purchased. Knowing that non-design students are unlikely to use T-squares and architectural scale rulers beyond this class, we tell the students to check with classmates who have taken the class in the past. This course has been part of our department's curriculum for a very long time, and there must be tools out there that can be handed down.

We are able to send emails to registered students over the summer, so about a month before the semester begins we contact those enrolled in the class. The students are encouraged to look for deals before they arrive on campus and it becomes difficult to get to an art supply store. It is not essential that students have all the items present and ready on the first day of class. As you go through each chapter, the lists at the beginning of each will give you an idea of what is needed at which point.

Perishable materials (papers, glue, etc.) can often be shared. Students can purchase some items with a classmate to save pennies. Tools (T-square, X-Acto knife, etc.) are difficult to share, especially when working in class on projects – sharing will just slow all parties down. We have accumulated a classroom supply of items like scissors and glue sticks, and it's usually easier for the instructor to bring a pad of cardstock and 3 x 5 cards rather than expect the students to bring their own.

Supplies for Instructors

- Collage materials. Have a box of clippings that can be pulled for exercises as needed. Avoid images with text or faces
- Unlined 3 x 5 notecards
- Croquis (see Chapter 2 for an explanation of these)
- Handouts of fashion components
- Light box/graphite paper (for tracing and copying)
- Color copies of the color wheel
- Large fabric samples (to observe pattern at a distance)

- Scrap fabric (for swatching)
- Color images for swatching project (Chapter 4)
- Workable Fixatif (to fix charcoal sketches)
- Example groundplans
- Images of scenic designs
- Human Heights handout
- Handout of Images of Furniture
- Tape measures
- Blank Large Stage House groundplan (Chapter 9)
- Camera (to photograph light lab work)
- Light Lab (see Chapters 11 through 14 for further details)
- Four to eight moveable lighting units
- A way to control the intensity of individual lighting units
- A black background
- A white background
- A doll or figure
- Objects to use as walls and furniture
- Small set to use in the light lab for the short play (see Chapter 12)
- Gel (a wide assortment of colors)
- Gel swatchbooks (to distribute to the students)
- A prism
- Playback and recording system for sound
- Classroom computer with photo and word processing software

Supplies for Students

- ¼" thick foamcore or gator board (white and black) for models and presentations. They will need about four sheets of black for the two models we will build
- A pad of Bristol board (vellum surface) or cardstock for models, drawings, and watercolors
- White poster board
- Pad of drawing paper, no smaller than 14" x 17"
- Copier paper. A ream is not expensive and certainly something that can be shared.
- Drawing pencils of various hardnesses

- Fine-point black Sharpie markers
- Graph paper
- Tracing paper
- Unlined paper
- Tacky glue
- Glue stick
- Cellophane tape
- Rubber cement
- X-Acto knife
- X-Acto knife blades
- Good scissors
- A metal straightedge to cut against (cheap wooden ruler with a metal strip works fine)
- A self-sealing cutting mat (this is nice, but not essential – what is required is a smooth surface that does not allow the blade to slice through into the desk top)
- Straight pins (to hold foamcore together while glue dries)
- Small binder clips (also useful to hold things together as they dry)
- Architect's scale rule (this is NOT a plain old ruler and is essential)
- T-square (no less than 24")
- Drafting triangles, both 45-degree and 30/60-degree; get them medium-sized – super tiny will be useless, super large will be annoying
- Compass
- Soft drawing charcoal
- White plastic eraser
- A set of inexpensive watercolors – don't go so cheap they're next to useless. Cake or tube, either works well. The set should have more than six colors, or it will become limiting and problematic
- Plastic watercolor mixing tray
- Cups for holding water while using watercolors
- A couple of watercolor brushes of various sizes. Stay on the small side – ¼" round is probably the biggest needed. A ¼" flat is also useful for laying in washes. Don't settle for the cheap little brush that comes with the tray of grammar school paints
- Blue painter's tape/drafting tape

Two Short Plays by Eric Appleton, Used for Design Exercises

(The author grants permission for the use of these two plays for non-public course-related activities.)

Play One:
The Return of the Living

Cast:

Devon   male, mid-twenties
Audrey   female, mid-twenties
Lawrence   Egyptologist, their father, dead

Location:

The parlor

Time:

A dark and stormy night

> *A dark and stormy night. A crash offstage. The maid screams. Audrey marches in from the other side of the stage, wielding an axe, muttering under her breath:*

AUDREY

. . . goddam mummy coming here and I have to deal with it because no one else is going to deal with the goddam mummy I always have to deal with everything around here no else is going to deal with—

> *Devon sits in a chair, sullenly drinking whiskey.*

DEVON

Audrey, what are you doing?

> *She stops and steams at this ridiculously obvious question.*

AUDREY

What does it look like I'm doing?

DEVON

Finally cutting down the dead cherry tree out back.

AUDREY

No. I am going to dispatch the mummy that is currently rampaging through the house. In case you didn't notice.

DEVON

You can't do that. Not with an axe.

AUDREY

Why not with an axe?

DEVON

It's the undead, for Pete's sake.

AUDREY

It moves slowly with its arms stuck out in front of it. Ungh. Ungh. I'm pretty sure I can get in a few good whacks before—

DEVON

You can't go whacking at the undead—

AUDREY

If dad had one lesson to teach us—

DEVON

It's that death always wins, Audrey.

AUDREY

At least he went down swinging. (*there's another scream off stage*) May I go now? The thing's terrorizing poor Mrs. Radjeski.

DEVON

Little Miss Action. Father always liked you better anyway.

AUDREY

If you'd become an Egyptologist like he wanted –

DEVON

Oh, so this mummy's curse thing is all my fault, is it? Like if I'd walked in dear old dad's footsteps I could banish this – thing with a mysterious incantation I just happened across while lounging about perusing some fabled ancient book of the dead. Ooooo. Mummy begone . . . Fear me, for I am Professor Devon Mason, tenured Egyptologist with twenty-seven journal articles and far too many conference panels to my credit!

Mrs. Radjeski screams again.

AUDREY

Are we done here? The thing's probably half way across the room to Mrs. Radjeski by now. I would like to try to save her.

DEVON

Go. Go on. I'll just be the sniveling coward left in the rear. Again.

AUDREY

You are a coward, Devon. That has nothing to do with me.

She marches past him and exits.

DEVON

I – well, you don't have to make it so apparent, then. Do you.

He sips his whiskey. His father, a ghost, appears.

LAWRENCE

Well, that's disappointing.

DEVON

What? Who's there?

LAWRENCE

Letting your sister go up against that cursed hell-being all by herself. I'm very, very disappointed in you.

DEVON

Dad, stay dead, please. We have enough of the undead running about this evening.

LAWRENCE

And you're drinking the wedding scotch.

DEVON

Like anyone's marriage is looming.

LAWRENCE

That distillery no longer even exists.

DEVON

This seemed like a singular enough occasion. If you're not going to be useful, dad, please let me sulk alone. I'd rather not stare death in the face all evening.

Mrs. Radjeski screams again.

LAWRENCE

Helpless women screaming in terror and you just sit there.

DEVON

Audrey's taking care of it.

LAWRENCE

I hardly think that's the point, young man.

DEVON

She's much more capable than I am. We all know that.

LAWRENCE

Why can't you ever prove me wrong for once?

DEVON

Why couldn't you appreciate whatever qualities I already have?

LAWRENCE

And what fine qualities would these be, pray tell?

DEVON

I am an excellent watercolorist, you know.

LAWRENCE

"And this, senator, is my son, who has excellent brush control and a good eye for color."

DEVON

And this, senator, is my father, who opened a cursed tomb and loosed unspeakable evil upon the world, getting himself horribly killed in the process. Whoopee.

LAWRENCE

I've paid for my mistakes, Devon.

DEVON

No. You paid for a mistake. And might I add, you're acting awfully smug and self-righteous for someone who made a mistake of such – staggering dimension. If you weren't already dead, father—

Audrey marches back in, without the axe.
She heads for the fireplace and grabs a poker.

AUDREY

Damned thing's tougher than I expected.

DEVON

I told you, you just don't go whacking at the undead and expect them to fall down – um, not undead.

AUDREY

Daddy?

DEVON

She can see you?

LAWRENCE

Audrey, darling.

DEVON

Wonderful. I don't even get personal visitations.

AUDREY

Oh, I knew you wouldn't go and leave everything all unfinished.

DEVON

No, he just returned to tell me how disappointed he was in me. Can't even leave me alone after death.

AUDREY

Oh, shut up, Devon.

Mrs. Radjeski screams again.

AUDREY

Hurry up and tell me. It's almost all the way across the room and I don't know how much longer poor Mrs. Radjeski can hold up.

LAWRENCE

Oh, well. Audrey. Here's – the thing, then. I'm – unfortunately—

AUDREY

You do know how to reverse the curse, don't you?

LAWRENCE

It's never really – that simple, darling.

DEVON

You don't know how to undo it, do you?

AUDREY

Don't tell me. Oh, don't tell me.

DEVON

So we're still screwed, then, is that it?

LAWRENCE

Devon, don't make me—

DEVON

Make you what? Spank me? Make me go without supper? Guess what! You're dead! Dead dead dead! You can't do anything!

AUDREY

You're not being helpful.

DEVON

I don't feel like being helpful.

AUDREY

Devon, what's this in my hand?

DEVON

A poker. So?

AUDREY

As I am quite alive at the moment, and holding a metal implement, I think I am quite capable of making you shut up if you don't do so voluntarily.

LAWRENCE

Right. Back to the grave, then—

AUDREY

Don't you dare, father. I'm not done with you, either.

LAWRENCE

Dead or not, Audrey, I do not appreciate your tone.

AUDREY

I need you to tell me what to do about the mummy. The axe was – not a success.

DEVON

Whacking at the undead.

She brandishes the poker at him.

LAWRENCE

Well, for starters. Um, I expect holy items would be a good choice. Sacred bits. Wave them about. Isis commands you, that sort of thing.

AUDREY

Do we have any sacred bits in the house?

LAWRENCE

Not as such. Um. I donated them all to the university museum just before my – demise.

AUDREY

Incantations. Parchments, books of lore, that sort of thing.

LAWRENCE

Darling, I don't – didn't have the facilities for their proper preservation here. I'm – was – a scientist. Not a magician. I was looking for pottery shards, historical inscriptions, which pharaoh came before this other pharaoh, that sort of thing. There were no courses at Harvard to prepare us for the undead.

AUDREY

You didn't go down swinging, did you.

LAWRENCE

What's that supposed to mean, young lady?

AUDREY

Doctor Mathers told us you went down "swinging." Valiant. Lots of swash and buckle. That sort of thing. That's why there was – so little of you left. How exactly did you die, father?

LAWRENCE

That's a rather personal question.

Mrs. Radjeski screams.

AUDREY

(*yells in return*) Try to hold on a little longer, Mrs. Radjeski!

LAWRENCE

Er – we don't really have time for this, do we? What with poor Mrs. Radjeski being menaced and all?

AUDREY

Devon.

DEVON

What?

AUDREY

Take this and go buy us some time.

DEVON

You're not seriously thinking—

AUDREY

Take the damned poker and save poor Mrs. Radjeski or I will personally pick you up and fling you into the goddamned mummy's arms! Go! Now! Do it!

Devon runs off with the poker.

LAWRENCE

When did you develop a mouth like a sailor, young lady?

AUDREY

Do not change the subject, daddy.

LAWRENCE

And to think you were my little princess.

AUDREY

How did you die?

LAWRENCE

I hardly see the relevance, considering the situation.

AUDREY

I no longer care about relevance. We're down to owed explanations.

LAWRENCE

It was the – mummy's curse. Yes.

AUDREY

All you need to do is tell me you went down singlehandedly saving the expedition from a horde of living skeletons and you can go back to your grave and we'll pretend you never showed up here and was absolutely useless.

LAWRENCE

Yes, that. The skeletons. A horde. It was horrible. Bony arms waving and all.

AUDREY

I will go out and dig up your grave and scatter that handful of bits Dr. Mather brought back from Egypt from here to – to – Timbuktu, old man! I will make you an unhappy wandering ghost, doomed to walk restlessly through all eternity!

LAWRENCE

You're really taking this undead thing a little too seriously, Audrey. Darling.

AUDREY

I've been hacking at the living dead all evening! Don't you talk to me about taking it a little too seriously! I am tired of always picking up all the goddamned pieces!

LAWRENCE

It's just that I mean—

AUDREY

I'm going to go get a shovel, right now!

LAWRENCE

No, wait. I – I—

AUDREY

Yes?

LAWRENCE

I – slipped. Off the boat. On the Nile. Hippopotamus got me.
        Beat.

AUDREY

All these years, treating Devon like that, and you were just as bad as he was.

LAWRENCE

I was a highly respected Egyptologist!

AUDREY

All those stories you told. And the whole time it was all just pottery and inscriptions. No swash or buckle. I guess it doesn't really matter now. We're all going to die horribly at the mummy's hands anyway.

LAWRENCE

I really don't think you can compare my exemplary career with Devon's exploits as a layabout watercolorist.

AUDREY

He really is quite good, you know.

LAWRENCE

There is a world out there, and I fully expected my children to go out there and engage it in some meaningful and active manner!

AUDREY

So between poor, languishing, housebound mom and an absentee father we were supposed to figure out this engagement on our own, is that it?

LAWRENCE

You're a reasonably attractive, intelligent young woman. What kept you from striking out on your own?

AUDREY

Like it's that easy.

LAWRENCE

Well, yes. It is, actually.

AUDREY

Go back to your grave, we'll forget any of this ever happened, and Devon and I will just deal with the mummy ourselves.

LAWRENCE

You really blame me for making your life boring?

AUDREY

I'm not going to talk about it.

LAWRENCE

Alright, yes, I had my flaws. Perhaps I wasn't around as much as I should have been, perhaps I embellished the telling of some of my expeditions, but you know, it was important to me that you think I was, well, a little bigger than life. I wanted to be a bit of a hero to you.

AUDREY

A hero.

LAWRENCE

The swash and buckle stuff.

AUDREY

Bedtime stories.

LAWRENCE

It worked when you were my little princess.

AUDREY

I was only a princess when mother dressed me for your visits.

LAWRENCE

Visits. This was my home! You are my family!

AUDREY

You were a houseguest who showed up at irregular intervals and stayed only as long as was convenient for you!

LAWRENCE

Egypt called! Science does not wait!

AUDREY

Did you ever take me with you?

LAWRENCE

Egypt is no place for a reasonably attractive young lady.

AUDREY

I see.

LAWRENCE

I was going to invite young Peterson from anthropology over to dinner when I returned from that ill-fated expedition. He had – expressed interest in you.

AUDREY

I dream of Egypt and you think I'd be happy with a young anthropologist?

LAWRENCE

He's been to Borneo, you know.

AUDREY

Would he take me with him to Borneo?

LAWRENCE

Well, the university seldom funds spouses on these expeditions—

AUDREY

You thought I would be happy to be like mother, didn't you. Waiting, waiting, waiting – and then hanging on your every word when you returned because she was convinced that was all she was capable of!

LAWRENCE

Don't speak of your mother like that!

AUDREY

Why not? I knew her better than you did!

LAWRENCE

If you're going to upbraid me and insult your mother, I will be returning to the grave, then.

AUDREY

I know where you're buried, father.

LAWRENCE

Perhaps, if you'd ever actually asked me to bring you along to Egypt, I might have figured out how to do so once you were old enough. As much as the reasons for watercolor elude me, at least your brother found his own interests. Theodore Vance, who is buried a few plots down from me, mentioned that Devon's actually showing a few pieces at a gallery in town next month.

Lawrence vanishes.

Devon runs in, elatedly brandishing the poker.

DEVON

O my god, Audrey! That was amazing! Whack! Whack! Beating back the mummy, step by step by step; Mrs. Radjeski, huddled into the corner, screaming horrifically as I did battle *mano-a-mano* with the dread hell-fiend, fighting it step by step back across the room through the French doors, onto the patio! Forcing the doors shut as it slowly struggled to get back in! He's out in the garden somewhere, now. I've never felt more, more – what's the matter?

AUDREY

(*she grabs the poker out of his hands*) Why didn't you tell me you had a gallery showing?!

DEVON

You never seemed interested. You never asked.

AUDREY

(*she brandishes the poker at Devon , then flings it to the ground*) Augh!

Audrey stomps out.

DEVON

What?

Devon sees something moving in the garden outside the French doors. He crosses to the doors, and with a roar, brandishes the poker before giving chase.

Black.

End of Play.

Play Two: *That Horrible Human Condition*

Cast:

Horace
Betsy
Gregory
The Maid
Father

Betsy sits, reading a collection of Gertrude Stein plays. Horace enters from the garden, swinging his tennis racket

HORACE

What ho, Betsy! Lovely day for tennis!

BETSY

Do you think Gertrude Stein would have played tennis?

HORACE

I'm sure she would have. Who's Gertrude Stein?

BETSY

A writer.

HORACE

For sure, then. I hear writers love tennis.

Gregory enters from the hall, carrying a book of Eugene O'Neill's plays.

GREGORY

Gertrude Stein, Gertrude Stein, Gertrude Stein. Always with the Gertrude Stein. You should read a real playwright.

BETSY

Like Mr. Dark and Gloomy?

GREGORY

Like the greatest American playwright who ever lived.

HORACE

Did he write plays about tennis?

GREGORY

He wrote about the human condition.

BETSY

And how it's a sad and horrible condition. Yuck.

HORACE

Certainly nothing to be reading on a bright sunny day! Play tennis with me!

The phone rings. Betsy answers it.

BETSY

Claire! Lovely, yourself?

HORACE

Say hullo to Claire for me, will you?

GREGORY

You have a thing for Claire, don't you?

HORACE

It is not a "thing."

GREGORY

She hasn't the slightest idea you even exist, you know.

HORACE

She does too!

BETSY

Hang on, Claire. There's all this – racket. (*to Gregory and Horace*) Claire hates you both. (*she sticks out her tongue and exits into the garden*)

HORACE

I refuse to believe she hates us both.

GREGORY

Such are women.

HORACE

Dash it all, Gregory! When will I find a girl who loves tennis as much as I do?

The Maid enters. She rings a bell.

MAID

Luncheon is served.

HORACE

Excellent! What's on the menu today?

MAID

Sandwiches, sir.

HORACE

Hooray! I love sandwiches!

GREGORY

If only you could find a girl who loved sandwiches as much as you.

HORACE

She must be out there somewhere, don't you think?

MAID

I wouldn't know, sir.

HORACE

Coming, Mr. Gloomy Puss?

GREGORY

No, I think I shall wallow a bit longer.

HORACE

Your loss!

GREGORY

Wait – do me a favor.

He hands the Maid Betsy's book.

MAID

I beg your pardon, sir?

HORACE

But that's Betsy's book!

GREGORY

I refuse to be in the same room as Gertrude Stein. Hide this somewhere.

MAID

Yes, sir.

The Maid exits.

HORACE

You're a snot, Gregory.

GREGORY

You're just jealous I'm having an existential crisis and you're not.

HORACE

I don't need one. I have tennis.

Horace exits.

GREGORY

I think I shall run away to Sea.

Betsy enters, with phone and instant camera.
She snaps a photo of Gregory.

GREGORY

Stop that! You know I don't photograph well!

Betsy looks at the photo.

BETSY

You're absolutely right.

GREGORY

Where did you find that camera?

BETSY

It was on the garden wall. I expect Father forgot it.

GREGORY

What was he taking pictures of?

BETSY

Birds, probably. He's had an obsession with flying things of late.

GREGORY

The merchant marine is looking better and better.

Father enters, attempting to juggle.

FATHER

I have taken up juggling!

BETSY

That's wonderful, Father.

FATHER

Good for the circulation. And hand–eye coordination.

BETSY

We are so happy for you.

FATHER

I'm going to juggle for a bit in the garden. Call me when lunch is ready, will you?

BETSY

Of course, Father.

FATHER

You should take up a hobby, Gregory. It's no good to be so pale so often.

GREGORY

I'm running away to a life on the Sea, Father.

FATHER

Excellent! I hear sea air is quite healthy!

Father juggles his way into the garden.

GREGORY

Does Mother know about this?

BETSY

I haven't seen Mother in three days.

GREGORY

She's not lost in the East Wing again, is she?

BETSY

You're running away for a life on the sea?

GREGORY

Yes.

BETSY

Take me with you?

Black.

Appendix D

Sample Cue
Synopses

This appendix contains two sample lighting cue synopses, one from the Milwaukee Chamber Theatre's production of *Master Class* and one from the Children's Theater of Madison's production of *Lilly's Purple Plastic Purse*. A column for Counts has been included, but has yet to have estimated durations noted.

Both are revised synopses that include information gathered from production meetings and rehearsal observation. Some descriptions include questions about things that occurred to the designer but have yet to be proposed to the director or logistically fleshed out.

Master Class
Revised Cue Synopsis 7/28/14
Milwaukee Chamber Theatre
August 2014
LD: Eric Appleton

Cue	Page	Cnt	On	What
1	7		preset and house	set-up for class; house lights, "work lights" a hastily built cue for the class; visibility into backstage areas; we see stage still being arranged
2	7		end preshow announcement	brighten stage slightly after live announcement (Maria's entrance); as though the grand master was bumped a notch
3	9		"If you don't, get one."	Cascade of house flicks flicking out, ending with final sconces dimming to a glow – as though technician flicked off a series of switches after running to the booth
9	23		"Show us *that* truth"	a slow slow drift, Maria and Sophia focus, Maria watching Sophie as all else drops away
10	23		with music	(slide 31:1) begin a shift to Maria alone with her music; terrifying moment, my voice filling the void
12	23		"Ari always said . . ."	a change, memories shift (Ari), images get closer and closer, the blurred image on stage . . . we are part of the audience at La Scala
13	24		"This part."	Gentle shift; gentler color on Maria; Memory as she listens
14	24		"You give me class"	return to harsher Ari light
15	25		"Sing it anyway"	music ends; gentle light again – a silhouette as the slide arrives at shadowy figure (a magical moment?); we listen with her
16	25		"I never heard their"	open Maria as she speaks (she's talking to us) (slide 36.2)
16.5	26		"I keep thinking of a"	stronger on Maria – into the past
17	26		"the universe right now"	crossfade from chair to down center as Maria moves (slide 37.1)
18	26		"Now the genius part . . ."	shift to a footlight on Maria – do what Visconti did . . . house lights (sconces . . .) the Cabot in reds and golds . . .

Cue	Page	Cnt	On	What
19	26		"with fresh roses hung"	build house reds and golds, Maria crosses DSL, shift footlight
20	27		"I only have one note"	slow lose house, Maria in footlights surrounded by void (headlights slide comes up with applause)
21	27		end of applause	restore: house lights to full
22	27		with Sop. and Manny's exit	houselights up; stage dims a little
23	28		during intermission	a sweeter, more "planned" cue for stage – perhaps this might change in stages to suggest someone playing with the look live
24	28		when ready	the house lights dim – back to lower level sconces? – firm up sweeter look on stage for Act Two (more front light)
30	45		with *Macbeth* slide	adjust for slides, begin shift into making the stage look like an extension of the slide image/set (clouds, depth, highlighting architecture)
32	45		"they're waiting for you"	continue *Macbeth* shift; add downstage leg scrapers
33	46		"led up to this moment"	add midstage leg scrapers (continue *Macbeth* look)
34	46		"heard anything yet"	add backwall leg scrapers
35	46		"this costume is so heavy"	change quality of Maria special (tense past)
36	46		"I know what they're saying"	change quality of Maria special; triumphant
37	47		"Why can't you say you"	change quality of Maria special; Battista
38	47		"and his Lady"	change quality of Maria special; applause (slides go to black)
39	47		"I told him"	change quality of Maria special: Ari
40	48		"I have news Ari"	change quality of Maria special: pleading with Ari
41	48		"It's done Ari"	change quality of Maria special; despair
42	48		"They fired me at La Scala"	exit slides; *il palco funesto*
43	48		with applause track	restore to class lighting

Cue	Page	Cnt	On	What
44	49		"So. Po pop o."	begin shift to highlight Maria's concluding remarks (at table)
45	50		"If I have seemed harsh"	pull center with Maria's cross; slow pull down of stage – a pool, not a special; these are the concluding remarks and Maria is speaking to us
46	50		after Maria exits	fade to black (exterior La Scala slide)
47	50		when ready	bows
48	50		actors break	postset and house lights

Lilly's Purple Plastic Purse
Preliminary Cue Synopsis
Children's Theater of Madison
LD: Eric Appleton
January, 2010

Cue	Pg	Cnt	On	What
1	3		before house opens	preset and house
2	3		house closes	house to ½
3	3		house settles	house out
4	3		house out	preset out
5	3		actors ready	cyc silhouette for C&W's entrance
6	3		C&W comes downstage	add texture across stage
7	3		C&W arrive picnic area	add picnic light
8	3		"Perfect. Yes."	basket opens – perfect picnic light from within
10	6		Lilly's 1st entrance	star path around periphery
11	6		Lilly gone	stars out
12	6		Lilly's 2nd entrance	upstage brighten for cross
13	6		Lilly's gone	fade upstage
14	6		Lilly's final entrance	brighten/open center/downstage
15	8		"I like Everything!!!"	restore to Q8

Cue	Pg	Cnt	On	What
16	8		"Okay."	crossfade to upstage house area
17	10		"... diva once and for all."	heighten for Opera moment
18	10		end of opera	restore Q16
19	11		wall flies out/Garland enters	cross fade from houselight to specials for Lilly and Garland
20	11		"Me Me ..." Garland's exit	Garland's special out
21	11		"I know."	special up for C&W
22	12		"Bye, Wilson." Lilly exits.	Lilly's special out
23	12		"... practice hand signals."	crossfade from special to bike path
24	12		bikes set	pull to bikes, begin ride movement
25	13		1st wheeeee	shift
26	13		2nd wheeee	shift
27	13		3rd wheeee	shift
28	13		4th wheeeee	shift
29	13		"end up in China ..."	1st flat drops
30	13		"or Africa"	2nd flat drops
31	13		"New York"	3rd flat drops
32	13		"outer space!"	4th flat drops, add stars?
33	13		flats fall	bike path – bully downlight
34	14		"Peas in a pod."	open downstage for bully movement (downlight remains upstage)
35	15		"What was that?"	bullies return to downlight; C&W in specials for Zora's threatening ...
36	16		"MEOWWWWWW."	open stage, lose bully downlight
37	18		"Thanks for saving our"	pull up right slightly for trio
38	20		"Three peas in a pod."	interesting series of looks to transition into house
41	20		Julius revealed	Julius revealed
42	20		entrance of actors	scene light – house, around crib
43	22		"Look he's blowing bubbles!"	Lilly Xs DSL; open for cross

Cue	Pg	Cnt	On	What
44	23		"All right."	Pull to crib for tea party and story
45	24		Mom pulls lever	Reveal uncooperative chair (spooky uplight)
46	24		Black	time passage
47	24		First Sign	Lilly with sign
48	24		Black	time passage
49	24		Second Sign	Lilly with sign
50	24		Black	time passage
51	24		Third Sign	Lilly with sign
52	24		"It's all your fault Julius."	Crossfade into nightmare lighting – upstage of proscenium
56	24		"Time's up."	Restore to scene light (Q44?)
57	25		". . . germ of the world."	Crossfade to first going to school pool DSL
58	26		"Love it, love it, love it."	Crossfade to second pool DSR
59	27		"And pencils, sharp and"	Crossfade to third pool USR
60	29		Bell rings	Open up into school look (full stage)
61	30		"Snacks!"	Heavenly glow on Mr. Slinger DSC
62	30		music ends	Glow out
63	30		"this place is very special."	weak lightbulb table area
64	31		students converge on table	pull to lightbulb table area (but don't lose school look)
65	32		"best teacher in the world."	Lilly's picture enters
66	32		picture exits	restore (Q64)
67	33		". . . zipped, and snapped."	pull USR as table rolls away for L and Mr. S
68	33		"Excellent choice!"	House look
69	35		"Let's go."	Shift from house look to shop look
70	35		"is bound to . . ."	Ping the purse
70.5	35		pick up purse	lose pedestal special

Cue	Pg	Cnt	On	What
71	36		". . . beautiful but wise."	tweak area where L and G dance
72	36		end of dance	restore shop look (Q70.5)
73	37		"My purple plastic purse."	into fantasy sequence
74	37		"MUSIC!!!!"	dance sequence (disco floor?)
80	37		end of dance sequence	specials DL and DR for CW and LG
81	38		" . . . seems to be a problem."	pull to hole – light up from hole
82	39		"Hooray!!!"	lose hole after Mr. S pulled to safety
83	40		". . . brother into space."	Proscenium look for rocket ship
84	40		"Bye, Lilly!"	Button
85	40		as they exit	settle – darkness in preparation
86	40		C&W enter	establish strip of light (tennis net)
87	40		C&W take their places	open tennis court for play
88	43		"Now you owe me . . ."	Lose tennis court, open center for Lilly and Garland
89	43		"Garland! Chester!"	Pull upstage for Mom and Julius
90	44		"He's a lump."	Slight shift USR for C&W entrance
91	44		"You'll see."	Change to school look (full stage)
92	47		". . . there was cheese."	slight pull for cheese presentation (maintain school look); should there be a special on Lilly?
94	49		" . . . visit the lightbulb lab."	Pull to Lilly (students in glow)
95	49		Lilly picture comes on	Light picture
96	49		Picture exits	restore to school look for end of presentation
97	50		"EVER!!!!"	crossfade to outside look
98	51		"Okay."	crossfade into House look
99	52		". . . what I have to do."	uncooperative chair descends
100	52		"I deserve it."	nightmare sequence begins
105	54		"Tomorrow will be better."	transition back to normal House look

Cue	Pg	Cnt	On	What
108	56		". . . long as possible."	crossfade to school look
110	59		"Three peas in a pod."	lose school look/ house silhouette for party
111	60		with banner in	open House look for party
115	62		"Four peas in a pod."	transition into picnic look
117	64		double take at Victor	Black
118	64		bows	bow light
119	64		actors break and exit	postset and house

Sample Blank Cue Synopsis Chart for Handout

The cue synopsis is introduced in Chapter 12. This format works
well for a handout; it was created as a table in Word.

Title:

Designer:

Date:

Page #	Cue #	Est. Count	On	What

Standard Lighting Positions and Unit Numbering

While we don't get much into standard lighting positions in the class, once you start talking about breaking the stage up into areas of control and determining beam throws it's good to know what positions are available in the average theatre. If you have a student who is going further along the path of a realized design, this appendix also provides information on labeling lighting units as they are drawn on the light plot.

Proscenium Spaces

Onstage

Electrics

Pipes (battens) running laterally across the stage, normally raised and lowered by a fly system: "A batten with a light on it becomes an electric." Electrics are numbered from the proscenium toward the upstage; the 1st Electric is the electric closest to the proscenium. If an electric is used exclusively for lighting a cyclorama, it may be called the 'Cyc Electric' rather than have a numeric designation. Units on electrics are numbered from stage left to stage right. Each electric begins with its own unit #1: 1st Electric #1, 2nd Electric #1, etc.

If a space has dedicated electrics, additional pipes are lettered from the downstage dedicated electric (#1A, #1B, #2A, #2B, etc.): Electric #1, Electric #1A, Electric #2, Electric #2A, Electric #2B, Electric #3, etc. Even if a dedicated electric is not used, additional electrics between it and the next dedicated electric upstage of it are still lettered from that electric (dedicated Electric #2 is not used, but #2A, #2B are still named from it).

Booms

Vertical pipes (usually in weighted bases) sitting on the stage floor. May be located anywhere the designer deems necessary. On the plot the floor position is noted, with the pipe itself exploding outward or included on a separate detail plate. Booms are numbered according to side of stage and their order from the proscenium toward the upstage. SR Boom #1 is the boom closest to the proscenium on stage right; SL Boom #1 is the boom closest to the proscenium on stage left.

Units on booms are numbered from the top down. Each boom begins with its own Unit #1. If multiple units are hung on horizontal side-arms, begin numbering at the uppermost downstage units. For side-arms with multiple units, on each level of the boom the lowest number of that level should be consistently downstage.

Tail-Downs

A vertical pipe suspended from a batten or electric. For clarity, this is better designated a separate hanging position if it is suspended from an electric. As with booms, the placement of the tail-down is located on the plot, with the pipe itself shown in exploded view or on a detail plate.

Boom numbering rules also apply to tail-downs.

Ladders

Runged pipe structures. They look like short, squat ladders, often with two or three horizontal pipes and are often suspended in the wings. Ladders are numbered with regard to both side of the stage and order upstage from the proscenium. SR Ladder #1 is the ladder closest to the proscenium on stage right; SL Ladder #1 is the ladder closest to the proscenium on stage left. Location of the ladder is shown on the plot, with units shown on an exploded view or on a detail plate. Use boom and tail-down rules for unit numbering.

Torms

Torms are vertical pipes (booms) fastened directly to the upstage side of the proscenium on either side of the proscenium. There are typically only two torms in a proscenium theatre – stage right (SR Torm) and stage left (SL Torm). Location of the torm is shown on the plot, with units shown on an exploded view or on a detail plate. Units on torms are numbered as per boom, tail-down, and ladder rules.

Groundrows

Typically a row of striplights or far-cyc units set in a row on the floor to light a cyclorama or drop. If there are multiple ground-rows, each is named in order from the proscenium upstage. Groundrow #1 is closest to the proscenium. If the only ground-row is to light a cyc, it may be called 'Cyc Groundrow.' If units in the groundrow are multi-cell strip-type units, the overall fix-tures are lettered from stage left to stage right, with each cell within the unit receiving a number, also from stage left to stage right (Unit A1, A2, A3, Unit B1, B2, B3, etc.). The numbering and lettering convention also holds for strip units hung on battens. Since groundrows typically sit on the deck, they are cross-hatched to show that they sit below the level of the rest of the plot.

Set Mounts

Any unit that is mounted on a scenic element. Numbering sys-tems may vary, depending on number of scenic units and whether they travel. A scenic unit with multiple set mounts might be labeled Porch Unit #1, Porch Unit #2, etc. Set mounts are cross-hatched to show that they sit below the level of the rest of the plot.

Rovers

Units that are placed in position for short durations during the performance, often for specific effects that a permanently mounted unit cannot achieve. Naming and Numbering systems may vary, depending on number of rovers, rovers with multiple uses, and scenes in which it is used. Be sure labels are clear.

Footlights

A groundrow placed along the front lip of the stage apron. Some older theatres may have built-in footlights (typically located in a footlight trough). If units in the footlights are multi-cell strip units, the overall fixtures are lettered from stage left to stage right, with each cell within the unit receiving a number, also from stage left to stage right (Unit A1, A2, A3, Unit B1, B2, B3, etc.). This numbering and lettering convention also holds for strip units hung on battens. If the footlight system is composed of separate units or fixtures, they are numbered individually from stage left to stage right, as per electric numbering conventions. Since the footlights are on the deck, they are cross-hatched.

Front of House

Front of house architecture can vary widely from theatre to theatre and the names attached to front of house positions can vary due to the traditions of the individual venue. However, positions still fall within general categories.

Apron

Many venues have been retrofitted with a batten or truss over the apron of the stage. The name of this position will often vary from theatre to theatre. Because it is *downstage* of the prosce-nium, even if it is a suspended batten it is *not* an electric. Units on an Apron position are numbered from stage left to stage right. If there are multiple parts of an Apron position, each portion begins from #1 (SL Truss Unit #1, SR Truss Unit #1).

Box Booms

Generally, vertical pipes attached to the side walls of the audi-torium. Depending on theatre architecture these may be concealed within alcoves, may be horizontal pipes or ladders, etc. The name comes from the early practice of placing a boom in the box seats to achieve front lighting.

Box Booms are numbered in order from the proscenium outward to the rear of the auditorium and are named for the side of the house they are located. House Left Box Boom #1 is the box boom closest to the proscenium on house left. Units on Box Booms are numbered from the top down. Each box boom begins with Unit #1 (SR Box Boom #1 Unit #1, SR Box Boom #2 Unit #1). Follow conventions for booms, ladders, and torms, keeping in mind the proscenium is now in the other direction.

Balcony Rail

If the auditorium has a balcony, this is usually a horizontal pipe attached to the front of the balcony. Theatres with multiple balconies will typically name the rail for the balcony to which it attaches: Mezzanine Rail, Gallery Rail, etc. If the auditorium does not have a balcony, a pipe mounted to the back wall of the theatre is also typically called a Balcony Rail. Units on a Balcony Rail are numbered from stage left (house right) to stage right (house left).

Coves, Beams, Slots, Catwalks

These are positions located in the ceiling of the auditorium, and range from individually suspended pipes to catwalk systems. The designation (cove, beam, etc.) of these positions is perhaps the most varied of all lighting positions and depends upon the traditions of the venue.

If the auditorium has multiple ceiling positions, they are named in order from the proscenium to the rear of the house. For example, Cove #1 is closest to the proscenium. Units in ceiling positions are numbered from stage left (house right) to stage right (house left).

Thrust and Black Box Theatres

Thrust and Black Box theatres combine familiar positions of the proscenium theatre with positions often unique to the architecture of that individual theatre. A boom is still a boom, though, and a balcony rail continues to be a balcony rail. Always check with the venue's electrics staff to learn the naming conventions in non-traditional spaces.

Thrust

Thrust theatres are often a combination of standard upstage proscenium positions (such as electrics) and an array of unique front of house positions determined by the architecture of the space. The Mitchell Theatre at the University of Wisconsin–Madison, for example, has an overstage position called "The Eggcrate." There is often some sort of grid or catwalk system over the thrust stage itself; naming of the positions will generally begin from the proscenium (Catwalk #1 is closest to the proscenium). Numbering of units per position is typically from stage left (house right) to stage right (house left) and from proscenium out toward the rear of the auditorium.

Black Box

Black Box theatres will typically feature a grid of catwalks or pipes. These are often named along the axes – the pipes running north/south, for instance, may be lettered (A, B, C, D), while the pipes running east/west will be numbered (1, 2, 3, 4). They are typically called 'pipes' rather than 'electrics.' An additional pipe located between positions will typically be given a letter designation to note that it is between two permanent pipes. A short pipe added between Pipes #5 and #6 will be named Pipe #5A; a pipe added between Pipes #B and #C will be Pipe #BB.

Numbering units on pipes crossing the stage is from stage left to stage right (including those pipes that run over the seating areas). Numbering units on pipes that run upstage/downstage is often done from the stage toward the rear of the seating area.

Design Timelines

The process we follow in our class attempts to adhere to the first steps in a typical production timeline. Production calendars vary depending on a venue's scale and resources, but the order in which events occur is fairly standard. We have done our best to base the production timeline we use in class on a professional model.

The timelines below illustrate how and where the class content aligns with production schedules, from first readings through opening night. We use these timelines to structure further student design work; if a student is working on a realized design for a departmental production, we use the timeline to create a practicum syllabus with appropriate process deadlines. The steps are also useful as a handout, reminding students not to skip things and providing a fall-back map for those times they feel lost.

A production calendar for Milwaukee Chamber Theatre's production of *Boeing Boeing* is included at the end of the appendix.

Costume Design: The Steps

Note: At every step of the way, conversation with the director and fellow design team members is *essential* and should be more or less constant, regardless of regularity of production meetings.

1. Read the script (perhaps participate in the play selection process)
2. Develop a metaphor, or take it from member(s) of the production
3. Early production meetings; discussion/alignment with directional goals/approach
4. Script analysis
5. Develop costume plot
6. Research
7. Reread the script, focusing on the various types and idiosyncrasies of the characters; keep the research and metaphor in mind
8. Present non-direct research
9. Draw costumes, with detail but without color
10. Further production meetings
11. Consider set color when painting renderings
12. Paint renderings
13. Present renderings
14. Adjust renderings
15. Create a book of actors' measurements
16. Create a book with renderings, to help if needed, to organize the build process
17. Pull items from stock (even if it is just socks and t-shirts and the rest is built)
18. Pull for fabric (There is some chance that lining fabric, interfacing, accent fabric may be in the shop, and therefore, available at no additional cost.)
19. Buy fabric, shop for clothing
20. Sort and assign the work of building the costumes
21. Further production meetings
22. Build costumes
23. Fitting(s)
24. Dress rehearsals
25. Notes
26. Opening
27. Maintenance
28. Strike

Note: Some directors or producers will ask for a costume parade, in which actors in finished costumes walk the set under stage lights prior to the first technical rehearsal. Whether this is desired and feasible depends greatly on the time and resources available to the costume shop.

Scenic Design: The Steps

Note: It bears repeating, at every step of the way, that conversation with the director and fellow design team members is *essential* and should be more or less constant, regardless of regularity of production meetings.

1. Read the script
2. Develop preliminary design metaphor
3. Read the script again
4. Discussion with director; style, goals, approaches, etc.
5. Early production meetings
6. Script analysis
7. Research
8. Thumbnail sketches and diagrams
9. More production meetings
10. Read the script again
11. More research
12. More thumbnails and diagrams
13. More talks with the director
14. Preliminary groundplan/Experimental model
15. Preliminary sketches
16. Discuss color with Costume Designer
17. Discussion with Props Manager
18. Finalize groundplan
19. Renderings/Exhibition model construction
20. Detail plates
21. Paint elevations
22. Send drawings to shop
23. Groundplan to Stage Manager
24. Groundplan and section to Lighting Designer
25. Prop drawings to Props Manager
26. Paint elevations to Scenic Artists
27. More production meetings
28. Rehearsals begin
29. Check in with shop regularly
30. Set dressing shopping and pulling
31. Watch rehearsals; revise as necessary/possible
32. Check in with Shop/Props
33. More production meetings
34. Check in with Shop/Props
35. Supervise set dressing
36. Paper tech
37. Dry tech
38. Technical rehearsals
39. Notes
40. Dress rehearsals
41. Notes
42. Opening Night
43. Maintenance and strike

Lighting Design: The Steps

Note: And we'll say it again – at every step of the way, conversation with your director and fellow design team members is *essential* and should be more or less constant, regardless of regularity of production meetings.

1. Read the script
2. Develop metaphor/concept
3. Script analysis
4. Research
5. Develop preliminary cue synopsis
6. Early production meetings
7. Coordinate with venue lighting staff
8. Watch rehearsals
9. Get drawings from Set Designer
10. Storyboard
11. More production meetings
12. Magic sheets
13. Purpose list
14. Watch more rehearsals
15. Division of stage into areas of control
16. Preliminary channel hookup
17. Watch more rehearsals
18. Revised channel hookup
19. Lighting section
20. Production meetings
21. Revised cue synopsis
22. Rough plot
23. Light plot and finalized paperwork

24. Designer run-through
25. Revise plot and paperwork as dictated by designer run-through
26. Light hang
27. Focus
28. Troubleshoot
29. Write cuing reference sheet
30. Paper tech
31. Build cues
32. Dry tech
33. First tech
34. Notes
35. More tech
36. Notes
37. More tech
38. Notes
39. Dress rehearsal
40. Notes
41. Final dress
42. Opening Night
43. Maintenance
44. Strike

A Production Calendar

In order to get a sense of how all three of these timelines can work together, Brandy Kline, the current production manager at Milwaukee Chamber Theatre, has allowed us to include her calendar for their August 2015 production of *Boeing Boeing*.

Milwaukee Chamber Theatre

Production Deadlines: BOEING BOEING

Updated by bkline 4/14/2015

*target dates, subject to change based on designer availability

DATE	EVENT	NOTES
March 25, 2015	Design Conference	Designers & Director
May 12, 2015	**Scenic Plan Prelims Due**	Scenic Designer > PM > TD
June 2, 2015	TD Feasibility Report	TD > PM
June 9, 2015*	Production Meeting #1	Design Team, Director, PM + Props Present & Discuss Prelims
	Costume Measurements Due	PM > Costume Designer
June 23, 2015	**Final Scenic Plans & Model Due**	Scenic Designer > PM > TD
As per Shop Schedule	Scenic Build Begins	TD/Shop Staff
As per Shop Schedule	Scenic Paint Begins	
July 14, 2015*	Production Meeting #2	Designers Present Total Design to SM Status Reports Review Tech Schedule
	Costume Renderings Due	Designer > Director & SM

DATE	EVENT	NOTES
	Sound Prelim Cue List Due	Designer > Director & SM
July 21, 2015	First Rehearsal	Designers are invited, but not required, to present designs to the cast & guests.
July 26, 2015	**Light, Sound & Soft Goods Plots Due to MCT**	Lighting, Sound & Scenic Designers > PM
August 2, 2015	Designer Run	
	Production Meeting #3	Status Reports Finalize Tech Schedule
August 3, 2015	Light Hang	ME, LX Crew
August 4–6, 2015	Scenic Load-in	TD & Scenic Crew Scenic Designer Check-in
August 7, 2015 9am–5pm	Lighting Focus	ME, LX Crew & Lighting Designer
1pm–2pm	Prop Check-in Sound Check	Propmaster, ASM & Deck Chief Sound Designer & A/V Supervisor
6pm–10pm	Onstage Spacing Rehearsal	Designers welcome to observe
August 8–14, 2015	Tech Week	All Personnel
August 8, 2015 morning	Wardrobe Setup Costume Load-in	Wardrobe Supervisor ADD Costume Designer
August 12, 2015 afternoon	Photo Call	Dress Run or posed shots TBD
7:30pm	PWYC Preview (Studio) Curtain or Invited Dress (Cabot) Curtain	
August 13, 2015 7:30pm	Subscriber Series Preview Curtain	
August 14, 2015 8:00pm	Opening Curtain	
August 30, 2015	Close/Strike	
September 6, 2015	Final Expenses/Receipts Due	

Glossary

ALD Assistant Lighting Designer

Arena playing space completely surrounded by audience

Background the region in a composition containing items that appear to be behind other items or appear furthest from the viewer

Backlight illumination from behind (upstage) the performer

Balance an equilibrium and stability achieved by arranging objects with different sizes so that an equal 'weight' is perceived on either side of an axis

Batten a pipe hung horizontally and laterally across the stage, used to suspend scenery or lighting equipment; in a proscenium stage, usually attached to ropes and pulleys to allow the pipe vertical movement

Black Box flexible space that can accommodate a variety of configurations

Blackout (*snap to black*) a zero-second crossfade into no light on stage

Blocking determining when, where, and how performers move around the stage environment

Border a horizontal curtain used to hide overhead equipment and pipes from the audience

Bows or, *curtain call*. A lighting look for the performers' bows at the end of the show

Box Set removal of the 'fourth wall' to view the space; often used for interiors, realistic or otherwise

Button in comedies and musicals, there may be a tag-line or final beat to a song or gag that requires a quick pop in the light-ing as a finale; often this entails brightening the performer, letting applause begin, and then fading into the next look

CAD Computer Aided Drafting; refers to any number of computer programs such as AutoCAD and Vectorworks

Center Line the axis of the stage, from downstage to upstage, splitting the playing space equally in half right and left (the Y axis)

Console or light board, also called a desk; the piece of equipment that tells the dimmers how much electricity (or data) to send to the units

Conventional a lighting unit that uses an incandescent light source and has no in-built motorized movement

Cool refers to colors of light that are, or contain, blue. A cool green is a green that contains more blue than yellow, but not so much it becomes cyan

Croquis photos/line drawings of human beings used as templates for costume renderings. Using fashion sketches will create renderings with inaccurate proportions

Crossfade a smooth transition from one lighting look into another; generally, the first look is gone by the time the second look is fully established

Cross Grain threads perpendicular to the grain

Curtain Warmer for proscenium theatres, the preset illuminating the act or show curtain as the audience enters the theatre

DAT Digital Audio Tape

Deck the bare stage floor

Diagetic a sound whose source is visible on the stage (such as music from a radio) or emerges from the stage environment (such as birdsong)

Diagonal Backlight illumination from behind the performer but off to the side

Dimmer the piece of equipment which controls how much electricity is sent out to an incandescent unit, and therefore determines how bright the light is that is emitted

Downlight illumination from directly above the performer

Dramaturgy (also, *dramaturgical*) According to director John Caird: "the craft of analyzing the structure of dramatic texts and the theatrical style in which they are performed . . . may be used more loosely to describe the dramatic structure of a play or the theoretical basis of a production."[1]

Drop large, flat, usually painted fabric scenic element; usually hangs laterally across the full stage space and is most often used in proscenium-style theatres

Fade to Black a smooth crossfade into no light on stage, usually three to four seconds in duration

Flats refers to the temporary walls built for theatrical production; these can range from fabric-covered wooden frames to plywood-covered steel frames

Flying / Flown refers to the act of raising and lowering items in the stage space; to fly something out is to raise it up off the stage

Fly Rail the fly rail is the area in which the linesets are operated; normally located against either the stage left or stage right wall of the stage area

FOH Front of House; or the seating area of the theatre; the auditorium

Foley a Foley artist is someone who creates the sound effects and background noises that are added in post-production to film and video. Foley can also refer to the craft of creating sound effects in a live theatrical environment

Footprint of an Object the perimeter of an object; the outline of an object when placed on the floor

Foreground the region in a composition containing items that appear to be in front of other items or appear nearest to the viewer

Frontlight illumination from the front of the performer, applying to the full range of angles possible from in front of the stage

Gel transparent color media, also called simply 'color' (as in "go drop color into those units"). Commonly called gel because it was once made from gelatins and lacquers. Color media is now made from plastic

Gobo also called a 'pattern' or 'template.' Traditionally, a stamped piece of thin metal placed in an ERS to project textures and shapes. They can also be made of glass or plastic imprinted with photographic images

Grain in fabric, all threads parallel to the selvage

Groundplan a drawing generated by the scenic designer to show where all items of the set are to be placed; can be thought of as a map of the stage

H, 2H, HB, etc. in pencils, the grading scale of graphite hardness. 'H' denotes harder leads, 'B' denotes softer leads. The higher the number, the harder or softer the lead. The average No. 2 pencil is HB, which is a middle grade

Hidden Line on a drawing, a dashed line indicating that an object is behind or underneath another object

Hook-up a spreadsheet of almost all of the non-graphically expressed information required to execute a lighting design

House Lights auditorium lighting for the audience, usually up during the preset, intermission, and postset

House to Half lighting cue that partially dims the house lights in preparation for the start of the show

Incandescent light source with a filament enclosed in a glass bulb; light is produced by the wire's resistance to the electricity sent through it

Lamp non-theatre people call this a lightbulb

LD Lighting Designer

LED Light Emitting Diode; electronic light source that is fast replacing incandescent light sources due to color-changing capability and reduced energy usage. Requires a high degree of electronic control

Leg a vertical curtain used to hide the offstage (wings) from the audience

Light Plot drawing that shows where each and every lighting unit is to be placed in the venue

Light, Unit, Fixture, Luminaire terms that refer to the piece of theatrical stage equipment that emits light. Often used interchangeably

Line Drawing an unpainted sketch or nearly finalized drawing that depicts the costume

Line Schedule a diagram included on a groundplan to show the placement of linesets; placed on the drawing where the fly rail is found in the venue

Line Weight the darkness, thickness, and pattern of a line on a drawing; the various types of lines indicate the purpose and importance of the object drawn

Lineset refers to a single complete arrangement of ropes, pulleys and batten

Load-in the day or process of bringing the scenery from the shop into the performance space and setting it up

Masking refers to the various curtains (soft-goods) and flats used to hide the backstage and overhead equipment from the audience

ME Master Electrician. The person in charge of executing the technical aspects of the design, such as hanging the lighting units

Motivated light on the stage that appears to come from an identifiable source such as a sconce, chandelier, window, or the sun

MP3 a common digital recording format used in many consumer audio players

Phantom Line on a drawing, a type of dashed line that denotes items that move

Plaster Line a reference line through the proscenium arch that denotes the plane of the upstage side of the architectural proscenium

Postset lighting cue that the audience sees after the performers have left the stage, as the house clears

Practical most often refers to lighting fixtures that are part of the scenic environment, such as sconces and chandeliers. Can also refer to appliances and other electrical devices

Preset lighting look that the audience sees as they enter the theatre

Proportion the comparison of size, small to large. Scenic design drawings are small in proportion to reality, but the use of scale provides accuracy in measurement

Proscenium Arch the 'picture frame' through which an audience views the stage; depending on the venue, the proscenium arch may be a permanent architectural feature

Purpose refers to the effect a particular direction of light is intended to accomplish on stage, such as 'afternoon daylight,' 'light through window,' 'moonlight,' or 'light spilling in through open kitchen door.' A purpose can also be generalized to describe *only* the direction of light (where it comes from in the theatre), such as 'frontlight' or 'downlight.' It may also be linked to a specific part of the stage, such as 'frontlight downstage left.' However, once you stop describing the *quality* of the light it becomes less a purpose and more simply a note on where the lighting unit is to be focused

Rendering any drawing or painting that is intended to depict a costume

Scale ratios of measurement used to describe real objects at reduced sizes

Scenographer a person who is in charge of all design aspects of the production: scenery, costumes, *and* lights. It is more common to find scenographers in European practice

Selvage the manufacturer's tightly woven edge of fabric that prevents it from unraveling

Sidelight illumination from the side of the performer, ranging from floor units ('shinbusters') to those hung above the performer

Sightlines designers will use the extreme seats in the audience to determine if offstage and overhead spaces are masked properly; if someone sitting in those seats cannot see it, the rest of the audience can't either

Sittable might be a Midwestern term; used to denote anything on a stage which can be sat upon before a specific furniture piece has been determined

Sound Plot a spreadsheet containing all the information about sound that the designer plans to incorporate into a production

Special usually refers to a single lighting unit that serves a highly specialized purpose, such as providing a small pool of stationary light for a monologue or song; typically, a special picks a performer or object out of the overall stage lighting to attract the audience's attention

Square in drafting and scenic construction refers to whether an object or line is at a right angle (perpendicular – 90 degrees) to another object or line

Stadium playing space as strip between halves of the audience

Straightedge any drawing tool used to draw straight lines on a technical drawing, such as a T-square or drafting triangles

Swatch small pieces of fabric, usually 2" x 2", usually attached to a rendering, depicting the fabric and trim choices for that costume.

Symmetry when a composition of items on one side of an axis is mirrored on the other side of the axis

The Flies in a proscenium theatre, the portion of the building over the stage where the battens are located

Thrust audience on two or more adjacent sides of playing space

Transition Light a very low intensity look that allows stagehands to reset the stage or actors to get into place between scenes; the audience will see them, but the low level of light is a signal that this activity is not part of the action of the play

Turntable a large, rotating platform

Unit Set generalized architectural structure meant to support a variety of locales with only minor scenic changes

Uplight illumination from below the performer, such as from footlights

Value the lightness or darkness of a color, especially when compared to the graduated steps moving from white through grey to black

Vellum a high quality semi-transparent paper traditionally used in hand-drafting

Wagon a wheeled scenic unit, usually large enough to accommodate actors

Warm refers to colors of light that are, or contain, red, orange, and/or yellow. A warm blue, for example, is a blue that contains red, but not so much red that the color becomes violet or magenta

Wing and Drop typically created by flat painted surfaces, such as drops and legs

Note

1. John Caird, *Theatre Craft: A Director's Practical Companion from A to Z* (London: Faber and Faber, 2010), pp. 242–243.

Index